X-FACTOR

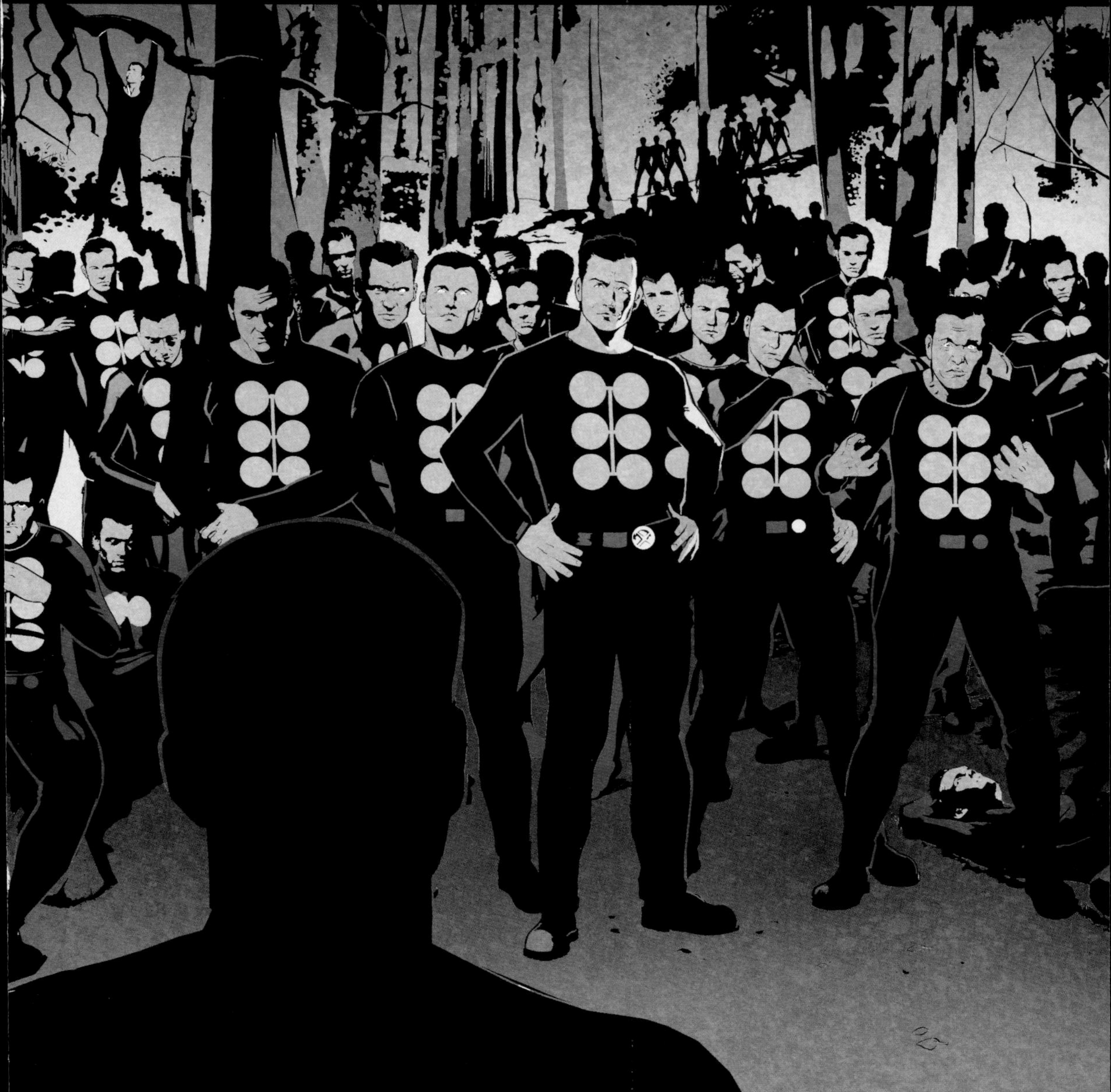

THE LONGEST NIGHT

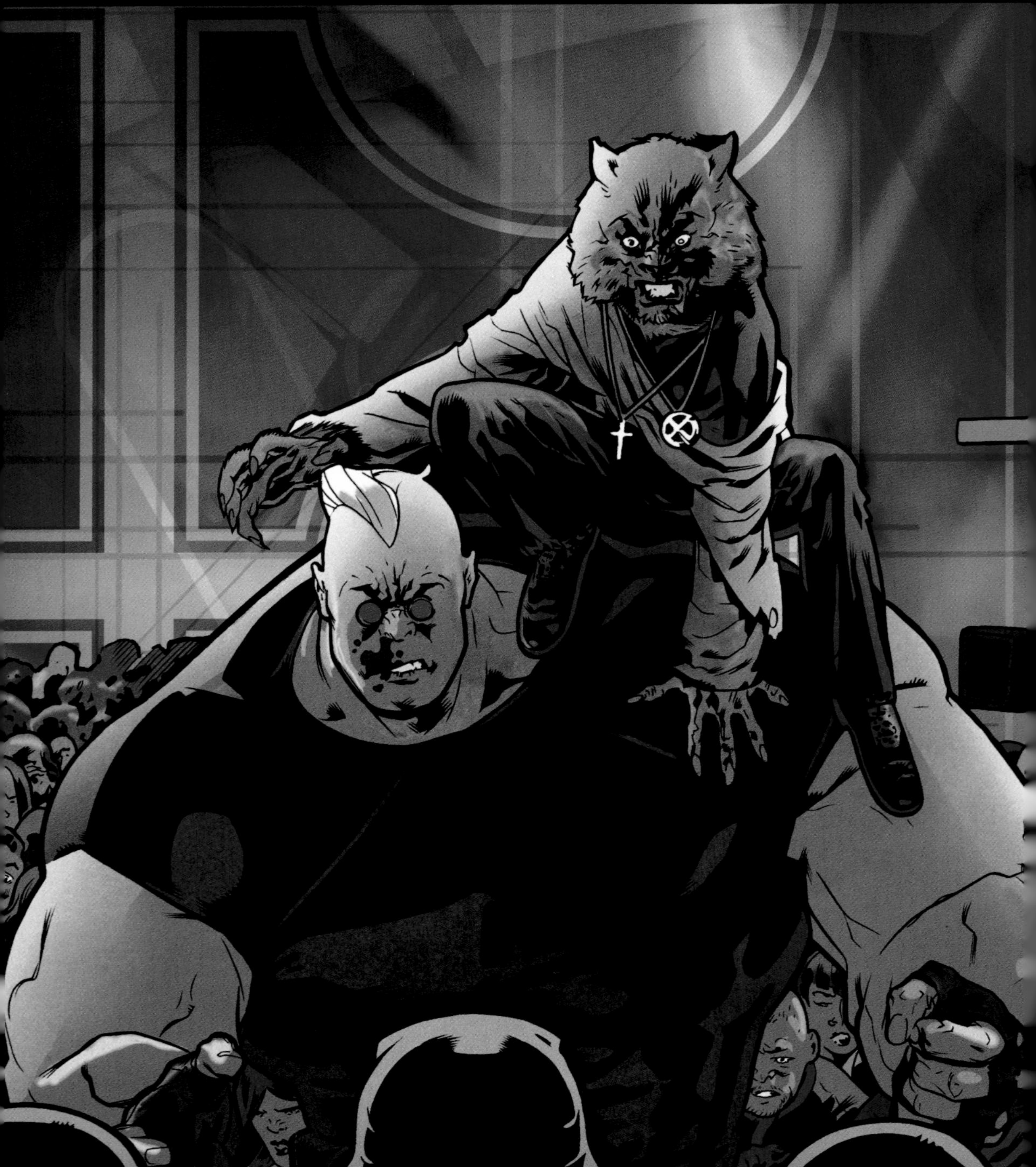

X-FACTOR

THE LONGEST NIGHT

Writer: **PETER DAVID**
Pencils: **RYAN SOOK & DENNIS CALERO**
Inks: **WADE VON GRAWBADGER & DENNIS CALERO**
Color Art: **JOSE VILLARRUBIA**

Letters: **VIRTUAL CALLIGRAPHY'S CORY PETIT**
Cover Art: **RYAN SOOK & JOSE VILLARRUBIA (ISSUES #1-3 & 5)**
AND GABRIELE DELL'OTTO & JOSE VILLARRUBIA (ISSUES #4 & 6)
Assistant Editors: **MOLLY LAZER & AUBREY SITTERSON**
Editor: **ANDY SCHMIDT**

Collection Editor: **JENNIFER GRÜNWALD**
Assistant Editor: **MICHAEL SHORT**
Senior Editor, Special Projects: **JEFF YOUNGQUIST**
Vice President of Sales: **DAVID GABRIEL**
Book Designer: **PATRICK McGRATH**
Vice President of Creative: **TOM MARVELLI**

Editor in Chief: **JOE QUESADA**
Publisher: **DAN BUCKLEY**

X-FACTOR: THE LONGEST NIGHT. Contains material originally published in magazine form as X-FACTOR #1-6. First printing 2006. ISBN# 0-7851-2351-2. Published by MARVEL PUBLISHING, INC., a subsidiary of MARVEL ENTERTAINMENT, INC. OFFICE OF PUBLICATION: 417 5th Avenue, New York, NY 10016. Copyright © 2005 and 2006 Marvel Characters, Inc. All rights reserved. $19.99 per copy in the U.S. and $32.00 in Canada (GST #R127032852); Canadian Agreement #40668537. All characters featured in this issue and the distinctive names and likenesses thereof, and all related indicia are trademarks of Marvel Characters, Inc. No similarity between any of the names, characters, persons, and/or institutions in this magazine with those of any living or dead person or institution is intended, and any such similarity which may exist is purely coincidental. **Printed in the U.S.A.** AVI ARAD, Chief Creative Officer; ALAN FINE, President & CEO Of Marvel Toys and Marvel Publishing, Inc.; DAVID BOGART, VP Of Publishing Operations; DAN CARR, Executive Director of Publishing Technology; JUSTIN F. GABRIE, Managing Editor; STAN LEE, Chairman Emeritus. For information regarding advertising in Marvel Comics or on Marvel.com, please contact Joe Maimone, Advertising Director, at jmaimone@marvel.com or 212-576-8534.

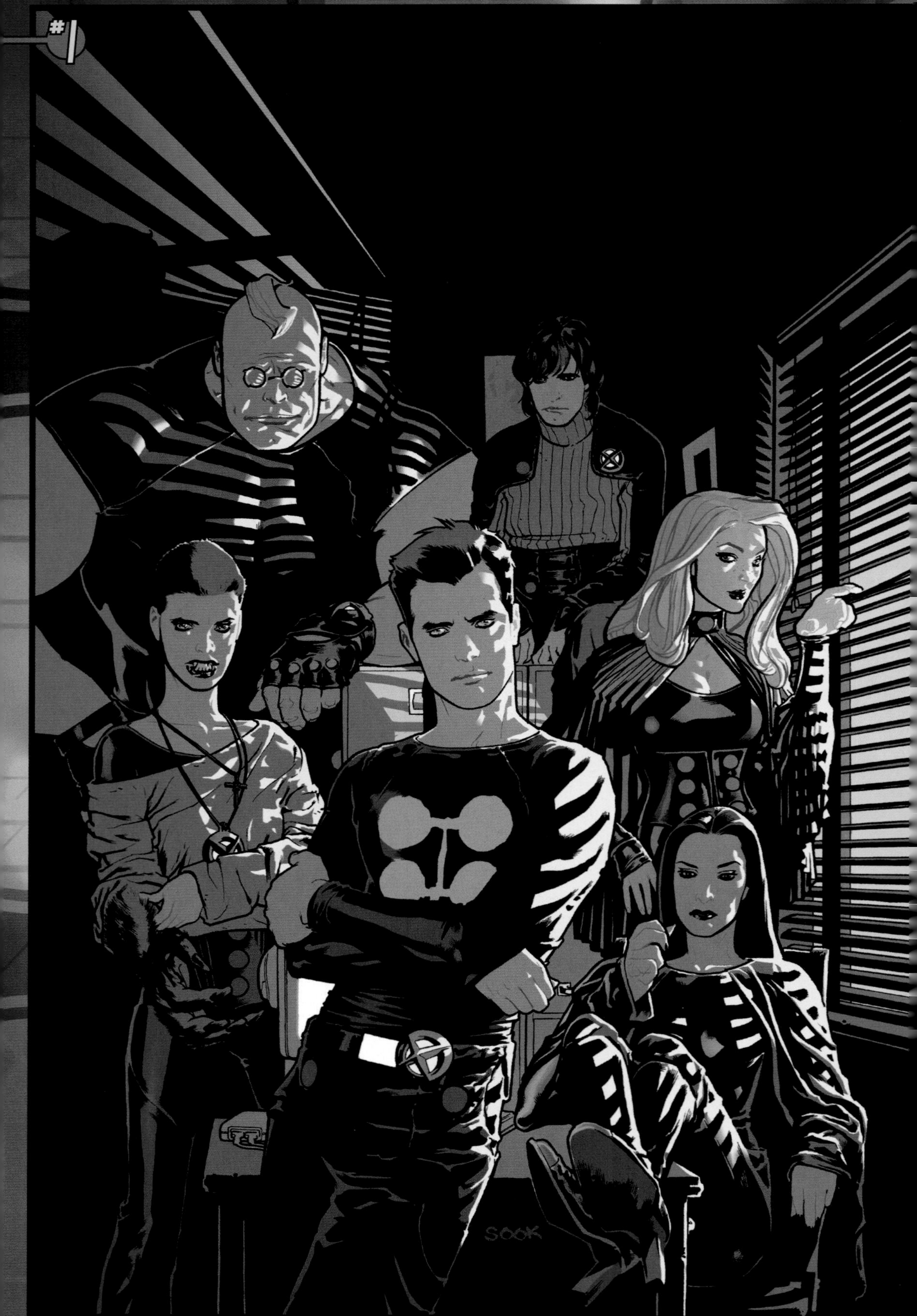
#1
SOOK

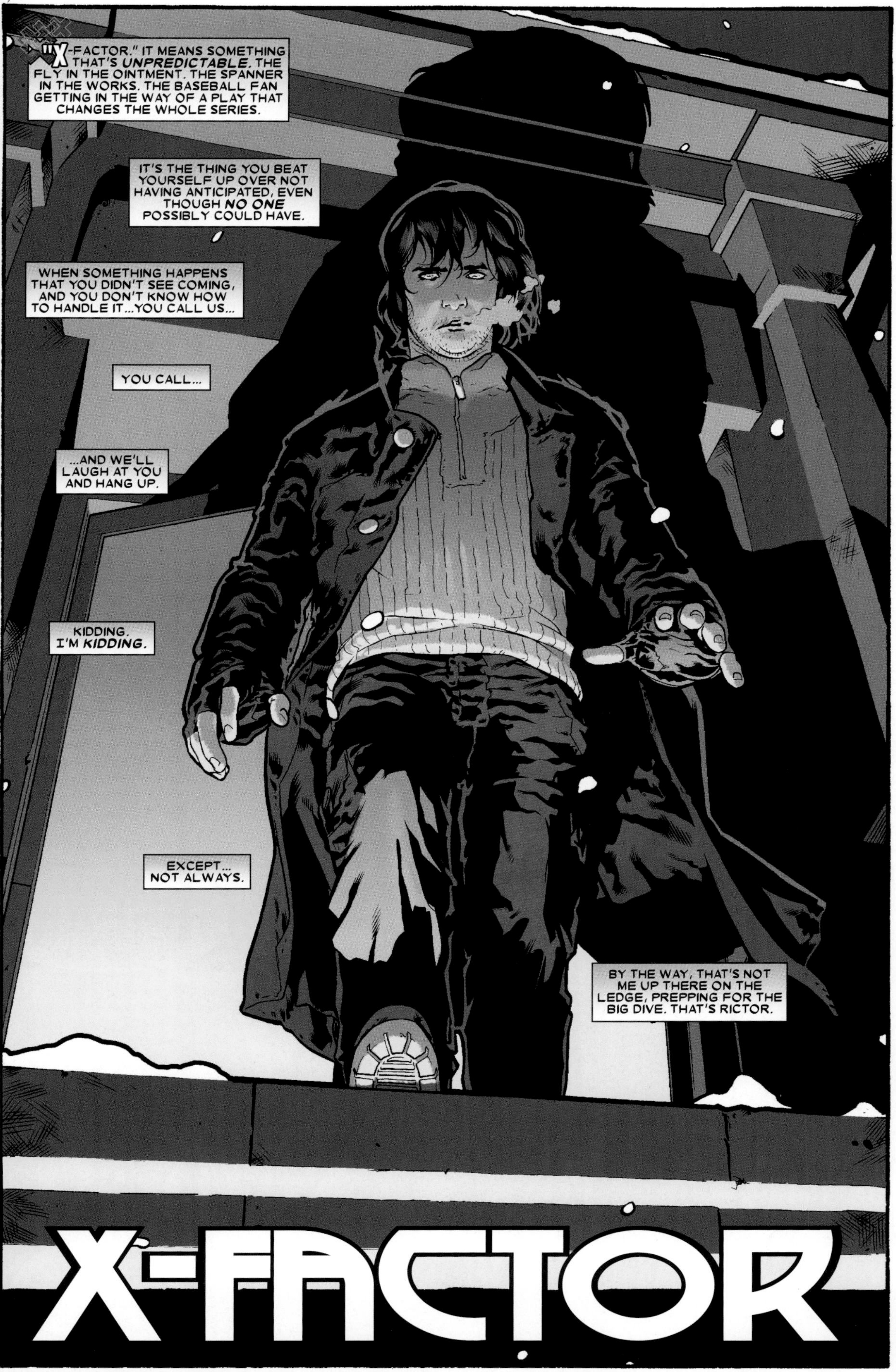
"X-FACTOR." IT MEANS SOMETHING THAT'S *UNPREDICTABLE.* THE FLY IN THE OINTMENT. THE SPANNER IN THE WORKS. THE BASEBALL FAN GETTING IN THE WAY OF A PLAY THAT CHANGES THE WHOLE SERIES.
IT'S THE THING YOU BEAT YOURSELF UP OVER NOT HAVING ANTICIPATED, EVEN THOUGH *NO ONE* POSSIBLY COULD HAVE.
WHEN SOMETHING HAPPENS THAT YOU DIDN'T SEE COMING, AND YOU DON'T KNOW HOW TO HANDLE IT...YOU CALL US...
YOU CALL...
...AND WE'LL LAUGH AT YOU AND HANG UP.
KIDDING. I'M *KIDDING.*
EXCEPT... NOT ALWAYS.
BY THE WAY, THAT'S NOT ME UP THERE ON THE LEDGE, PREPPING FOR THE BIG DIVE. THAT'S RICTOR.
X-FACTOR

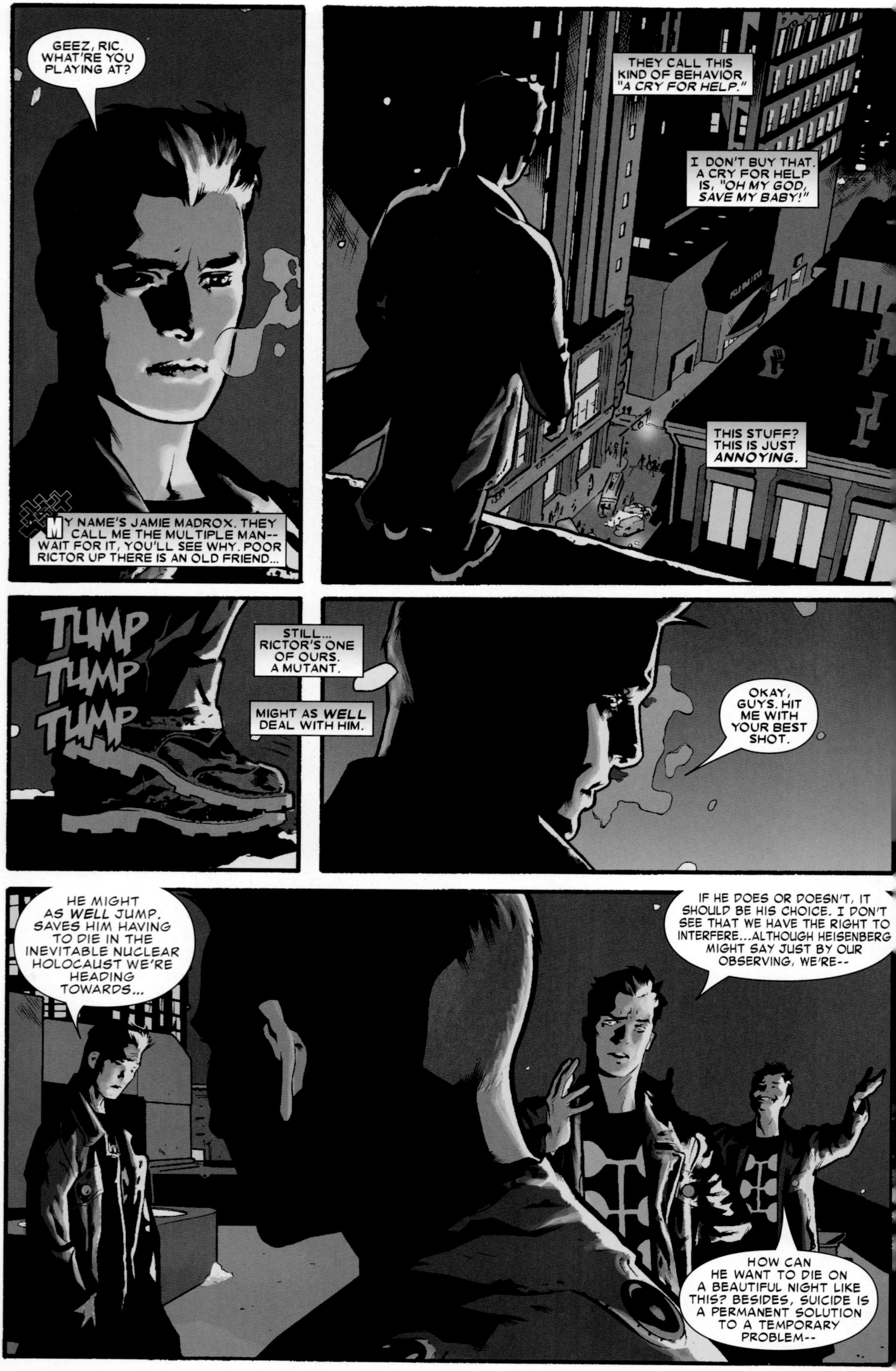
GEEZ, RIC. WHAT'RE YOU PLAYING AT?
MY NAME'S JAMIE MADROX. THEY CALL ME THE MULTIPLE MAN-- WAIT FOR IT, YOU'LL SEE WHY. POOR RICTOR UP THERE IS AN OLD FRIEND...
THEY CALL THIS KIND OF BEHAVIOR "A CRY FOR HELP."
I DON'T BUY THAT. A CRY FOR HELP IS, "OH MY GOD, SAVE MY BABY!"
THIS STUFF? THIS IS JUST ANNOYING.
TUMP TUMP TUMP
STILL... RICTOR'S ONE OF OURS. A MUTANT.
MIGHT AS WELL DEAL WITH HIM.
OKAY, GUYS. HIT ME WITH YOUR BEST SHOT.
HE MIGHT AS WELL JUMP. SAVES HIM HAVING TO DIE IN THE INEVITABLE NUCLEAR HOLOCAUST WE'RE HEADING TOWARDS...
IF HE DOES OR DOESN'T, IT SHOULD BE HIS CHOICE. I DON'T SEE THAT WE HAVE THE RIGHT TO INTERFERE...ALTHOUGH HEISENBERG MIGHT SAY JUST BY OUR OBSERVING, WE'RE--
HOW CAN HE WANT TO DIE ON A BEAUTIFUL NIGHT LIKE THIS? BESIDES, SUICIDE IS A PERMANENT SOLUTION TO A TEMPORARY PROBLEM--

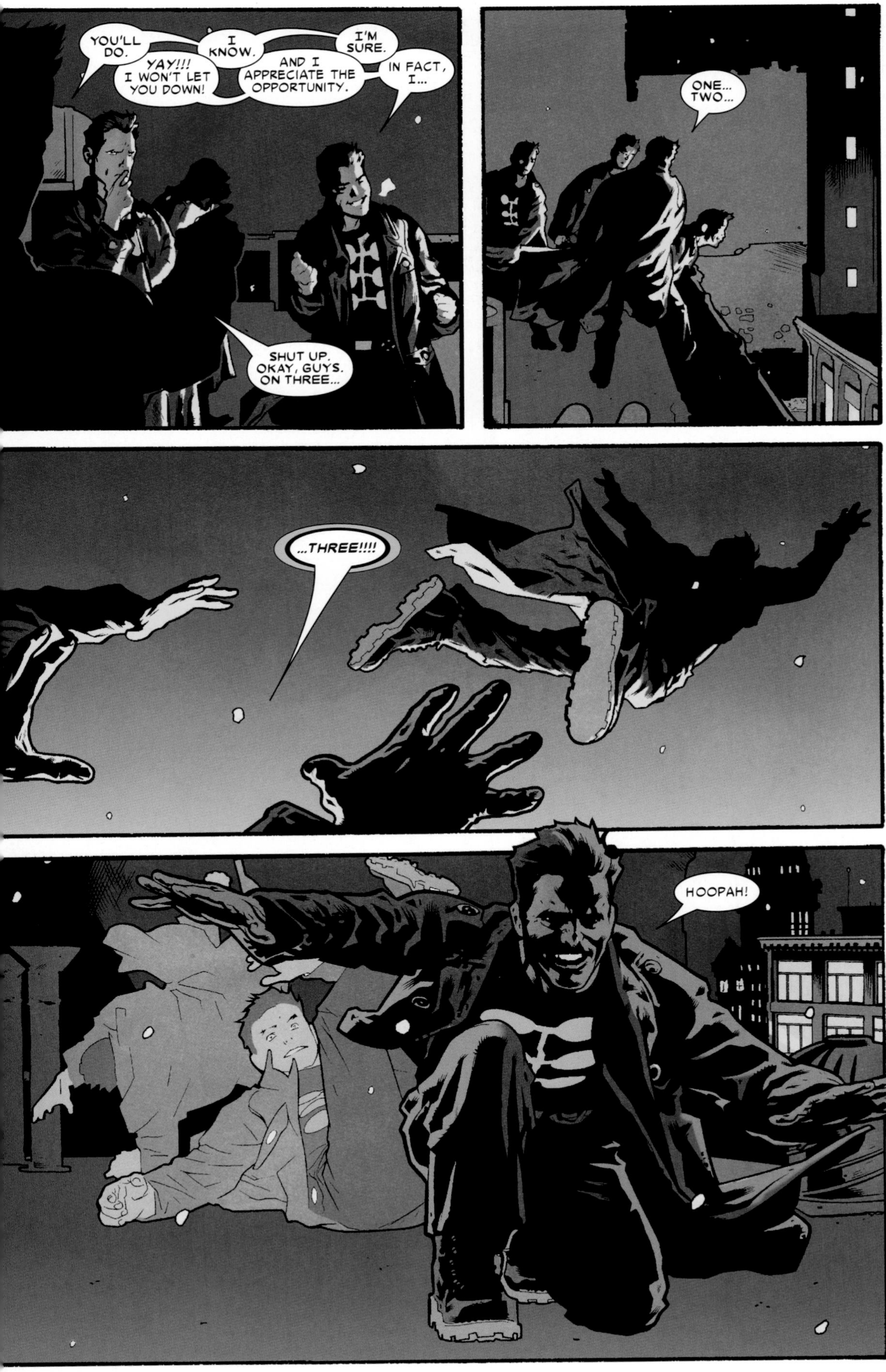
YOU'LL DO.
YAY!!! I WON'T LET YOU DOWN!
I KNOW.
AND I APPRECIATE THE OPPORTUNITY.
I'M SURE.
IN FACT, I...
SHUT UP. OKAY, GUYS. ON THREE...
ONE... TWO...
...THREE!!!!
HOOPAH!

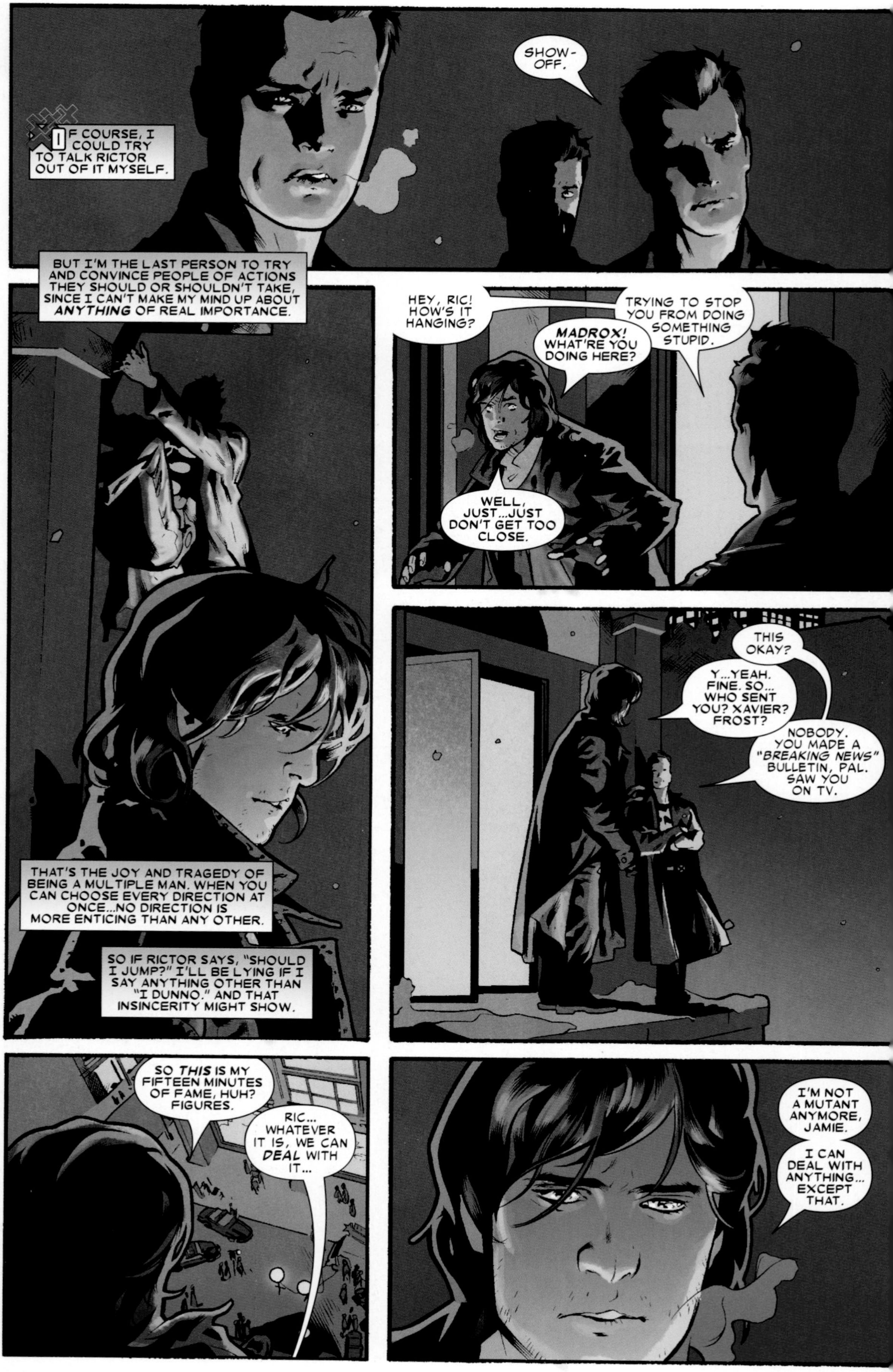

OF COURSE, I COULD TRY TO TALK RICTOR OUT OF IT MYSELF.
SHOW-OFF.
BUT I'M THE LAST PERSON TO TRY AND CONVINCE PEOPLE OF ACTIONS THEY SHOULD OR SHOULDN'T TAKE, SINCE I CAN'T MAKE MY MIND UP ABOUT *ANYTHING* OF REAL IMPORTANCE.
THAT'S THE JOY AND TRAGEDY OF BEING A MULTIPLE MAN. WHEN YOU CAN CHOOSE EVERY DIRECTION AT ONCE...NO DIRECTION IS MORE ENTICING THAN ANY OTHER.
SO IF RICTOR SAYS, "SHOULD I JUMP?" I'LL BE LYING IF I SAY ANYTHING OTHER THAN "I DUNNO." AND THAT INSINCERITY MIGHT SHOW.
HEY, RIC! HOW'S IT HANGING?
MADROX! WHAT'RE YOU DOING HERE?
TRYING TO STOP YOU FROM DOING SOMETHING STUPID.
WELL, JUST...JUST DON'T GET TOO CLOSE.
THIS OKAY?
Y...YEAH. FINE. SO... WHO SENT YOU? XAVIER? FROST?
NOBODY. YOU MADE A "*BREAKING NEWS*" BULLETIN, PAL. SAW YOU ON TV.
SO *THIS* IS MY FIFTEEN MINUTES OF FAME, HUH? FIGURES.
RIC... WHATEVER IT IS, WE CAN *DEAL* WITH IT...
I'M NOT A MUTANT ANYMORE, JAMIE.
I CAN DEAL WITH ANYTHING... EXCEPT THAT.

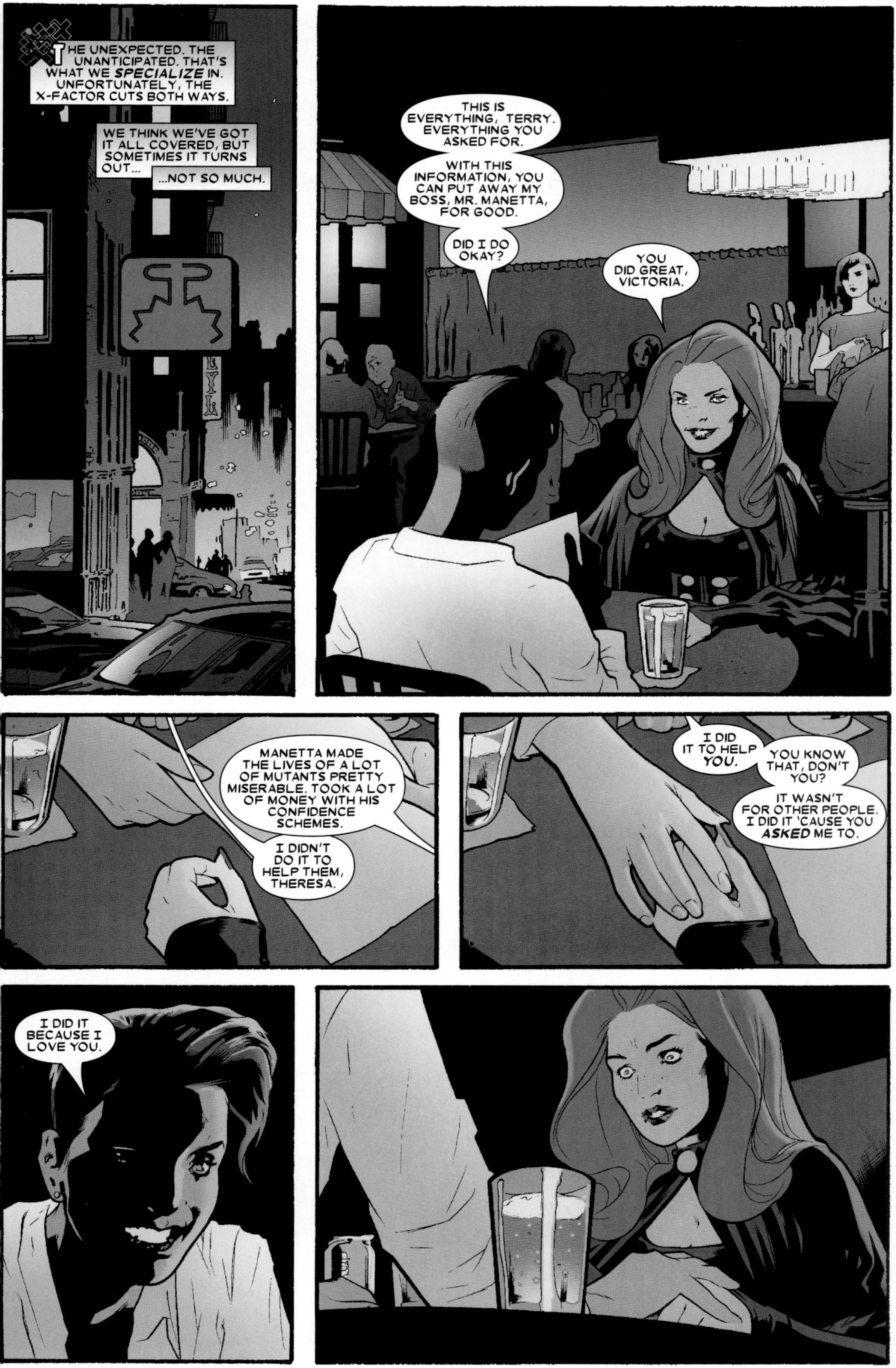
THE UNEXPECTED. THE UNANTICIPATED. THAT'S WHAT WE SPECIALIZE IN. UNFORTUNATELY, THE X-FACTOR CUTS BOTH WAYS.
WE THINK WE'VE GOT IT ALL COVERED, BUT SOMETIMES IT TURNS OUT...
...NOT SO MUCH.
THIS IS EVERYTHING, TERRY. EVERYTHING YOU ASKED FOR.
WITH THIS INFORMATION, YOU CAN PUT AWAY MY BOSS, MR. MANETTA, FOR GOOD.
DID I DO OKAY?
YOU DID GREAT, VICTORIA.
MANETTA MADE THE LIVES OF A LOT OF MUTANTS PRETTY MISERABLE. TOOK A LOT OF MONEY WITH HIS CONFIDENCE SCHEMES.
I DIDN'T DO IT TO HELP THEM, THERESA.
I DID IT TO HELP YOU.
YOU KNOW THAT, DON'T YOU?
IT WASN'T FOR OTHER PEOPLE. I DID IT 'CAUSE YOU ASKED ME TO.
I DID IT BECAUSE I LOVE YOU.

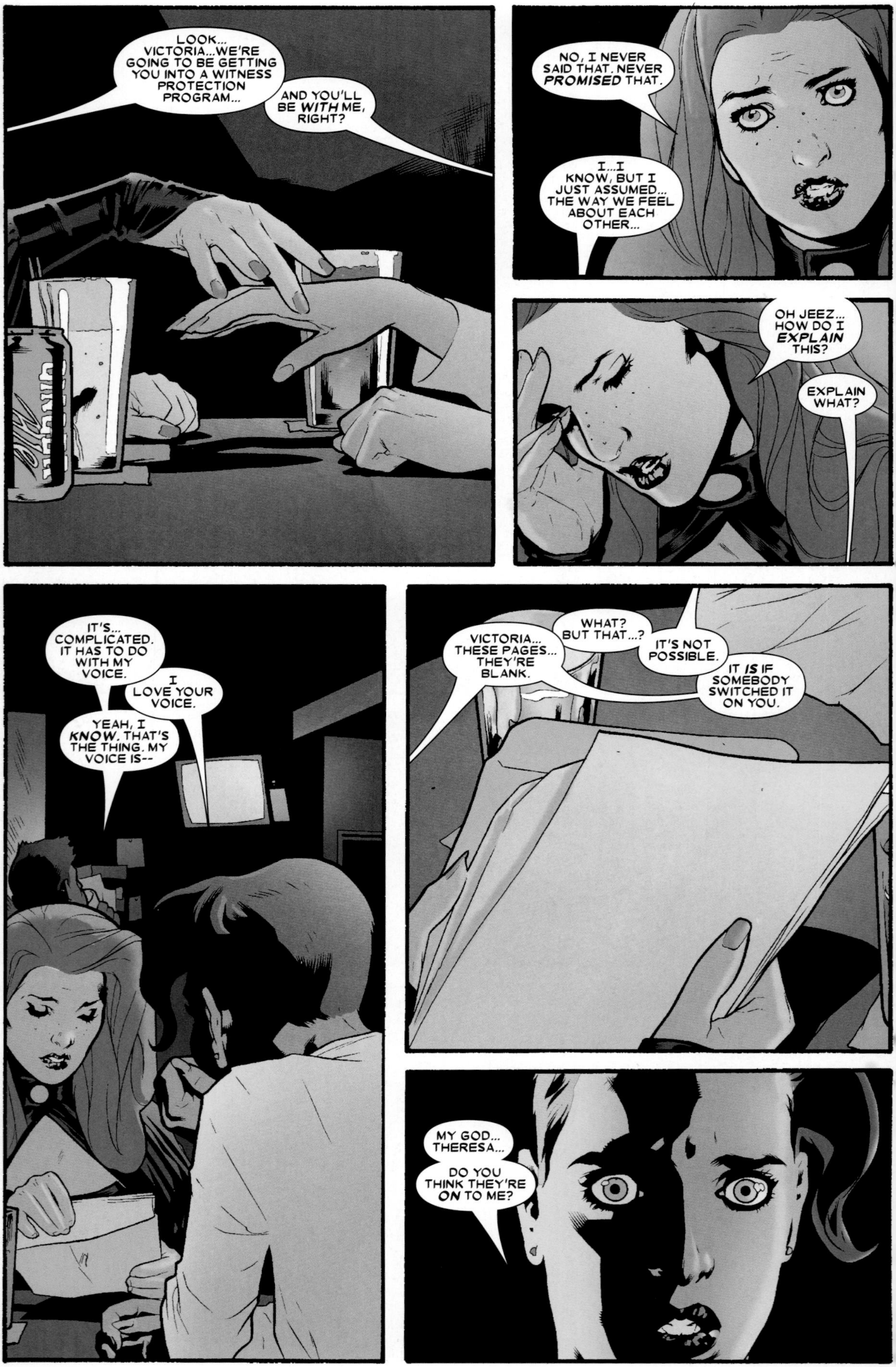
LOOK... VICTORIA...WE'RE GOING TO BE GETTING YOU INTO A WITNESS PROTECTION PROGRAM...
AND YOU'LL BE WITH ME, RIGHT?
NO, I NEVER SAID THAT. NEVER PROMISED THAT.
I...I KNOW, BUT I JUST ASSUMED... THE WAY WE FEEL ABOUT EACH OTHER...
OH JEEZ... HOW DO I EXPLAIN THIS?
EXPLAIN WHAT?
IT'S... COMPLICATED. IT HAS TO DO WITH MY VOICE.
I LOVE YOUR VOICE.
YEAH, I KNOW. THAT'S THE THING. MY VOICE IS--
VICTORIA... THESE PAGES... THEY'RE BLANK.
WHAT? BUT THAT...?
IT'S NOT POSSIBLE.
IT IS IF SOMEBODY SWITCHED IT ON YOU.
MY GOD... THERESA...
DO YOU THINK THEY'RE ON TO ME?

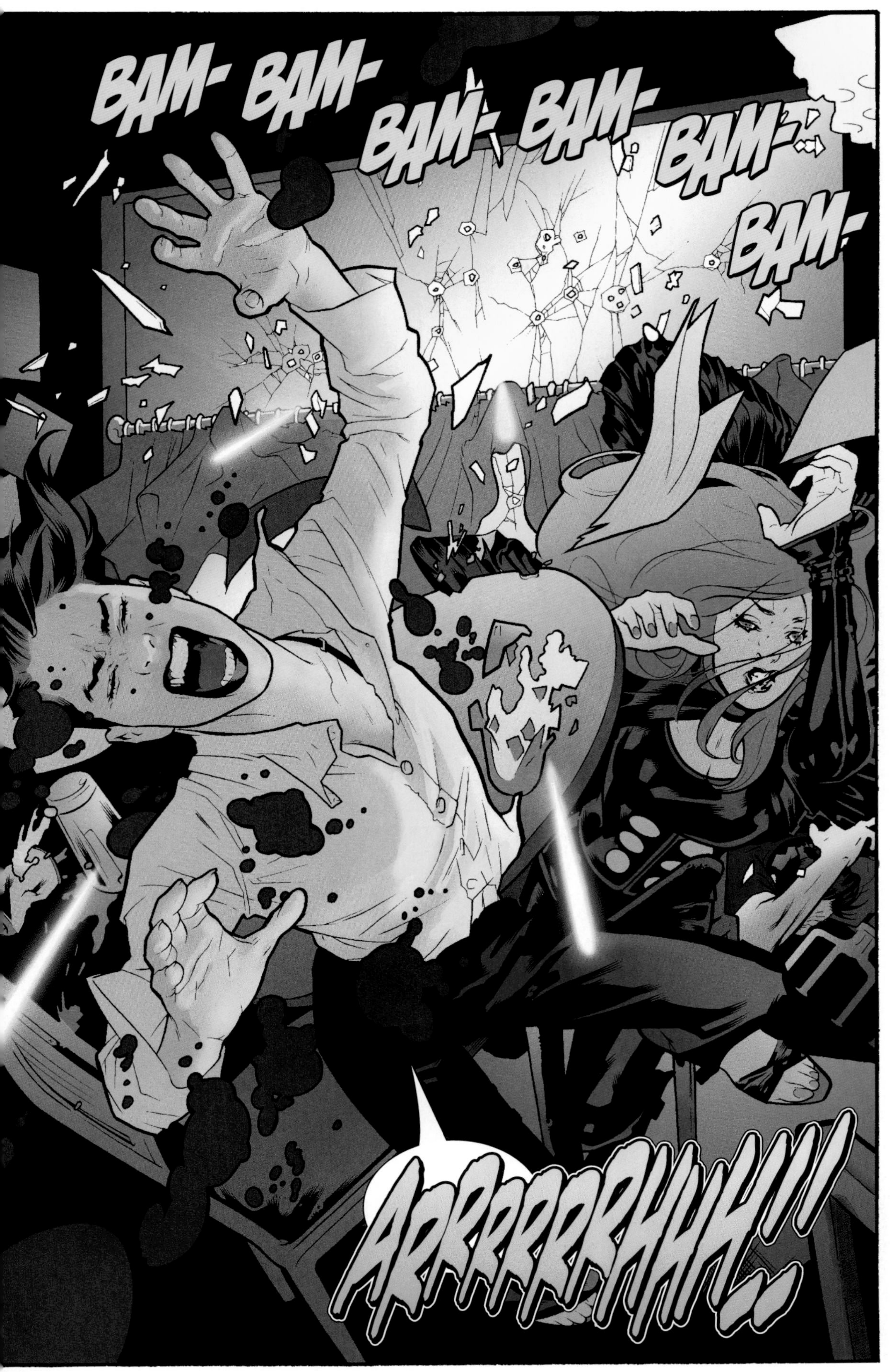
BAM- BAM-
BAM- BAM- BAM-
BAM-
ARRRRRRHHH!!..

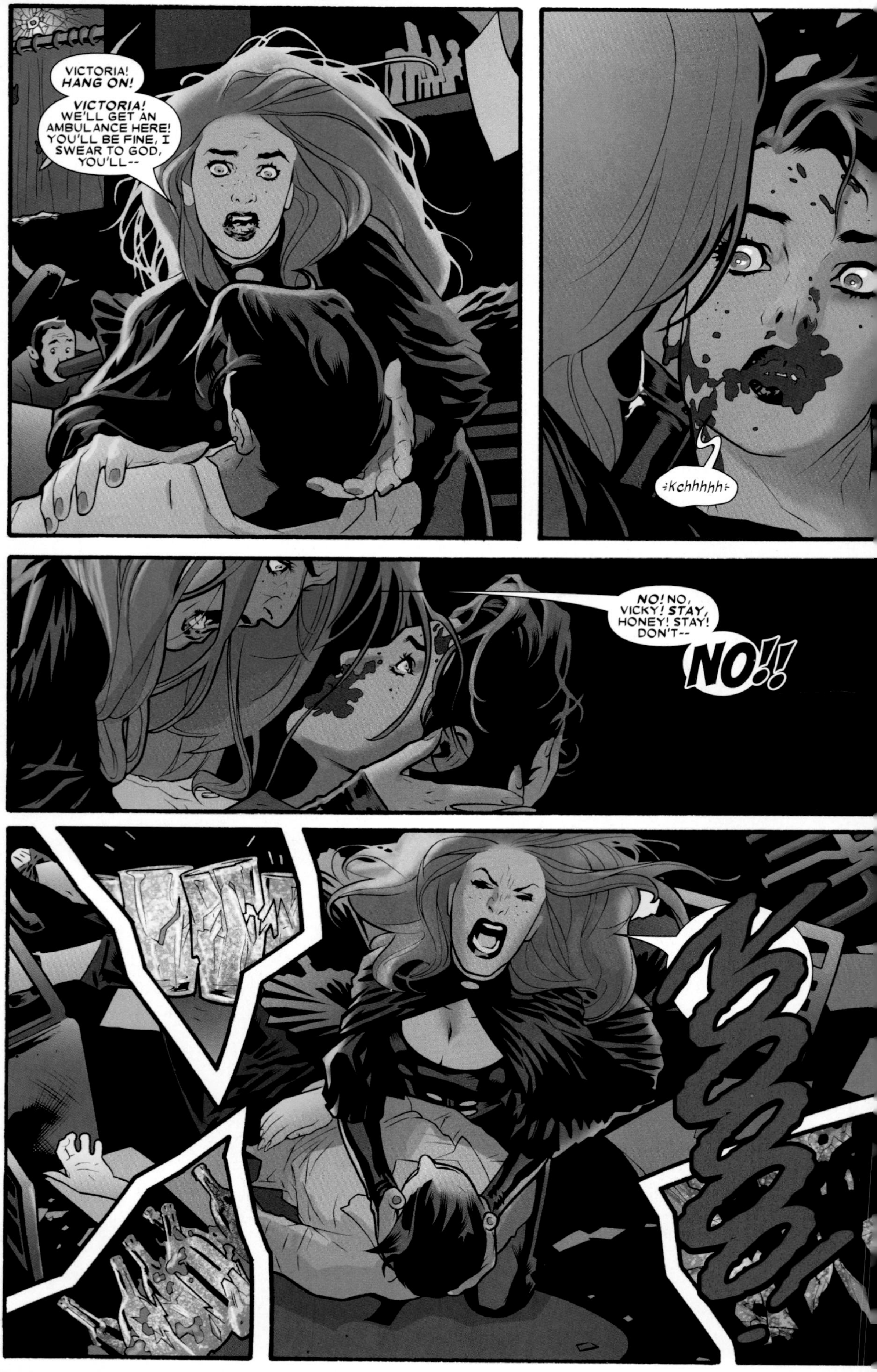
VICTORIA! **HANG ON!**
VICTORIA! WE'LL GET AN AMBULANCE HERE! YOU'LL BE FINE, I SWEAR TO GOD, YOU'LL--
kchhhhh
NO! NO, VICKY! **STAY,** HONEY! **STAY!** DON'T--
NO!!

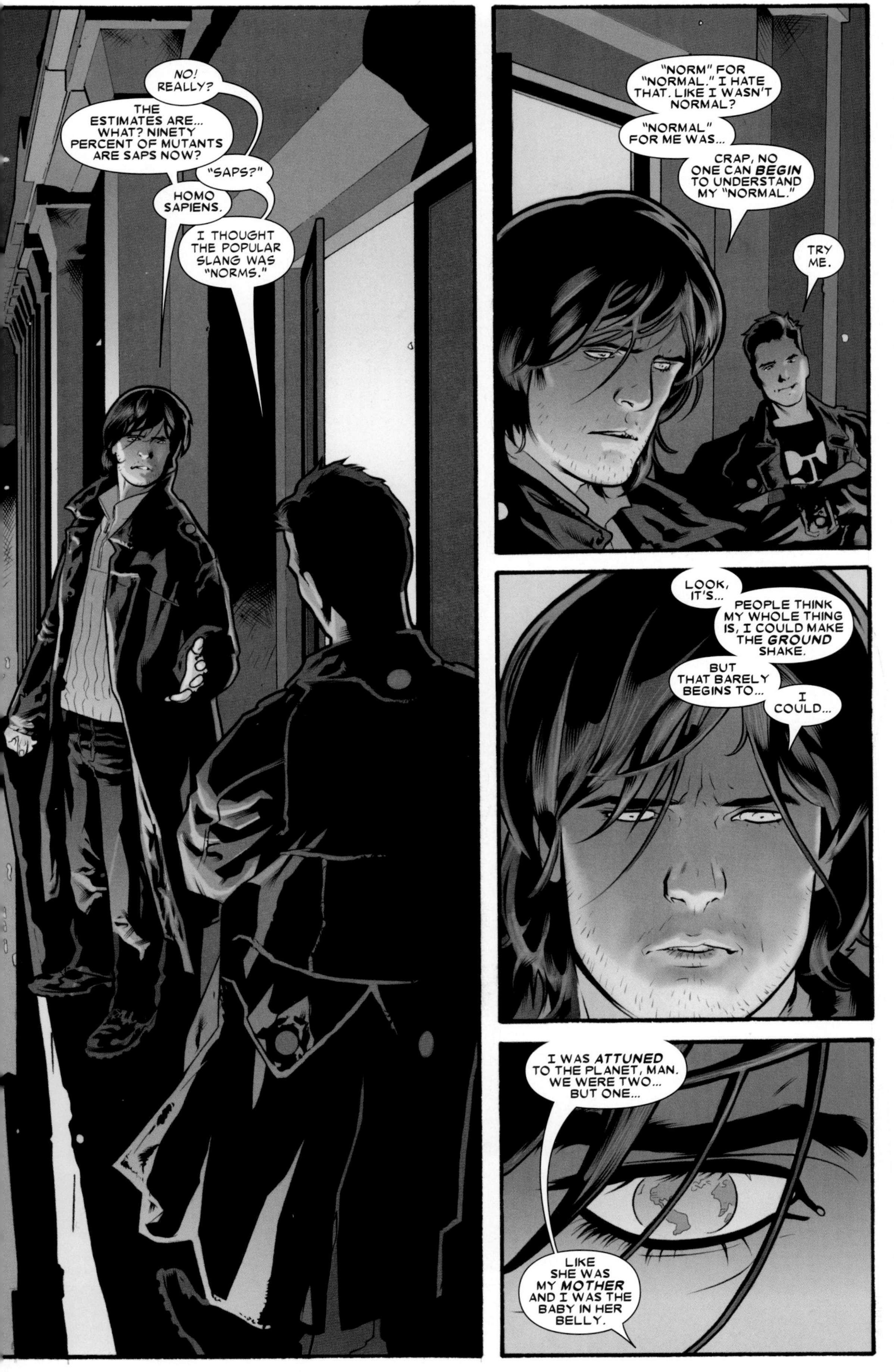
NO! REALLY?
THE ESTIMATES ARE... WHAT? NINETY PERCENT OF MUTANTS ARE SAPS NOW?
"SAPS?"
HOMO SAPIENS.
I THOUGHT THE POPULAR SLANG WAS "NORMS."
"NORM" FOR "NORMAL." I HATE THAT. LIKE I WASN'T NORMAL?
"NORMAL" FOR ME WAS...
CRAP, NO ONE CAN BEGIN TO UNDERSTAND MY "NORMAL."
TRY ME.
LOOK, IT'S...
PEOPLE THINK MY WHOLE THING IS, I COULD MAKE THE GROUND SHAKE.
BUT THAT BARELY BEGINS TO...
I COULD...
I WAS ATTUNED TO THE PLANET, MAN. WE WERE TWO... BUT ONE...
LIKE SHE WAS MY MOTHER AND I WAS THE BABY IN HER BELLY.

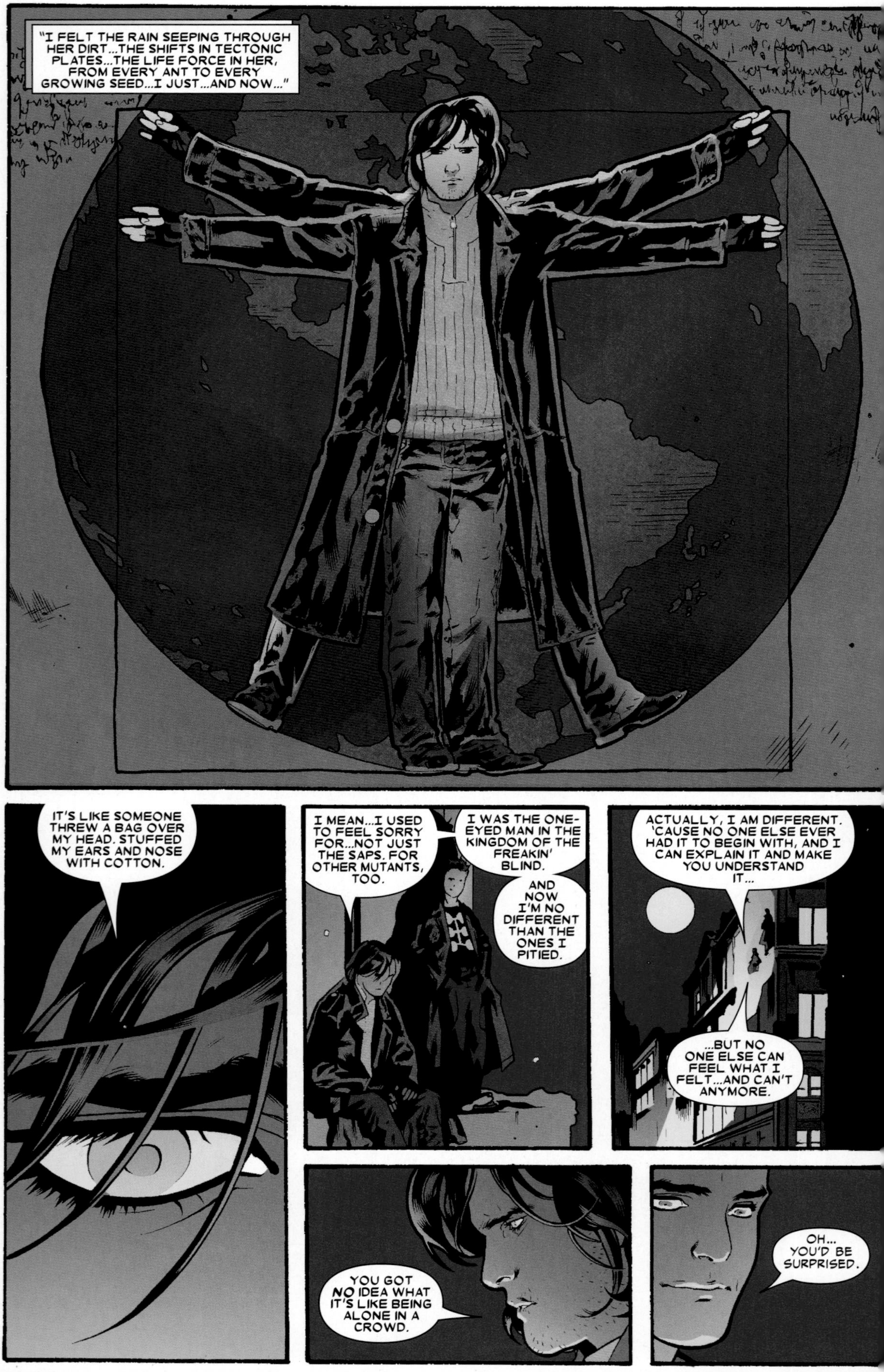
"I FELT THE RAIN SEEPING THROUGH HER DIRT...THE SHIFTS IN TECTONIC PLATES...THE LIFE FORCE IN HER, FROM EVERY ANT TO EVERY GROWING SEED...I JUST...AND NOW..."
IT'S LIKE SOMEONE THREW A BAG OVER MY HEAD. STUFFED MY EARS AND NOSE WITH COTTON.
I MEAN...I USED TO FEEL SORRY FOR...NOT JUST THE SAPS. FOR OTHER MUTANTS, TOO.
I WAS THE ONE-EYED MAN IN THE KINGDOM OF THE FREAKIN' BLIND.
AND NOW I'M NO DIFFERENT THAN THE ONES I PITIED.
ACTUALLY, I AM DIFFERENT. 'CAUSE NO ONE ELSE EVER HAD IT TO BEGIN WITH, AND I CAN EXPLAIN IT AND MAKE YOU UNDERSTAND IT...
...BUT NO ONE ELSE CAN FEEL WHAT I FELT...AND CAN'T ANYMORE.
YOU GOT NO IDEA WHAT IT'S LIKE BEING ALONE IN A CROWD.
OH... YOU'D BE SURPRISED.

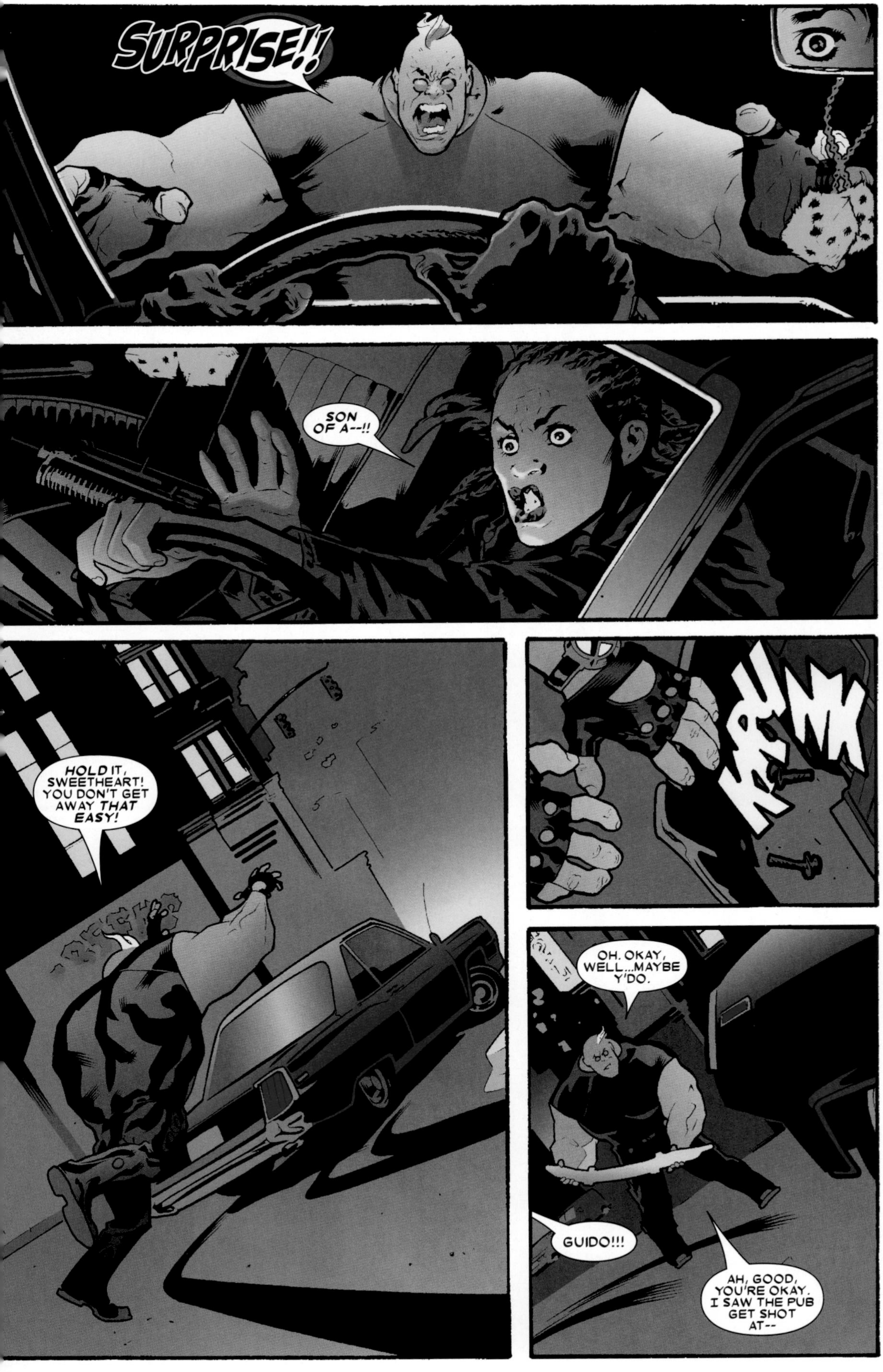
SURPRISE!!
SON OF A--!!
HOLD IT, SWEETHEART! YOU DON'T GET AWAY THAT EASY!
KRUNK
OH. OKAY, WELL...MAYBE Y'DO.
GUIDO!!!
AH, GOOD, YOU'RE OKAY. I SAW THE PUB GET SHOT AT--

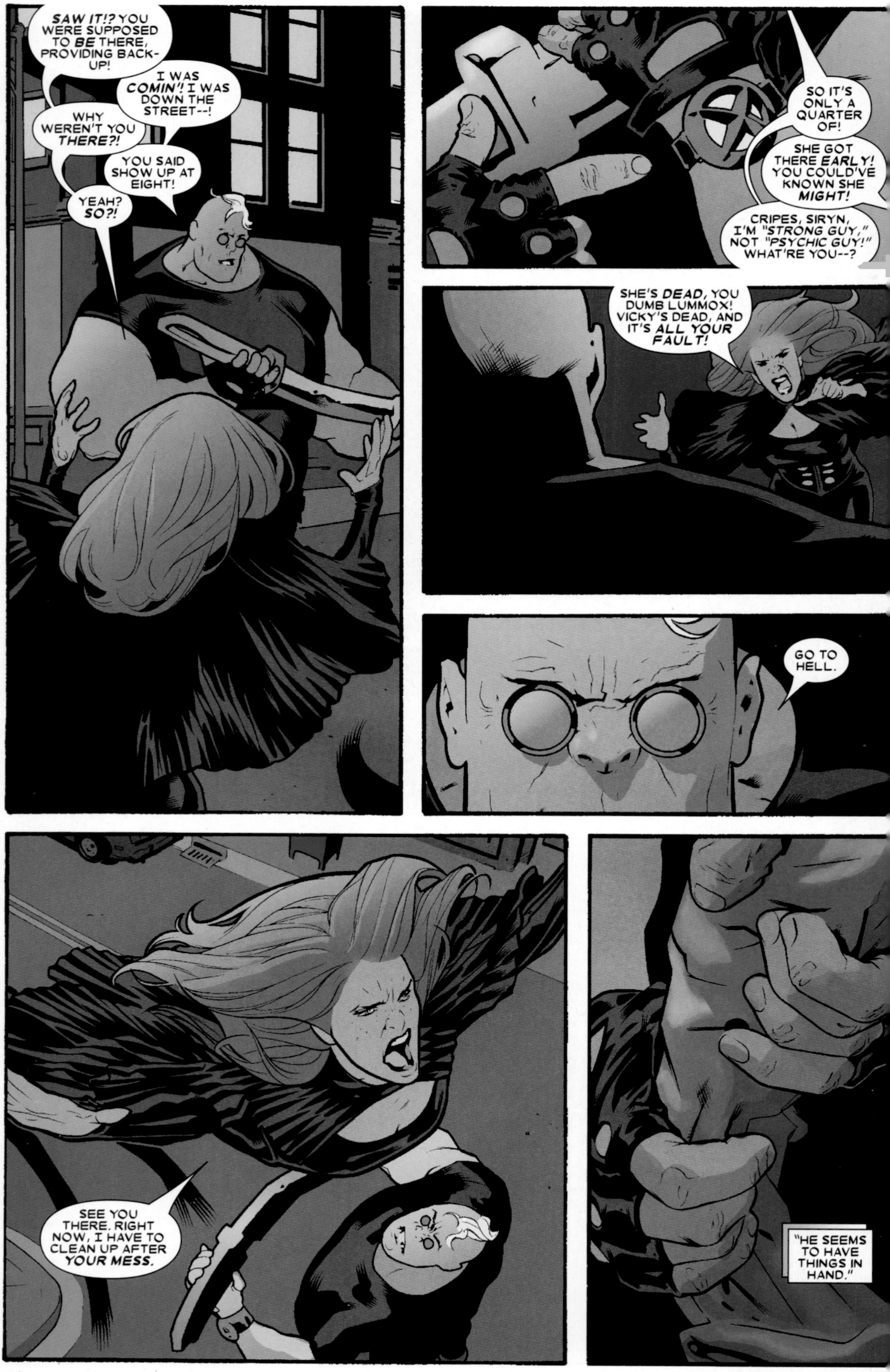
SAW IT!? YOU WERE SUPPOSED TO BE THERE, PROVIDING BACK-UP!
I WAS COMIN'! I WAS DOWN THE STREET--!
WHY WEREN'T YOU THERE?!
YOU SAID SHOW UP AT EIGHT!
YEAH? SO?!
SO IT'S ONLY A QUARTER OF!
SHE GOT THERE EARLY! YOU COULD'VE KNOWN SHE MIGHT!
CRIPES, SIRYN, I'M "STRONG GUY," NOT "PSYCHIC GUY!" WHAT'RE YOU--?
SHE'S DEAD, YOU DUMB LUMMOX! VICKY'S DEAD, AND IT'S ALL YOUR FAULT!
GO TO HELL.
SEE YOU THERE. RIGHT NOW, I HAVE TO CLEAN UP AFTER YOUR MESS.
"HE SEEMS TO HAVE THINGS IN HAND."

HE'S KEEPING RIC TALKING, WHICH IS THE IMPORTANT THING. NO ONE EVER JUMPS IN THE MIDDLE OF A SENTENCE. IT'S...

...I DUNNO... *RUDE*.

SHOULD YOU COME *HERE*? BY ALL MEANS. AND *HURRY*.

NO, I *WASN'T* IMPLYING YOU WERE GOING TO *STROLL*. I WAS--

JUST GET *OVER* HERE AND DON'T GIMME GRIEF, OKAY? JEEZ.

Y'KNOW...*I'D* DO IT. JUMP IN THE MIDDLE OF A SENTENCE.

I HAVE A PERVERSE SIDE OF ME THAT COMPELS ME TO DO THE UNEXPECTED. I CAN JUST SEE IT--

"THAT'S AN INTERESTING POINT I HADN'T CONSID--*AHHHHHH!*"

THAT WOULD BE FUNNY...BUT NOT REALLY.

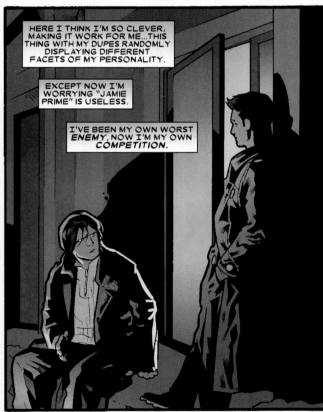

HERE I THINK I'M SO CLEVER, MAKING IT WORK FOR ME...THIS THING WITH MY DUPES RANDOMLY DISPLAYING DIFFERENT FACETS OF MY PERSONALITY.

EXCEPT NOW I'M WORRYING "JAMIE PRIME" IS USELESS.

I'VE BEEN MY OWN WORST *ENEMY*. NOW I'M MY OWN *COMPETITION*.

X-FACTOR?" EALLY? AND OU'RE THE BOSS?

YUP. IT STARTED OUT AS A SMALL DETECTIVE AGENCY. ME, STRONG GUY, WOLFSBANE...

"WOLFSBANE?" RAHNE JOINED UP?

PART-TIME, YEAH. STRICTLY LOW-RENT...UNTIL I GOT A MILLION BUCKS TO UPGRADE.

WHERE'D YOU GET A MILLION DOLLARS FROM?

FUNNY STORY, ACTUALLY...

OKAY, JAMIE, YOU'RE USING YOUR PHONE-A-FRIEND LIFELINE FOR THE HALF-MILLION DOLLAR QUESTION... YOUR FRIEND'S NAME IS "JAMIE" ALSO, IS THAT RIGHT?

YEAH.

YOU GOT THIRTY SECONDS, AND...*GO!*

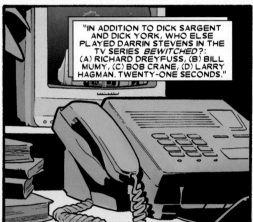

"IN ADDITION TO DICK SARGENT AND DICK YORK, WHO ELSE PLAYED DARRIN STEVENS IN THE TV SERIES *BEWITCHED*?: (A) RICHARD DREYFUSS, (B) BILL MUMY, (C) BOB CRANE, (D) LARRY HAGMAN. TWENTY-ONE SECONDS."

OOOO... LEMME THINK. UHM...

ISN'T THIS KIND OF *CHEATING?*

WHY? HE'S ONLY CALLING *ONE* FRIEND.

IT'S MUMY! HE PLAYED DARRIN WHEN ENDORA CHANGED HIM INTO A KID!

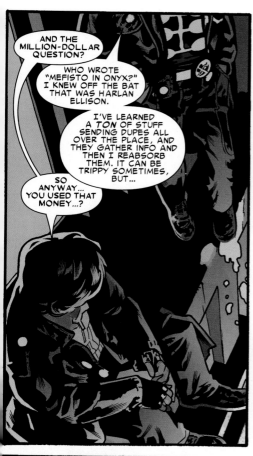

AND THE MILLION-DOLLAR QUESTION?

WHO WROTE "MEFISTO IN ONYX?" I KNEW OFF THE BAT THAT WAS HARLAN ELLISON.

I'VE LEARNED A *TON* OF STUFF SENDING DUPES ALL OVER THE PLACE, AND THEY GATHER INFO AND THEN I REABSORB THEM. IT CAN BE TRIPPY SOMETIMES, BUT...

SO ANYWAY... YOU USED THAT MONEY...?

"YEAH, I DID...TO BUY THE BUILDING WE WERE IN. THE OFFICES ARE THERE, WE TOOK ON A FEW MORE OPERATIVES, AND WE'VE GOT APARTMENTS SET UP SO WE CAN LIVE THERE..."

"...WHICH ISN'T EXACTLY WITHIN BUILDING CODE, BUT THE LOCAL LAW DOESN'T BOTHER US, AND THE BIG BOYS TEND TO STAY OUT OF MUTANT TOWN IF AT ALL POSSIBLE..."

X-FACTOR INVESTIGATIONS

OR AT LEAST WHAT'S LEFT OF MUTANT TOWN, AFTER THE...

THE GREAT POWER OUTAGE OF 2005. OVERNIGHT, HUNDREDS--MAYBE THOUSANDS OF MUTANTS-- WHO, JUST LIKE THAT... AREN'T ANYMORE.

YOU'RE DETECTIVES. WHY AREN'T YOU INVESTIGATING THAT-- WHAT ARE THEY CALLING IT... M-DAY?

WHO SAYS WE'RE NOT?

RICTOR, EVERYONE IN OUR NECK OF THE WOODS KNOWS US AS THE "MUTANT DETECTIVE AGENCY."

THE DUST BARELY SETTLED AND OUR PHONES WERE RINGING OFF THE *HOOK* FROM EX-MUTANTS...NO PUN INTENDED...ASKING US TO FIND OUT WHAT HAPPENED.

IT'S NOT THE ONLY CASE WE'RE WORKING ON, BUT WE *ARE* WORKING ON IT.

OKAY, SO...WAIT. WHO'S "WE" EXACTLY?

OH, SOME *GREAT* PEOPLE. TOP FLIGHT.

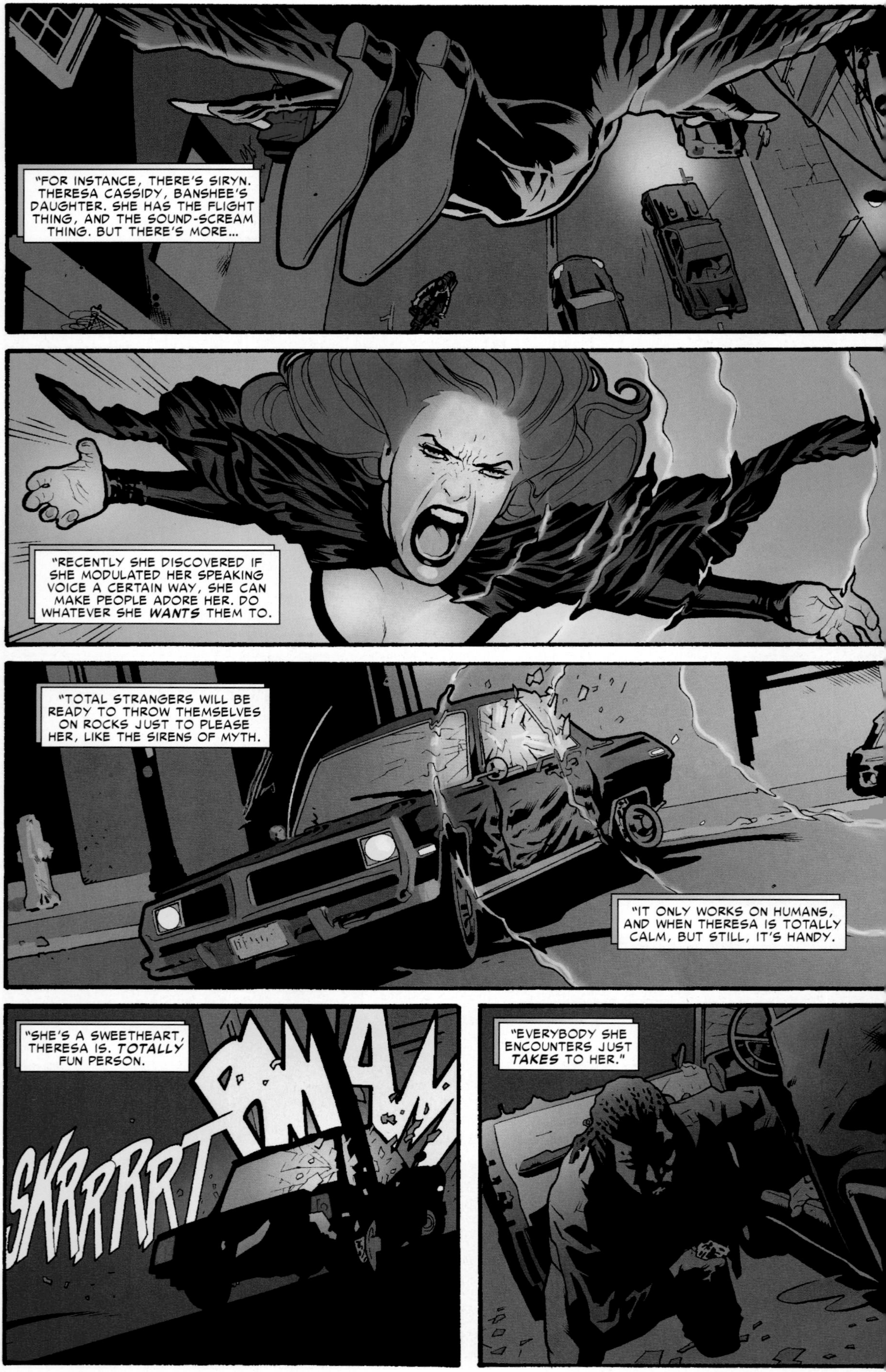
"FOR INSTANCE, THERE'S SIRYN. THERESA CASSIDY, BANSHEE'S DAUGHTER. SHE HAS THE FLIGHT THING, AND THE SOUND-SCREAM THING. BUT THERE'S MORE...
"RECENTLY SHE DISCOVERED IF SHE MODULATED HER SPEAKING VOICE A CERTAIN WAY, SHE CAN MAKE PEOPLE ADORE HER. DO WHATEVER SHE *WANTS* THEM TO.
"TOTAL STRANGERS WILL BE READY TO THROW THEMSELVES ON ROCKS JUST TO PLEASE HER, LIKE THE SIRENS OF MYTH.
"IT ONLY WORKS ON HUMANS, AND WHEN THERESA IS TOTALLY CALM, BUT STILL, IT'S HANDY.
"SHE'S A SWEETHEART, THERESA IS. *TOTALLY* FUN PERSON.
BMAM
SKRRRRT
"EVERYBODY SHE ENCOUNTERS JUST *TAKES* TO HER."

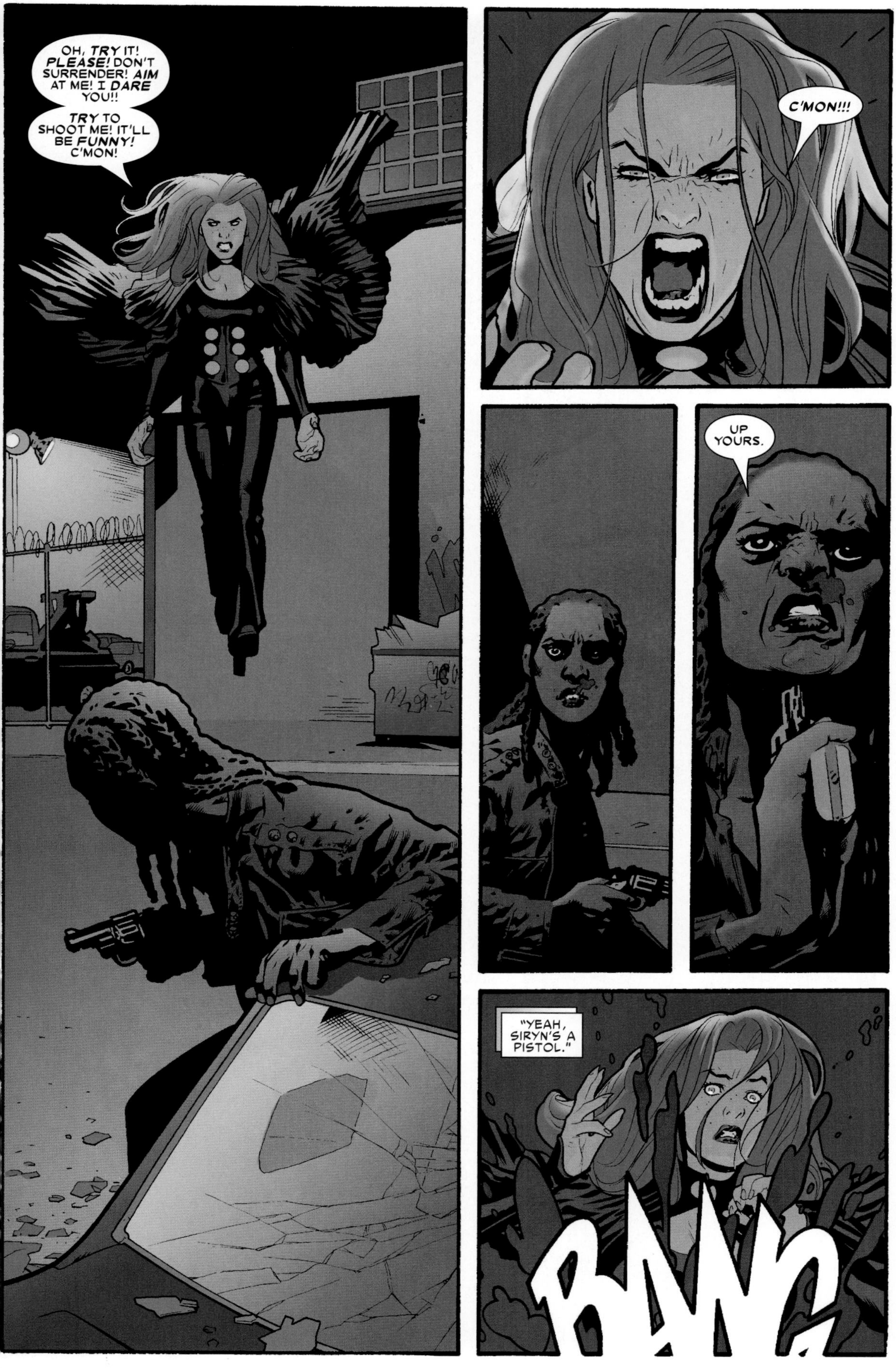
OH, TRY IT! PLEASE! DON'T SURRENDER! AIM AT ME! I DARE YOU!!
TRY TO SHOOT ME! IT'LL BE FUNNY! C'MON!
C'MON!!!
UP YOURS.
"YEAH, SIRYN'S A PISTOL."
BANG

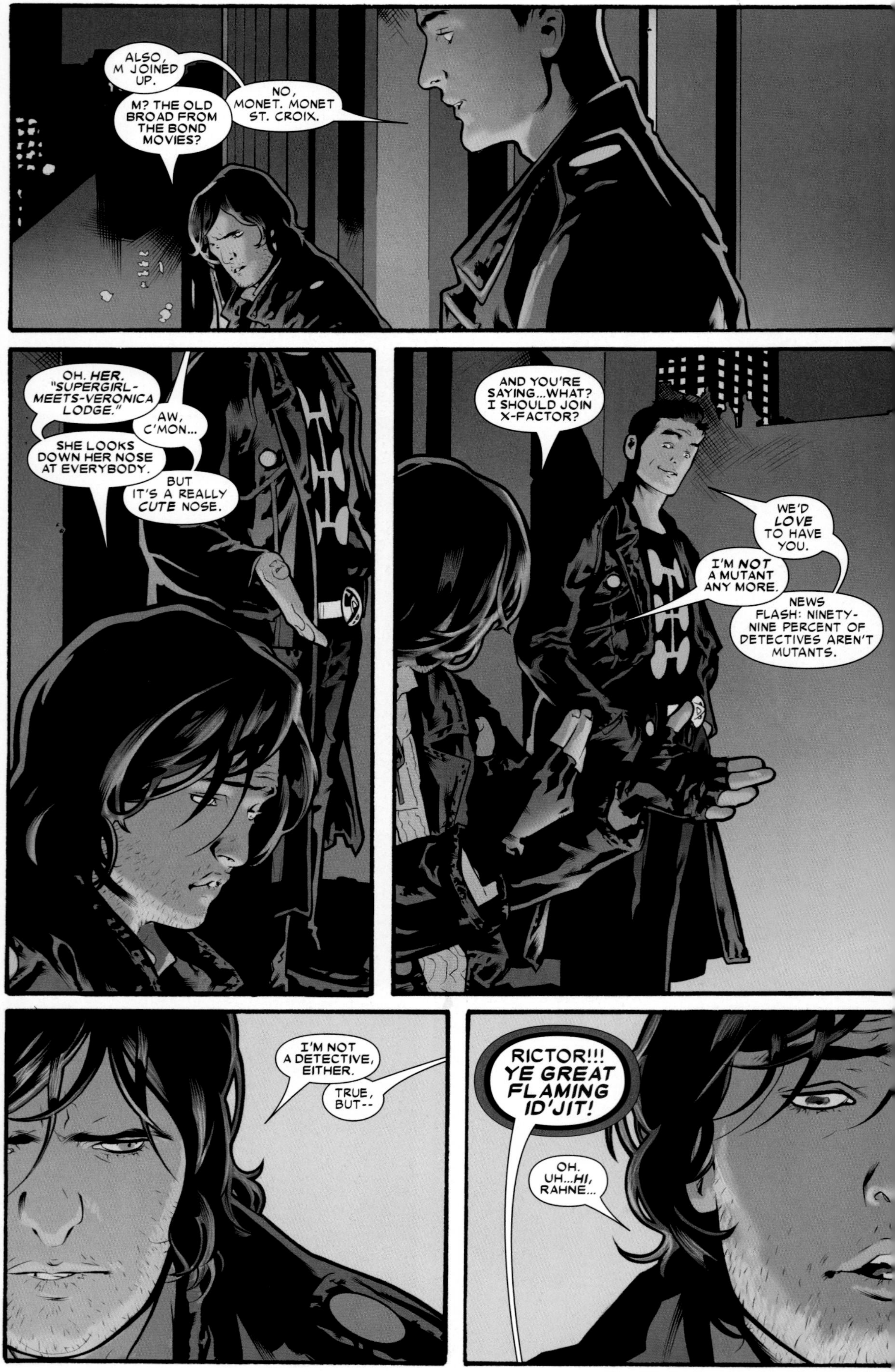
ALSO, M JOINED UP.
M? THE OLD BROAD FROM THE BOND MOVIES?
NO, MONET. MONET ST. CROIX.
OH. *HER.* "SUPERGIRL-MEETS-VERONICA LODGE."
AW, C'MON...
SHE LOOKS DOWN HER NOSE AT EVERYBODY.
BUT IT'S A REALLY *CUTE* NOSE.
AND YOU'RE SAYING...WHAT? I SHOULD JOIN X-FACTOR?
WE'D *LOVE* TO HAVE YOU.
I'M *NOT* A MUTANT ANY MORE.
NEWS FLASH: NINETY-NINE PERCENT OF DETECTIVES AREN'T MUTANTS.
I'M NOT A DETECTIVE, EITHER.
TRUE, BUT--
RICTOR!!! *YE GREAT FLAMING ID'JIT!*
OH. UH...*HI,* RAHNE...

DON'T YE BE "HI, RAHNE-ING" ME!

SUICIDE?! DO YE KNOW WHAT'LL HAPPEN IF YE KILL YUIRSELF? *DO YE?*

IT'S A *MORTAL SIN!* IT'S A *DEATH BLOW* TO YUIR SOUL!

YE'LL GO STRAIGHT TO HELL! HELL, RICTOR!

ETERNAL PUNISHMENT, BURNING IN TH' LAKE OF FIRE FOR EVER AND EVER!

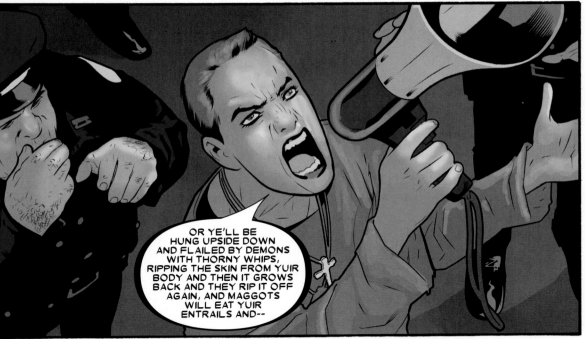

OR YE'LL BE HUNG UPSIDE DOWN AND FLAILED BY DEMONS WITH THORNY WHIPS, RIPPING THE SKIN FROM YUIR BODY AND THEN IT GROWS BACK AND THEY RIP IT OFF AGAIN, AND MAGGOTS WILL EAT YUIR ENTRAILS AND--

Y'KNOW...IN JAPAN, SUICIDE IS HISTORICALLY REGARDED AS AN HONORABLE MEANS OF--

DOES THIS LOOK LIKE JAPAN?! DOES IT?! YE SEE SHINTO *SHRINES* ANYWHERE?! A TOSHIRO MIFUNE FILM FESTIVAL DOWN THE STREET? *DO YE?*

UH... NO?

CORRECT! AND YE KNOW WHY? 'CAUSE YOU'RE NOT IN *BLEEDING JAPAN,* THAT'S WHY! DO YOU KNOW WHERE YE *ARE?!*

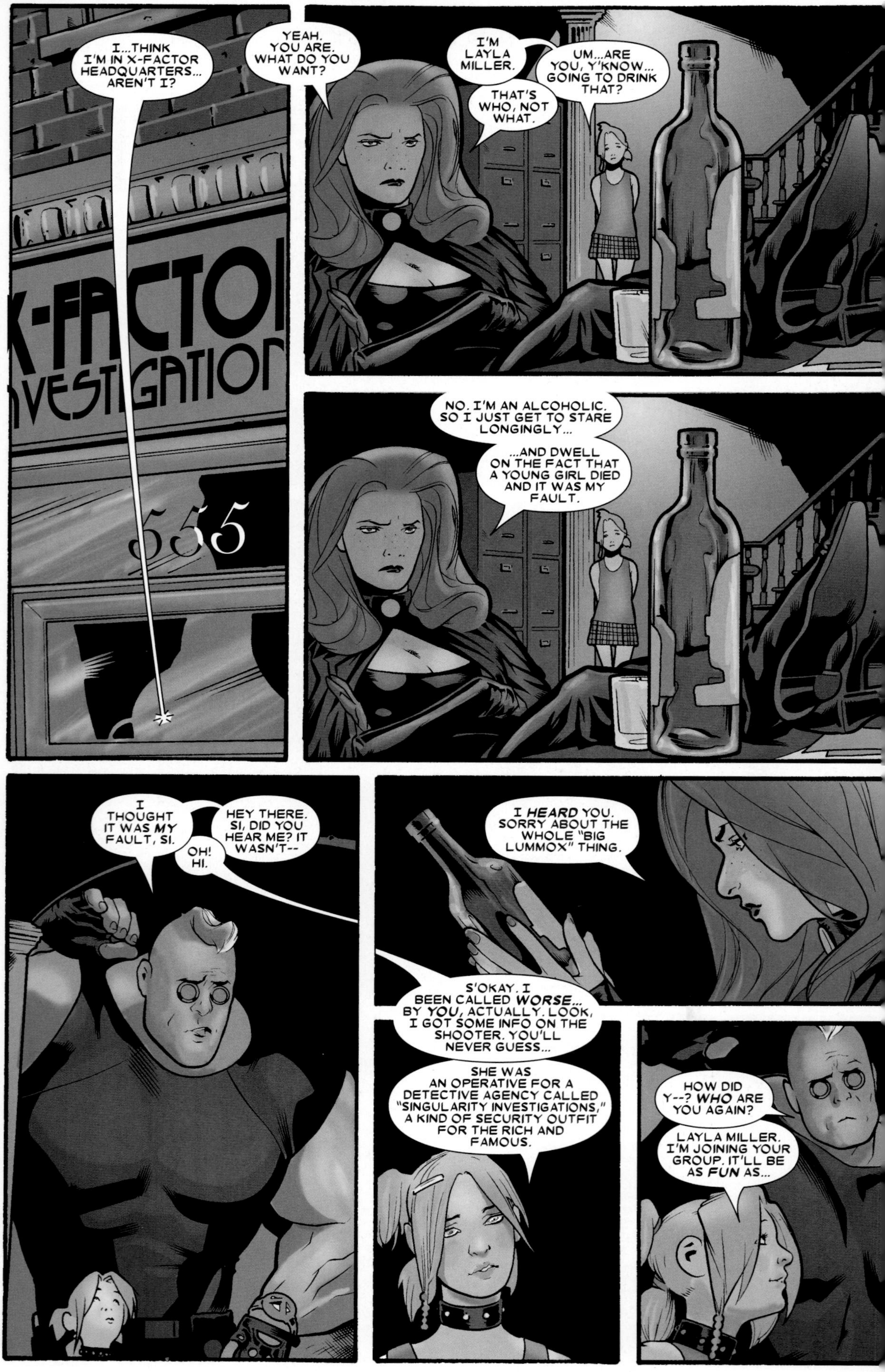
I...THINK I'M IN X-FACTOR HEADQUARTERS... AREN'T I?
X-FACTOR INVESTIGATION
555
YEAH. YOU ARE. WHAT DO YOU WANT?
I'M LAYLA MILLER.
THAT'S WHO, NOT WHAT.
UM...ARE YOU, Y'KNOW... GOING TO DRINK THAT?
NO. I'M AN ALCOHOLIC. SO I JUST GET TO STARE LONGINGLY...
...AND DWELL ON THE FACT THAT A YOUNG GIRL DIED AND IT WAS MY FAULT.
I THOUGHT IT WAS MY FAULT, SI.
HEY THERE. SI, DID YOU HEAR ME? IT WASN'T--
OH! HI.
I HEARD YOU. SORRY ABOUT THE WHOLE "BIG LUMMOX" THING.
S'OKAY. I BEEN CALLED WORSE... BY YOU, ACTUALLY. LOOK, I GOT SOME INFO ON THE SHOOTER. YOU'LL NEVER GUESS...
SHE WAS AN OPERATIVE FOR A DETECTIVE AGENCY CALLED "SINGULARITY INVESTIGATIONS," A KIND OF SECURITY OUTFIT FOR THE RICH AND FAMOUS.
HOW DID Y--? WHO ARE YOU AGAIN?
LAYLA MILLER. I'M JOINING YOUR GROUP. IT'LL BE AS FUN AS...

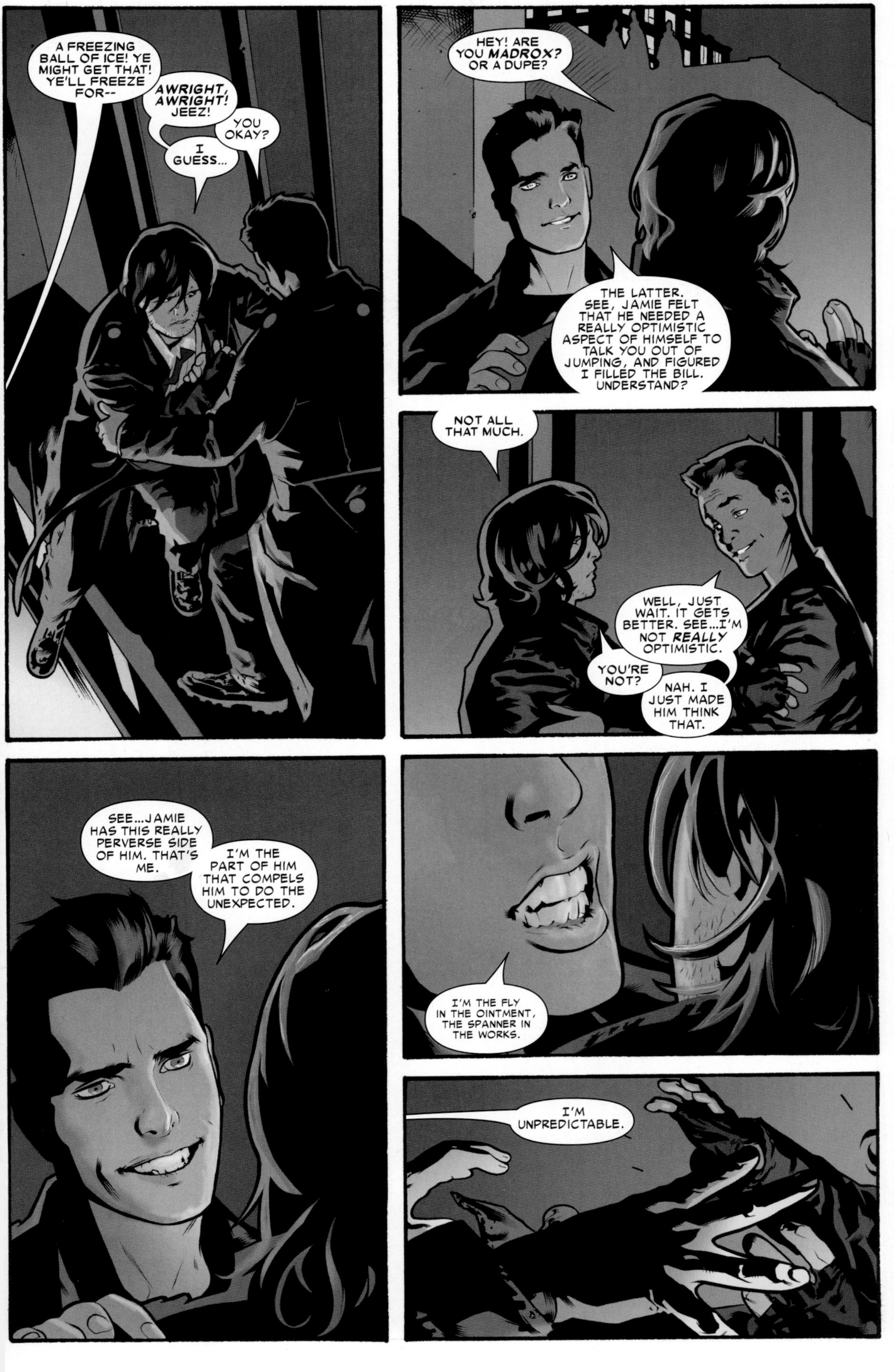
A FREEZING BALL OF ICE! YE MIGHT GET THAT! YE'LL FREEZE FOR--
AWRIGHT, AWRIGHT! JEEZ!
YOU OKAY?
I GUESS...
HEY! ARE YOU MADROX? OR A DUPE?
THE LATTER. SEE, JAMIE FELT THAT HE NEEDED A REALLY OPTIMISTIC ASPECT OF HIMSELF TO TALK YOU OUT OF JUMPING, AND FIGURED I FILLED THE BILL. UNDERSTAND?
NOT ALL THAT MUCH.
WELL, JUST WAIT. IT GETS BETTER. SEE...I'M NOT REALLY OPTIMISTIC.
YOU'RE NOT?
NAH. I JUST MADE HIM THINK THAT.
SEE...JAMIE HAS THIS REALLY PERVERSE SIDE OF HIM. THAT'S ME.
I'M THE PART OF HIM THAT COMPELS HIM TO DO THE UNEXPECTED.
I'M THE FLY IN THE OINTMENT, THE SPANNER IN THE WORKS.
I'M UNPREDICTABLE.

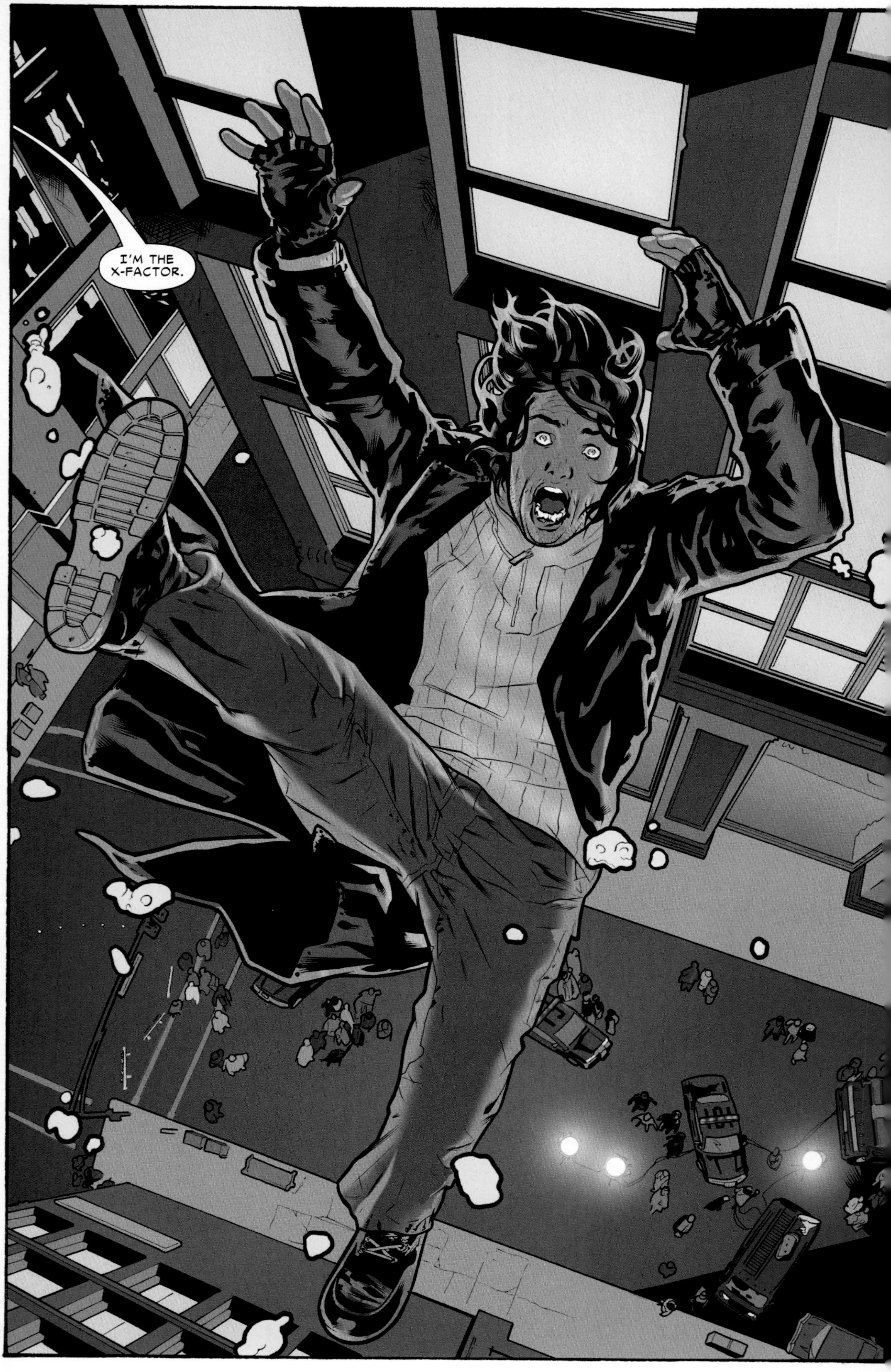
I'M THE X-FACTOR.

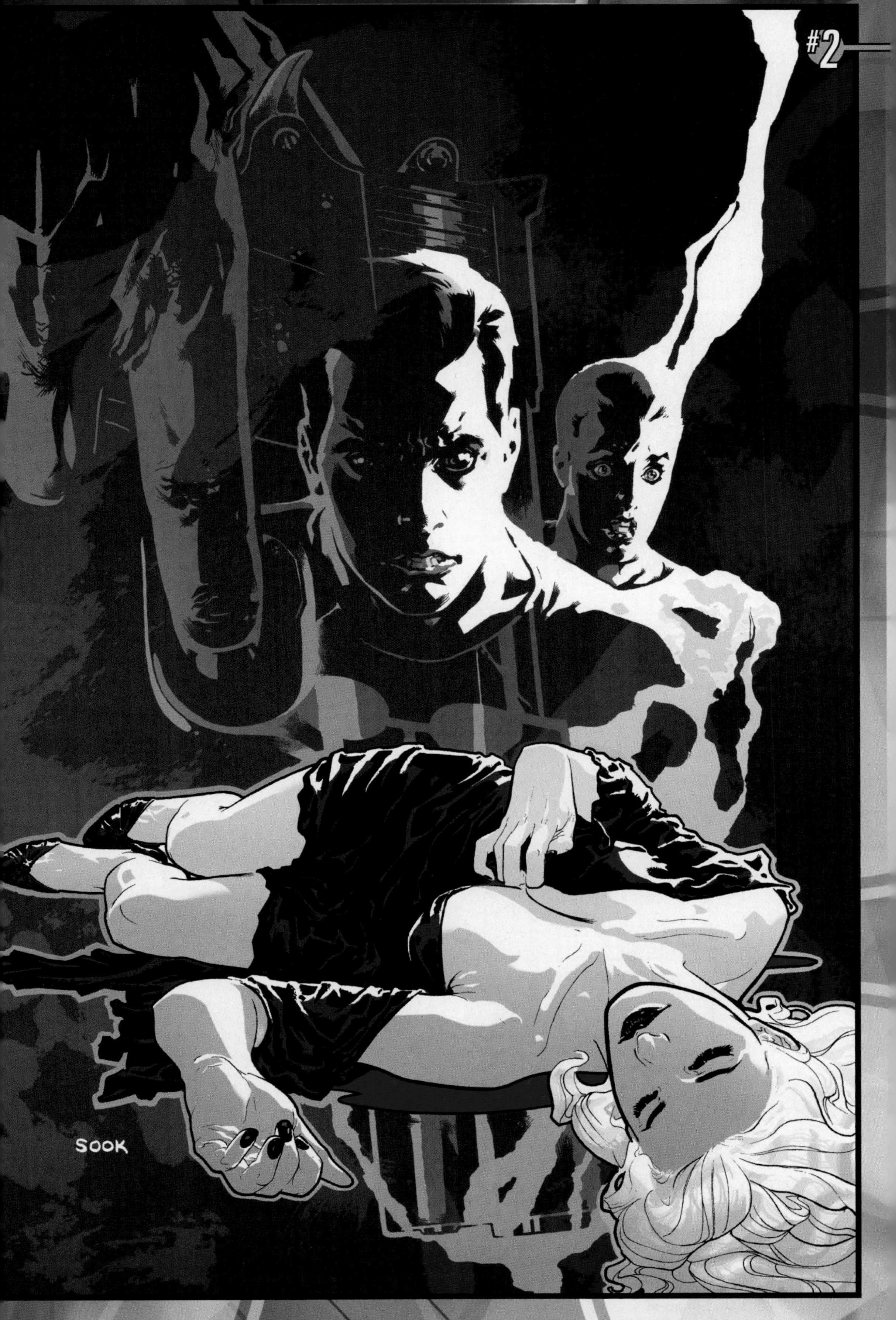
#2
SOOK

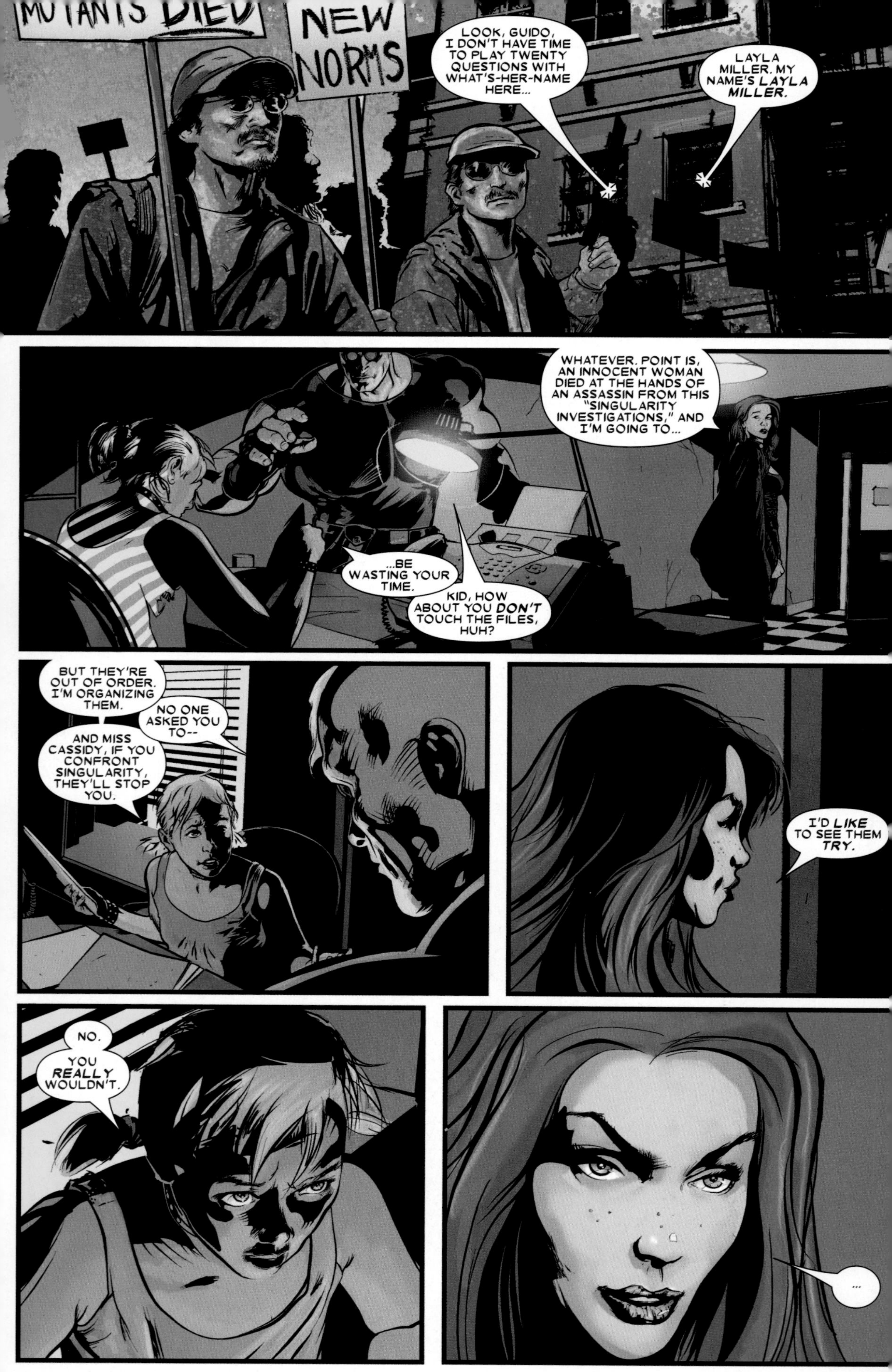
MUTANTS DIED
NEW NORMS
LOOK, GUIDO, I DON'T HAVE TIME TO PLAY TWENTY QUESTIONS WITH WHAT'S-HER-NAME HERE...
LAYLA MILLER. MY NAME'S *LAYLA MILLER.*
WHATEVER. POINT IS, AN INNOCENT WOMAN DIED AT THE HANDS OF AN ASSASSIN FROM THIS "SINGULARITY INVESTIGATIONS," AND I'M GOING TO...
...BE WASTING YOUR TIME.
KID, HOW ABOUT YOU *DON'T* TOUCH THE FILES, HUH?
BUT THEY'RE OUT OF ORDER. I'M ORGANIZING THEM.
NO ONE ASKED YOU TO--
AND MISS CASSIDY, IF YOU CONFRONT SINGULARITY, THEY'LL STOP YOU.
I'D *LIKE* TO SEE THEM *TRY.*
NO.
YOU *REALLY* WOULDN'T.
...

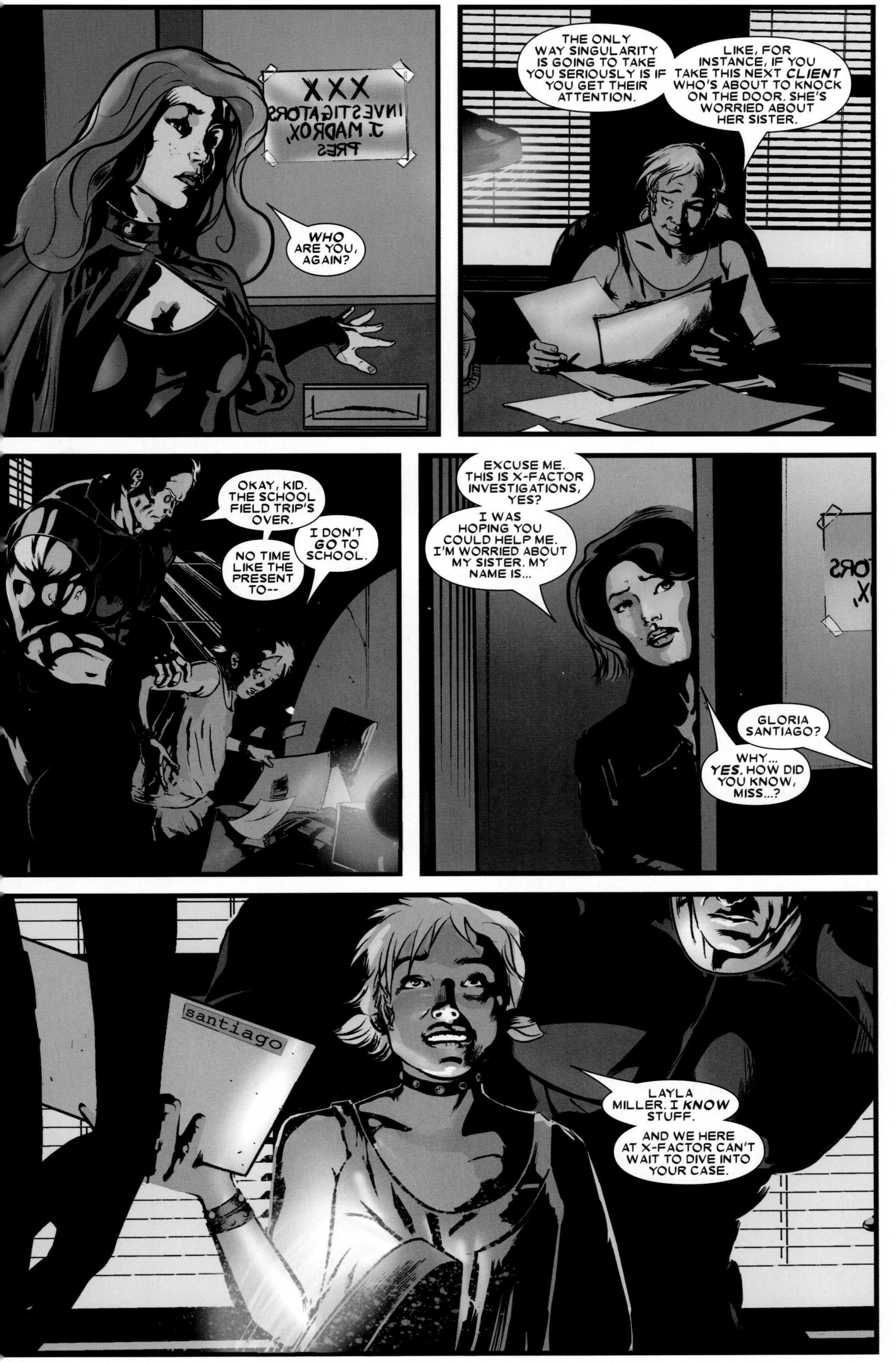

XXX INVESTIGATORS J. MADROX, PRES
WHO ARE YOU, AGAIN?
THE ONLY WAY SINGULARITY IS GOING TO TAKE YOU SERIOUSLY IS IF YOU GET THEIR ATTENTION.
LIKE, FOR INSTANCE, IF YOU TAKE THIS NEXT CLIENT WHO'S ABOUT TO KNOCK ON THE DOOR. SHE'S WORRIED ABOUT HER SISTER.
OKAY, KID. THE SCHOOL FIELD TRIP'S OVER.
NO TIME LIKE THE PRESENT TO--
I DON'T GO TO SCHOOL.
EXCUSE ME. THIS IS X-FACTOR INVESTIGATIONS, YES?
I WAS HOPING YOU COULD HELP ME. I'M WORRIED ABOUT MY SISTER. MY NAME IS...
GLORIA SANTIAGO?
WHY... YES. HOW DID YOU KNOW, MISS...?
santiago
LAYLA MILLER. I KNOW STUFF.
AND WE HERE AT X-FACTOR CAN'T WAIT TO DIVE INTO YOUR CASE.

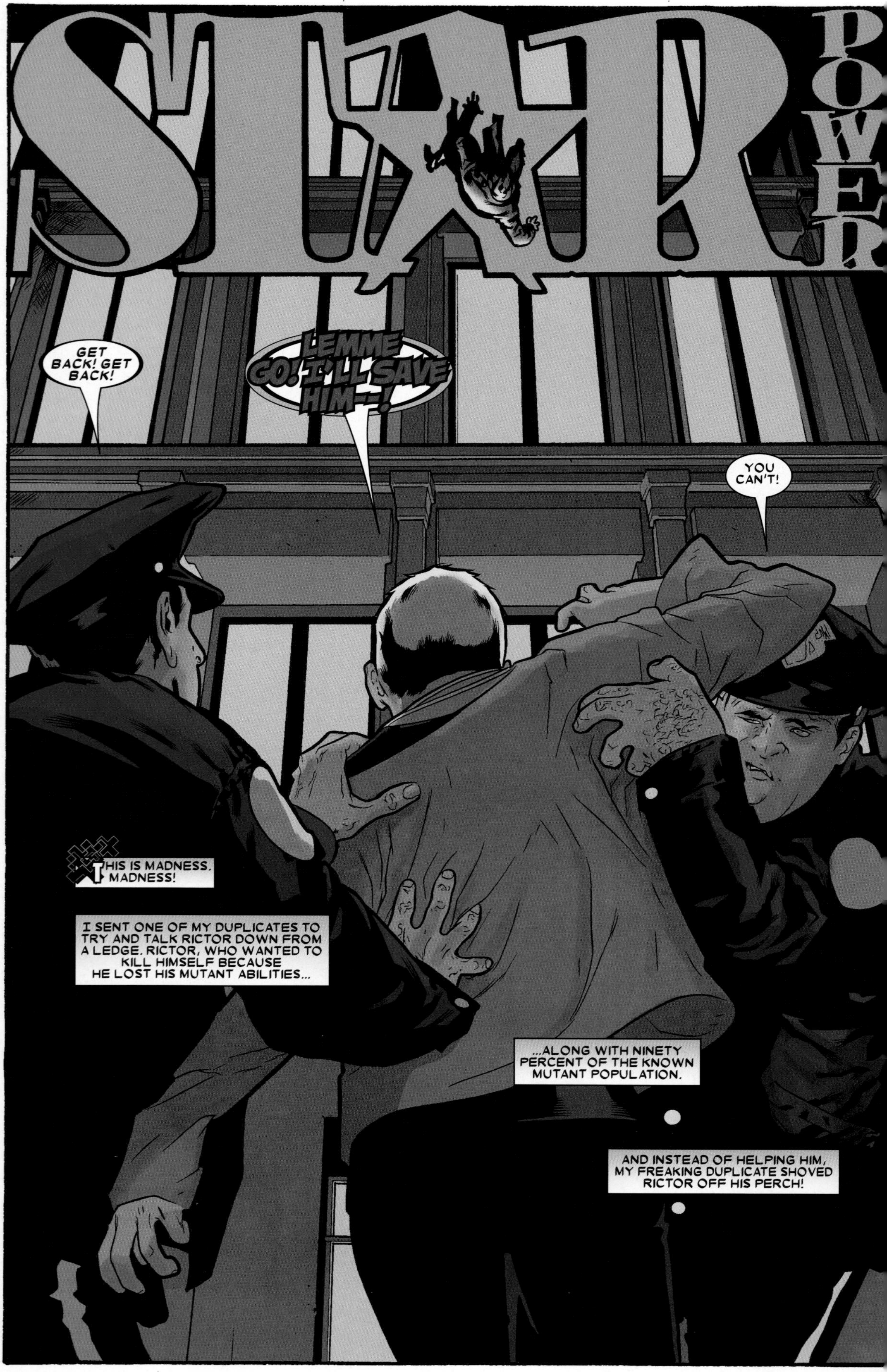
STAR POWER
GET BACK! GET BACK!
LEMME GO! I'LL SAVE HIM--!
YOU CAN'T!
THIS IS MADNESS. MADNESS!
I SENT ONE OF MY DUPLICATES TO TRY AND TALK RICTOR DOWN FROM A LEDGE. RICTOR, WHO WANTED TO KILL HIMSELF BECAUSE HE LOST HIS MUTANT ABILITIES...
...ALONG WITH NINETY PERCENT OF THE KNOWN MUTANT POPULATION.
AND INSTEAD OF HELPING HIM, MY FREAKING DUPLICATE SHOVED RICTOR OFF HIS PERCH!

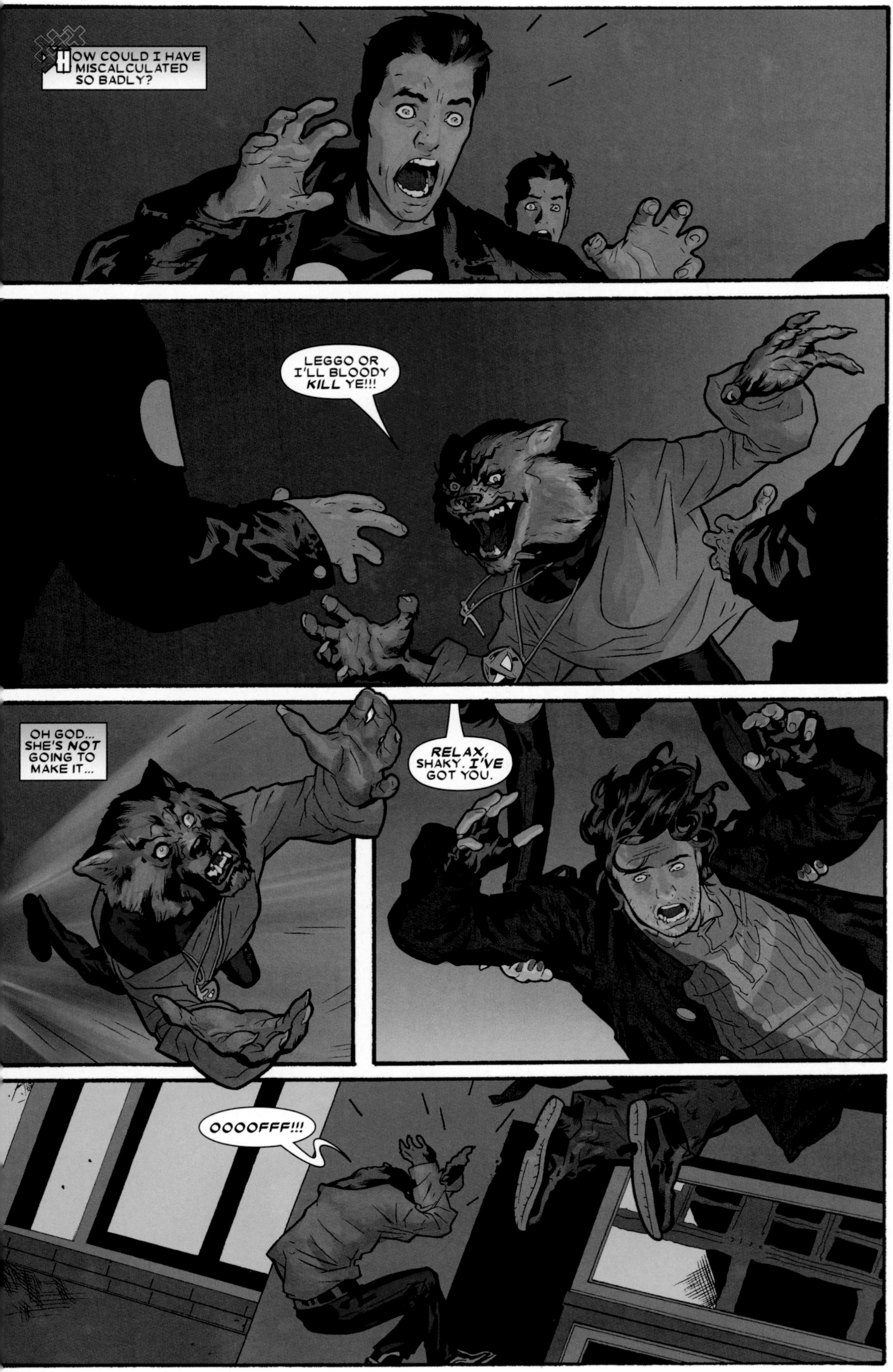
HOW COULD I HAVE MISCALCULATED SO BADLY?
LEGGO OR I'LL BLOODY KILL YE!!!
OH GOD... SHE'S NOT GOING TO MAKE IT...
RELAX, SHAKY. I'VE GOT YOU.
OOOOFFF!!!

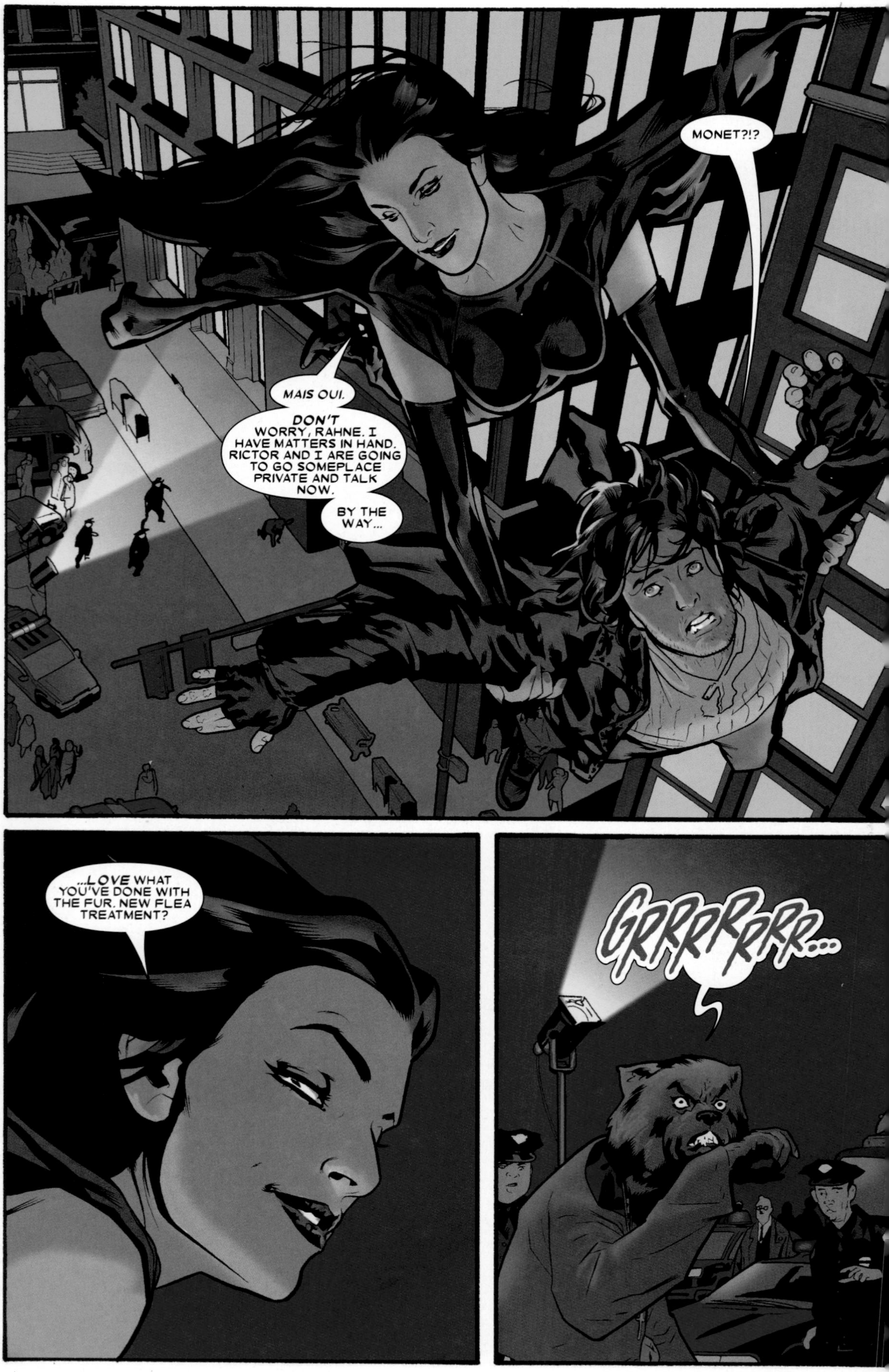
MONET?!?
MAIS OUI.
DON'T WORRY, RAHNE. I HAVE MATTERS IN HAND. RICTOR AND I ARE GOING TO GO SOMEPLACE PRIVATE AND TALK NOW.
BY THE WAY...
...LOVE WHAT YOU'VE DONE WITH THE FUR. NEW FLEA TREATMENT?
GRRRRRRR...

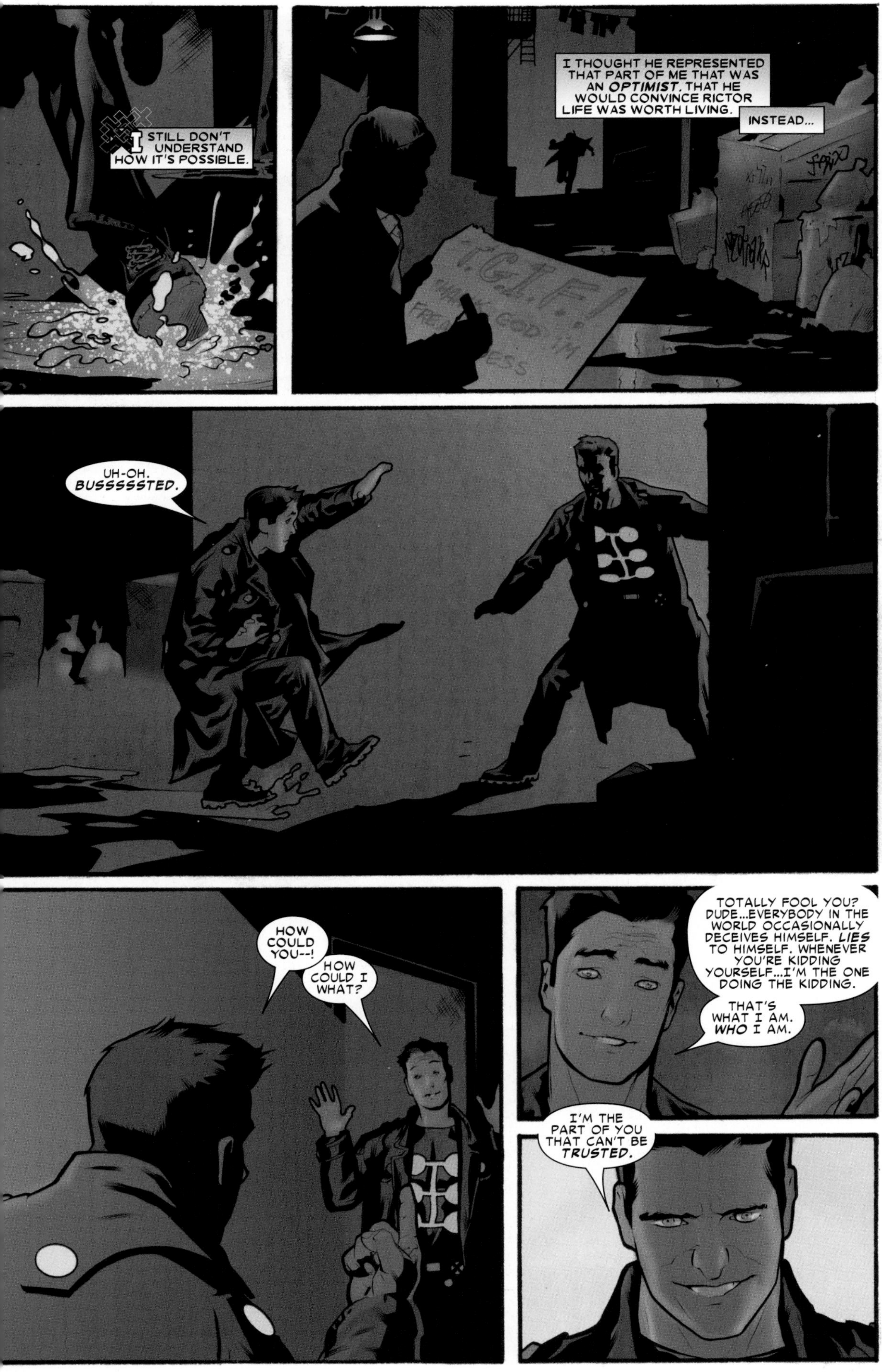
I STILL DON'T UNDERSTAND HOW IT'S POSSIBLE.
I THOUGHT HE REPRESENTED THAT PART OF ME THAT WAS AN OPTIMIST. THAT HE WOULD CONVINCE RICTOR LIFE WAS WORTH LIVING.
INSTEAD...
T.G.I.F.!
UH-OH. BUSSSSSTED.
HOW COULD YOU--!
HOW COULD I WHAT?
TOTALLY FOOL YOU? DUDE...EVERYBODY IN THE WORLD OCCASIONALLY DECEIVES HIMSELF. LIES TO HIMSELF. WHENEVER YOU'RE KIDDING YOURSELF...I'M THE ONE DOING THE KIDDING.
THAT'S WHAT I AM. WHO I AM.
I'M THE PART OF YOU THAT CAN'T BE TRUSTED.

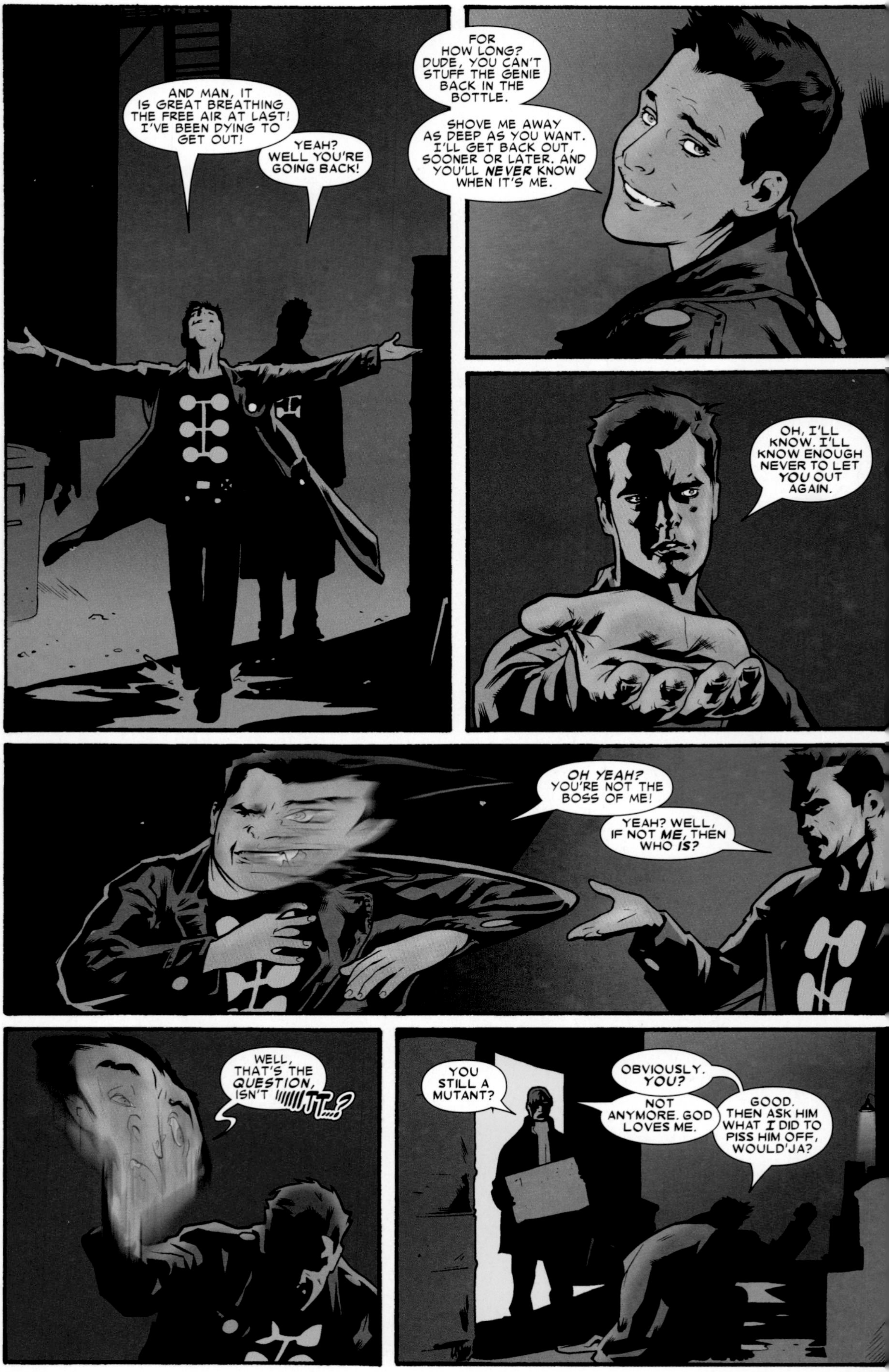
AND MAN, IT IS GREAT BREATHING THE FREE AIR AT LAST! I'VE BEEN DYING TO GET OUT!
YEAH? WELL YOU'RE GOING BACK!
FOR HOW LONG? DUDE, YOU CAN'T STUFF THE GENIE BACK IN THE BOTTLE.
SHOVE ME AWAY AS DEEP AS YOU WANT. I'LL GET BACK OUT, SOONER OR LATER. AND YOU'LL NEVER KNOW WHEN IT'S ME.
OH, I'LL KNOW. I'LL KNOW ENOUGH NEVER TO LET YOU OUT AGAIN.
OH YEAH? YOU'RE NOT THE BOSS OF ME!
YEAH? WELL, IF NOT ME, THEN WHO IS?
WELL, THAT'S THE QUESTION, ISN'T IIIIIITTT...?
YOU STILL A MUTANT?
OBVIOUSLY. YOU?
NOT ANYMORE. GOD LOVES ME.
GOOD. THEN ASK HIM WHAT I DID TO PISS HIM OFF, WOULD'JA?

"MUTANTISM?" IS THAT EVEN A WORD?

NO MUTANTS

MY SISTER, RACHEL--SHE'S A CLEANING GIRL AT THE MARQUIS--HAS UNDERGONE A...THERE'S NO OTHER WAY TO PUT IT...A *PERSONALITY* CHANGE.

Y'KNOW IT'S GETTING *WEIRD* OUT THERE.

QUIET, GUIDO. GO AHEAD, MISS.

SHE USED TO TELL ME EVERYTHING. WE HAD NO SECRETS FROM EACH OTHER. NOW SHE SKULKS AROUND... DOESN'T TALK TO ME... SHE'S HIDING SOMETHING...

I'M A LITTLE UNCLEAR, MS. SANTIAGO... WHAT MADE YOU THINK SOMETHING LIKE THIS WAS UP X-FACTOR'S ALLEY?

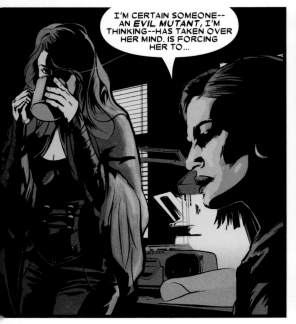

I'M CERTAIN SOMEONE-- AN *EVIL MUTANT*, I'M THINKING--HAS TAKEN OVER HER MIND. IS FORCING HER TO...

LOOK... MISS...

FIRST OF ALL, THE ODDS OF *ANY* MUTANT MENACING YOUR SISTER HAVE RECENTLY DROPPED PRECIPITOUSLY...

...AND SECOND, ANY "EVIL MUTANT" WORTH HIS SALT WOULDN'T BE DIDDLING WITH CLEANING GIRLS IF HE COULD CONTROL MINDS. HE'D GO AFTER WORLD LEADERS, THOSE SORTS.

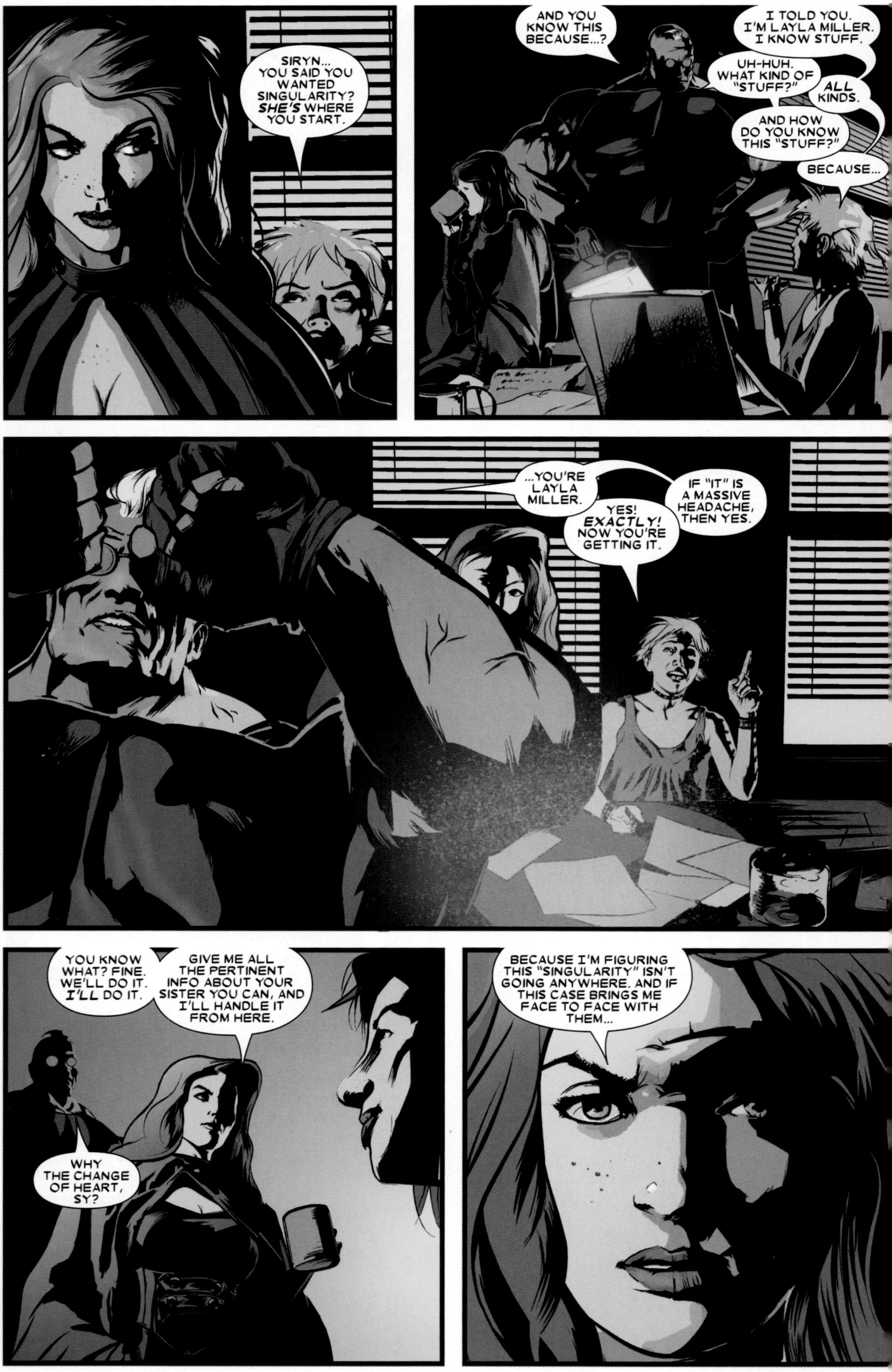
SIRYN... YOU SAID YOU WANTED SINGULARITY? *SHE'S* WHERE YOU START.
AND YOU KNOW THIS BECAUSE...?
I TOLD YOU. I'M LAYLA MILLER. I KNOW STUFF.
UH-HUH. WHAT KIND OF "STUFF?"
ALL KINDS.
AND HOW DO YOU KNOW THIS "STUFF?"
BECAUSE...
...YOU'RE LAYLA MILLER.
YES! *EXACTLY!* NOW YOU'RE GETTING IT.
IF "IT" IS A MASSIVE HEADACHE, THEN YES.
YOU KNOW WHAT? FINE. WE'LL DO IT. *I'LL* DO IT.
GIVE ME ALL THE PERTINENT INFO ABOUT YOUR SISTER YOU CAN, AND I'LL HANDLE IT FROM HERE.
WHY THE CHANGE OF HEART, SY?
BECAUSE I'M FIGURING THIS "SINGULARITY" ISN'T GOING ANYWHERE. AND IF THIS CASE BRINGS ME FACE TO FACE WITH THEM...

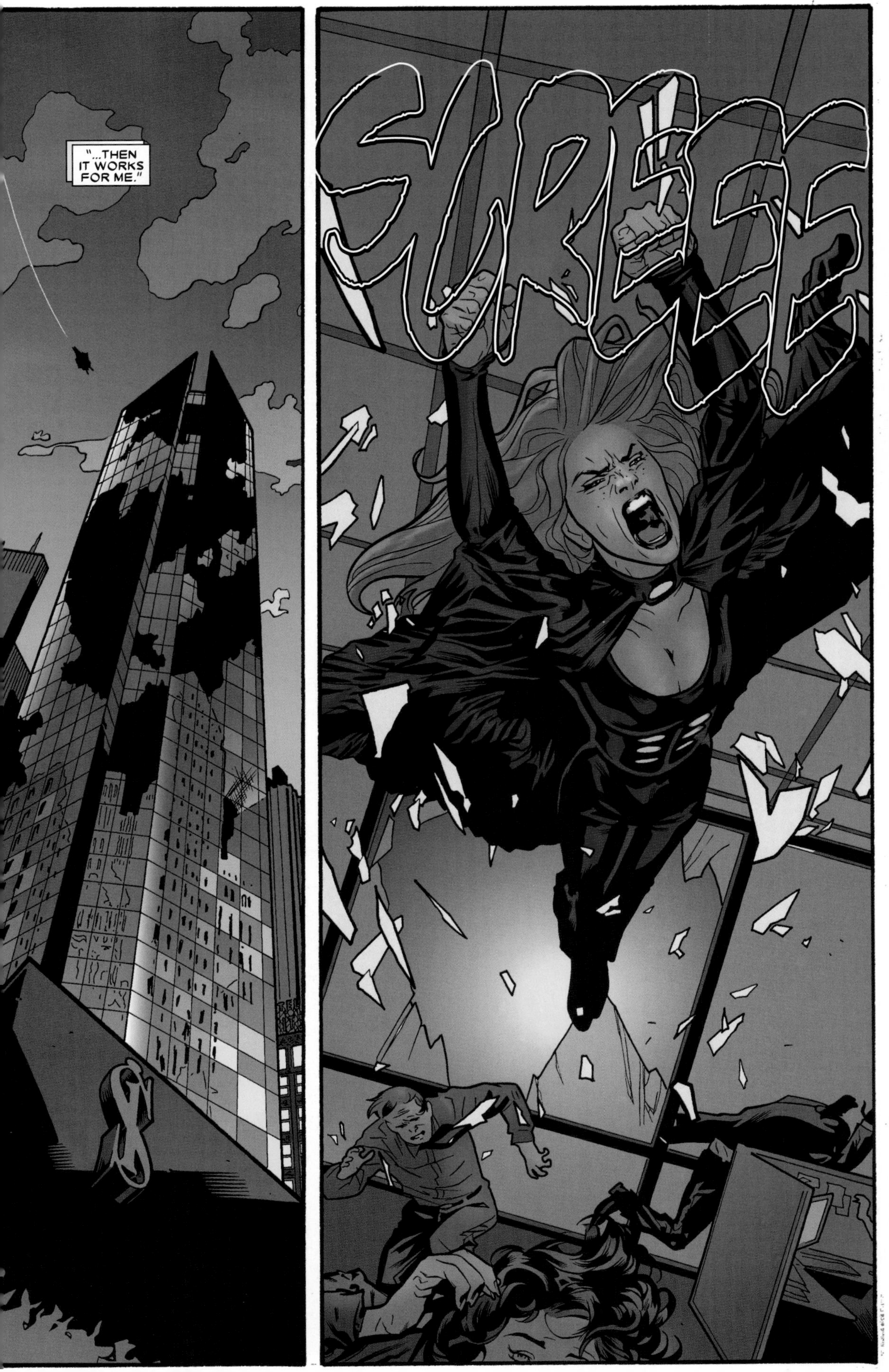
"...THEN IT WORKS FOR ME."

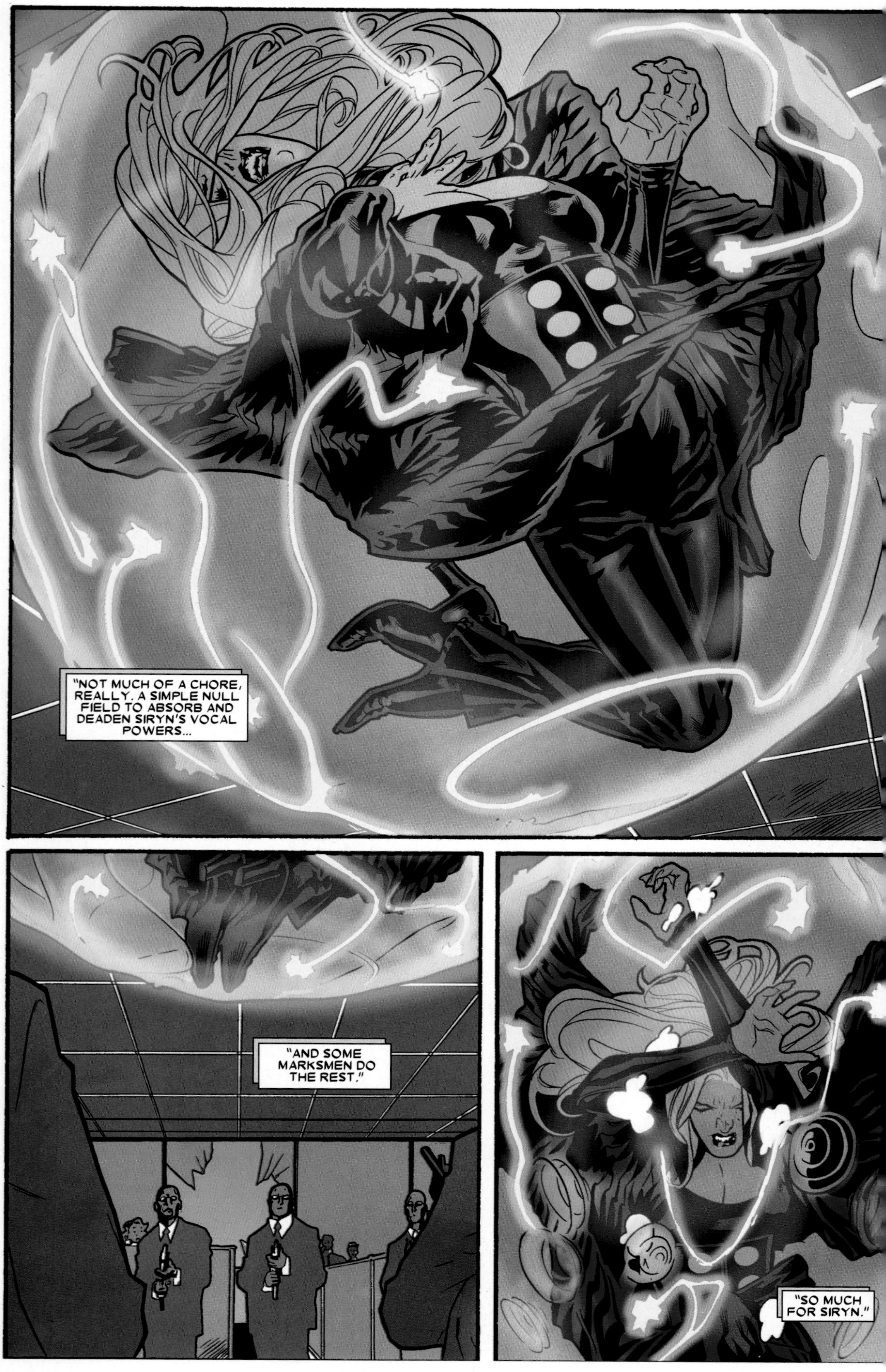
"NOT MUCH OF A CHORE, REALLY. A SIMPLE NULL FIELD TO ABSORB AND DEADEN SIRYN'S VOCAL POWERS...
"AND SOME MARKSMEN DO THE REST."
"SO MUCH FOR SIRYN."

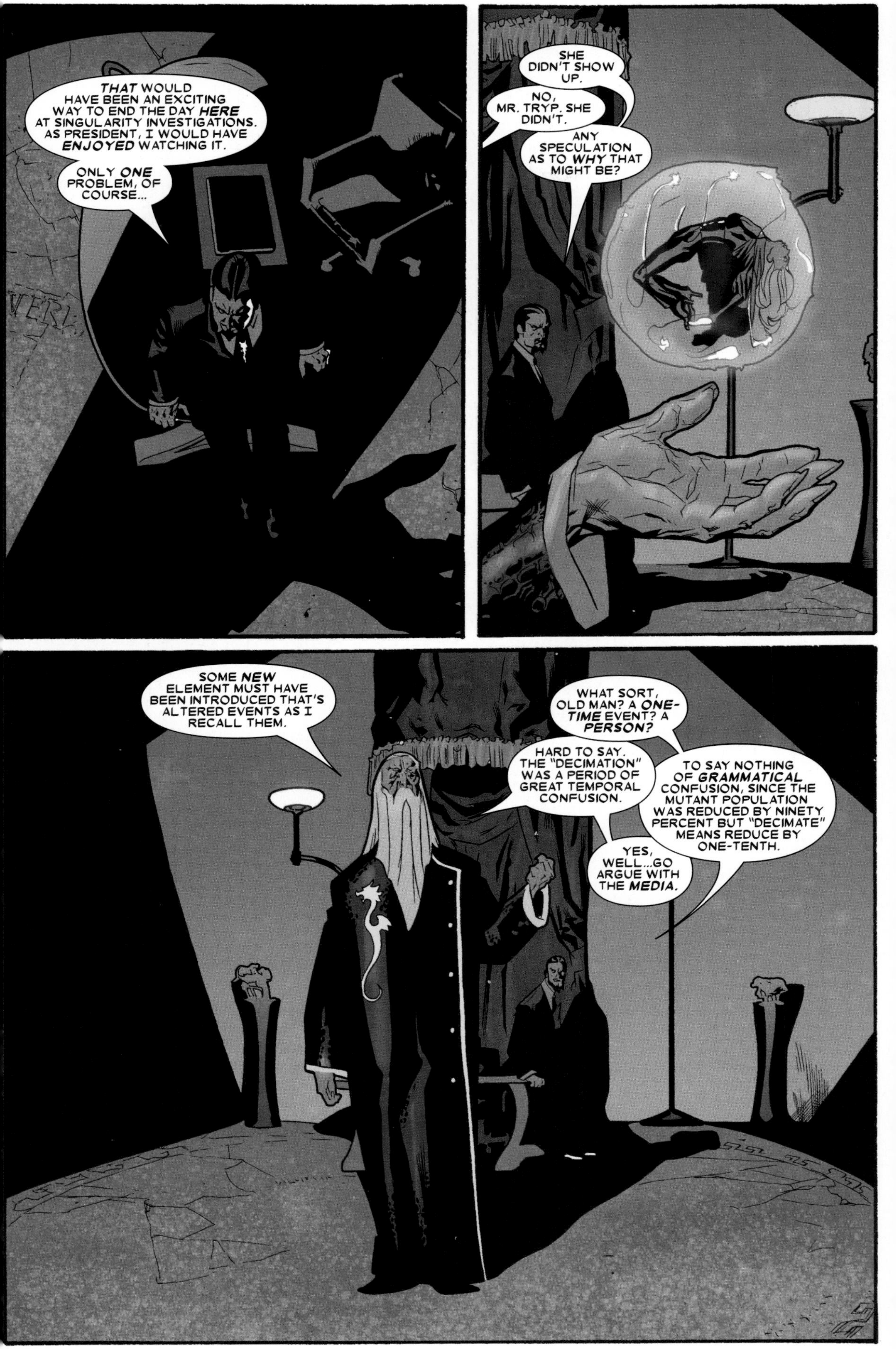
THAT WOULD HAVE BEEN AN EXCITING WAY TO END THE DAY HERE AT SINGULARITY INVESTIGATIONS. AS PRESIDENT, I WOULD HAVE ENJOYED WATCHING IT.
ONLY ONE PROBLEM, OF COURSE...
SHE DIDN'T SHOW UP.
NO, MR. TRYP. SHE DIDN'T.
ANY SPECULATION AS TO WHY THAT MIGHT BE?
SOME NEW ELEMENT MUST HAVE BEEN INTRODUCED THAT'S ALTERED EVENTS AS I RECALL THEM.
WHAT SORT, OLD MAN? A ONE-TIME EVENT? A PERSON?
HARD TO SAY. THE "DECIMATION" WAS A PERIOD OF GREAT TEMPORAL CONFUSION.
TO SAY NOTHING OF GRAMMATICAL CONFUSION, SINCE THE MUTANT POPULATION WAS REDUCED BY NINETY PERCENT BUT "DECIMATE" MEANS REDUCE BY ONE-TENTH.
YES, WELL...GO ARGUE WITH THE MEDIA.

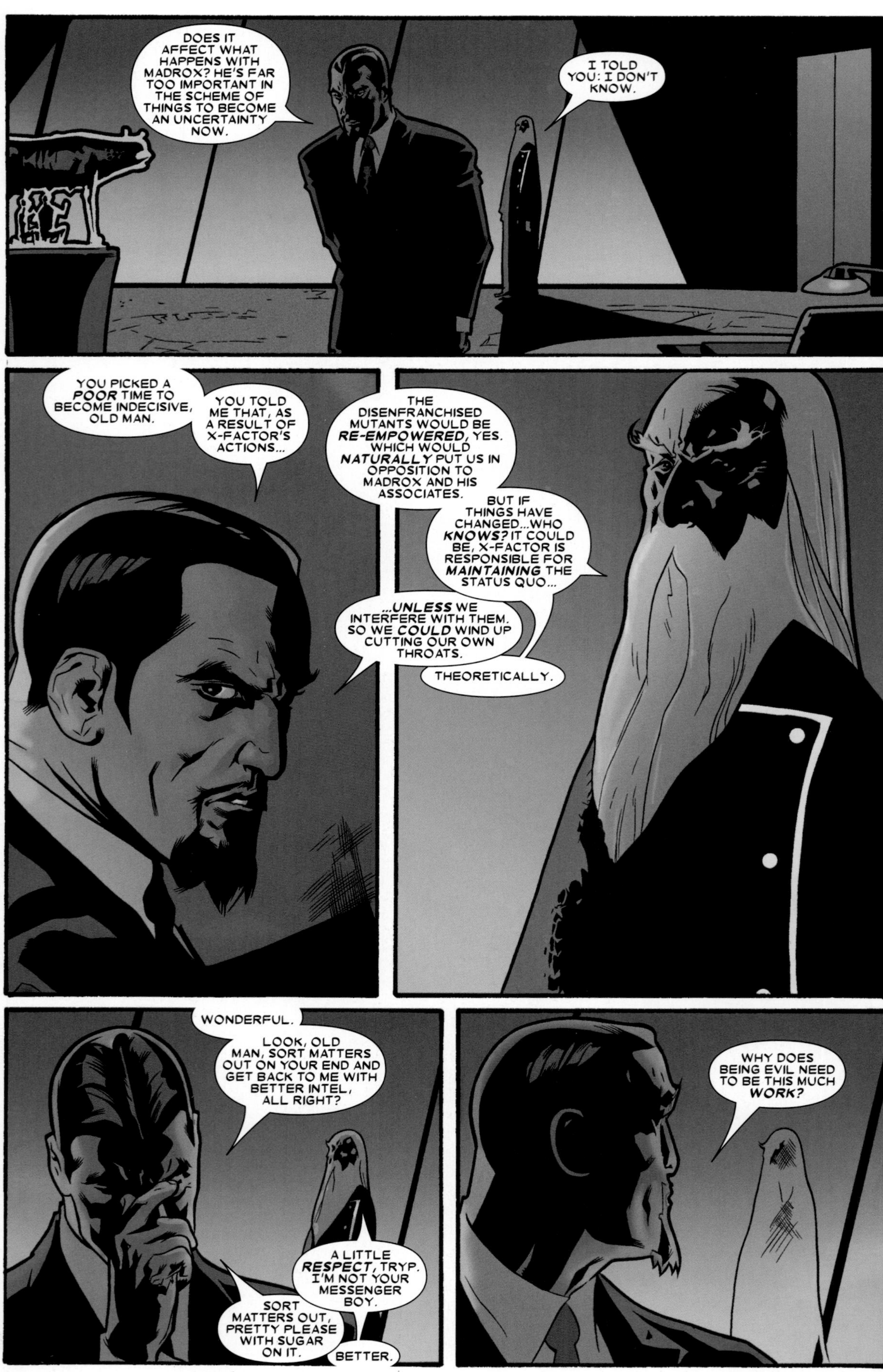
DOES IT AFFECT WHAT HAPPENS WITH MADROX? HE'S FAR TOO IMPORTANT IN THE SCHEME OF THINGS TO BECOME AN UNCERTAINTY NOW.
I TOLD YOU: I DON'T KNOW.
YOU PICKED A *POOR* TIME TO BECOME INDECISIVE, OLD MAN.
YOU TOLD ME THAT, AS A RESULT OF X-FACTOR'S ACTIONS...
THE DISENFRANCHISED MUTANTS WOULD BE *RE-EMPOWERED*, YES. WHICH WOULD *NATURALLY* PUT US IN OPPOSITION TO MADROX AND HIS ASSOCIATES.
BUT IF THINGS HAVE CHANGED...WHO *KNOWS?* IT COULD BE, X-FACTOR IS RESPONSIBLE FOR *MAINTAINING* THE STATUS QUO...
...UNLESS WE INTERFERE WITH THEM. SO WE *COULD* WIND UP CUTTING OUR OWN THROATS.
THEORETICALLY.
WONDERFUL.
LOOK, OLD MAN, SORT MATTERS OUT ON YOUR END AND GET BACK TO ME WITH BETTER INTEL, ALL RIGHT?
A LITTLE *RESPECT*, TRYP. I'M NOT YOUR MESSENGER BOY.
SORT MATTERS OUT, PRETTY PLEASE WITH SUGAR ON IT.
BETTER.
WHY DOES BEING EVIL NEED TO BE THIS MUCH *WORK?*

GIVE US BACK OUR POWERS!

WE'RE MUTANTS ON THE INSIDE

powers is as powers

I LIKE BEING SUPER!

WILL WORK FOR...

WE'RE BETTER THAN YOU

HEY! YOU! YOU DON'T HAVE TO FLAUNT IT!

TRAGICALLY... I DO.

IMPRESSIVE MOTORCYCLE, RICTOR. IF I'M UNAVAILABLE TO SAVE YOUR LIFE NEXT TIME, CAN I HAVE IT?

NICE ATTITUDE, M.

BITE ME, "R." THE OFFICE IS JUST UP AHEAD, BY THE WAY.

WHAT A DUMP. KIND OF A COME-DOWN FOR A HIGH-TONED GIRL LIKE MONET ST. CROIX.

ACTUALLY, I'VE DONE WONDERS WITH BEAUTIFYING THE INTERIOR.

YEAH? HOW?

TO BEGIN WITH, I MOVED IN. MY PRESENCE ALONE IMPROVES IT EXPONENTIALLY.

YOU SHOULD COME IN AND--

AND WHAT? JOIN UP? I'VE NO POWERS.

YOU'RE QUICK, YOU'RE SMART, AND YOU'RE ALMOST AS GOOD-LOOKING AS ME.

WHERE'S THE DOWNSIDE?

THE DOWNSIDE IS, HANGING WITH MUTANTS WILL MAKE ME WIND UP LIKE ANGER BOY BACK THERE, REMINDING ME OF WHAT I'M NOT. PLUS, YOUR BOSS TRIED TO FREAKIN' KILL ME.

LATER, MONET.

THERE'S A SERVICE STATION THREE BLOCKS NORTH. HERE'S A COUPON FOR TWENTY PERCENT OFF GASOLINE.

YEAH? THANKS, KID.

WHO ARE YOU?

LAYLA MILLER. I KNOW STUFF.

HOW SPECIAL FOR YOU.

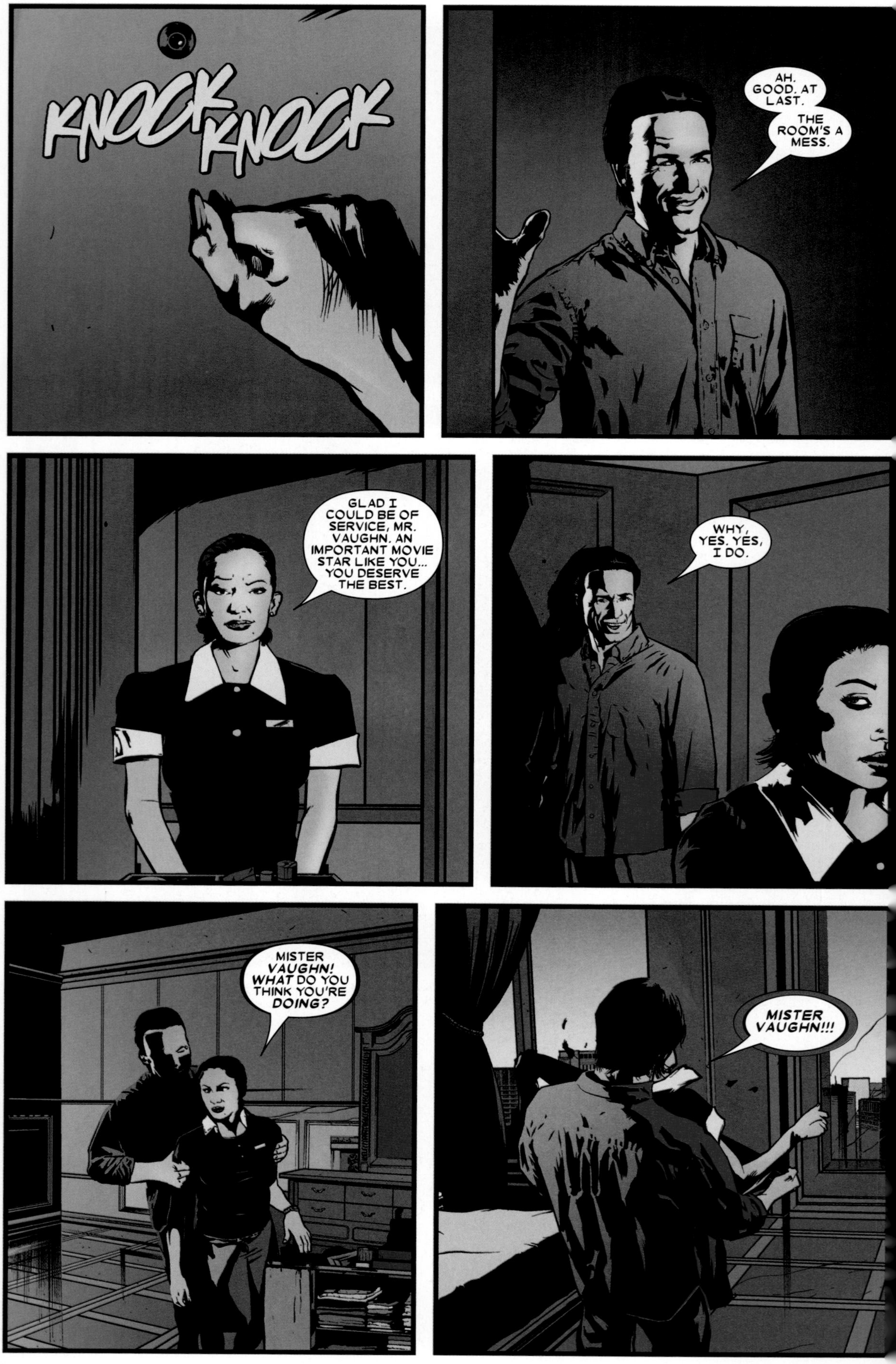

KNOCK KNOCK
AH. GOOD. AT LAST.
THE ROOM'S A MESS.
GLAD I COULD BE OF SERVICE, MR. VAUGHN. AN IMPORTANT MOVIE STAR LIKE YOU... YOU DESERVE THE BEST.
WHY, YES. YES, I DO.
MISTER *VAUGHN!* *WHAT* DO YOU THINK YOU'RE *DOING?*
MISTER VAUGHN!!!

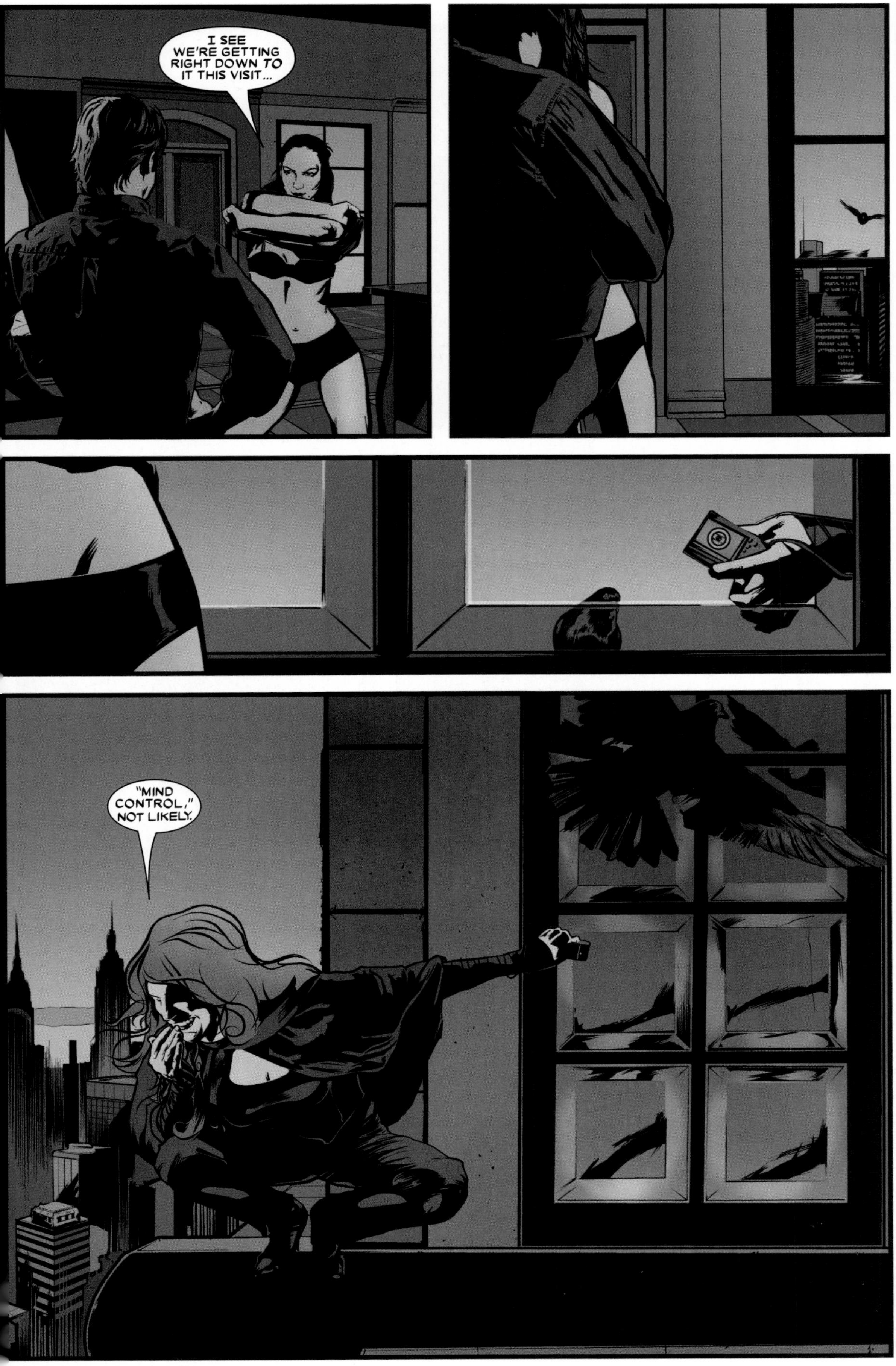
I SEE WE'RE GETTING RIGHT DOWN TO IT THIS VISIT...
"MIND CONTROL," NOT LIKELY.

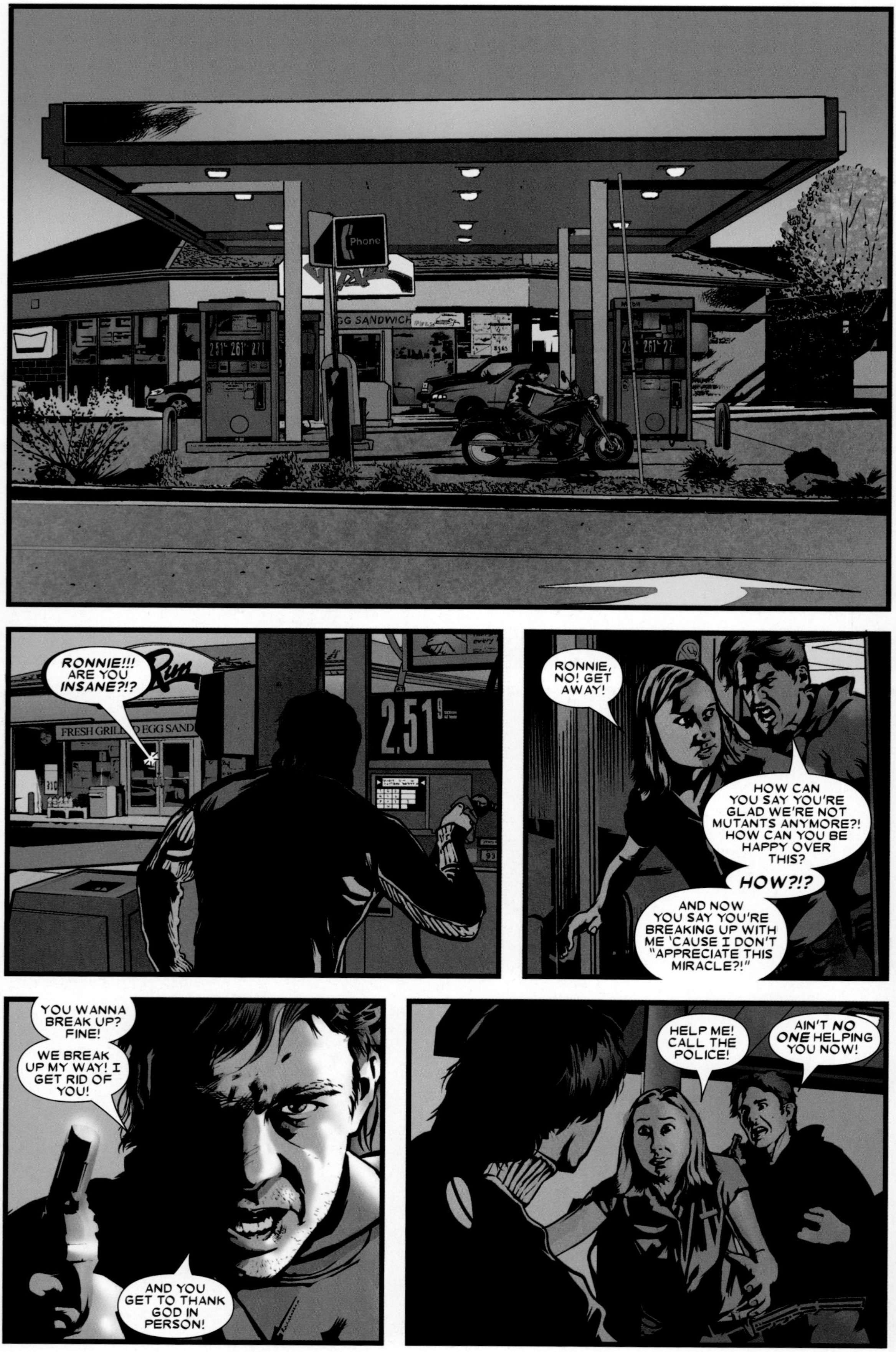

Phone
EGG SANDWICH
RONNIE!!! ARE YOU INSANE?!?
2,51
RONNIE, NO! GET AWAY!
HOW CAN YOU SAY YOU'RE GLAD WE'RE NOT MUTANTS ANYMORE?! HOW CAN YOU BE HAPPY OVER THIS?
HOW?!?
AND NOW YOU SAY YOU'RE BREAKING UP WITH ME 'CAUSE I DON'T "APPRECIATE THIS MIRACLE?!"
YOU WANNA BREAK UP? FINE!
WE BREAK UP MY WAY! I GET RID OF YOU!
AND YOU GET TO THANK GOD IN PERSON!
HELP ME! CALL THE POLICE!
AIN'T NO ONE HELPING YOU NOW!

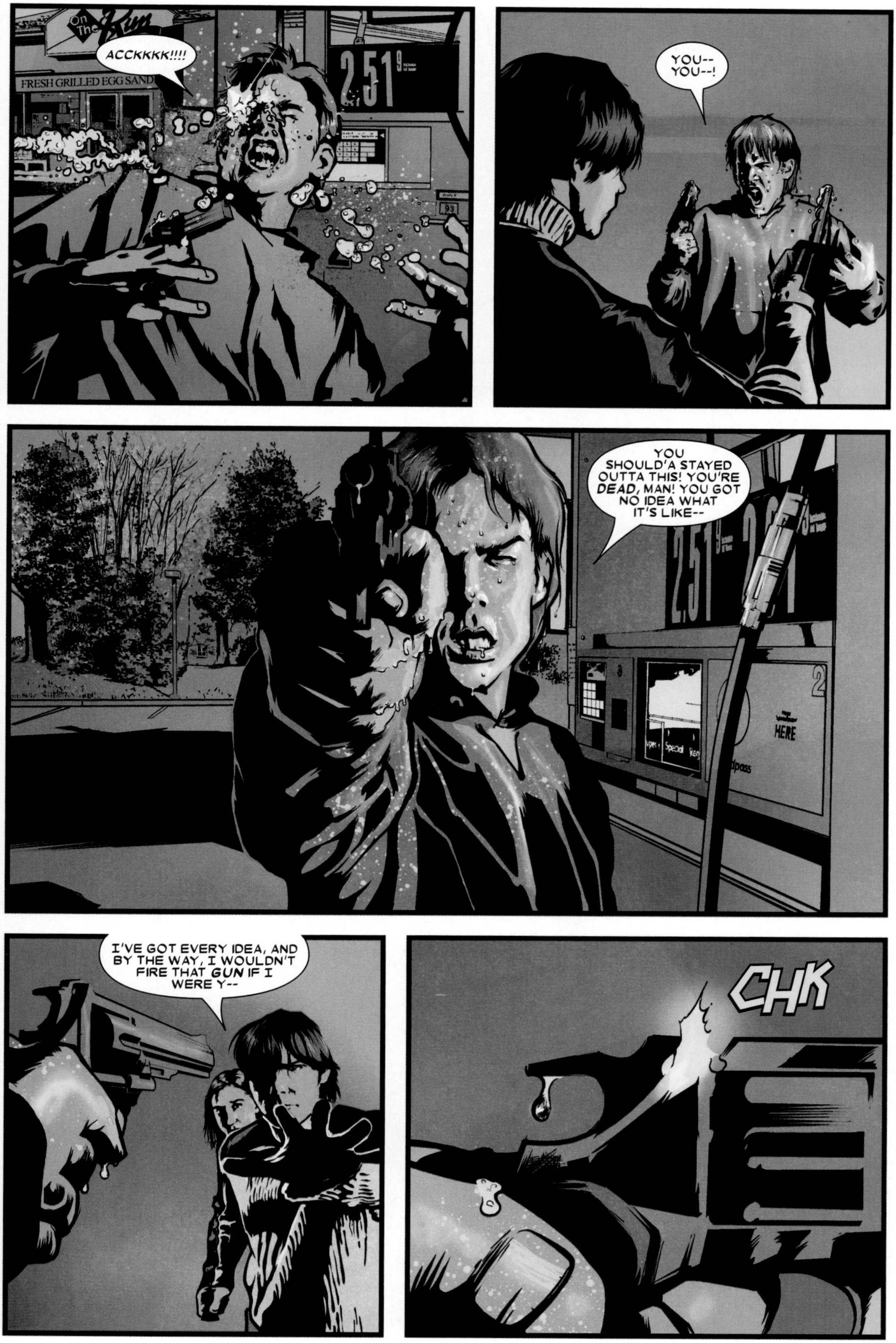
On The Run
ACCKKKK!!!!
FRESH GRILLED EGG SAND
2.51 9
YOU-- YOU--!
YOU SHOULD'A STAYED OUTTA THIS! YOU'RE DEAD, MAN! YOU GOT NO IDEA WHAT IT'S LIKE--
HERE
I'VE GOT EVERY IDEA, AND BY THE WAY, I WOULDN'T FIRE THAT GUN IF I WERE Y--
CHK

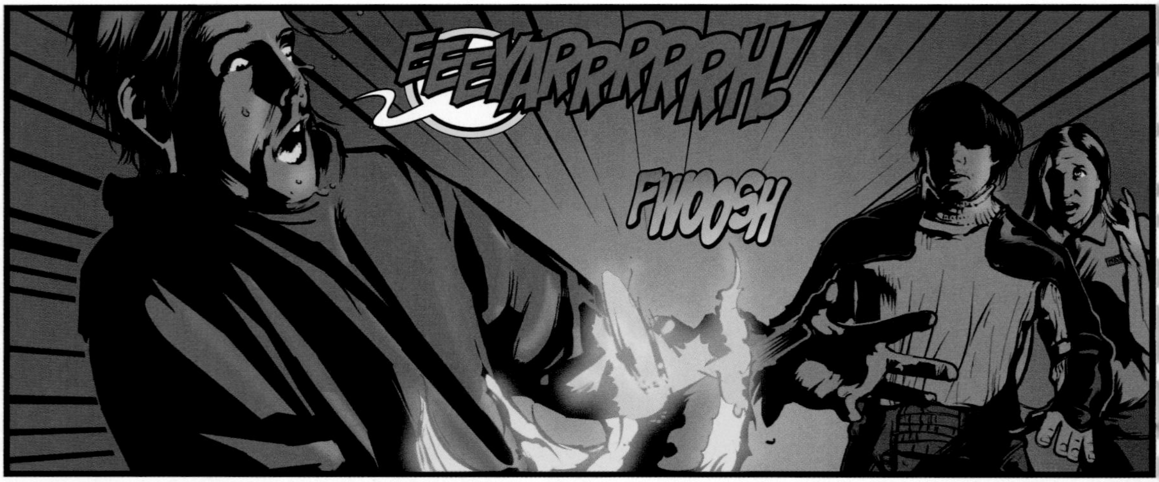
EEEYARRRRRRH!
FWOOSH

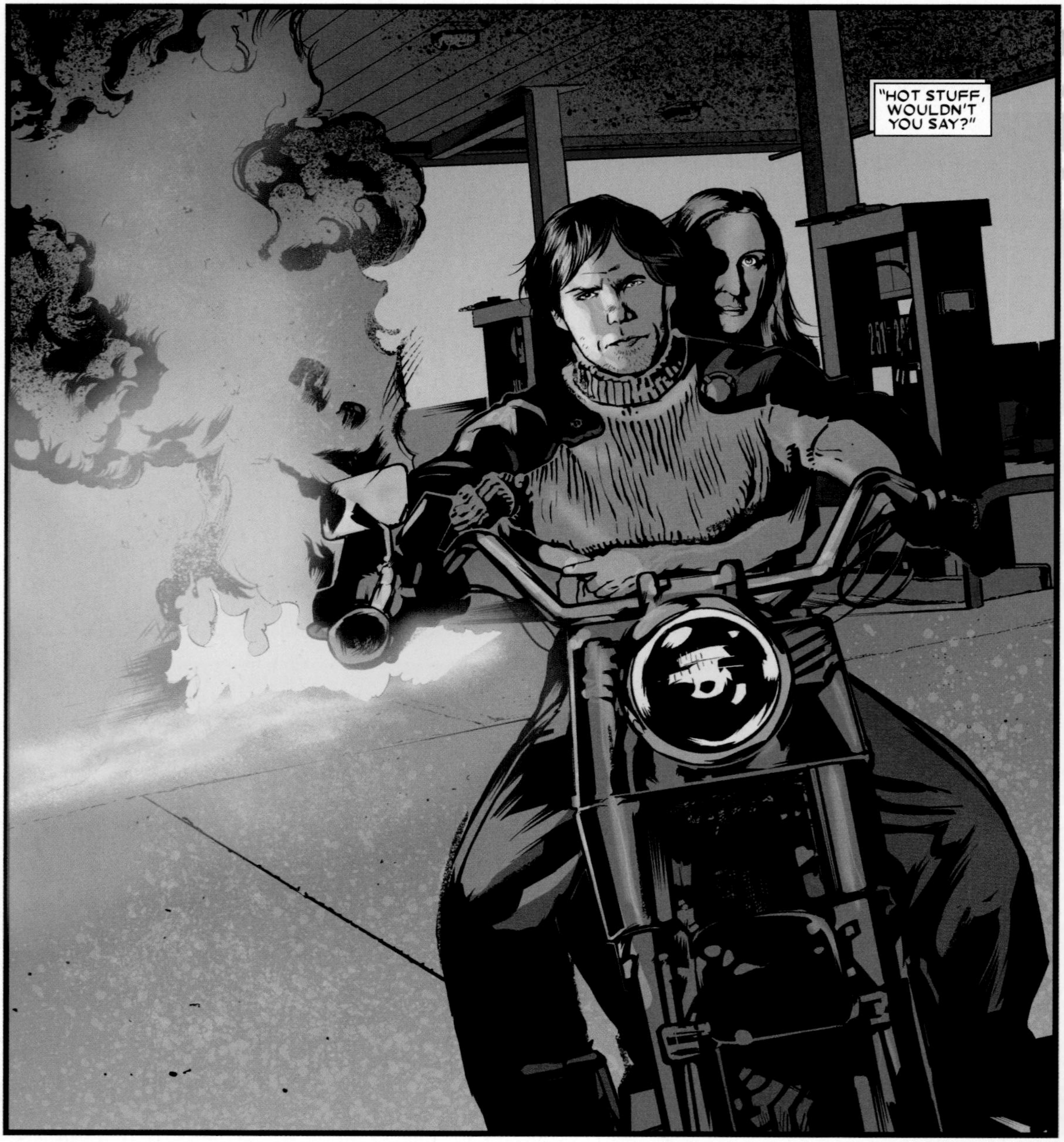
"HOT STUFF, WOULDN'T YOU SAY?"

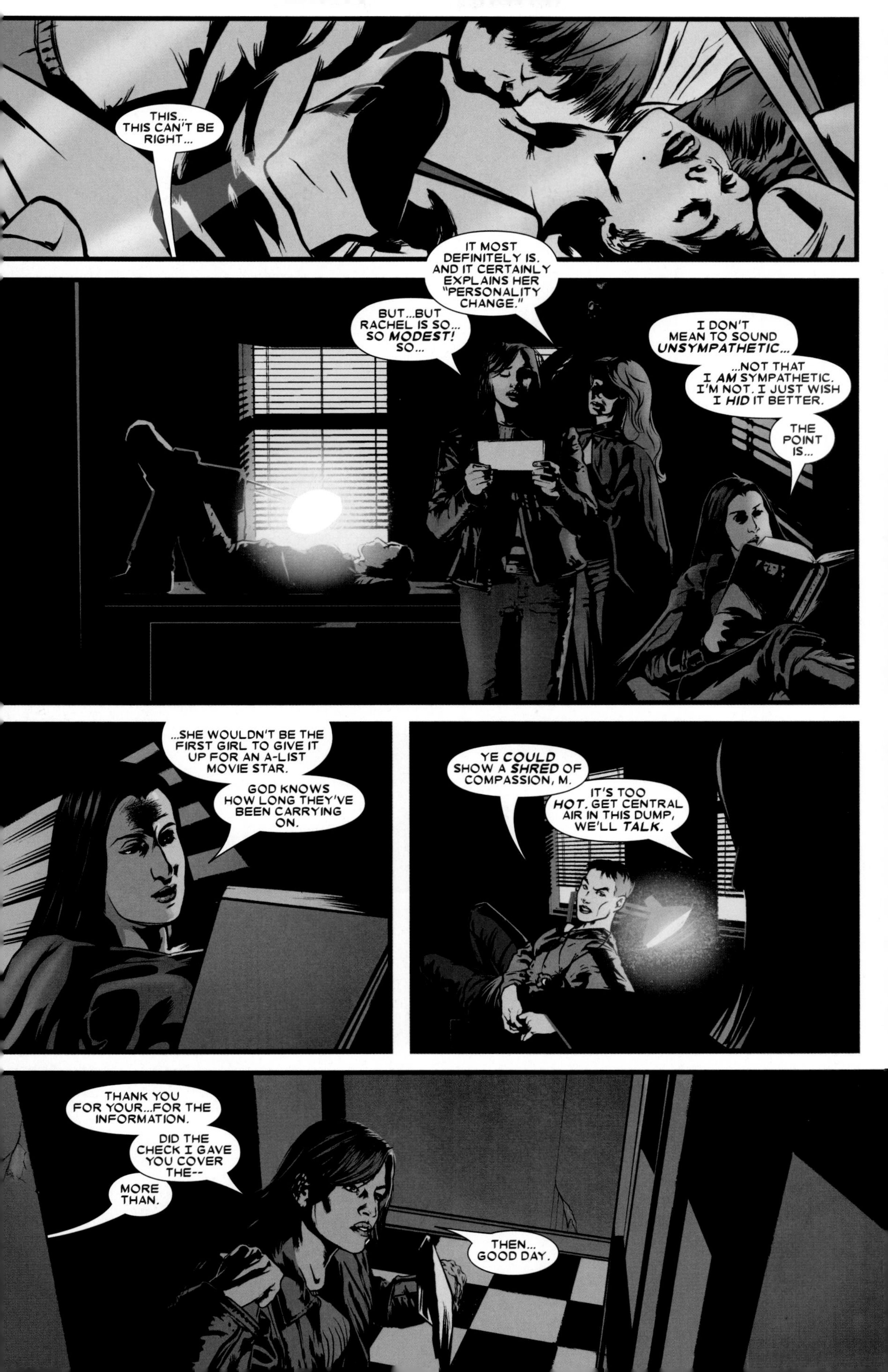
THIS... THIS CAN'T BE RIGHT...
IT MOST DEFINITELY IS. AND IT CERTAINLY EXPLAINS HER "PERSONALITY CHANGE."
BUT...BUT RACHEL IS SO... SO MODEST! SO...
I DON'T MEAN TO SOUND UNSYMPATHETIC...
...NOT THAT I AM SYMPATHETIC. I'M NOT. I JUST WISH I HID IT BETTER.
THE POINT IS...
...SHE WOULDN'T BE THE FIRST GIRL TO GIVE IT UP FOR AN A-LIST MOVIE STAR.
GOD KNOWS HOW LONG THEY'VE BEEN CARRYING ON.
YE COULD SHOW A SHRED OF COMPASSION, M.
IT'S TOO HOT. GET CENTRAL AIR IN THIS DUMP, WE'LL TALK.
THANK YOU FOR YOUR...FOR THE INFORMATION.
DID THE CHECK I GAVE YOU COVER THE--
MORE THAN.
THEN... GOOD DAY.

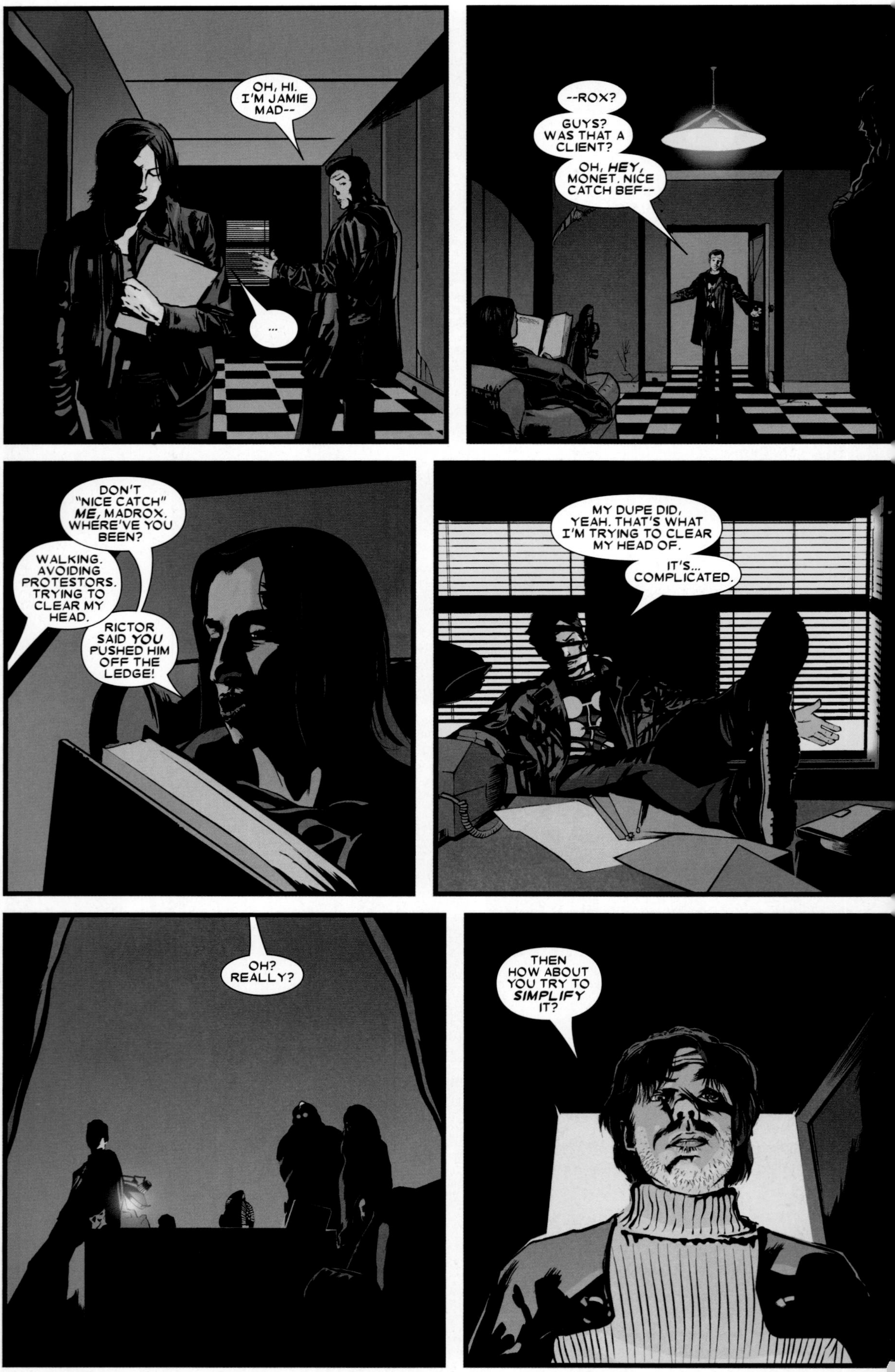
OH, HI. I'M JAMIE MAD--
...
--ROX?
GUYS? WAS THAT A CLIENT?
OH, HEY, MONET. NICE CATCH BEF--
DON'T "NICE CATCH" ME, MADROX. WHERE'VE YOU BEEN?
WALKING. AVOIDING PROTESTORS. TRYING TO CLEAR MY HEAD.
RICTOR SAID YOU PUSHED HIM OFF THE LEDGE!
MY DUPE DID, YEAH. THAT'S WHAT I'M TRYING TO CLEAR MY HEAD OF.
IT'S... COMPLICATED.
OH? REALLY?
THEN HOW ABOUT YOU TRY TO SIMPLIFY IT?

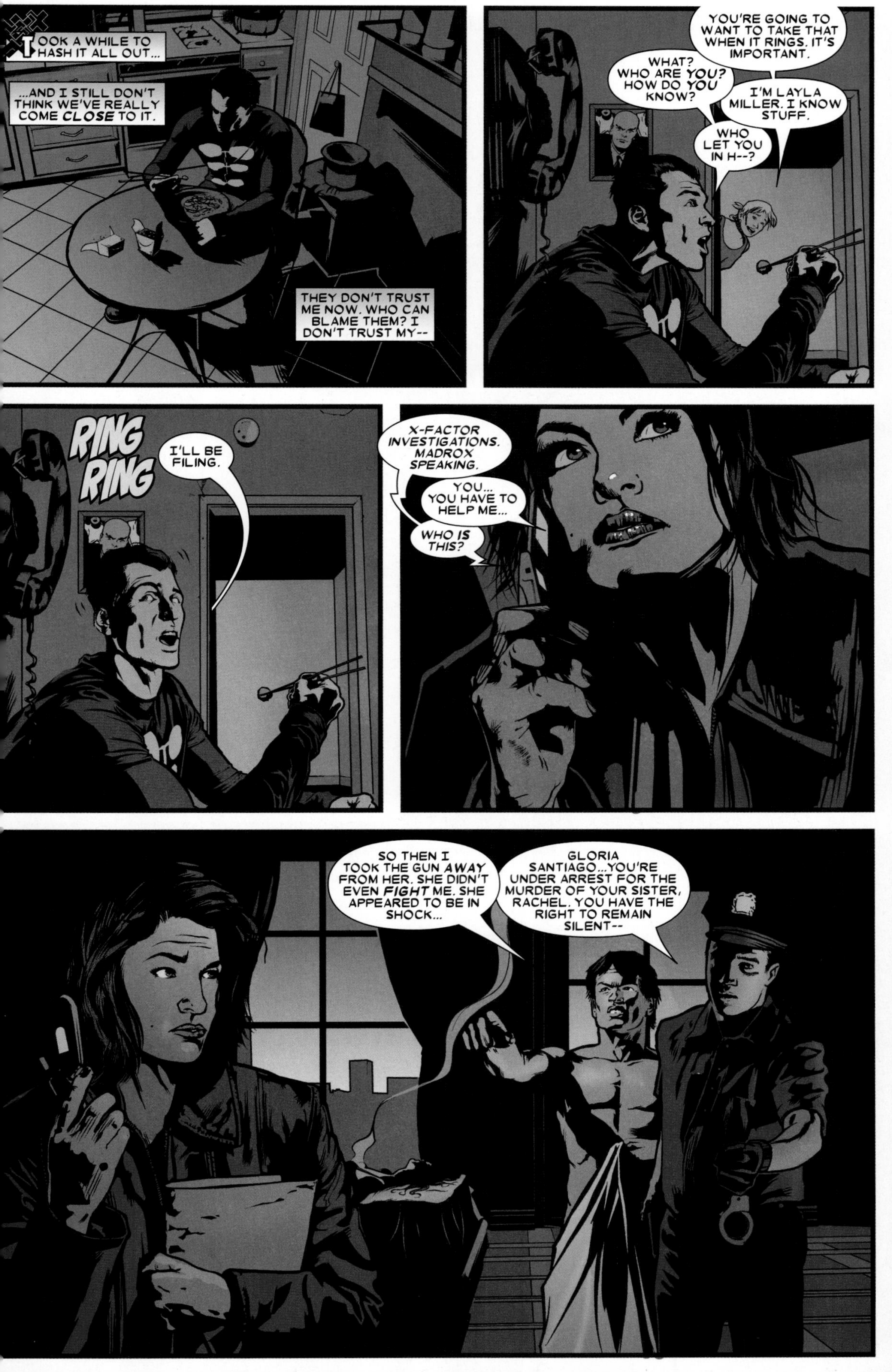

TOOK A WHILE TO HASH IT ALL OUT...
...AND I STILL DON'T THINK WE'VE REALLY COME CLOSE TO IT.
THEY DON'T TRUST ME NOW. WHO CAN BLAME THEM? I DON'T TRUST MY--
YOU'RE GOING TO WANT TO TAKE THAT WHEN IT RINGS. IT'S IMPORTANT.
WHAT? WHO ARE YOU? HOW DO YOU KNOW?
I'M LAYLA MILLER. I KNOW STUFF.
WHO LET YOU IN H--?
RING RING
I'LL BE FILING.
X-FACTOR INVESTIGATIONS. MADROX SPEAKING.
YOU... YOU HAVE TO HELP ME...
WHO IS THIS?
SO THEN I TOOK THE GUN AWAY FROM HER. SHE DIDN'T EVEN FIGHT ME. SHE APPEARED TO BE IN SHOCK...
GLORIA SANTIAGO...YOU'RE UNDER ARREST FOR THE MURDER OF YOUR SISTER, RACHEL. YOU HAVE THE RIGHT TO REMAIN SILENT--

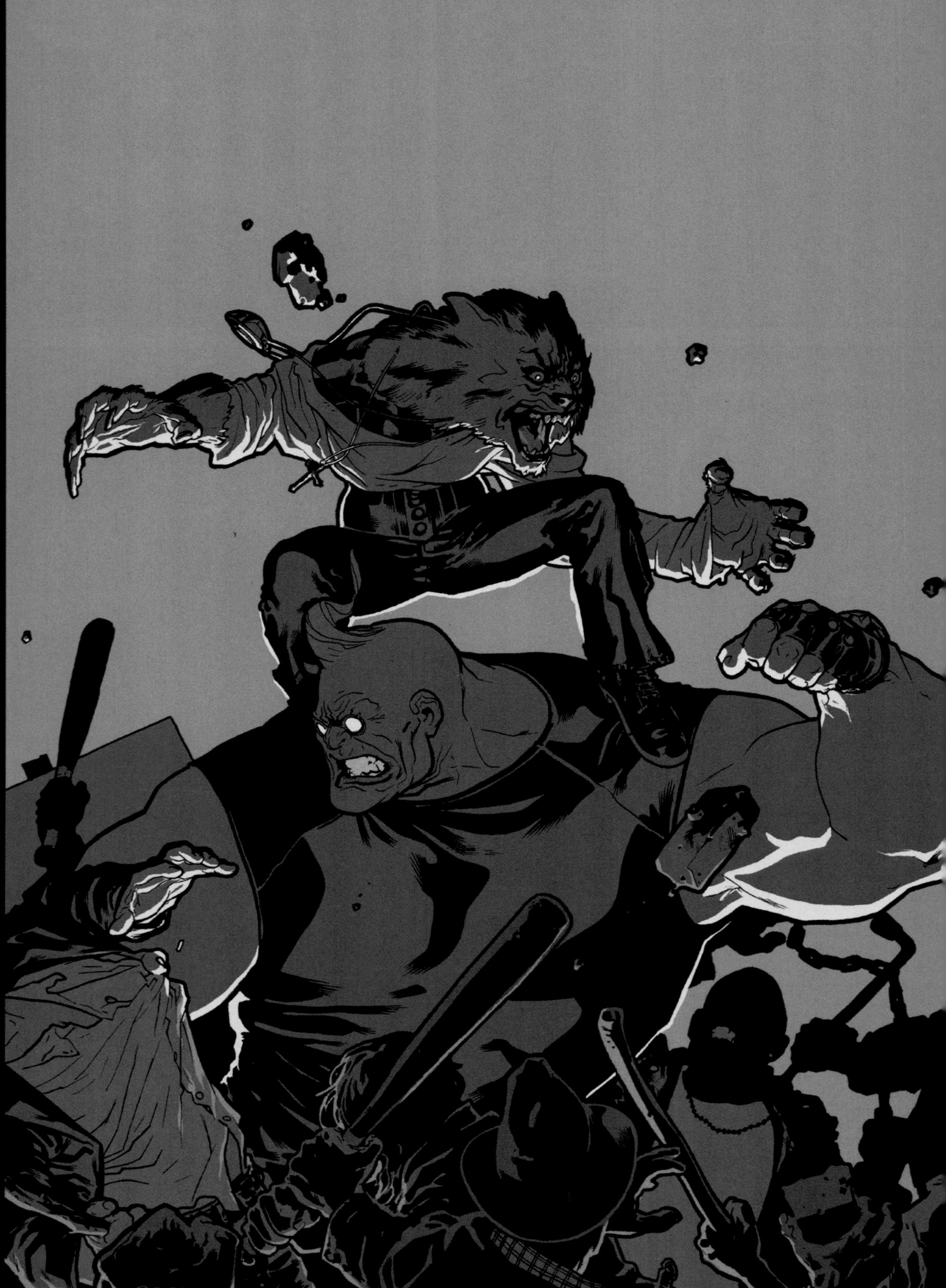
SOOK

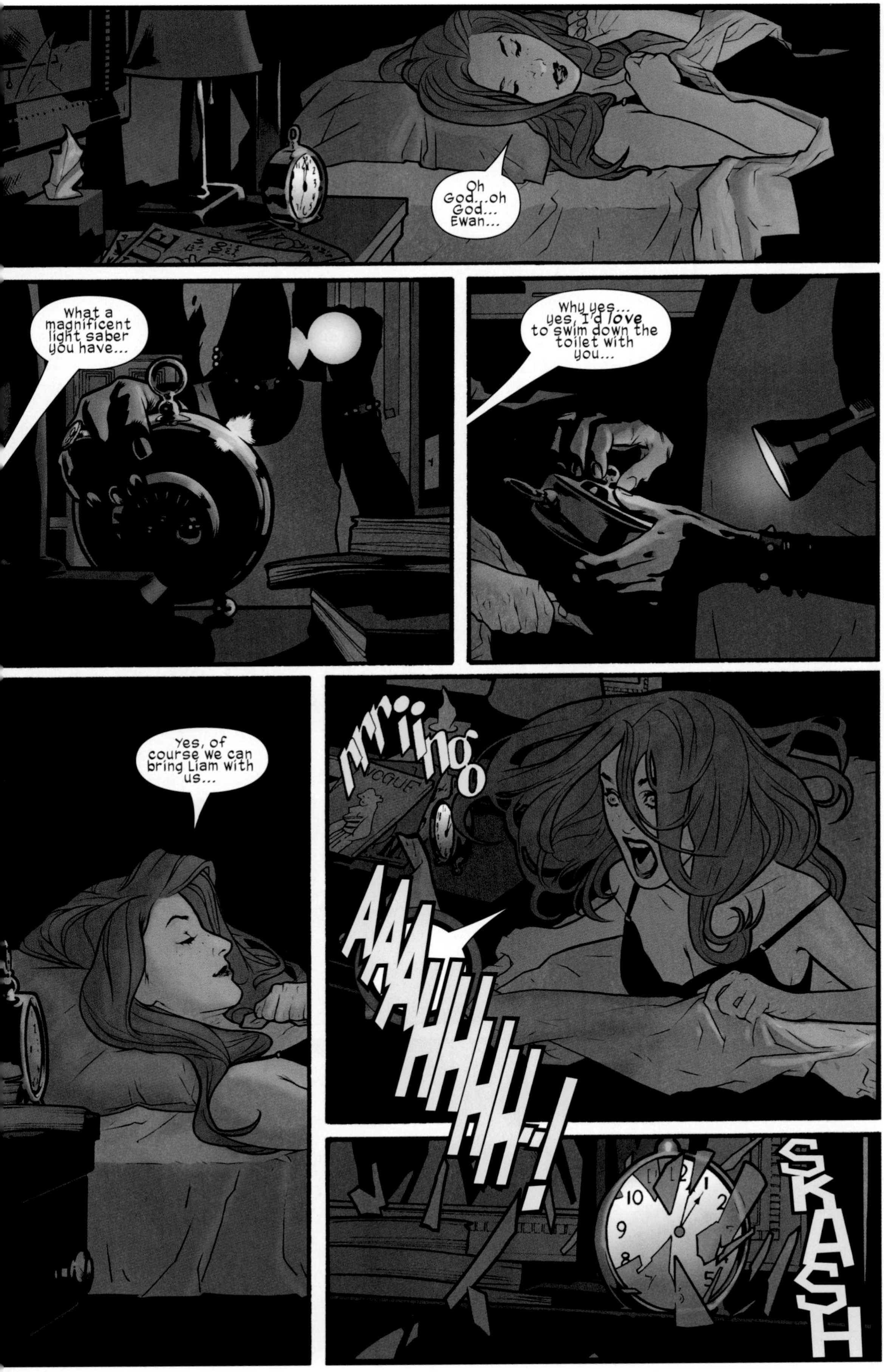
Oh God...oh God... Ewan...
What a magnificent light saber you have...
Why yes... yes, I'd love to swim down the toilet with you...
Yes, of course we can bring Liam with us...
rrriing
AAAHHHH..!
SKASH

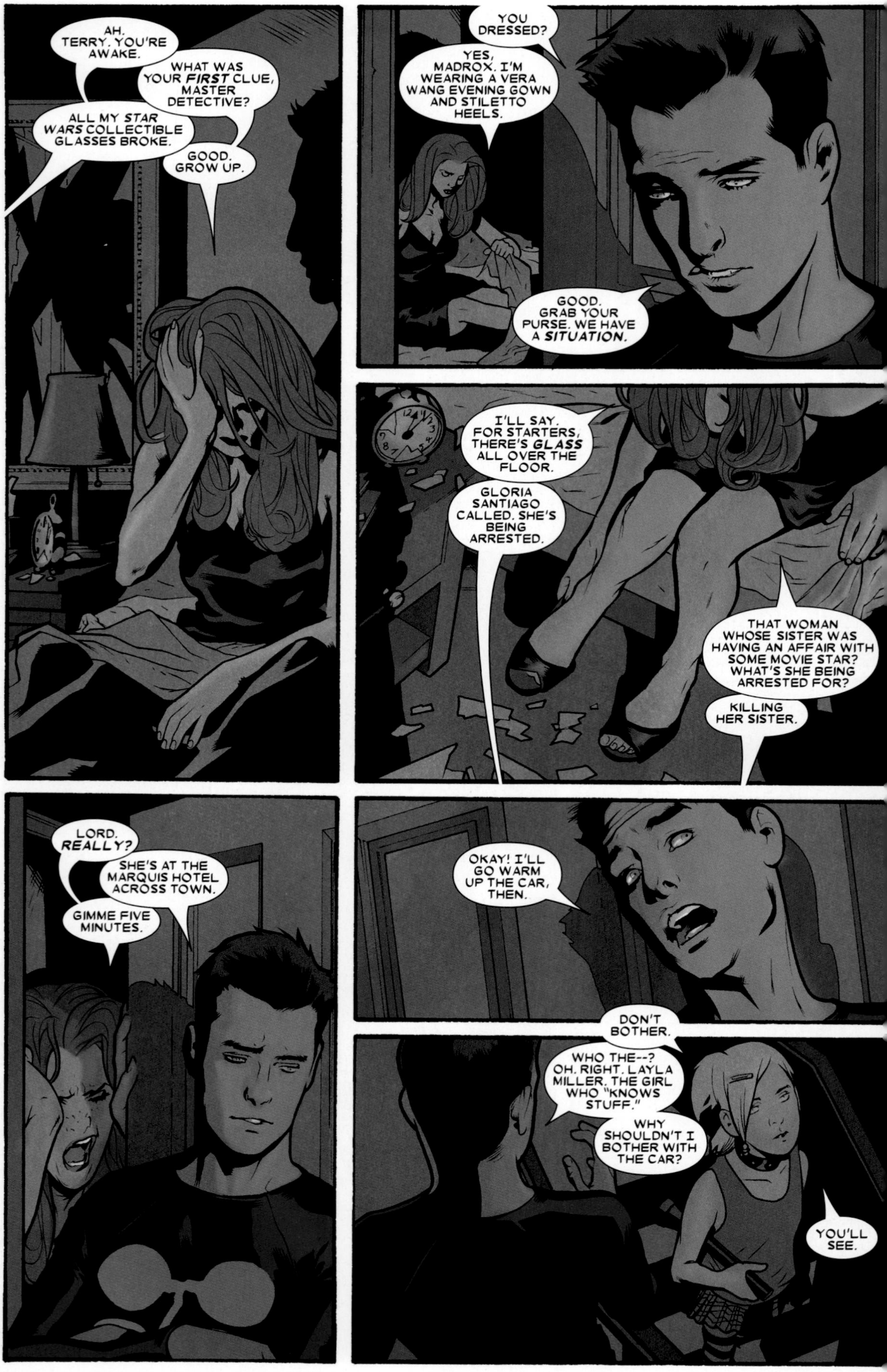
AH. TERRY. YOU'RE AWAKE.
WHAT WAS YOUR *FIRST* CLUE, MASTER DETECTIVE?
ALL MY *STAR WARS* COLLECTIBLE GLASSES BROKE.
GOOD. GROW UP.
YOU DRESSED?
YES, MADROX. I'M WEARING A VERA WANG EVENING GOWN AND STILETTO HEELS.
GOOD. GRAB YOUR PURSE. WE HAVE A *SITUATION.*
I'LL SAY. FOR STARTERS, THERE'S *GLASS* ALL OVER THE FLOOR.
GLORIA SANTIAGO CALLED. SHE'S BEING ARRESTED.
THAT WOMAN WHOSE SISTER WAS HAVING AN AFFAIR WITH SOME MOVIE STAR? WHAT'S SHE BEING ARRESTED FOR?
KILLING HER SISTER.
LORD. *REALLY?*
SHE'S AT THE MARQUIS HOTEL ACROSS TOWN.
GIMME FIVE MINUTES.
OKAY! I'LL GO WARM UP THE CAR, THEN.
DON'T BOTHER.
WHO THE--? OH. RIGHT. LAYLA MILLER. THE GIRL WHO "KNOWS STUFF."
WHY SHOULDN'T I BOTHER WITH THE CAR?
YOU'LL SEE.

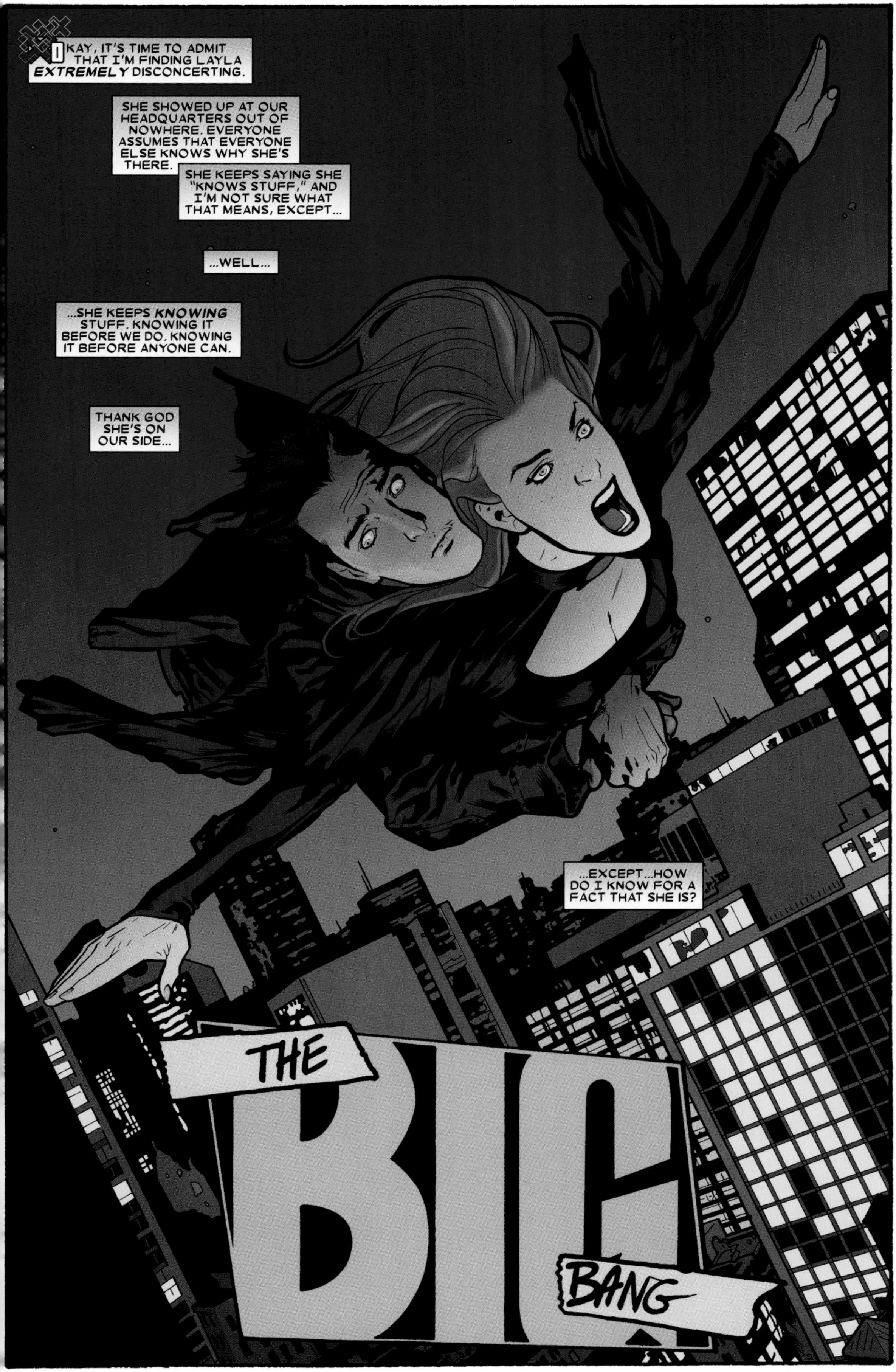
OKAY, IT'S TIME TO ADMIT THAT I'M FINDING LAYLA *EXTREMELY* DISCONCERTING.
SHE SHOWED UP AT OUR HEADQUARTERS OUT OF NOWHERE. EVERYONE ASSUMES THAT EVERYONE ELSE KNOWS WHY SHE'S THERE.
SHE KEEPS SAYING SHE "KNOWS STUFF," AND I'M NOT SURE WHAT THAT MEANS, EXCEPT...
...WELL...
...SHE KEEPS *KNOWING* STUFF. KNOWING IT BEFORE WE DO. KNOWING IT BEFORE ANYONE CAN.
THANK GOD SHE'S ON OUR SIDE...
...EXCEPT...HOW DO I KNOW FOR A FACT THAT SHE IS?
THE BIG BANG

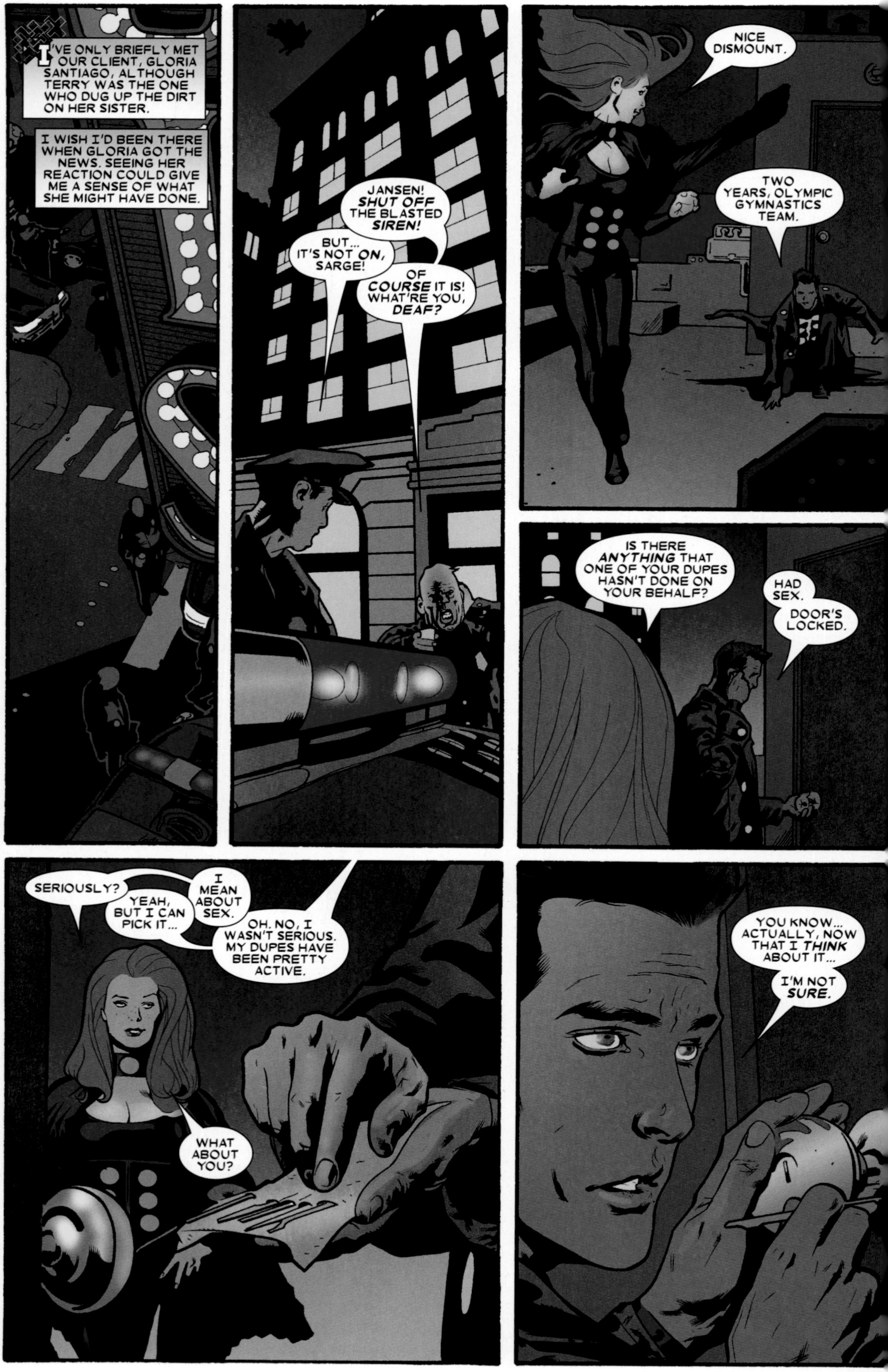
I'VE ONLY BRIEFLY MET OUR CLIENT, GLORIA SANTIAGO, ALTHOUGH TERRY WAS THE ONE WHO DUG UP THE DIRT ON HER SISTER.
I WISH I'D BEEN THERE WHEN GLORIA GOT THE NEWS. SEEING HER REACTION COULD GIVE ME A SENSE OF WHAT SHE MIGHT HAVE DONE.
JANSEN! SHUT OFF THE BLASTED SIREN!
BUT... IT'S NOT ON, SARGE!
OF COURSE IT IS! WHAT'RE YOU, DEAF?
NICE DISMOUNT.
TWO YEARS, OLYMPIC GYMNASTICS TEAM.
IS THERE ANYTHING THAT ONE OF YOUR DUPES HASN'T DONE ON YOUR BEHALF?
HAD SEX.
DOOR'S LOCKED.
SERIOUSLY?
I MEAN ABOUT SEX.
YEAH, BUT I CAN PICK IT...
OH. NO, I WASN'T SERIOUS. MY DUPES HAVE BEEN PRETTY ACTIVE.
WHAT ABOUT YOU?
YOU KNOW... ACTUALLY, NOW THAT I THINK ABOUT IT...
I'M NOT SURE.

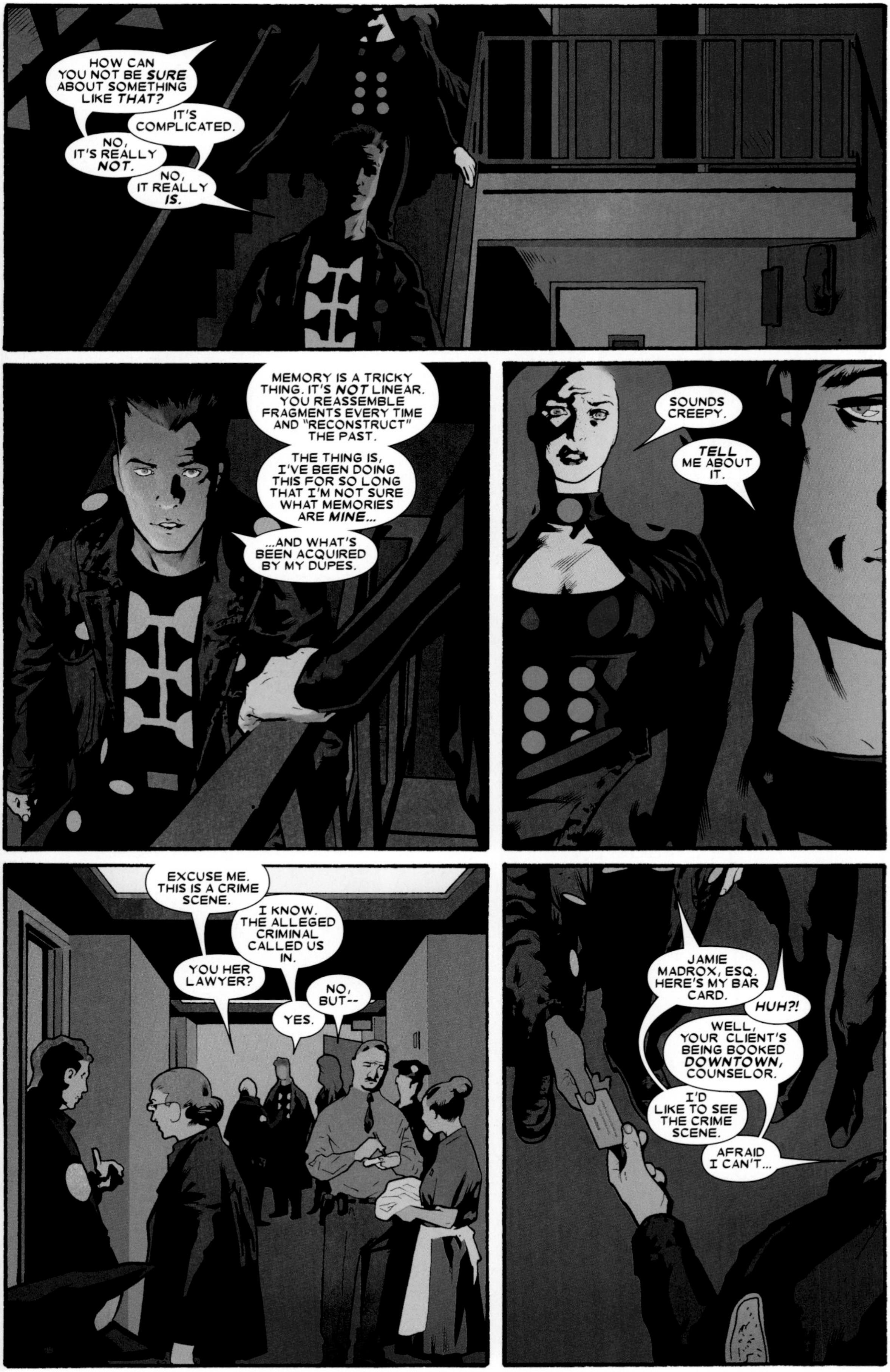
HOW CAN YOU NOT BE SURE ABOUT SOMETHING LIKE THAT?
IT'S COMPLICATED.
NO, IT'S REALLY NOT.
NO, IT REALLY IS.
MEMORY IS A TRICKY THING. IT'S NOT LINEAR. YOU REASSEMBLE FRAGMENTS EVERY TIME AND "RECONSTRUCT" THE PAST.
THE THING IS, I'VE BEEN DOING THIS FOR SO LONG THAT I'M NOT SURE WHAT MEMORIES ARE MINE...
...AND WHAT'S BEEN ACQUIRED BY MY DUPES.
SOUNDS CREEPY.
TELL ME ABOUT IT.
EXCUSE ME. THIS IS A CRIME SCENE.
I KNOW. THE ALLEGED CRIMINAL CALLED US IN.
YOU HER LAWYER?
NO, BUT--
YES.
JAMIE MADROX, ESQ. HERE'S MY BAR CARD.
HUH?!
WELL, YOUR CLIENT'S BEING BOOKED DOWNTOWN, COUNSELOR.
I'D LIKE TO SEE THE CRIME SCENE.
AFRAID I CAN'T...

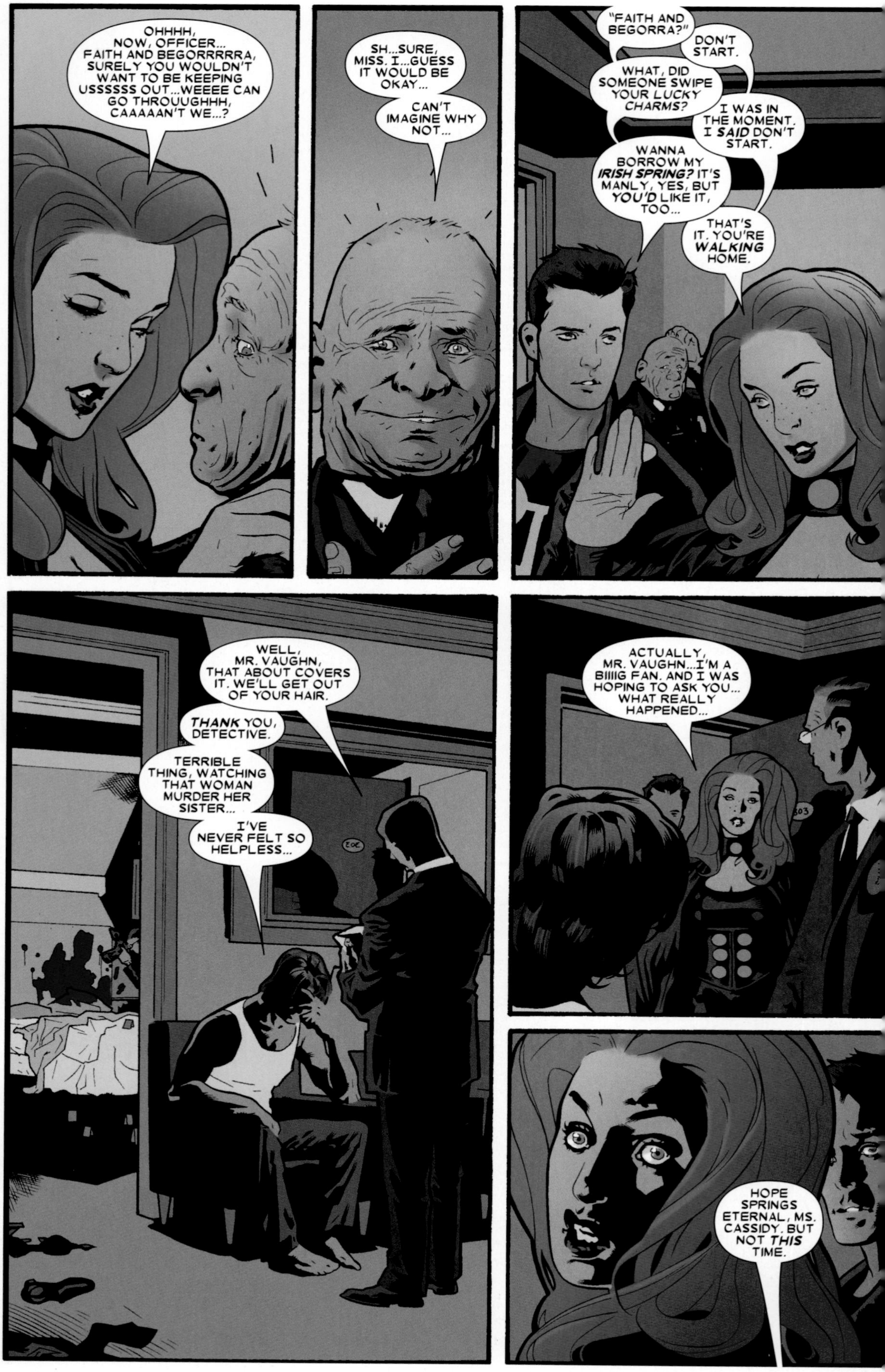
OHHHH, NOW, OFFICER... FAITH AND BEGORRRRRA, SURELY YOU WOULDN'T WANT TO BE KEEPING USSSSSS OUT...WEEEE CAN GO THROUUGHHH, CAAAAAN'T WE...?
SH...SURE, MISS. I...GUESS IT WOULD BE OKAY...
CAN'T IMAGINE WHY NOT...
"FAITH AND BEGORRA?"
DON'T START.
WHAT, DID SOMEONE SWIPE YOUR *LUCKY CHARMS?*
I WAS IN THE MOMENT. I *SAID* DON'T START.
WANNA BORROW MY ***IRISH SPRING?*** IT'S MANLY, YES, BUT ***YOU'D*** LIKE IT, TOO...
THAT'S IT. YOU'RE ***WALKING*** HOME.
WELL, MR. VAUGHN, THAT ABOUT COVERS IT. WE'LL GET OUT OF YOUR HAIR.
THANK YOU, DETECTIVE.
TERRIBLE THING, WATCHING THAT WOMAN MURDER HER SISTER...
I'VE NEVER FELT SO HELPLESS...
ACTUALLY, MR. VAUGHN...I'M A BIIIIG FAN. AND I WAS HOPING TO ASK YOU... WHAT REALLY HAPPENED...
HOPE SPRINGS ETERNAL, MS. CASSIDY. BUT NOT *THIS* TIME.

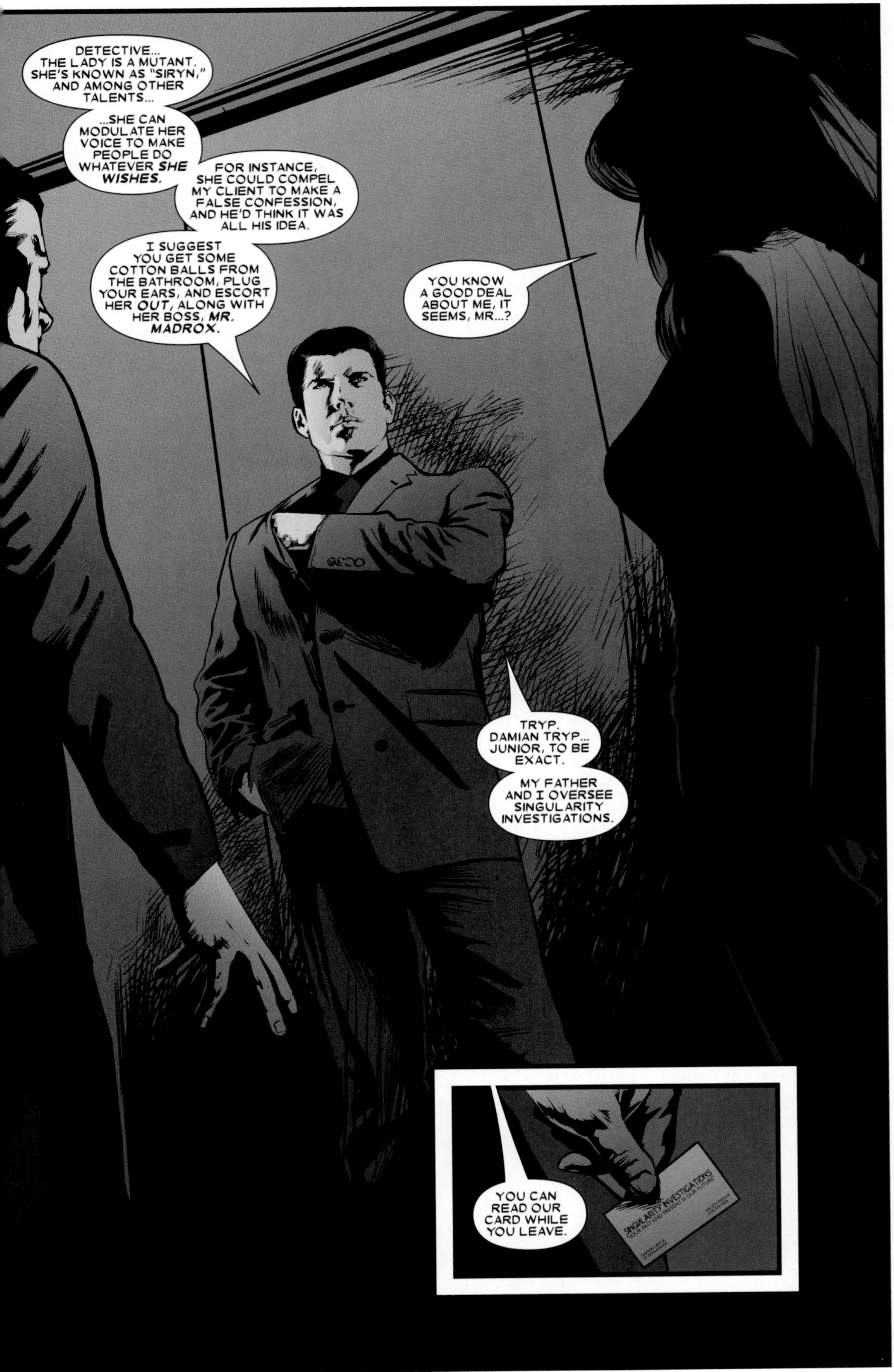
DETECTIVE... THE LADY IS A MUTANT. SHE'S KNOWN AS "SIRYN," AND AMONG OTHER TALENTS...
...SHE CAN MODULATE HER VOICE TO MAKE PEOPLE DO WHATEVER *SHE WISHES.*
FOR INSTANCE, SHE COULD COMPEL MY CLIENT TO MAKE A FALSE CONFESSION, AND HE'D THINK IT WAS ALL HIS IDEA.
I SUGGEST YOU GET SOME COTTON BALLS FROM THE BATHROOM, PLUG YOUR EARS, AND ESCORT HER *OUT,* ALONG WITH HER BOSS, *MR. MADROX.*
YOU KNOW A GOOD DEAL ABOUT ME, IT SEEMS, MR...?
TRYP. DAMIAN TRYP... JUNIOR, TO BE EXACT.
MY FATHER AND I OVERSEE SINGULARITY INVESTIGATIONS.
YOU CAN READ OUR CARD WHILE YOU LEAVE.
SINGULARITY INVESTIGATIONS

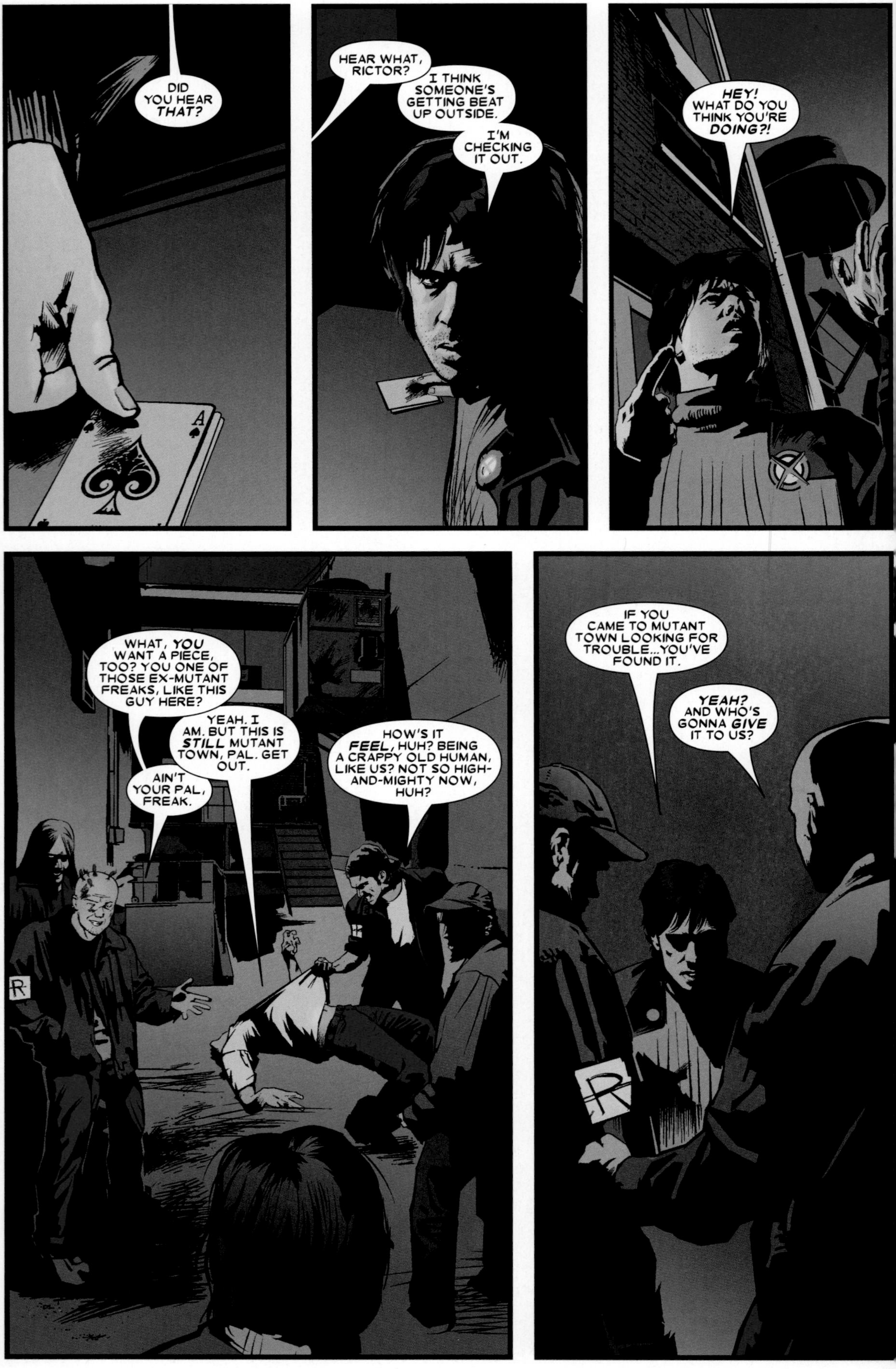
DID YOU HEAR *THAT?*
HEAR WHAT, RICTOR?
I THINK SOMEONE'S GETTING BEAT UP OUTSIDE.
I'M CHECKING IT OUT.
HEY! WHAT DO YOU THINK YOU'RE *DOING?!*
WHAT, *YOU* WANT A PIECE, TOO? YOU ONE OF THOSE EX-MUTANT FREAKS, LIKE THIS GUY HERE?
YEAH. I AM. BUT THIS IS *STILL* MUTANT TOWN, PAL. GET OUT.
AIN'T YOUR PAL, FREAK.
HOW'S IT *FEEL*, HUH? BEING A CRAPPY OLD HUMAN, LIKE US? NOT SO HIGH-AND-MIGHTY NOW, HUH?
IF YOU CAME TO MUTANT TOWN LOOKING FOR TROUBLE...YOU'VE FOUND IT.
YEAH? AND WHO'S GONNA *GIVE* IT TO US?

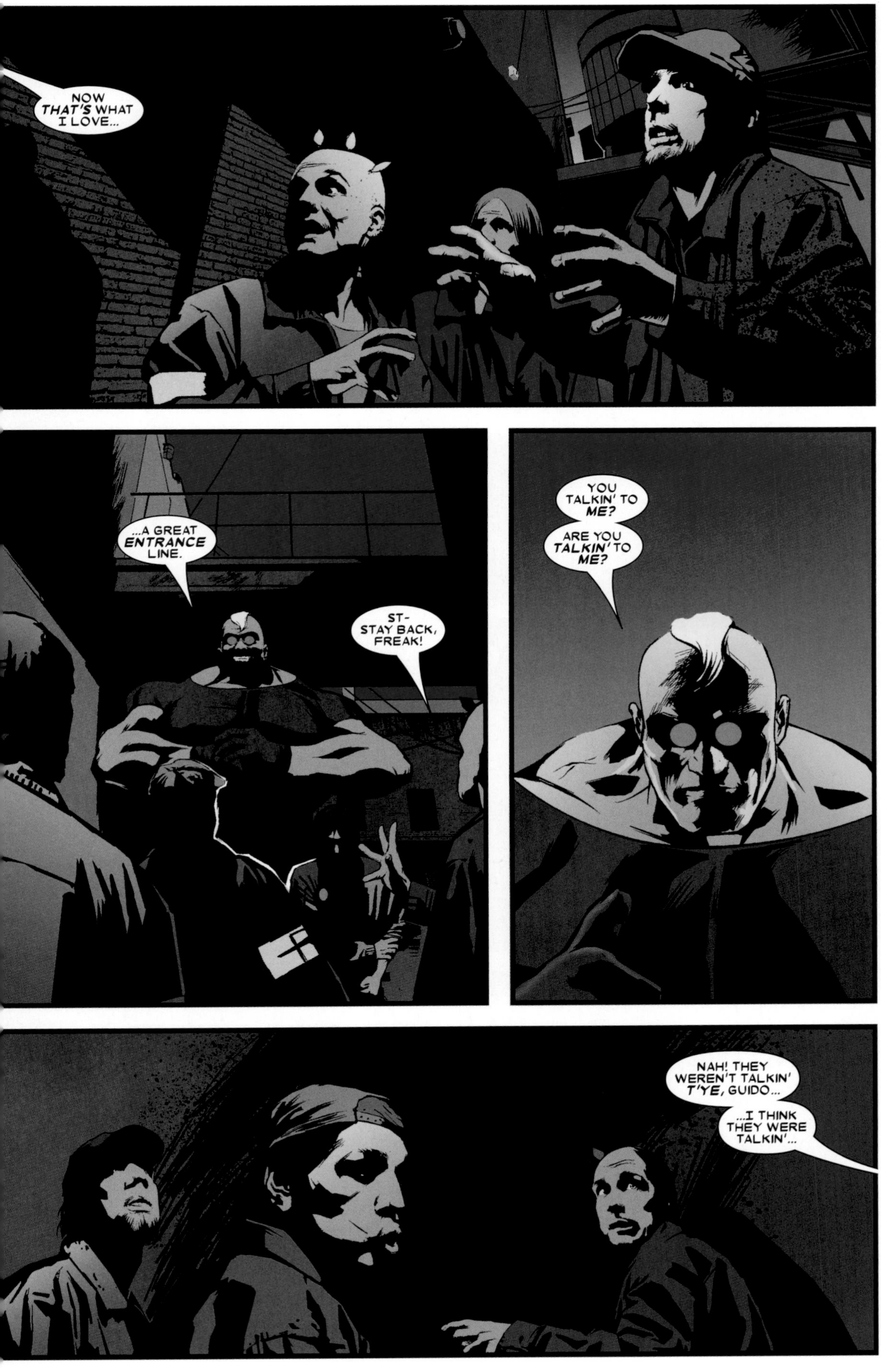
NOW THAT'S WHAT I LOVE...
...A GREAT ENTRANCE LINE.
ST- STAY BACK, FREAK!
YOU TALKIN' TO ME?
ARE YOU TALKIN' TO ME?
NAH! THEY WEREN'T TALKIN' T'YE, GUIDO...
...I THINK THEY WERE TALKIN'...

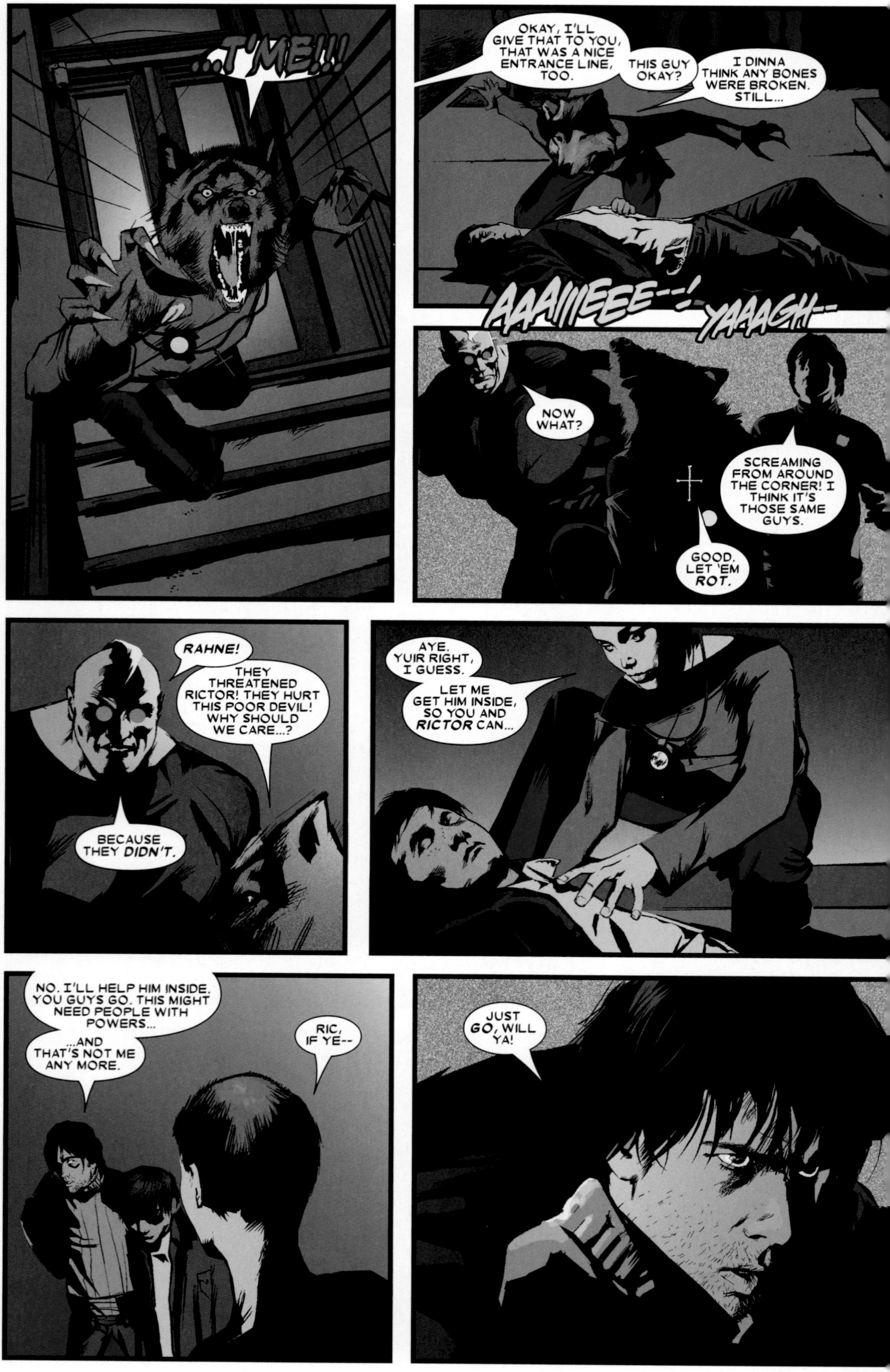

...T'ME!!!
OKAY, I'LL GIVE THAT TO YOU, THAT WAS A NICE ENTRANCE LINE, TOO.
THIS GUY OKAY?
I DINNA THINK ANY BONES WERE BROKEN. STILL...
AAAIIIEEE--!
YAAAGH--
NOW WHAT?
SCREAMING FROM AROUND THE CORNER! I THINK IT'S THOSE SAME GUYS.
GOOD. LET 'EM ROT.
RAHNE!
THEY THREATENED RICTOR! THEY HURT THIS POOR DEVIL! WHY SHOULD WE CARE...?
BECAUSE THEY DIDN'T.
AYE. YUIR RIGHT, I GUESS.
LET ME GET HIM INSIDE, SO YOU AND RICTOR CAN...
NO. I'LL HELP HIM INSIDE. YOU GUYS GO. THIS MIGHT NEED PEOPLE WITH POWERS...
...AND THAT'S NOT ME ANY MORE.
RIC, IF YE--
JUST GO, WILL YA!

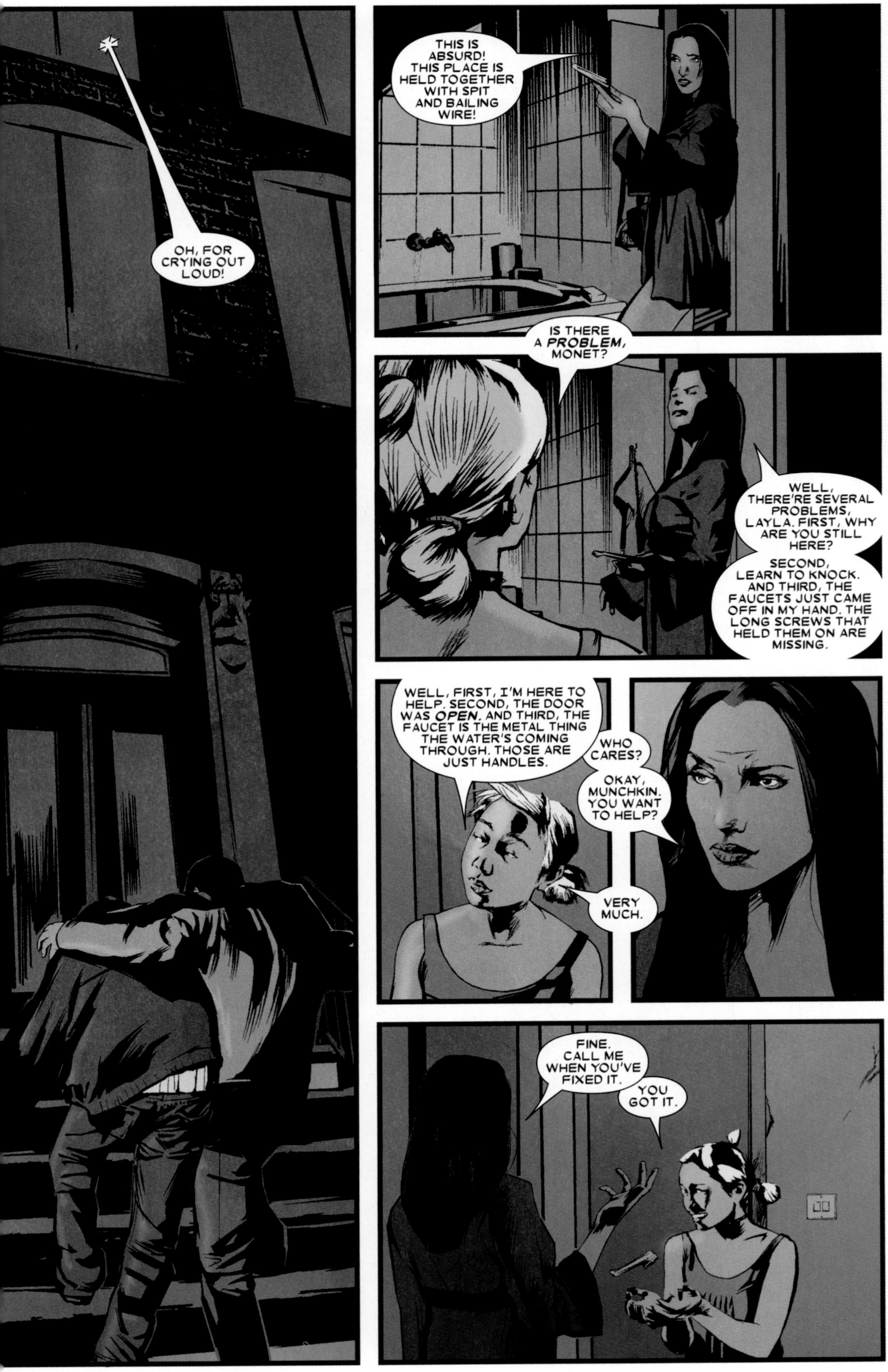

OH, FOR CRYING OUT LOUD!
THIS IS ABSURD! THIS PLACE IS HELD TOGETHER WITH SPIT AND BAILING WIRE!
IS THERE A PROBLEM, MONET?
WELL, THERE'RE SEVERAL PROBLEMS, LAYLA. FIRST, WHY ARE YOU STILL HERE?
SECOND, LEARN TO KNOCK. AND THIRD, THE FAUCETS JUST CAME OFF IN MY HAND. THE LONG SCREWS THAT HELD THEM ON ARE MISSING.
WELL, FIRST, I'M HERE TO HELP. SECOND, THE DOOR WAS OPEN. AND THIRD, THE FAUCET IS THE METAL THING THE WATER'S COMING THROUGH. THOSE ARE JUST HANDLES.
WHO CARES?
OKAY, MUNCHKIN. YOU WANT TO HELP?
VERY MUCH.
FINE. CALL ME WHEN YOU'VE FIXED IT.
YOU GOT IT.

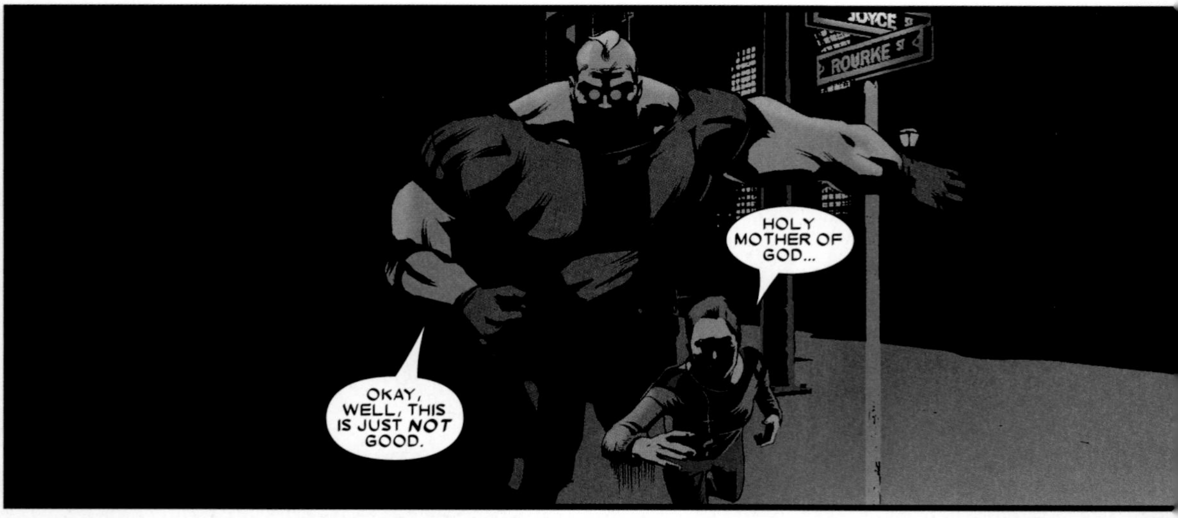
HOLY MOTHER OF GOD...
OKAY, WELL, THIS IS JUST **NOT** GOOD.
JOYCE ST
ROURKE ST

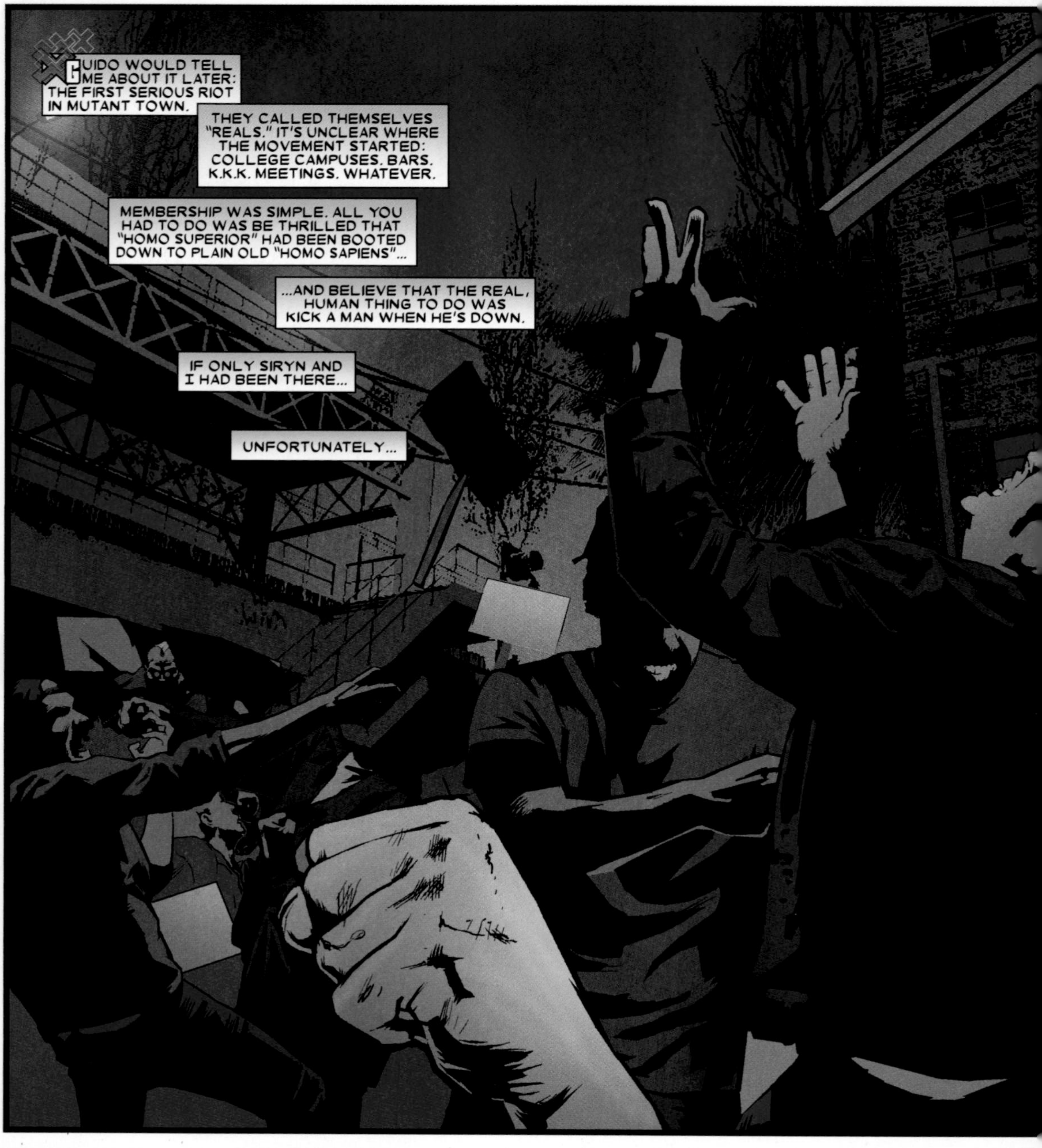
GUIDO WOULD TELL ME ABOUT IT LATER: THE FIRST SERIOUS RIOT IN MUTANT TOWN.
THEY CALLED THEMSELVES "REALS." IT'S UNCLEAR WHERE THE MOVEMENT STARTED: COLLEGE CAMPUSES. BARS. K.K.K. MEETINGS. WHATEVER.
MEMBERSHIP WAS SIMPLE. ALL YOU HAD TO DO WAS BE THRILLED THAT "HOMO SUPERIOR" HAD BEEN BOOTED DOWN TO PLAIN OLD "HOMO SAPIENS"...
...AND BELIEVE THAT THE REAL, HUMAN THING TO DO WAS KICK A MAN WHEN HE'S DOWN.
IF ONLY SIRYN AND I HAD BEEN THERE...
UNFORTUNATELY...

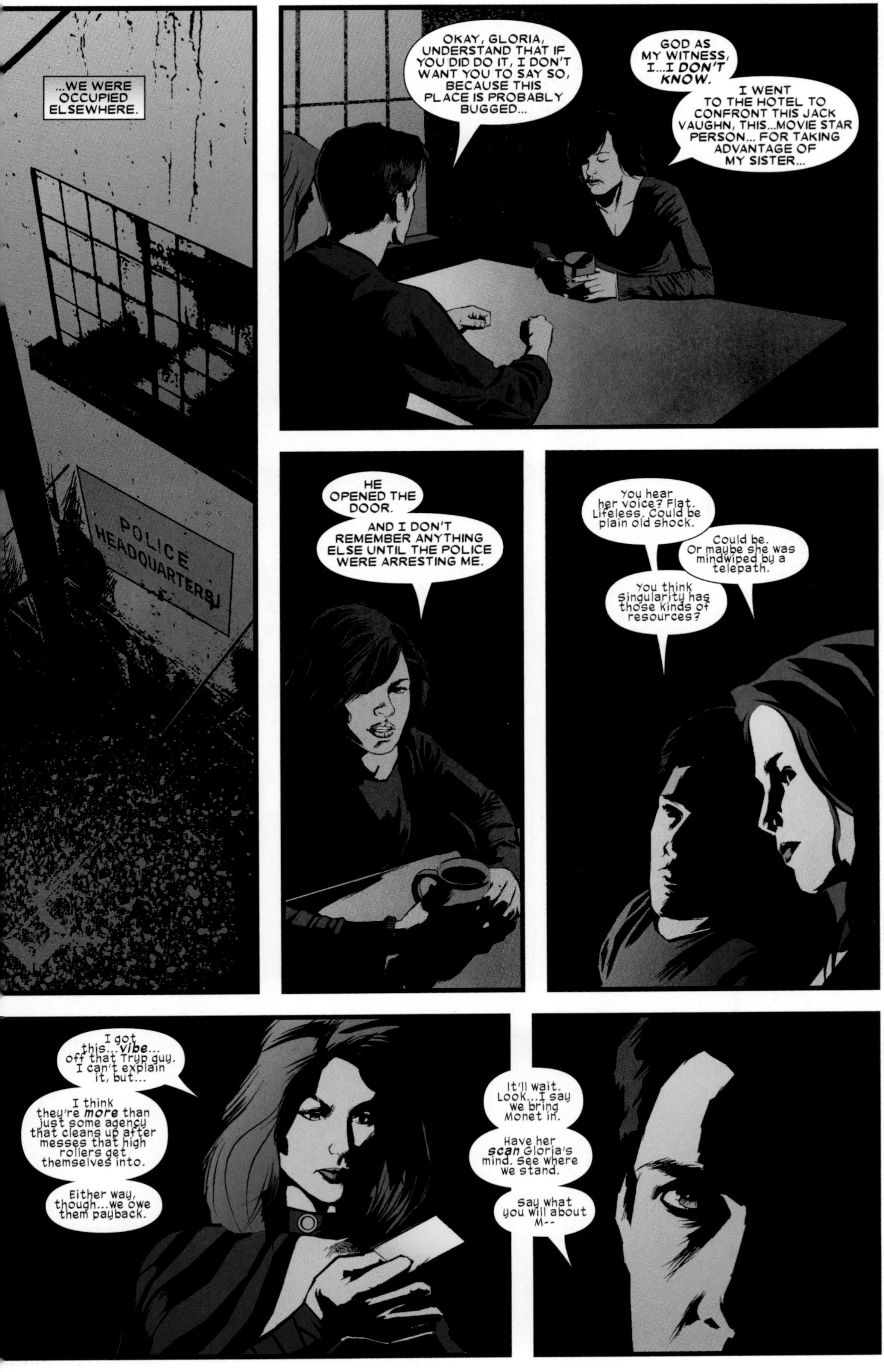

...WE WERE OCCUPIED ELSEWHERE.
POLICE HEADQUARTERS
OKAY, GLORIA, UNDERSTAND THAT IF YOU DID DO IT, I DON'T WANT YOU TO SAY SO, BECAUSE THIS PLACE IS PROBABLY BUGGED...
GOD AS MY WITNESS, I...I DON'T KNOW.
I WENT TO THE HOTEL TO CONFRONT THIS JACK VAUGHN, THIS...MOVIE STAR PERSON... FOR TAKING ADVANTAGE OF MY SISTER...
HE OPENED THE DOOR.
AND I DON'T REMEMBER ANYTHING ELSE UNTIL THE POLICE WERE ARRESTING ME.
You hear her voice? Flat. Lifeless. Could be plain old shock.
Could be. Or maybe she was mindwiped by a telepath.
You think Singularity has those kinds of resources?
I got this...vibe... off that Trup guy. I can't explain it, but...
I think they're more than just some agency that cleans up after messes that high rollers get themselves into.
Either way, though...we owe them payback.
It'll wait. Look...I say we bring Monet in.
Have her scan Gloria's mind. See where we stand.
Say what you will about M--

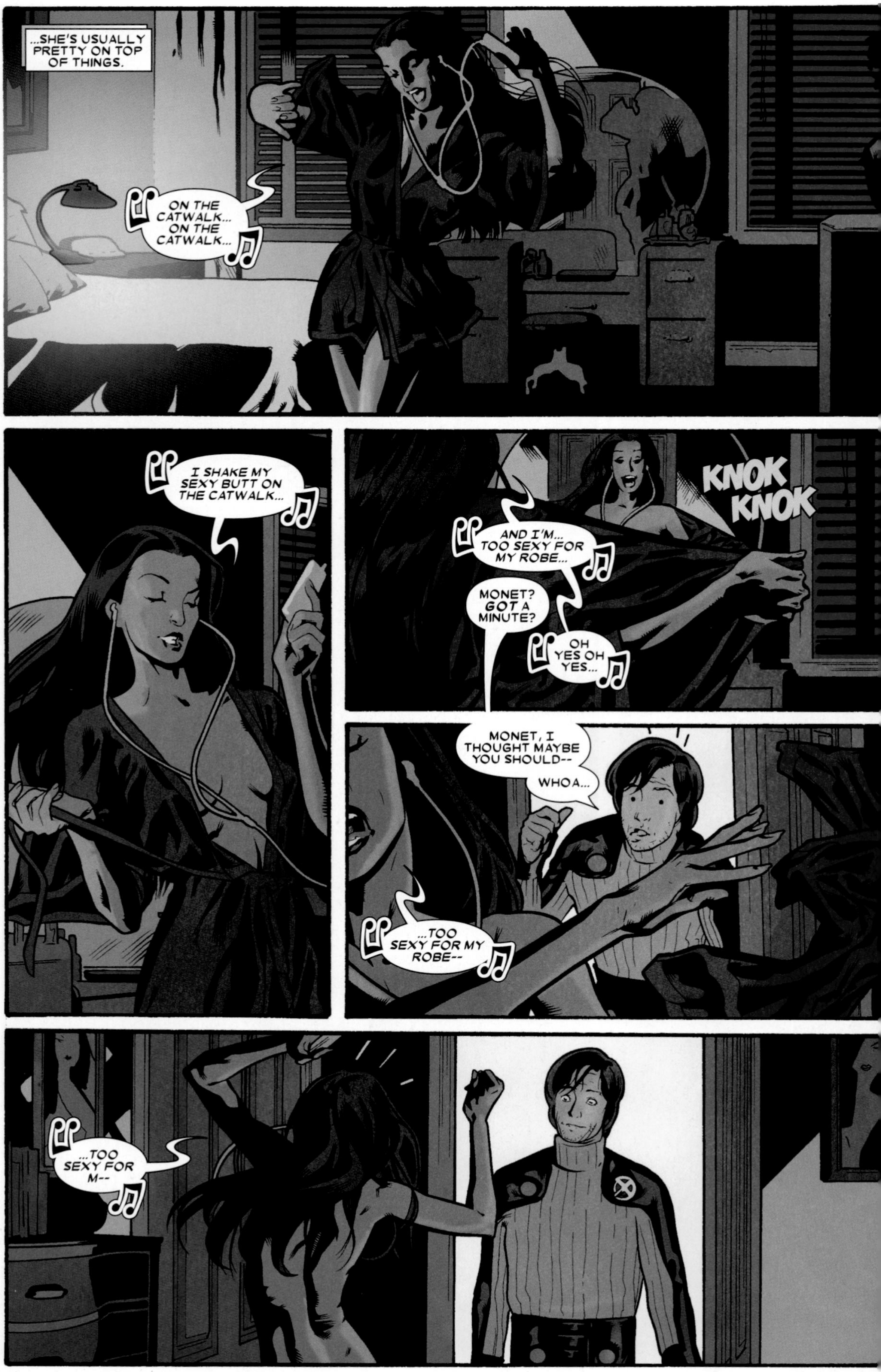

...SHE'S USUALLY PRETTY ON TOP OF THINGS.
ON THE CATWALK... ON THE CATWALK...
I SHAKE MY SEXY BUTT ON THE CATWALK...
KNOK KNOK
AND I'M... TOO SEXY FOR MY ROBE...
MONET? GOT A MINUTE?
OH YES OH YES...
MONET, I THOUGHT MAYBE YOU SHOULD--
WHOA...
...TOO SEXY FOR MY ROBE--
...TOO SEXY FOR M--

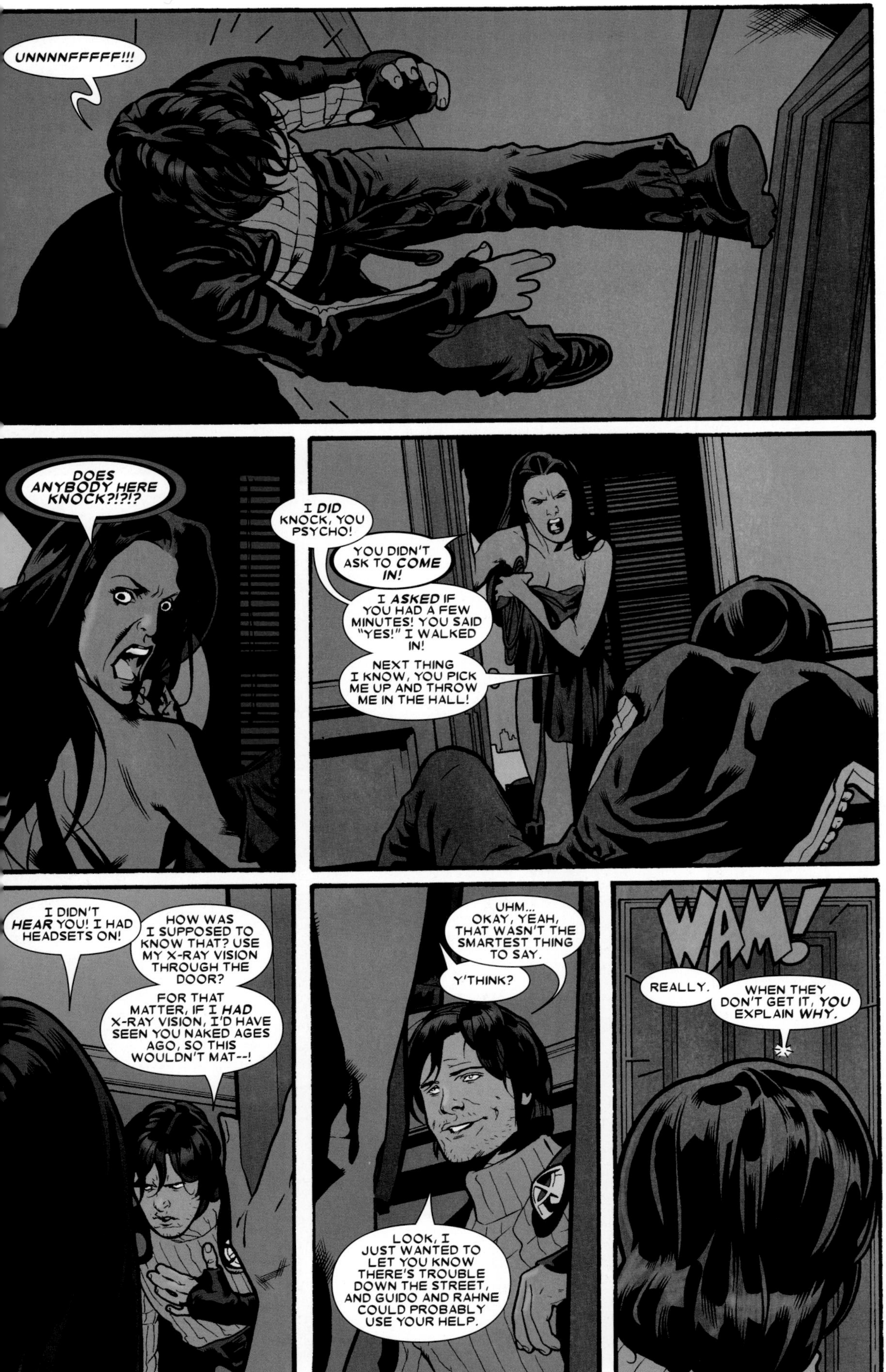
UNNNNFFFFF!!!
DOES ANYBODY HERE KNOCK?!?!?
I DID KNOCK, YOU PSYCHO!
YOU DIDN'T ASK TO COME IN!
I ASKED IF YOU HAD A FEW MINUTES! YOU SAID "YES!" I WALKED IN!
NEXT THING I KNOW, YOU PICK ME UP AND THROW ME IN THE HALL!
I DIDN'T HEAR YOU! I HAD HEADSETS ON!
HOW WAS I SUPPOSED TO KNOW THAT? USE MY X-RAY VISION THROUGH THE DOOR?
FOR THAT MATTER, IF I HAD X-RAY VISION, I'D HAVE SEEN YOU NAKED AGES AGO, SO THIS WOULDN'T MAT--!
UHM... OKAY, YEAH, THAT WASN'T THE SMARTEST THING TO SAY.
Y'THINK?
LOOK, I JUST WANTED TO LET YOU KNOW THERE'S TROUBLE DOWN THE STREET, AND GUIDO AND RAHNE COULD PROBABLY USE YOUR HELP.
WAM!
REALLY.
WHEN THEY DON'T GET IT, YOU EXPLAIN WHY.

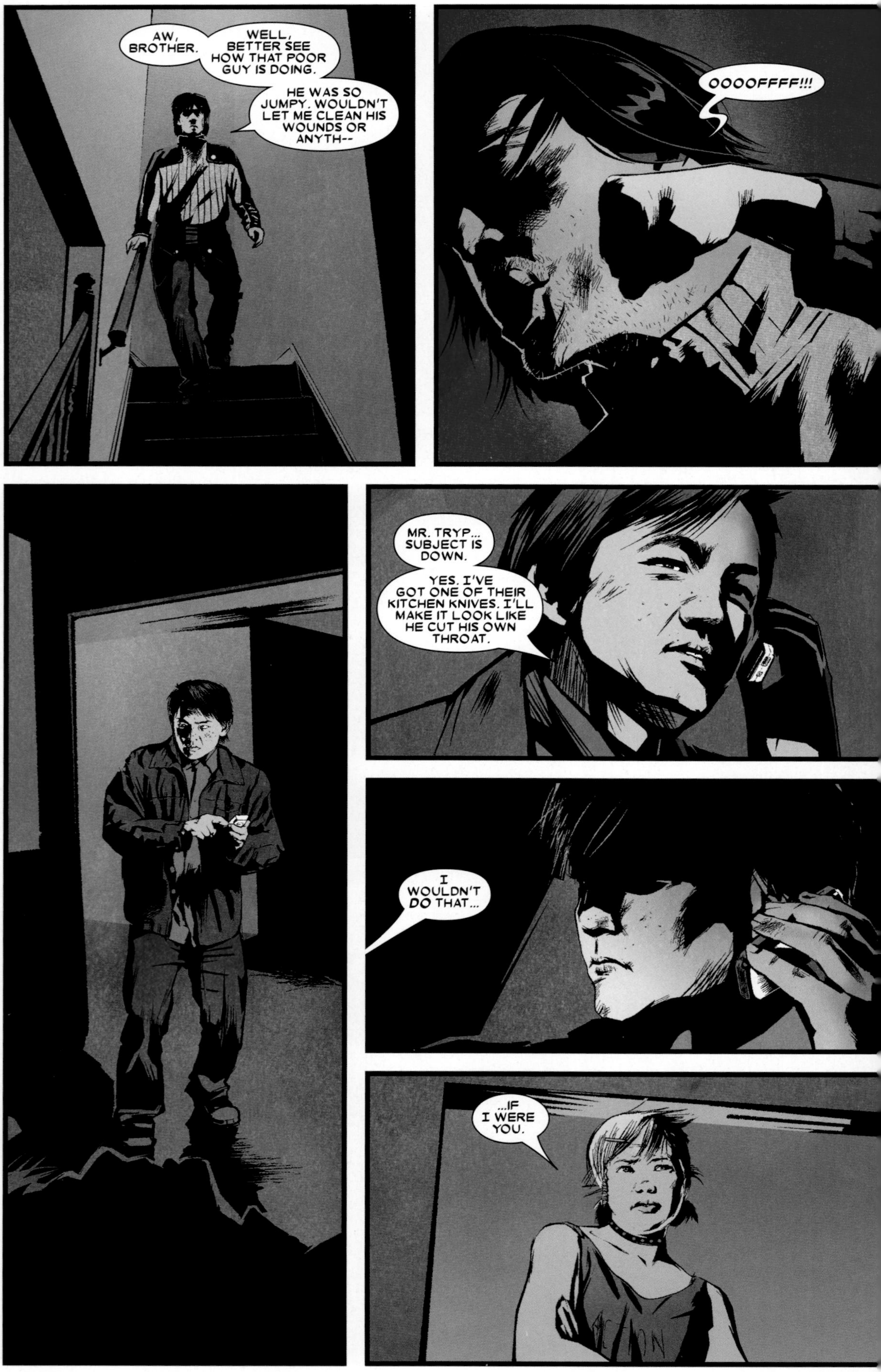
AW, BROTHER.
WELL, BETTER SEE HOW THAT POOR GUY IS DOING.
HE WAS SO JUMPY. WOULDN'T LET ME CLEAN HIS WOUNDS OR ANYTH--
OOOOFFFF!!!
MR. TRYP... SUBJECT IS DOWN.
YES. I'VE GOT ONE OF THEIR KITCHEN KNIVES. I'LL MAKE IT LOOK LIKE HE CUT HIS OWN THROAT.
I WOULDN'T *DO* THAT...
...IF I WERE YOU.

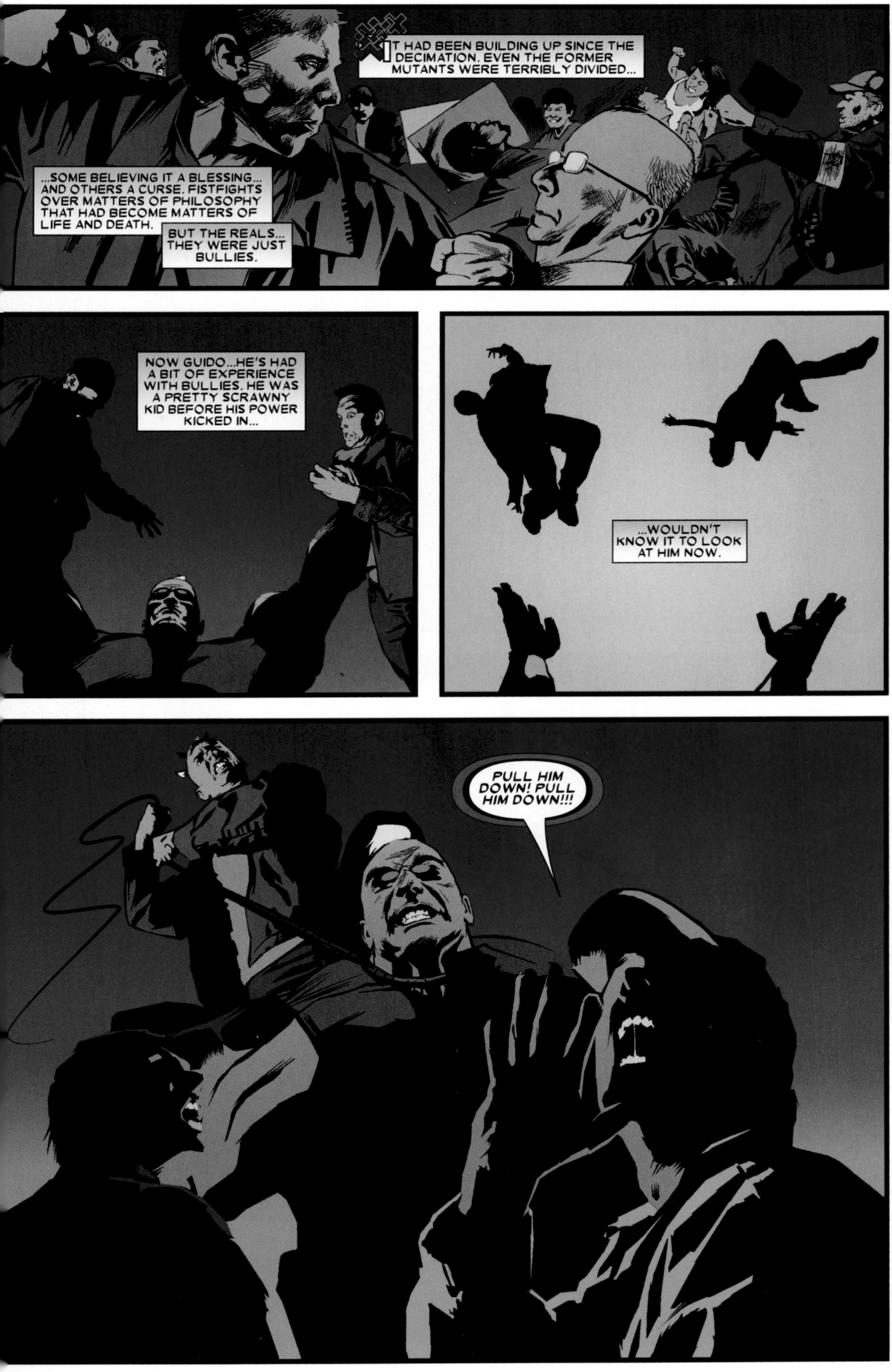
IT HAD BEEN BUILDING UP SINCE THE DECIMATION. EVEN THE FORMER MUTANTS WERE TERRIBLY DIVIDED...
...SOME BELIEVING IT A BLESSING... AND OTHERS A CURSE. FISTFIGHTS OVER MATTERS OF PHILOSOPHY THAT HAD BECOME MATTERS OF LIFE AND DEATH.
BUT THE REALS... THEY WERE JUST BULLIES.
NOW GUIDO...HE'S HAD A BIT OF EXPERIENCE WITH BULLIES. HE WAS A PRETTY SCRAWNY KID BEFORE HIS POWER KICKED IN...
...WOULDN'T KNOW IT TO LOOK AT HIM NOW.
PULL HIM DOWN! PULL HIM DOWN!!!

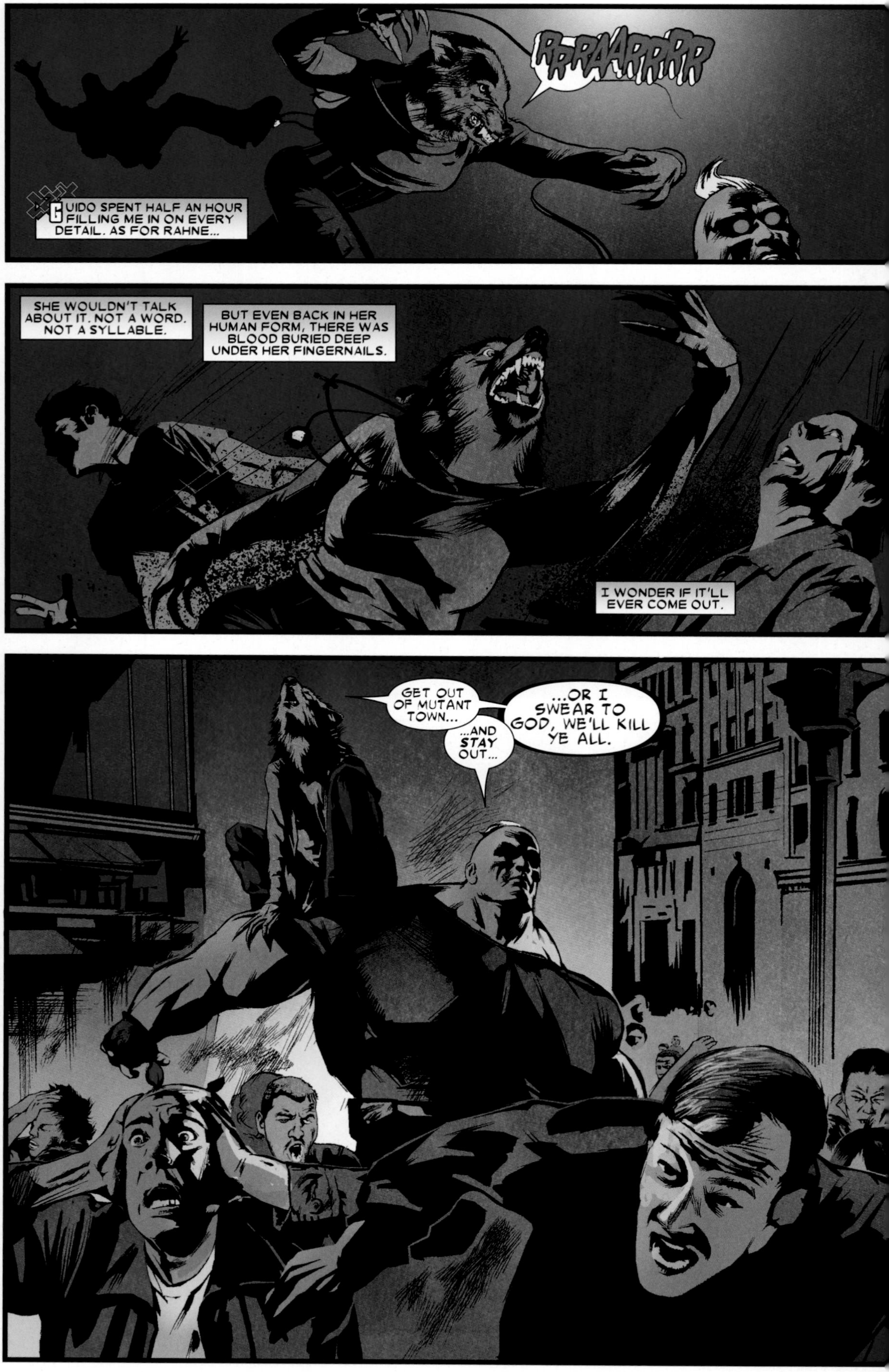
RRRAARRRRR
GUIDO SPENT HALF AN HOUR FILLING ME IN ON EVERY DETAIL. AS FOR RAHNE...
SHE WOULDN'T TALK ABOUT IT. NOT A WORD. NOT A SYLLABLE.
BUT EVEN BACK IN HER HUMAN FORM, THERE WAS BLOOD BURIED DEEP UNDER HER FINGERNAILS.
I WONDER IF IT'LL EVER COME OUT.
GET OUT OF MUTANT TOWN...
...AND STAY OUT...
...OR I SWEAR TO GOD, WE'LL KILL YE ALL.

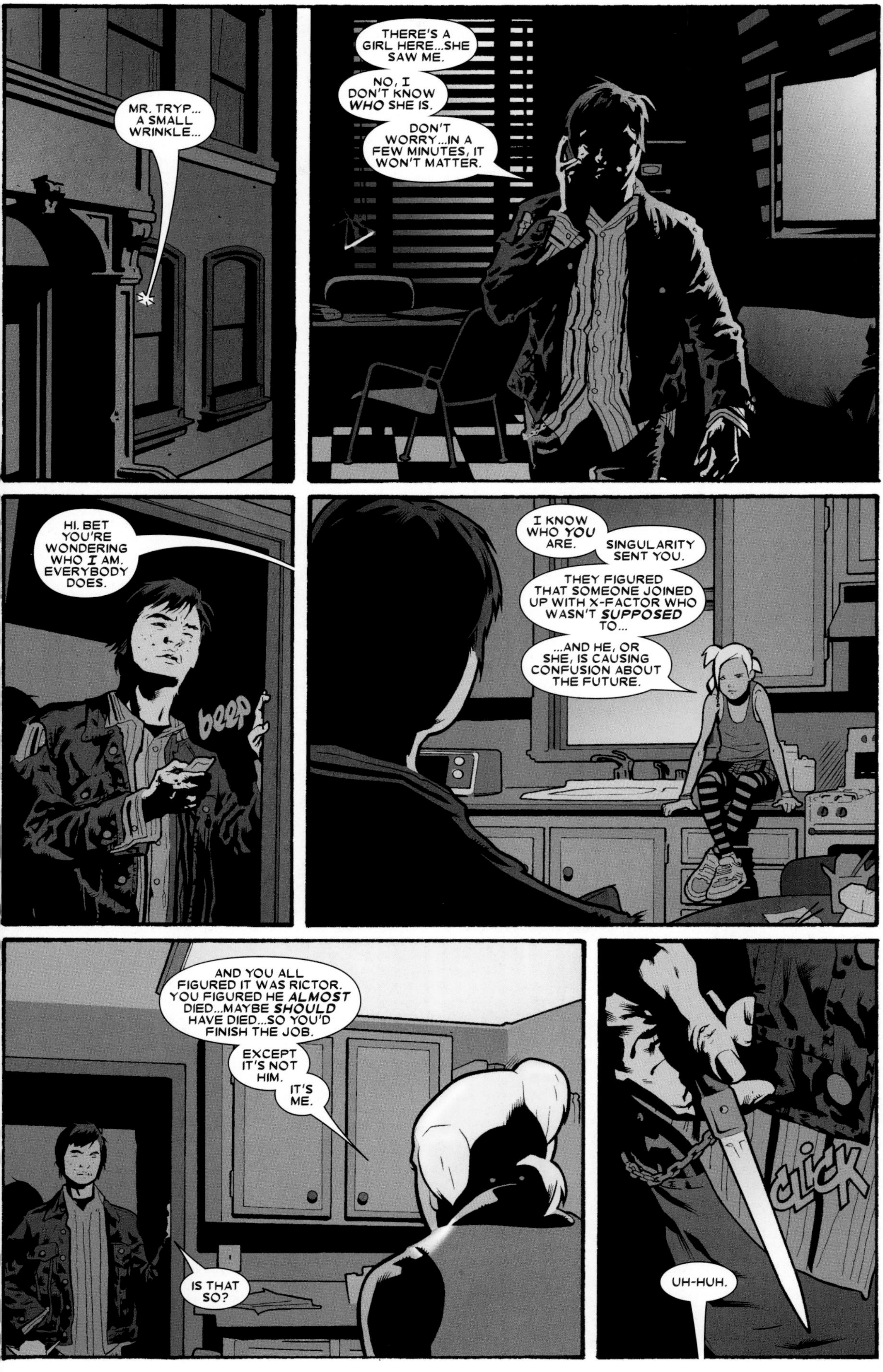
MR. TRYP... A SMALL WRINKLE...
THERE'S A GIRL HERE...SHE SAW ME.
NO, I DON'T KNOW WHO SHE IS.
DON'T WORRY...IN A FEW MINUTES, IT WON'T MATTER.
HI. BET YOU'RE WONDERING WHO I AM. EVERYBODY DOES.
beep
I KNOW WHO YOU ARE.
SINGULARITY SENT YOU.
THEY FIGURED THAT SOMEONE JOINED UP WITH X-FACTOR WHO WASN'T SUPPOSED TO...
...AND HE, OR SHE, IS CAUSING CONFUSION ABOUT THE FUTURE.
AND YOU ALL FIGURED IT WAS RICTOR. YOU FIGURED HE ALMOST DIED...MAYBE SHOULD HAVE DIED...SO YOU'D FINISH THE JOB.
EXCEPT IT'S NOT HIM.
IT'S ME.
IS THAT SO?
CLICK
UH-HUH.

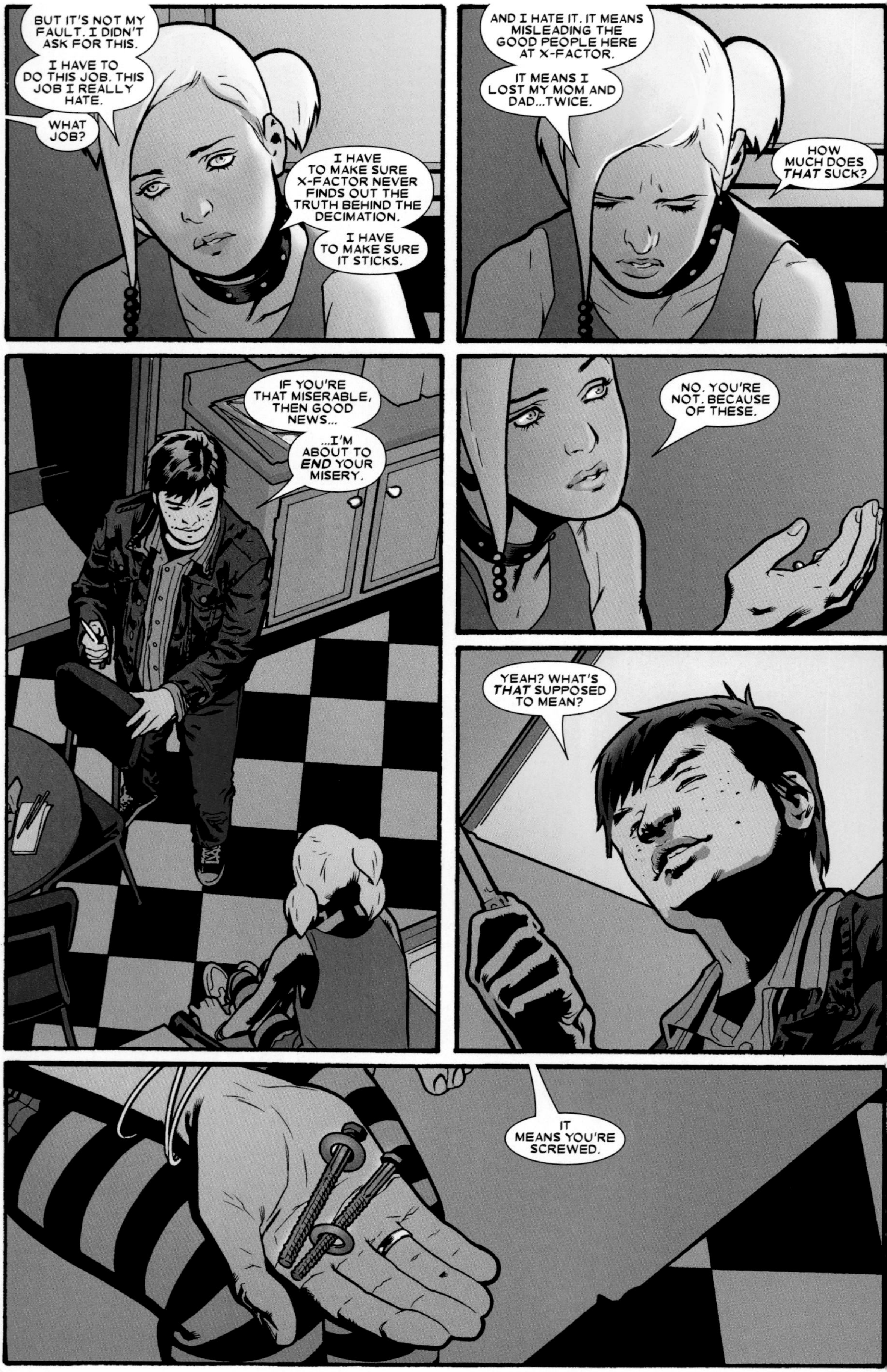
BUT IT'S NOT MY FAULT. I DIDN'T ASK FOR THIS.
I HAVE TO DO THIS JOB. THIS JOB I REALLY HATE.
WHAT JOB?
I HAVE TO MAKE SURE X-FACTOR NEVER FINDS OUT THE TRUTH BEHIND THE DECIMATION.
I HAVE TO MAKE SURE IT STICKS.
AND I HATE IT. IT MEANS MISLEADING THE GOOD PEOPLE HERE AT X-FACTOR.
IT MEANS I LOST MY MOM AND DAD...TWICE.
HOW MUCH DOES *THAT* SUCK?
IF YOU'RE THAT MISERABLE, THEN GOOD NEWS...
...I'M ABOUT TO ***END*** YOUR MISERY.
NO. YOU'RE NOT. BECAUSE OF THESE.
YEAH? WHAT'S ***THAT*** SUPPOSED TO MEAN?
IT MEANS YOU'RE SCREWED.

WHAT THE--?

HAH! MISSED ME!

EEEEYAARRRHHHHHHH!

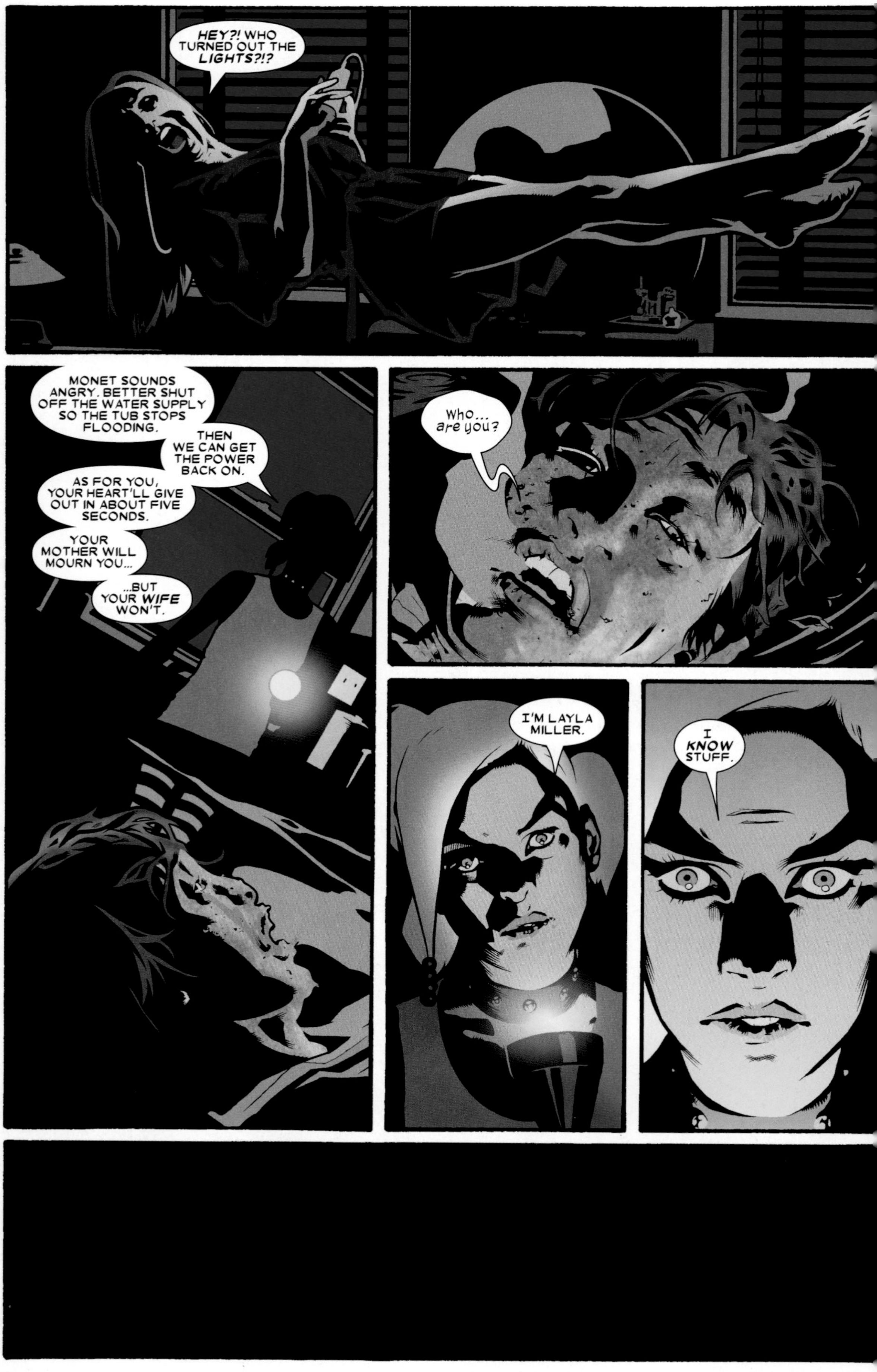
HEY?! WHO TURNED OUT THE LIGHTS?!?
MONET SOUNDS ANGRY. BETTER SHUT OFF THE WATER SUPPLY SO THE TUB STOPS FLOODING.
THEN WE CAN GET THE POWER BACK ON.
AS FOR YOU, YOUR HEART'LL GIVE OUT IN ABOUT FIVE SECONDS.
YOUR MOTHER WILL MOURN YOU...
...BUT YOUR WIFE WON'T.
Who... are you?
I'M LAYLA MILLER.
I KNOW STUFF.

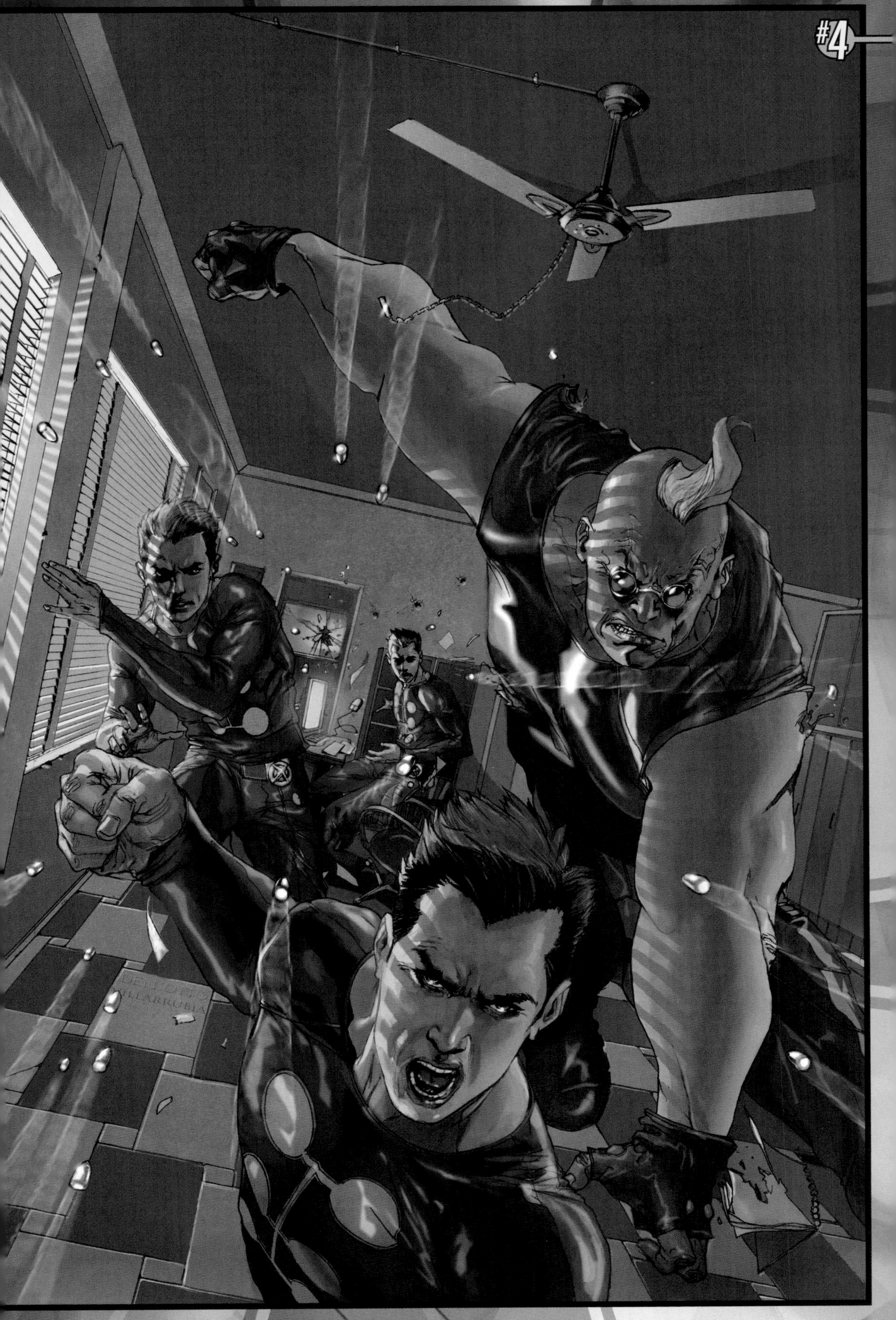
#4

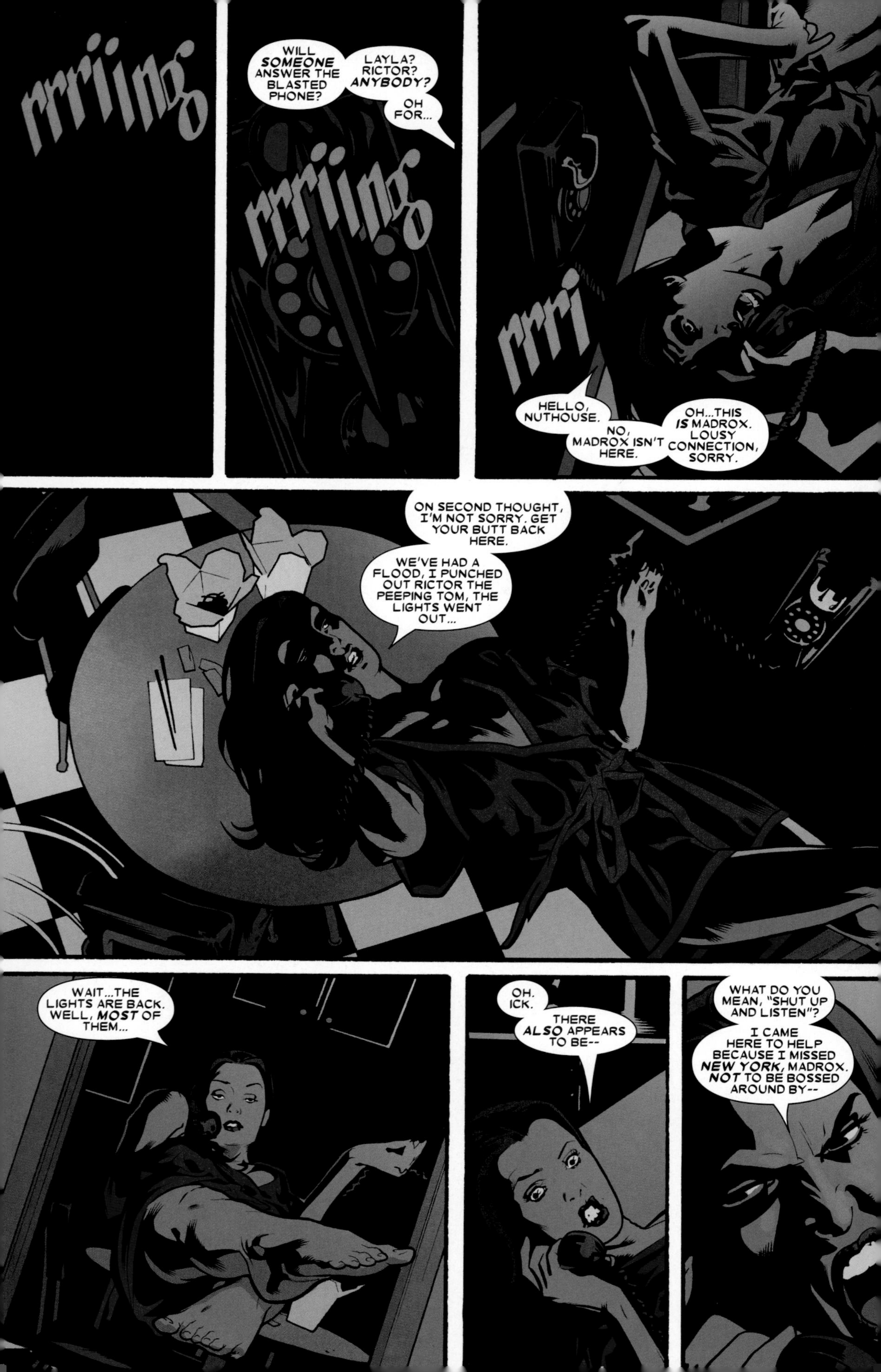
rrriing
WILL SOMEONE ANSWER THE BLASTED PHONE?
LAYLA? RICTOR? ANYBODY?
OH FOR...
rrriing
rrri
HELLO, NUTHOUSE.
NO, MADROX ISN'T HERE.
OH...THIS IS MADROX. LOUSY CONNECTION, SORRY.
ON SECOND THOUGHT, I'M NOT SORRY. GET YOUR BUTT BACK HERE.
WE'VE HAD A FLOOD, I PUNCHED OUT RICTOR THE PEEPING TOM, THE LIGHTS WENT OUT...
WAIT...THE LIGHTS ARE BACK. WELL, MOST OF THEM...
OH. ICK.
THERE ALSO APPEARS TO BE--
WHAT DO YOU MEAN, "SHUT UP AND LISTEN"?
I CAME HERE TO HELP BECAUSE I MISSED NEW YORK, MADROX. NOT TO BE BOSSED AROUND BY--

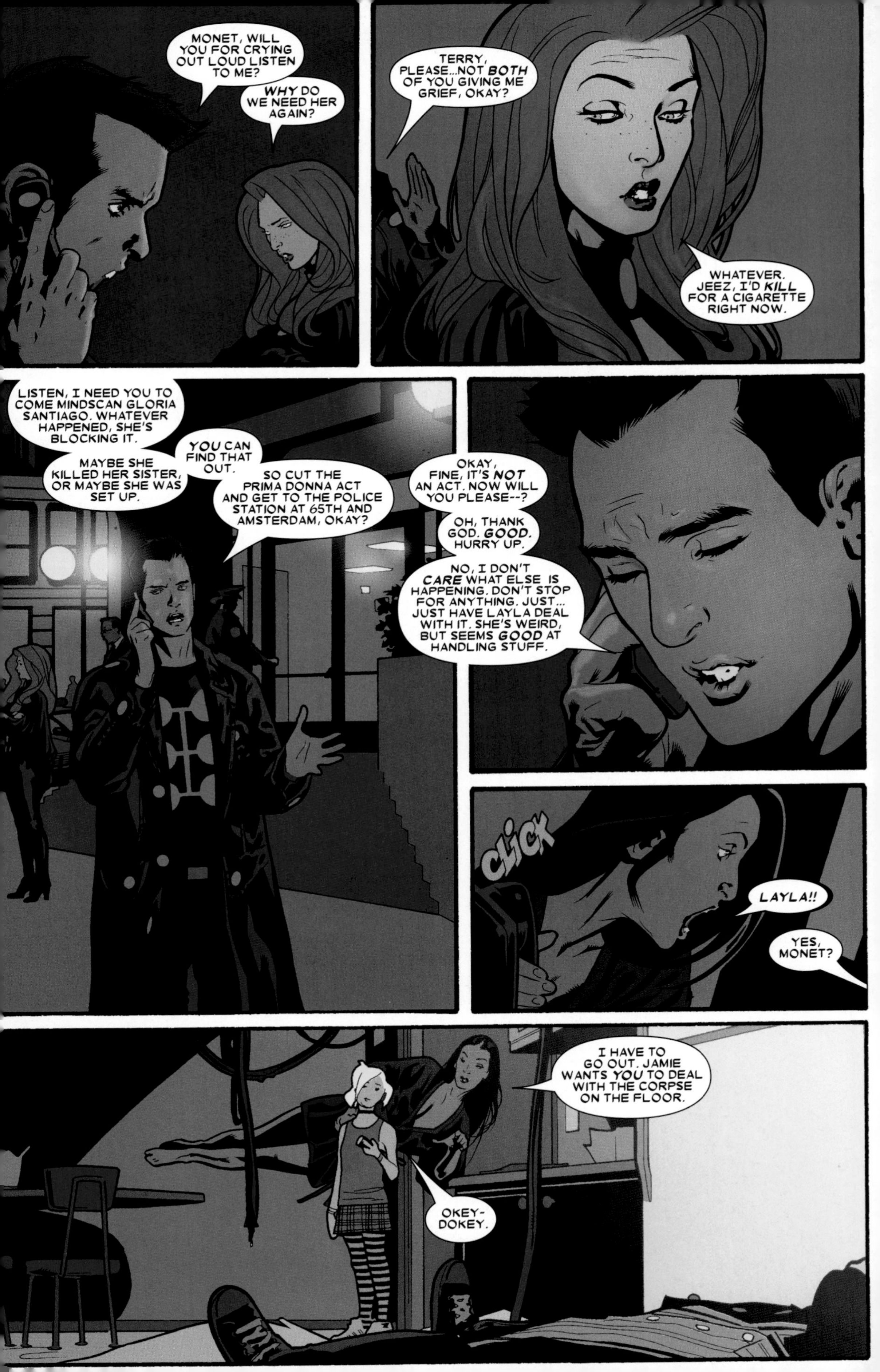
MONET, WILL YOU FOR CRYING OUT LOUD LISTEN TO ME?
WHY DO WE NEED HER AGAIN?
TERRY, PLEASE...NOT BOTH OF YOU GIVING ME GRIEF, OKAY?
WHATEVER. JEEZ, I'D KILL FOR A CIGARETTE RIGHT NOW.
LISTEN, I NEED YOU TO COME MINDSCAN GLORIA SANTIAGO. WHATEVER HAPPENED, SHE'S BLOCKING IT.
MAYBE SHE KILLED HER SISTER, OR MAYBE SHE WAS SET UP.
YOU CAN FIND THAT OUT.
SO CUT THE PRIMA DONNA ACT AND GET TO THE POLICE STATION AT 65TH AND AMSTERDAM, OKAY?
OKAY, FINE, IT'S NOT AN ACT. NOW WILL YOU PLEASE--?
OH, THANK GOD. GOOD. HURRY UP.
NO, I DON'T CARE WHAT ELSE IS HAPPENING. DON'T STOP FOR ANYTHING. JUST... JUST HAVE LAYLA DEAL WITH IT. SHE'S WEIRD, BUT SEEMS GOOD AT HANDLING STUFF.
CLICK
LAYLA!!
YES, MONET?
I HAVE TO GO OUT. JAMIE WANTS YOU TO DEAL WITH THE CORPSE ON THE FLOOR.
OKEY-DOKEY.

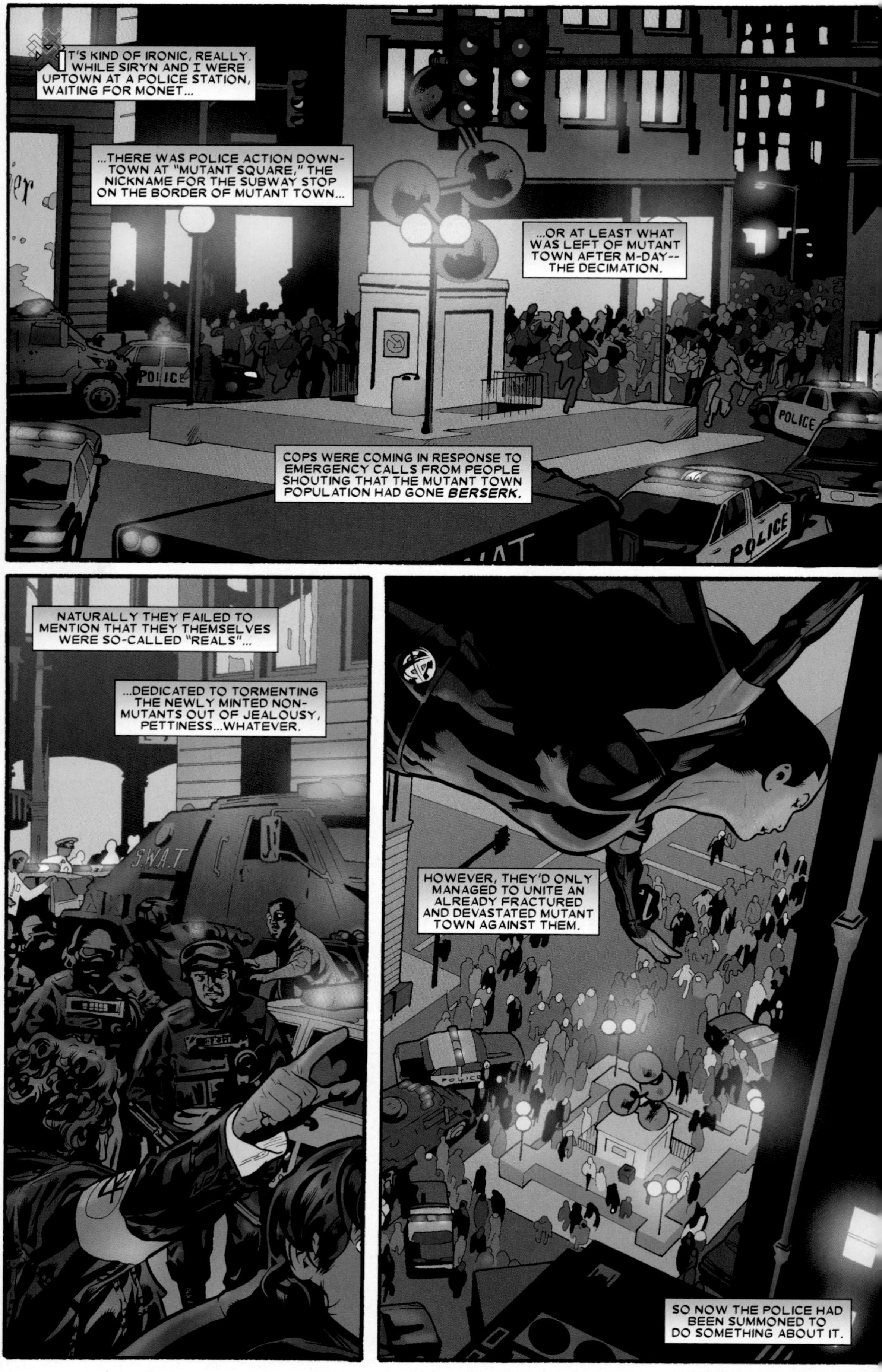
IT'S KIND OF IRONIC, REALLY. WHILE SIRYN AND I WERE UPTOWN AT A POLICE STATION, WAITING FOR MONET...
...THERE WAS POLICE ACTION DOWNTOWN AT "MUTANT SQUARE," THE NICKNAME FOR THE SUBWAY STOP ON THE BORDER OF MUTANT TOWN...
...OR AT LEAST WHAT WAS LEFT OF MUTANT TOWN AFTER M-DAY-- THE DECIMATION.
POLICE
POLICE
COPS WERE COMING IN RESPONSE TO EMERGENCY CALLS FROM PEOPLE SHOUTING THAT THE MUTANT TOWN POPULATION HAD GONE ***BERSERK.***
POLICE
NATURALLY THEY FAILED TO MENTION THAT THEY THEMSELVES WERE SO-CALLED "REALS"...
...DEDICATED TO TORMENTING THE NEWLY MINTED NON-MUTANTS OUT OF JEALOUSY, PETTINESS...WHATEVER.
S.W.A.T.
HOWEVER, THEY'D ONLY MANAGED TO UNITE AN ALREADY FRACTURED AND DEVASTATED MUTANT TOWN AGAINST THEM.
SO NOW THE POLICE HAD BEEN SUMMONED TO DO SOMETHING ABOUT IT.

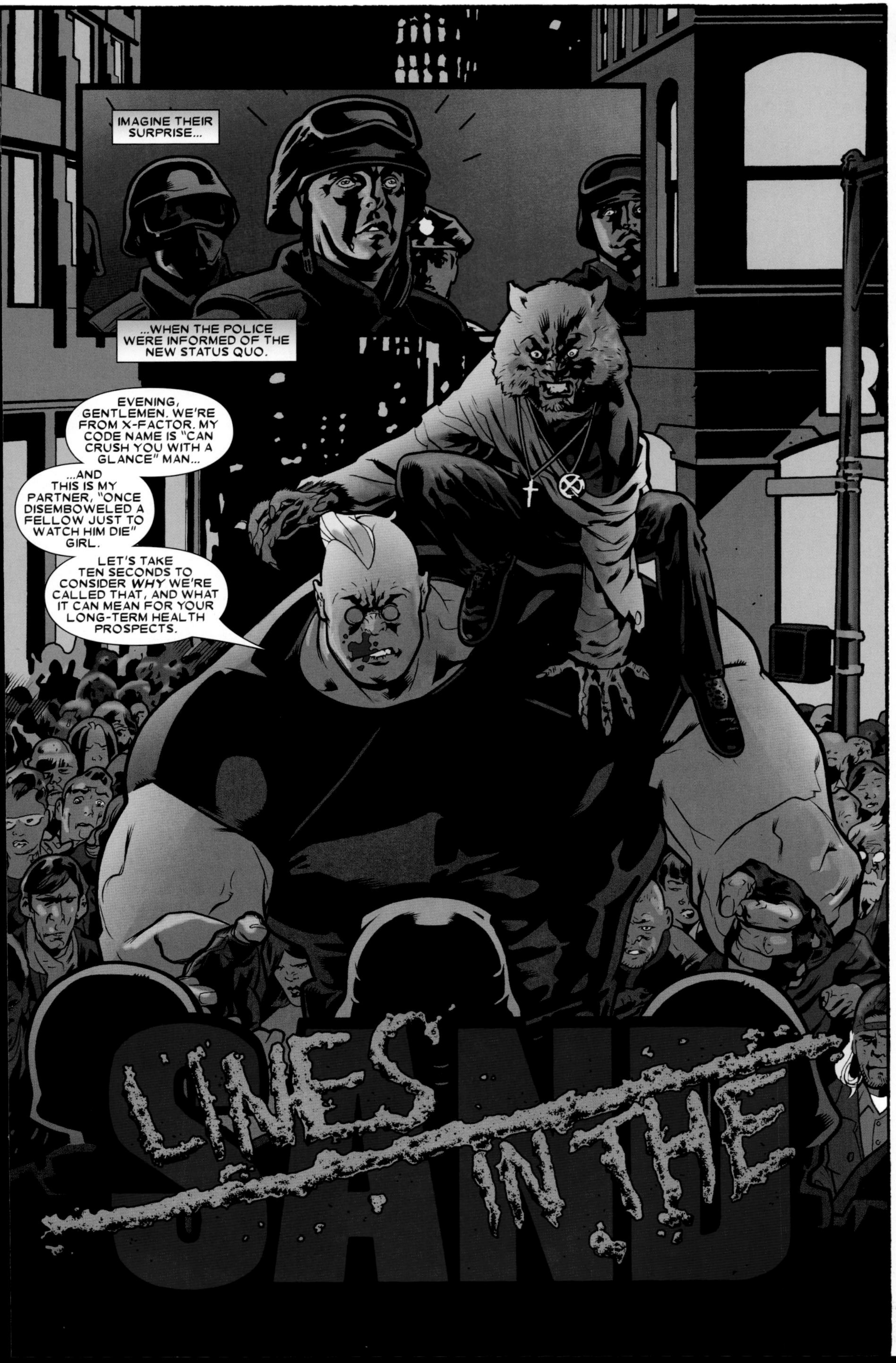
IMAGINE THEIR SURPRISE...
...WHEN THE POLICE WERE INFORMED OF THE NEW STATUS QUO.
EVENING, GENTLEMEN. WE'RE FROM X-FACTOR. MY CODE NAME IS "CAN CRUSH YOU WITH A GLANCE" MAN...
...AND THIS IS MY PARTNER, "ONCE DISEMBOWELED A FELLOW JUST TO WATCH HIM DIE" GIRL.
LET'S TAKE TEN SECONDS TO CONSIDER *WHY* WE'RE CALLED THAT, AND WHAT IT CAN MEAN FOR YOUR LONG-TERM HEALTH PROSPECTS.
LINES IN THE SAND

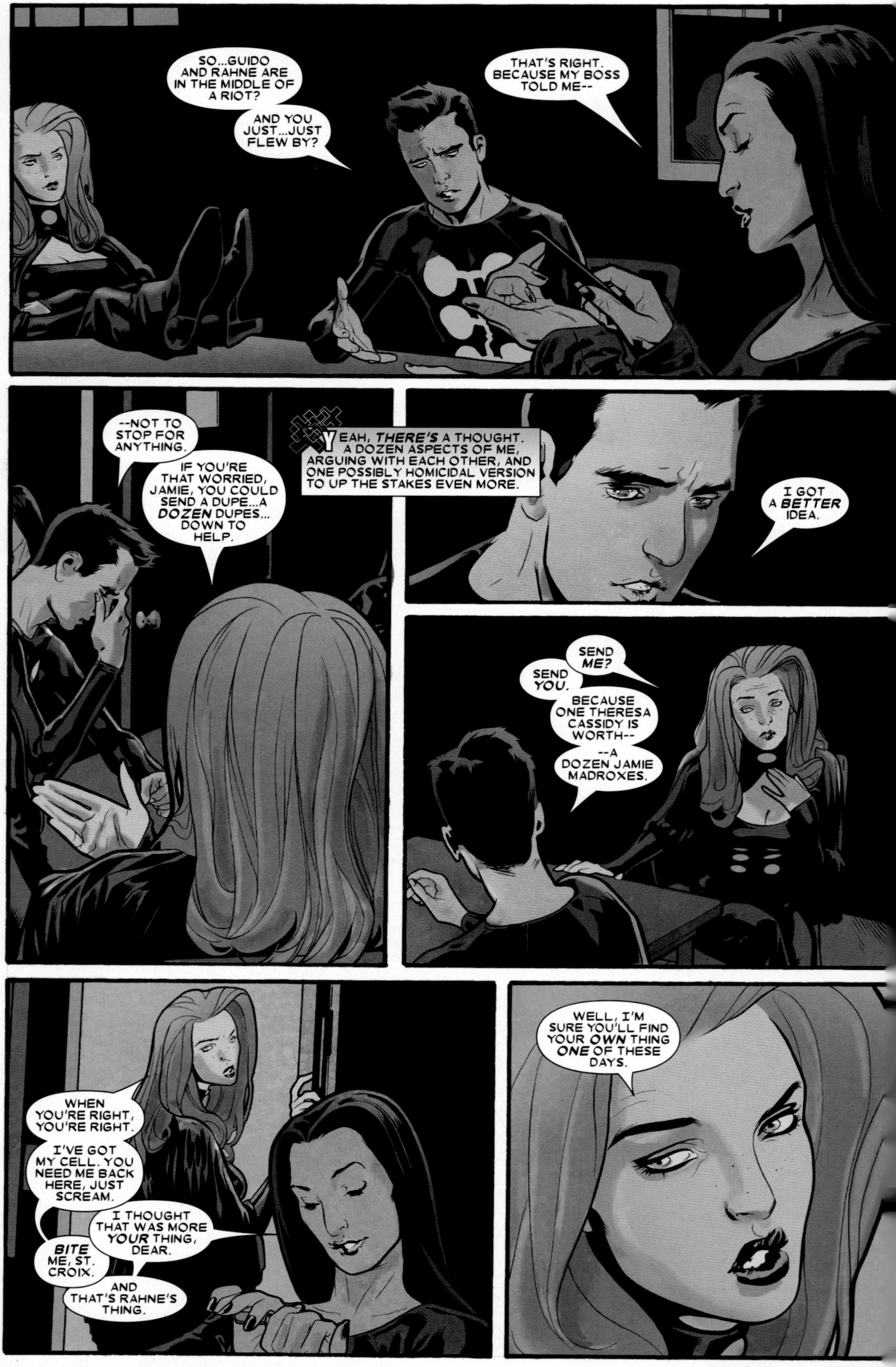
SO...GUIDO AND RAHNE ARE IN THE MIDDLE OF A RIOT?
AND YOU JUST...JUST FLEW BY?
THAT'S RIGHT. BECAUSE MY BOSS TOLD ME--
--NOT TO STOP FOR ANYTHING.
IF YOU'RE THAT WORRIED, JAMIE, YOU COULD SEND A DUPE...A DOZEN DUPES... DOWN TO HELP.
YEAH, THERE'S A THOUGHT. A DOZEN ASPECTS OF ME, ARGUING WITH EACH OTHER, AND ONE POSSIBLY HOMICIDAL VERSION TO UP THE STAKES EVEN MORE.
I GOT A BETTER IDEA.
SEND ME?
SEND YOU.
BECAUSE ONE THERESA CASSIDY IS WORTH--
--A DOZEN JAMIE MADROXES.
WHEN YOU'RE RIGHT, YOU'RE RIGHT.
I'VE GOT MY CELL. YOU NEED ME BACK HERE, JUST SCREAM.
I THOUGHT THAT WAS MORE YOUR THING, DEAR.
BITE ME, ST. CROIX.
AND THAT'S RAHNE'S THING.
WELL, I'M SURE YOU'LL FIND YOUR OWN THING ONE OF THESE DAYS.

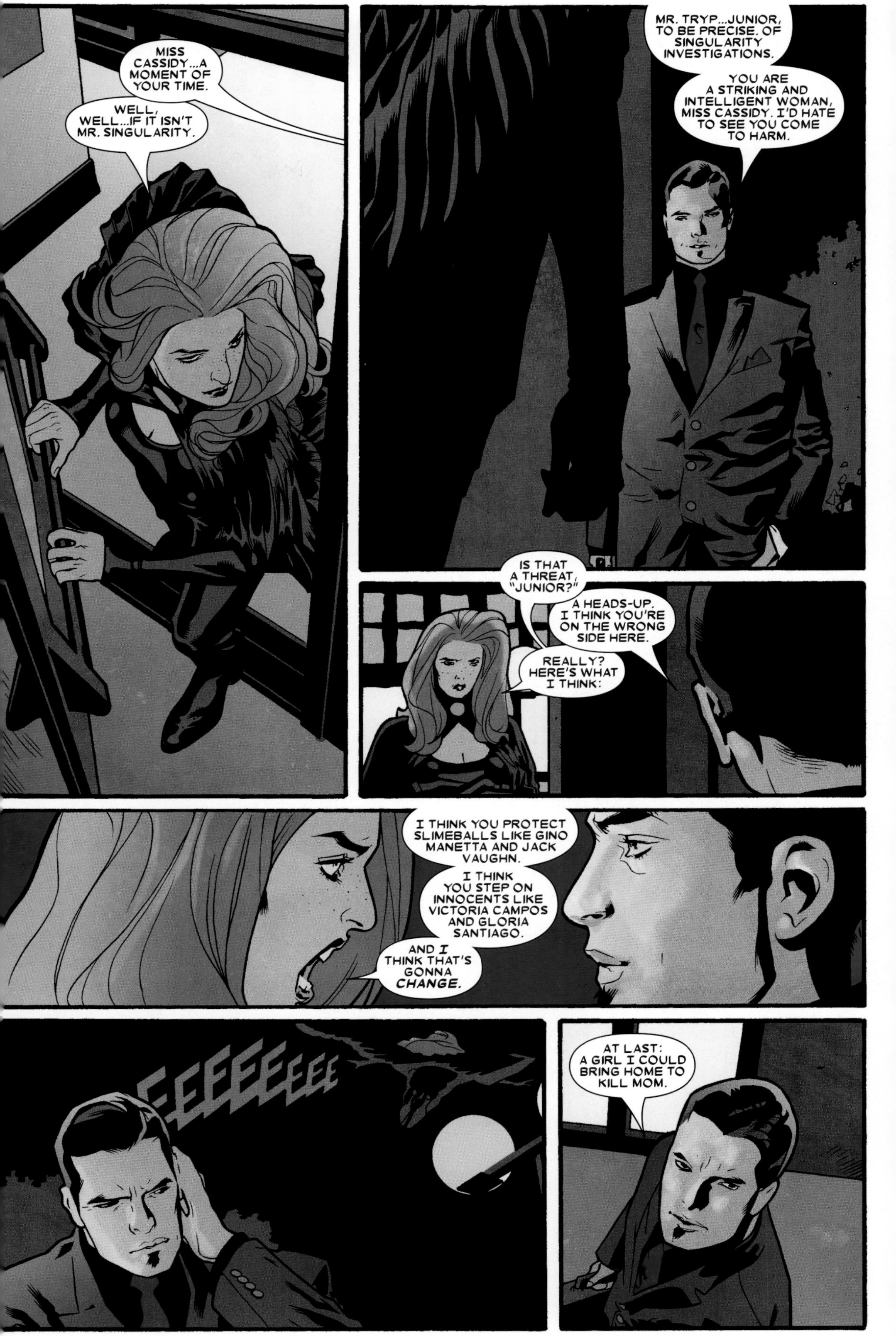
MISS CASSIDY...A MOMENT OF YOUR TIME.
WELL, WELL...IF IT ISN'T MR. SINGULARITY.
MR. TRYP...JUNIOR, TO BE PRECISE. OF SINGULARITY INVESTIGATIONS.
YOU ARE A STRIKING AND INTELLIGENT WOMAN, MISS CASSIDY. I'D HATE TO SEE YOU COME TO HARM.
IS THAT A THREAT, "JUNIOR?"
A HEADS-UP. I THINK YOU'RE ON THE WRONG SIDE HERE.
REALLY? HERE'S WHAT I THINK:
I THINK YOU PROTECT SLIMEBALLS LIKE GINO MANETTA AND JACK VAUGHN.
I THINK YOU STEP ON INNOCENTS LIKE VICTORIA CAMPOS AND GLORIA SANTIAGO.
AND *I* THINK THAT'S GONNA *CHANGE.*
EEEEEEeee
AT LAST: A GIRL I COULD BRING HOME TO KILL MOM.

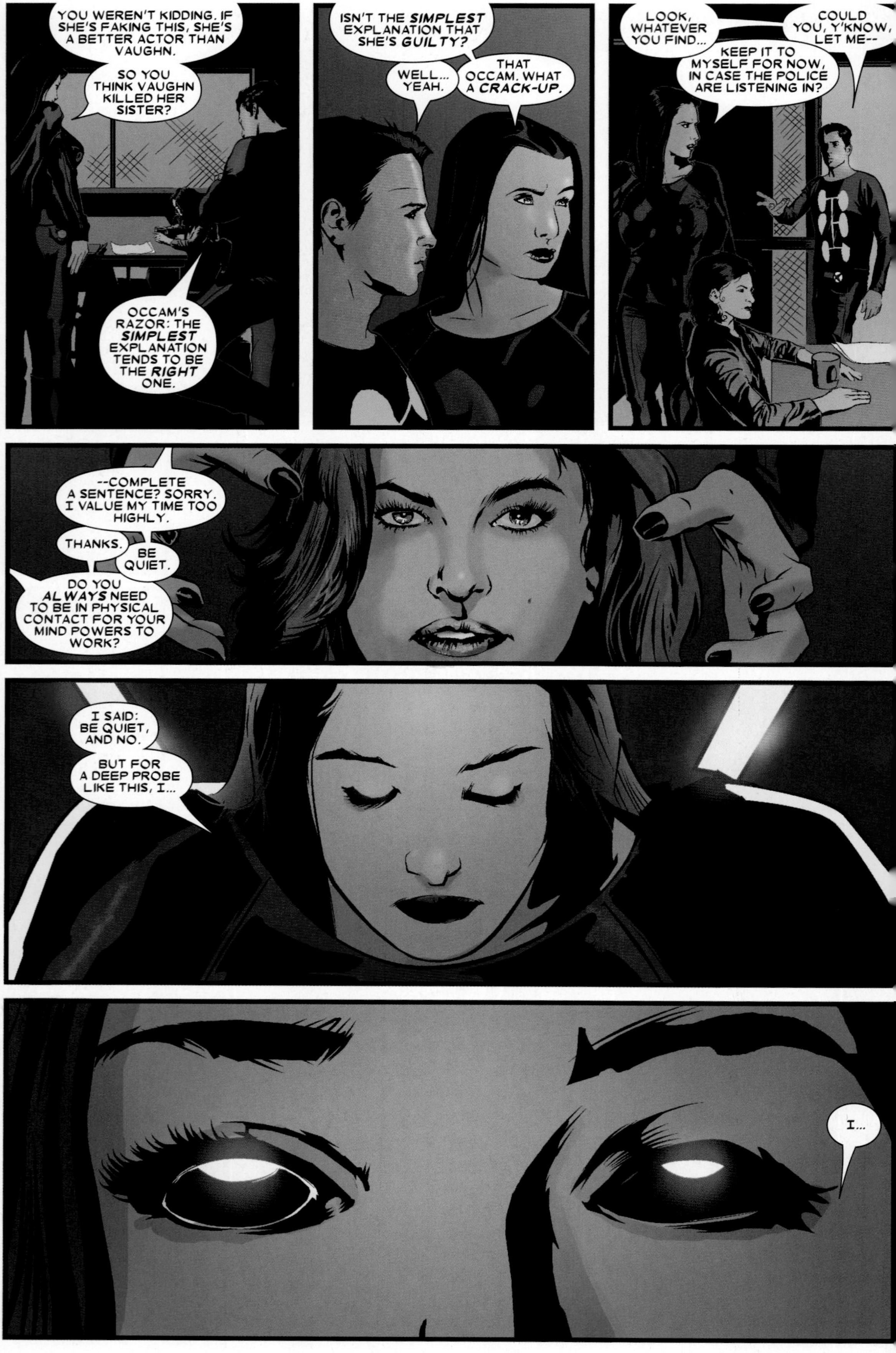
YOU WEREN'T KIDDING. IF SHE'S FAKING THIS, SHE'S A BETTER ACTOR THAN VAUGHN.
SO YOU THINK VAUGHN KILLED HER SISTER?
OCCAM'S RAZOR: THE SIMPLEST EXPLANATION TENDS TO BE THE RIGHT ONE.
ISN'T THE SIMPLEST EXPLANATION THAT SHE'S GUILTY?
WELL... YEAH.
THAT OCCAM. WHAT A CRACK-UP.
LOOK, WHATEVER YOU FIND...
COULD YOU, Y'KNOW, LET ME--
KEEP IT TO MYSELF FOR NOW, IN CASE THE POLICE ARE LISTENING IN?
--COMPLETE A SENTENCE? SORRY. I VALUE MY TIME TOO HIGHLY.
THANKS.
BE QUIET.
DO YOU ALWAYS NEED TO BE IN PHYSICAL CONTACT FOR YOUR MIND POWERS TO WORK?
I SAID: BE QUIET, AND NO.
BUT FOR A DEEP PROBE LIKE THIS, I...
I...

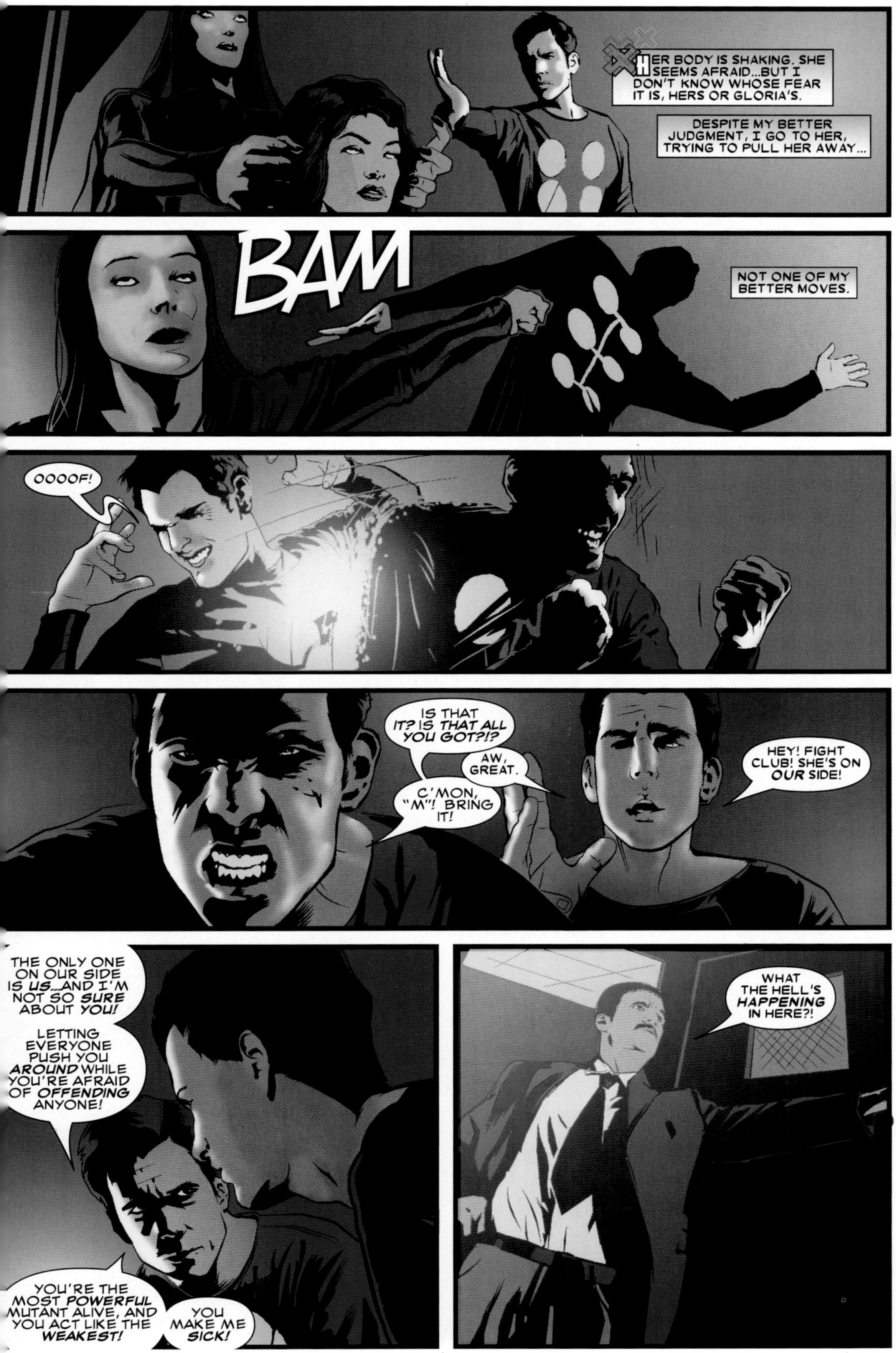
HER BODY IS SHAKING. SHE SEEMS AFRAID...BUT I DON'T KNOW WHOSE FEAR IT IS, HERS OR GLORIA'S.
DESPITE MY BETTER JUDGMENT, I GO TO HER, TRYING TO PULL HER AWAY...
BAM
NOT ONE OF MY BETTER MOVES.
OOOOF!
IS THAT IT? IS THAT ALL YOU GOT?!?
AW, GREAT.
C'MON, "M"! BRING IT!
HEY! FIGHT CLUB! SHE'S ON OUR SIDE!
THE ONLY ONE ON OUR SIDE IS US...AND I'M NOT SO SURE ABOUT YOU!
LETTING EVERYONE PUSH YOU AROUND WHILE YOU'RE AFRAID OF OFFENDING ANYONE!
YOU'RE THE MOST POWERFUL MUTANT ALIVE, AND YOU ACT LIKE THE WEAKEST!
YOU MAKE ME SICK!
WHAT THE HELL'S HAPPENING IN HERE?!

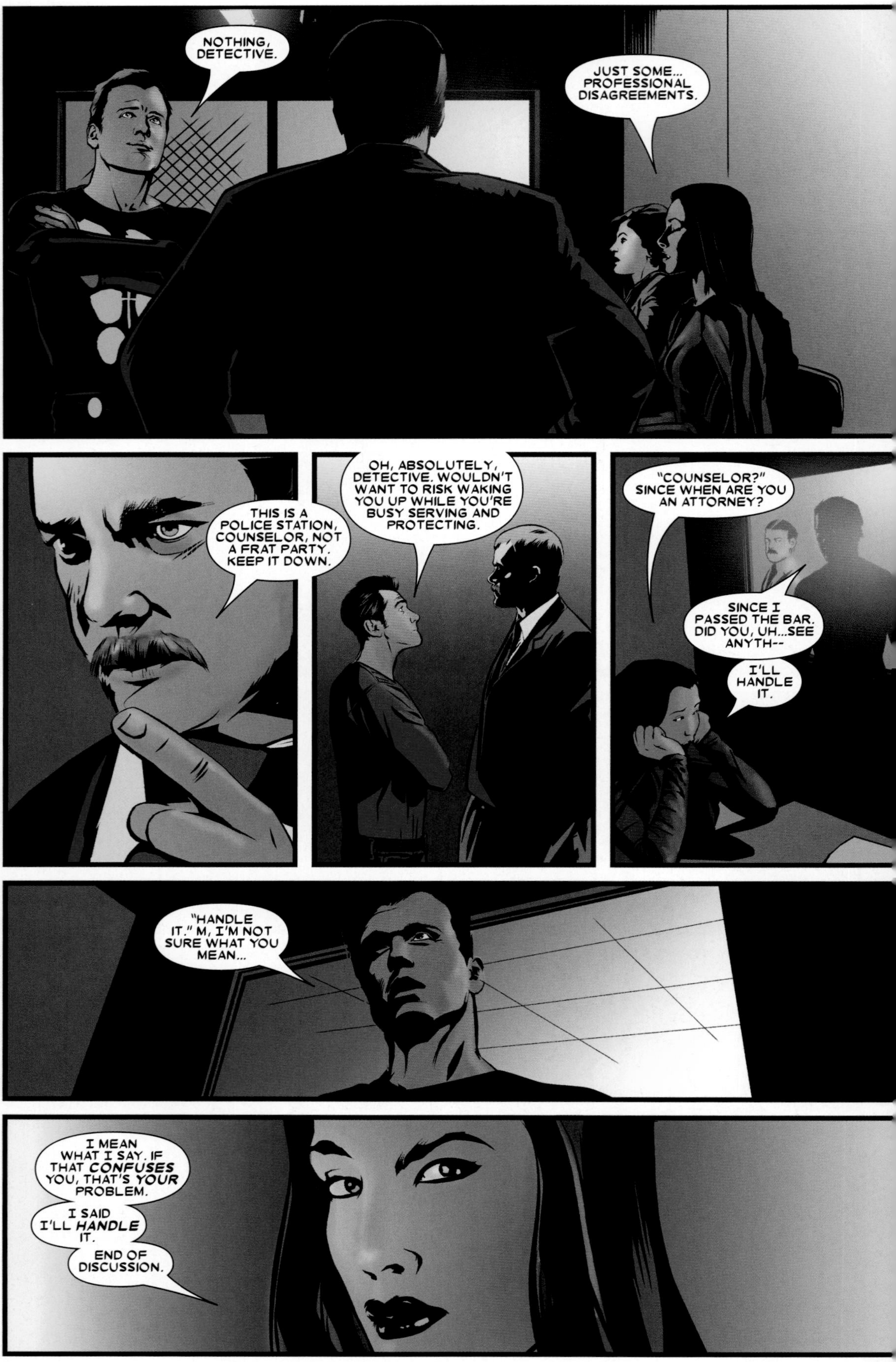
NOTHING, DETECTIVE.
JUST SOME... PROFESSIONAL DISAGREEMENTS.
THIS IS A POLICE STATION, COUNSELOR, NOT A FRAT PARTY. KEEP IT DOWN.
OH, ABSOLUTELY, DETECTIVE. WOULDN'T WANT TO RISK WAKING YOU UP WHILE YOU'RE BUSY SERVING AND PROTECTING.
"COUNSELOR?" SINCE WHEN ARE YOU AN ATTORNEY?
SINCE I PASSED THE BAR. DID YOU, UH...SEE ANYTH--
I'LL HANDLE IT.
"HANDLE IT." M, I'M NOT SURE WHAT YOU MEAN...
I MEAN WHAT I SAY. IF THAT *CONFUSES* YOU, THAT'S *YOUR* PROBLEM.
I SAID I'LL *HANDLE* IT.
END OF DISCUSSION.

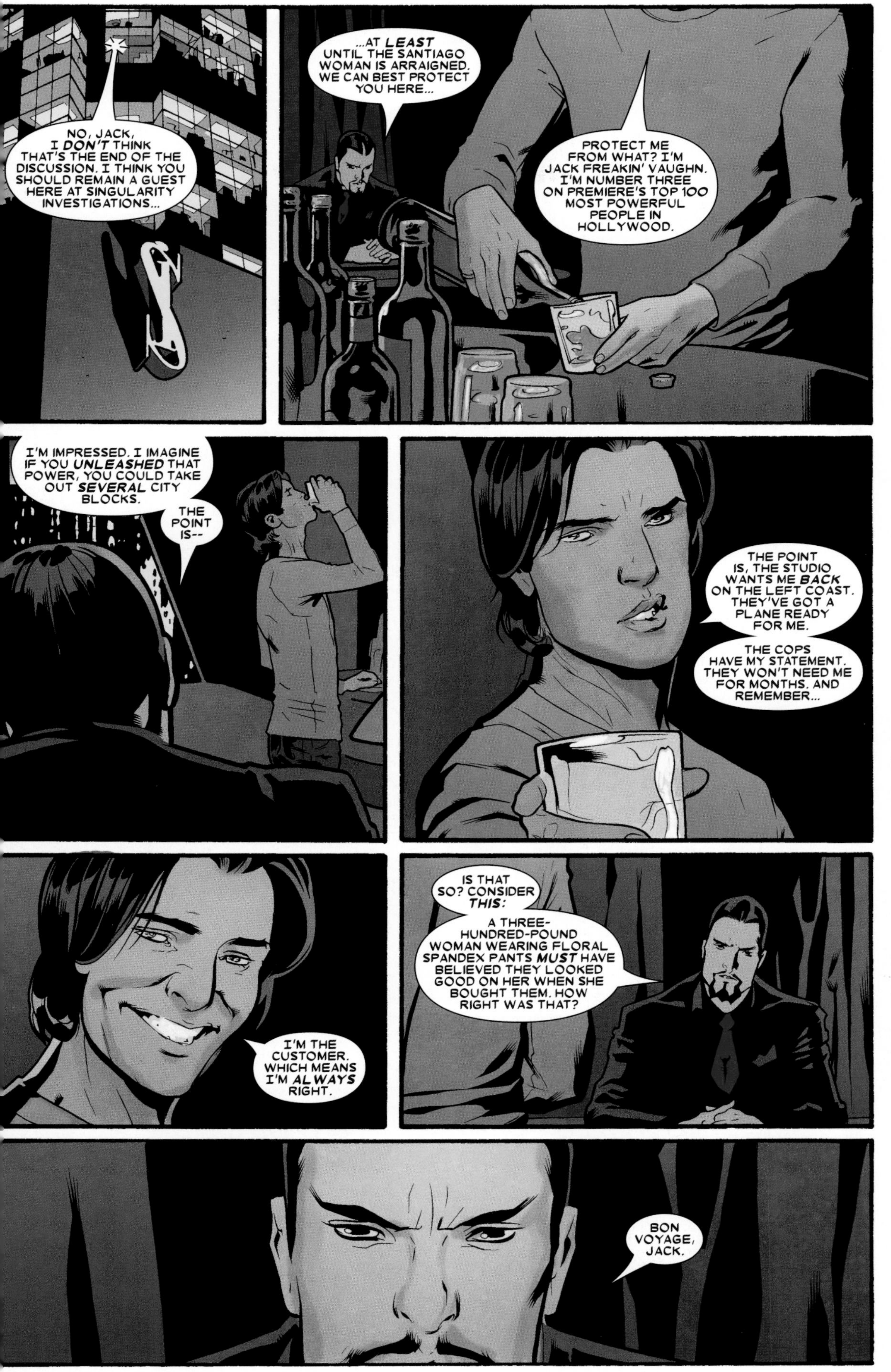

NO, JACK, I DON'T THINK THAT'S THE END OF THE DISCUSSION. I THINK YOU SHOULD REMAIN A GUEST HERE AT SINGULARITY INVESTIGATIONS...
...AT LEAST UNTIL THE SANTIAGO WOMAN IS ARRAIGNED. WE CAN BEST PROTECT YOU HERE...
PROTECT ME FROM WHAT? I'M JACK FREAKIN' VAUGHN. I'M NUMBER THREE ON PREMIERE'S TOP 100 MOST POWERFUL PEOPLE IN HOLLYWOOD.
I'M IMPRESSED. I IMAGINE IF YOU UNLEASHED THAT POWER, YOU COULD TAKE OUT SEVERAL CITY BLOCKS.
THE POINT IS--
THE POINT IS, THE STUDIO WANTS ME BACK ON THE LEFT COAST. THEY'VE GOT A PLANE READY FOR ME.
THE COPS HAVE MY STATEMENT. THEY WON'T NEED ME FOR MONTHS. AND REMEMBER...
I'M THE CUSTOMER. WHICH MEANS I'M ALWAYS RIGHT.
IS THAT SO? CONSIDER THIS:
A THREE-HUNDRED-POUND WOMAN WEARING FLORAL SPANDEX PANTS MUST HAVE BELIEVED THEY LOOKED GOOD ON HER WHEN SHE BOUGHT THEM. HOW RIGHT WAS THAT?
BON VOYAGE, JACK.

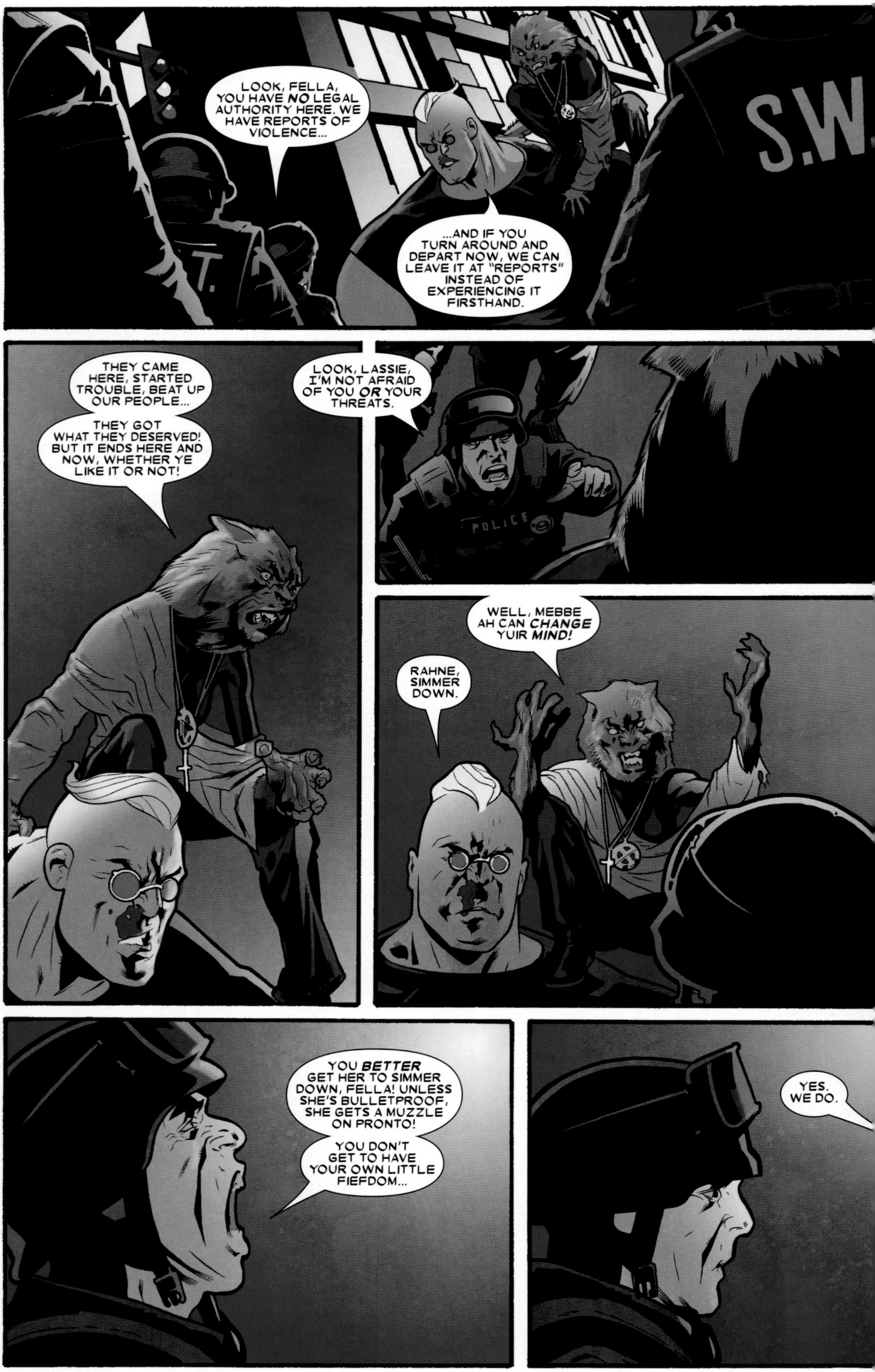

LOOK, FELLA, YOU HAVE NO LEGAL AUTHORITY HERE. WE HAVE REPORTS OF VIOLENCE...
...AND IF YOU TURN AROUND AND DEPART NOW, WE CAN LEAVE IT AT "REPORTS" INSTEAD OF EXPERIENCING IT FIRSTHAND.
S.W.
THEY CAME HERE, STARTED TROUBLE, BEAT UP OUR PEOPLE...
THEY GOT WHAT THEY DESERVED! BUT IT ENDS HERE AND NOW, WHETHER YE LIKE IT OR NOT!
LOOK, LASSIE, I'M NOT AFRAID OF YOU OR YOUR THREATS.
POLICE
WELL, MEBBE AH CAN CHANGE YUIR MIND!
RAHNE, SIMMER DOWN.
YOU BETTER GET HER TO SIMMER DOWN, FELLA! UNLESS SHE'S BULLETPROOF, SHE GETS A MUZZLE ON PRONTO!
YOU DON'T GET TO HAVE YOUR OWN LITTLE FIEFDOM...
YES. WE DO.

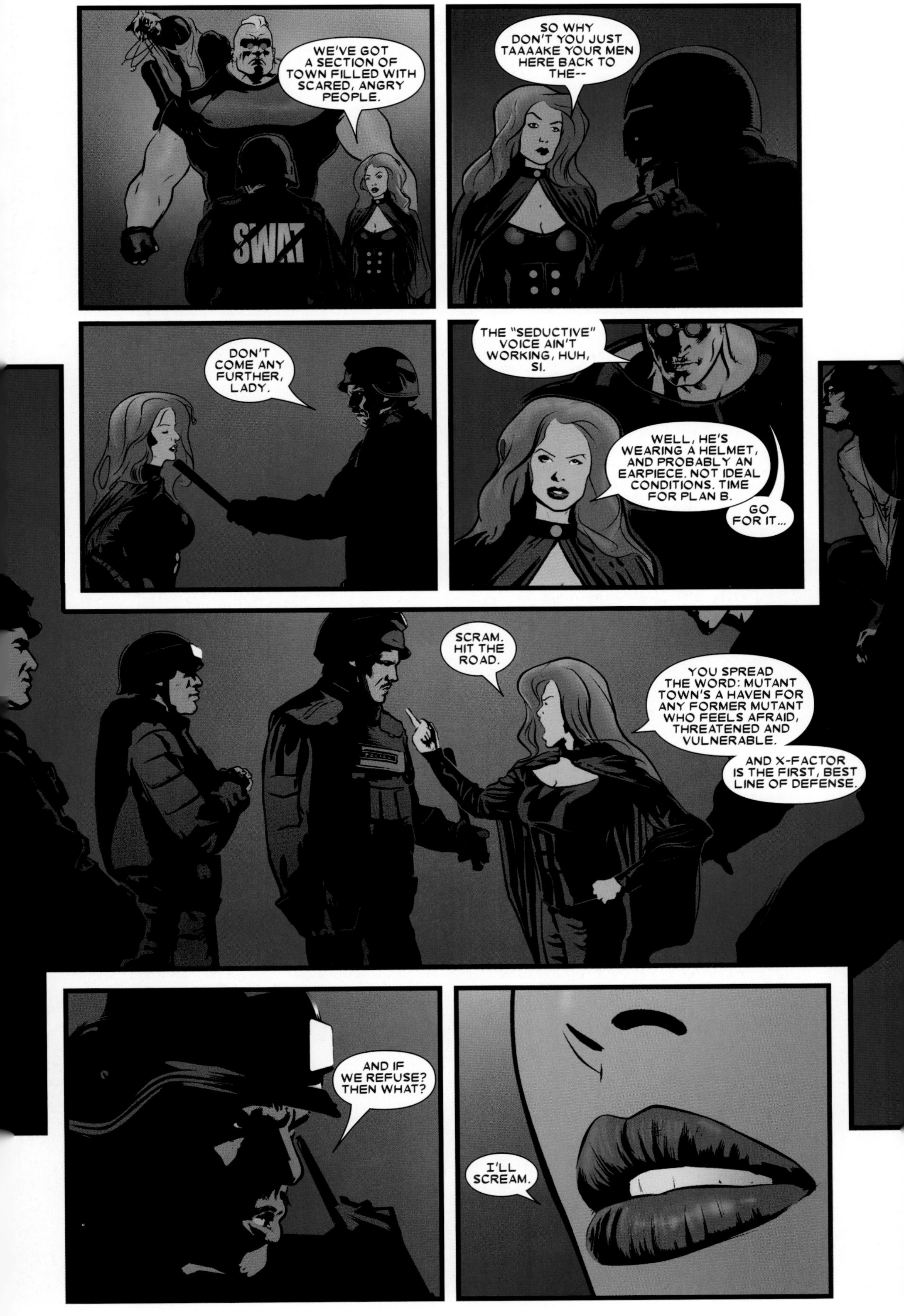
WE'VE GOT A SECTION OF TOWN FILLED WITH SCARED, ANGRY PEOPLE.
SO WHY DON'T YOU JUST TAAAAKE YOUR MEN HERE BACK TO THE--
SWAT
DON'T COME ANY FURTHER, LADY.
THE "SEDUCTIVE" VOICE AIN'T WORKING, HUH, SI.
WELL, HE'S WEARING A HELMET, AND PROBABLY AN EARPIECE. NOT IDEAL CONDITIONS. TIME FOR PLAN B.
GO FOR IT...
SCRAM. HIT THE ROAD.
YOU SPREAD THE WORD: MUTANT TOWN'S A HAVEN FOR ANY FORMER MUTANT WHO FEELS AFRAID, THREATENED AND VULNERABLE.
AND X-FACTOR IS THE FIRST, BEST LINE OF DEFENSE.
AND IF WE REFUSE? THEN WHAT?
I'LL SCREAM.

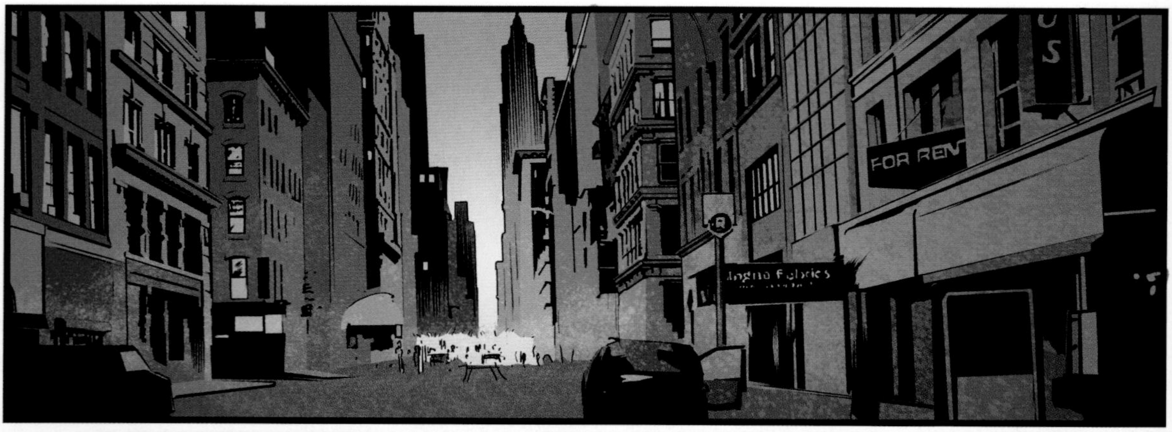
FOR RENT

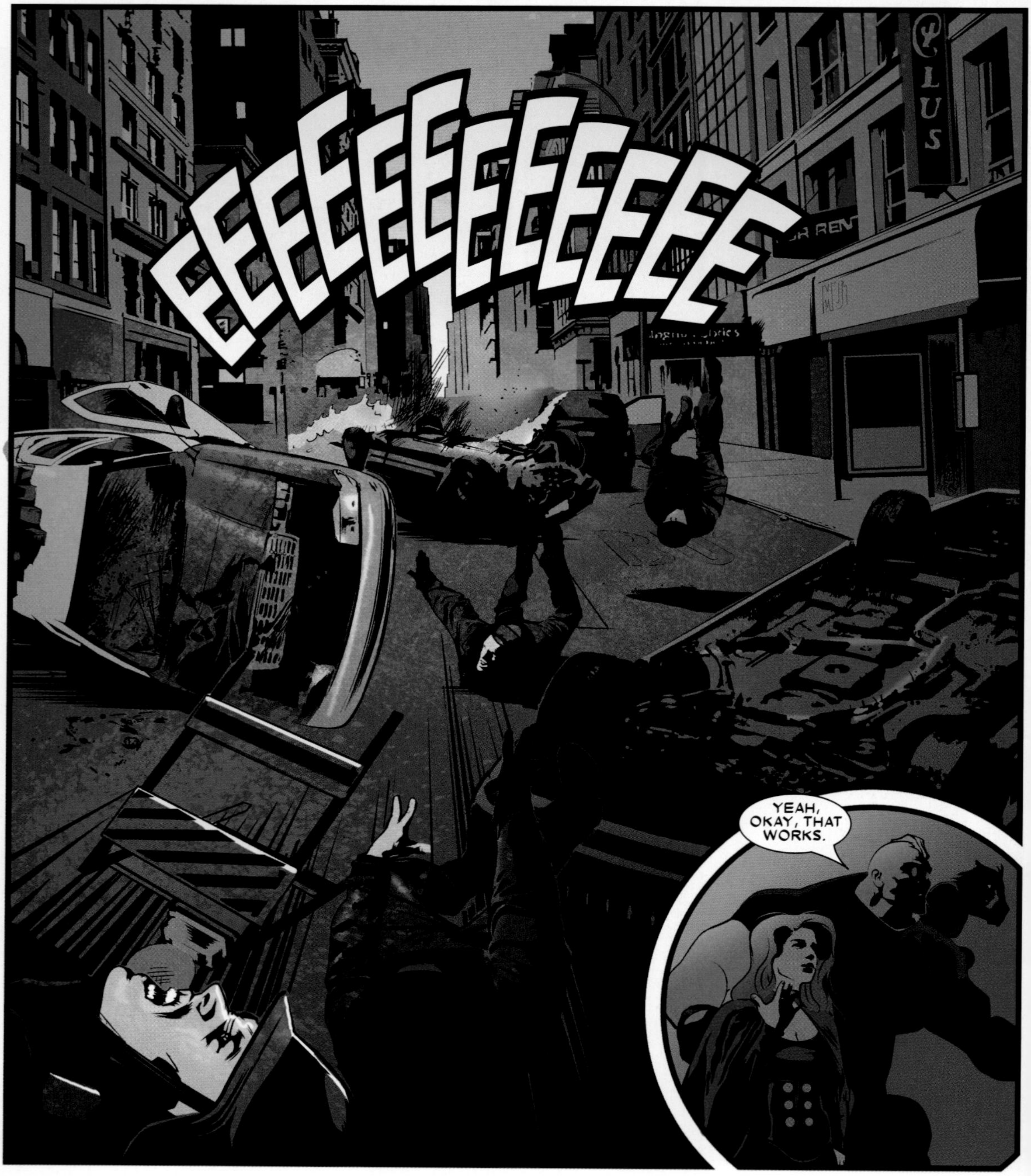
EEEEEEEEEEEE
YEAH, OKAY, THAT WORKS.

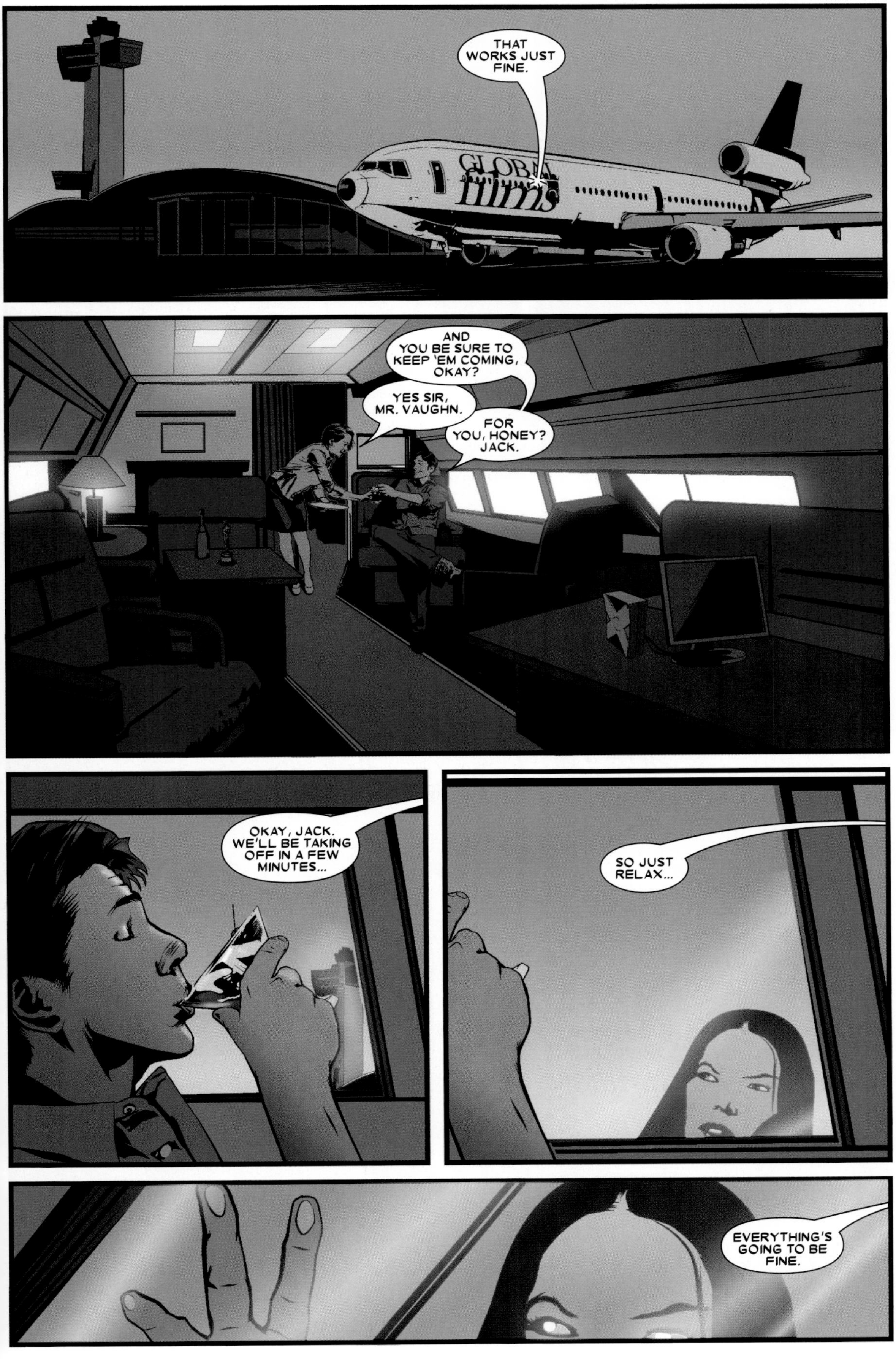
THAT WORKS JUST FINE.
GLOBAL FILMS
AND YOU BE SURE TO KEEP 'EM COMING, OKAY?
YES SIR, MR. VAUGHN.
FOR YOU, HONEY? JACK.
OKAY, JACK. WE'LL BE TAKING OFF IN A FEW MINUTES...
SO JUST RELAX...
EVERYTHING'S GOING TO BE FINE.

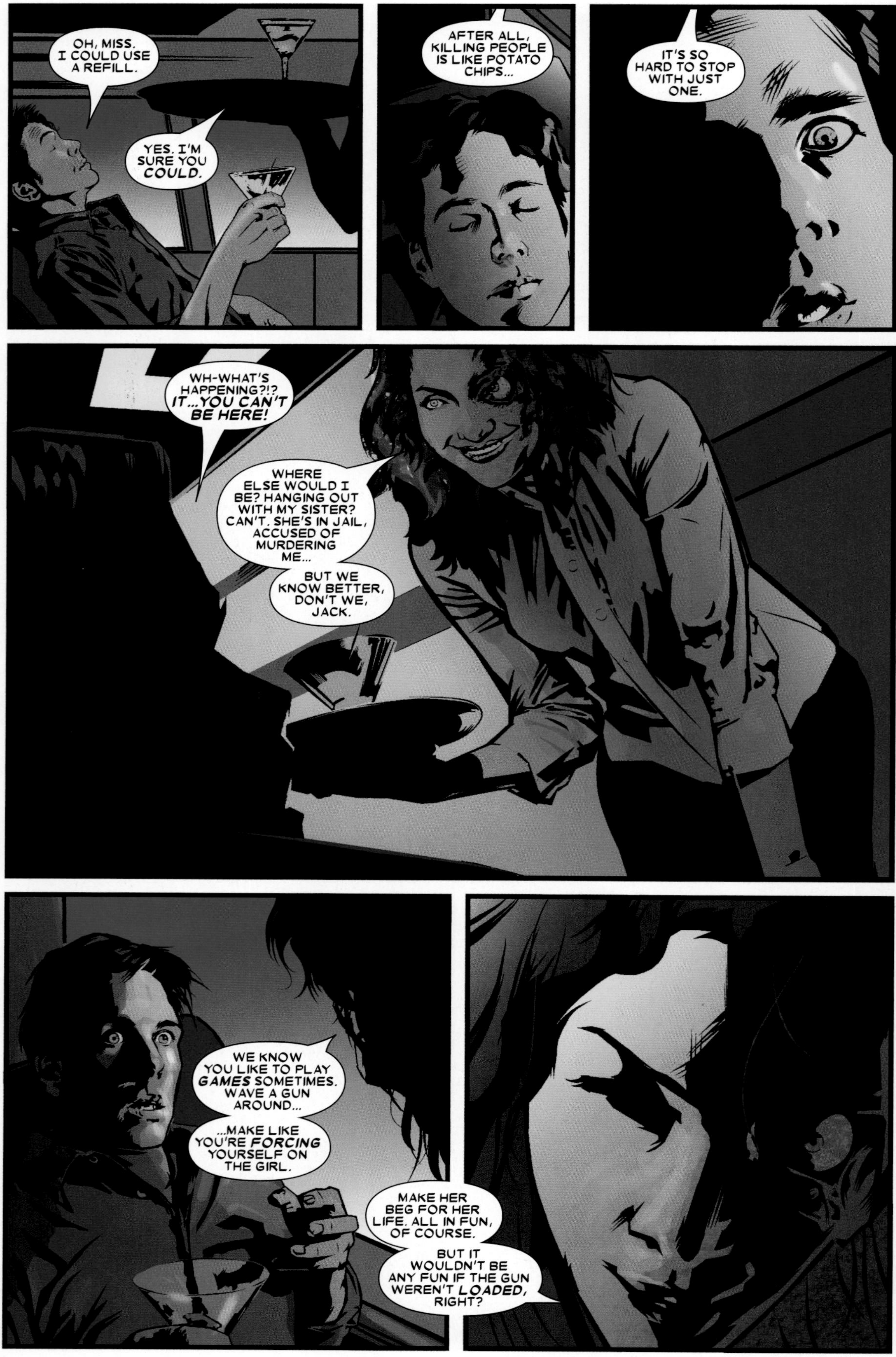
OH, MISS. I COULD USE A REFILL.
YES. I'M SURE YOU *COULD.*
AFTER ALL, KILLING PEOPLE IS LIKE POTATO CHIPS...
IT'S SO HARD TO STOP WITH JUST ONE.
WH-WHAT'S HAPPENING?!? *IT...YOU CAN'T BE HERE!*
WHERE ELSE WOULD I BE? HANGING OUT WITH MY SISTER? CAN'T. SHE'S IN JAIL, ACCUSED OF MURDERING ME...
BUT WE KNOW BETTER, DON'T WE, JACK.
WE KNOW YOU LIKE TO PLAY *GAMES* SOMETIMES. WAVE A GUN AROUND...
...MAKE LIKE YOU'RE *FORCING* YOURSELF ON THE GIRL.
MAKE HER BEG FOR HER LIFE. ALL IN FUN, OF COURSE.
BUT IT WOULDN'T BE ANY FUN IF THE GUN WEREN'T *LOADED,* RIGHT?

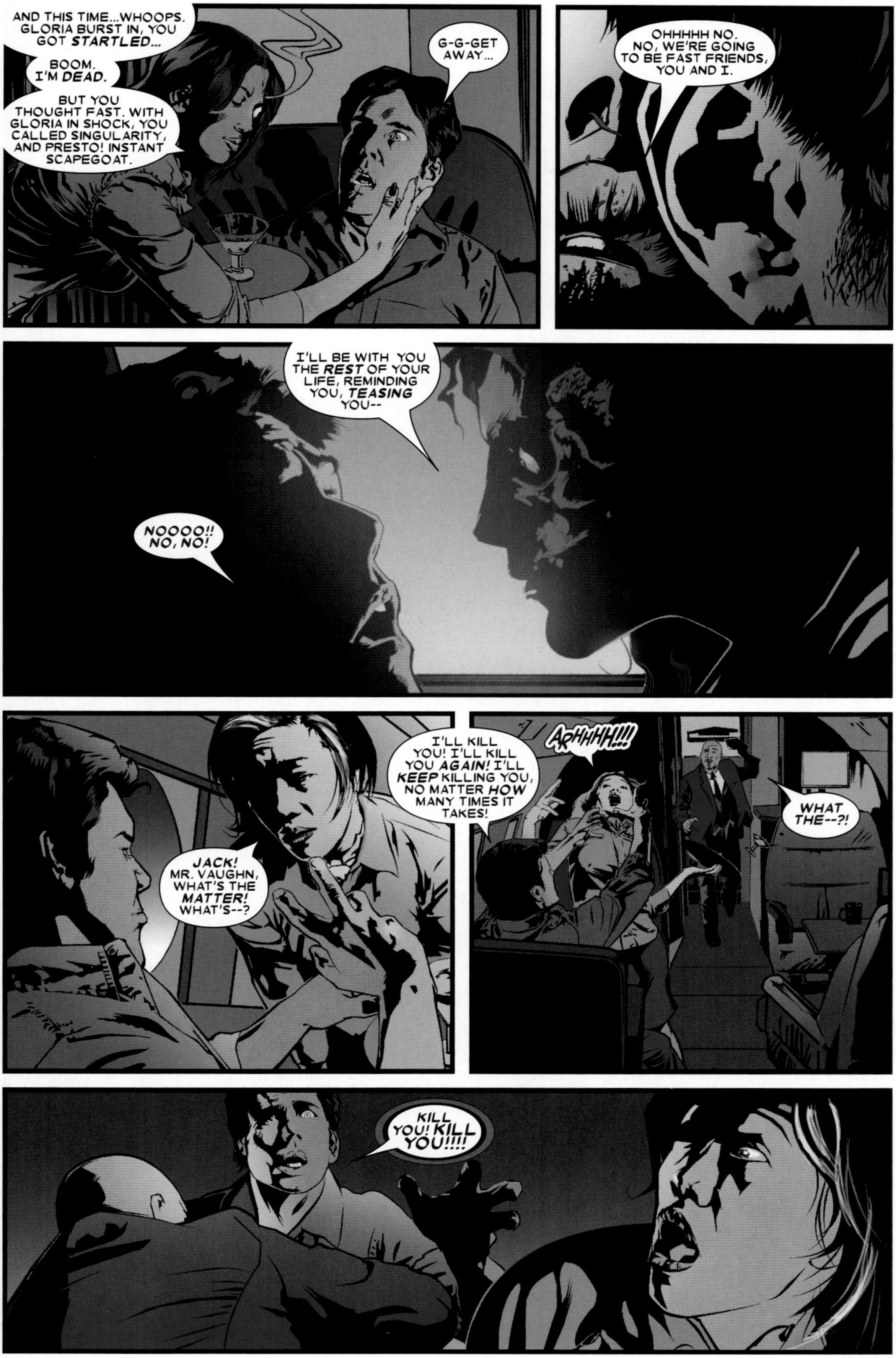
AND THIS TIME...WHOOPS. GLORIA BURST IN, YOU GOT STARTLED...
BOOM. I'M DEAD.
BUT YOU THOUGHT FAST. WITH GLORIA IN SHOCK, YOU CALLED SINGULARITY, AND PRESTO! INSTANT SCAPEGOAT.
G-G-GET AWAY...
OHHHHH NO. NO, WE'RE GOING TO BE FAST FRIENDS, YOU AND I.
I'LL BE WITH YOU THE REST OF YOUR LIFE, REMINDING YOU, TEASING YOU--
NOOOO!! NO, NO!
JACK! MR. VAUGHN, WHAT'S THE MATTER! WHAT'S--?
I'LL KILL YOU! I'LL KILL YOU AGAIN! I'LL KEEP KILLING YOU, NO MATTER HOW MANY TIMES IT TAKES!
ARHHHH!!!
WHAT THE--?!
KILL YOU! KILL YOU!!!!

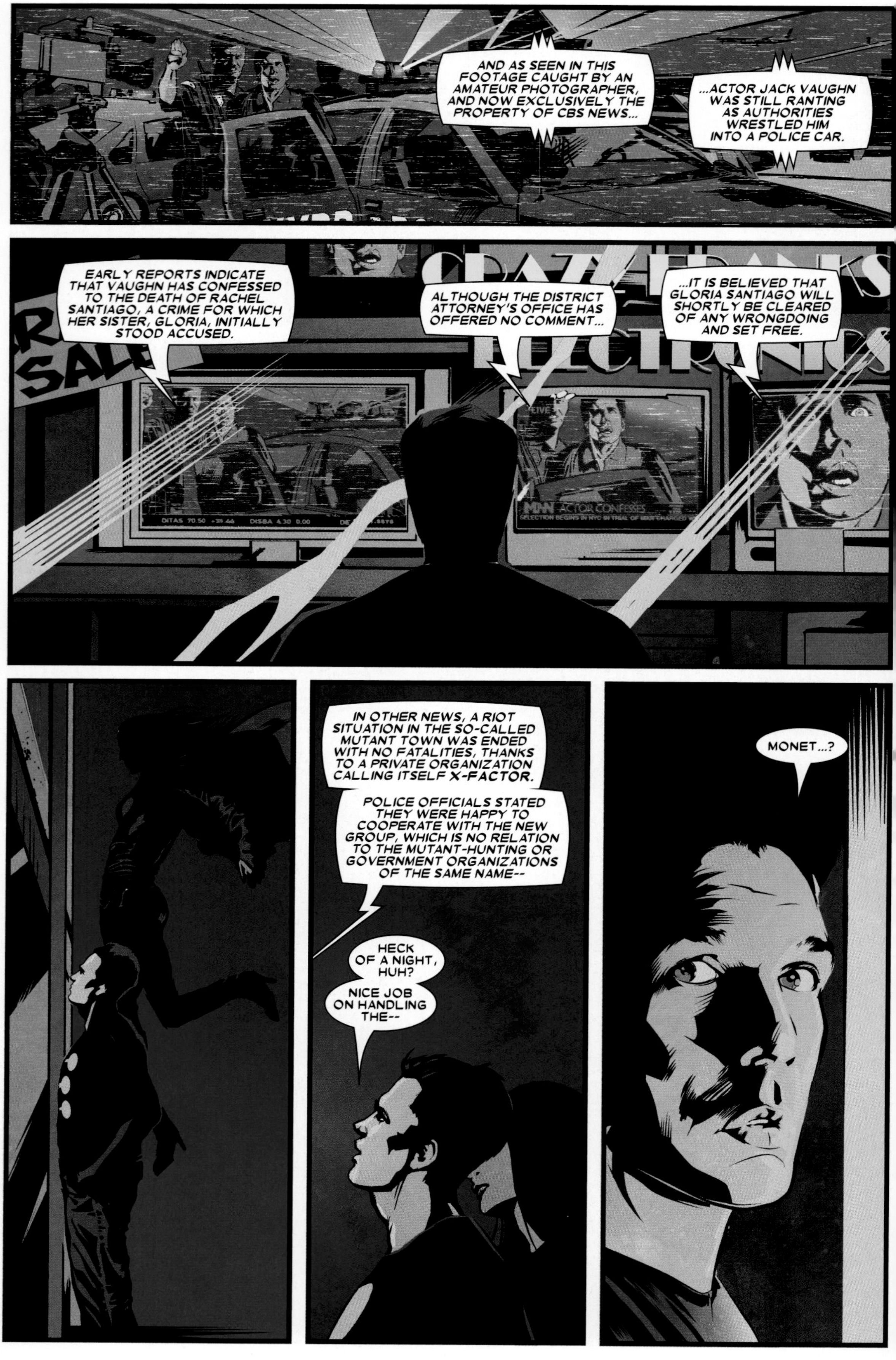
AND AS SEEN IN THIS FOOTAGE CAUGHT BY AN AMATEUR PHOTOGRAPHER, AND NOW EXCLUSIVELY THE PROPERTY OF CBS NEWS...
...ACTOR JACK VAUGHN WAS STILL RANTING AS AUTHORITIES WRESTLED HIM INTO A POLICE CAR.
EARLY REPORTS INDICATE THAT VAUGHN HAS CONFESSED TO THE DEATH OF RACHEL SANTIAGO, A CRIME FOR WHICH HER SISTER, GLORIA, INITIALLY STOOD ACCUSED.
ALTHOUGH THE DISTRICT ATTORNEY'S OFFICE HAS OFFERED NO COMMENT...
...IT IS BELIEVED THAT GLORIA SANTIAGO WILL SHORTLY BE CLEARED OF ANY WRONGDOING AND SET FREE.
SALE
ACTOR CONFESSES
IN OTHER NEWS, A RIOT SITUATION IN THE SO-CALLED MUTANT TOWN WAS ENDED WITH NO FATALITIES, THANKS TO A PRIVATE ORGANIZATION CALLING ITSELF X-FACTOR.
POLICE OFFICIALS STATED THEY WERE HAPPY TO COOPERATE WITH THE NEW GROUP, WHICH IS NO RELATION TO THE MUTANT-HUNTING OR GOVERNMENT ORGANIZATIONS OF THE SAME NAME--
HECK OF A NIGHT, HUH?
NICE JOB ON HANDLING THE--
MONET...?

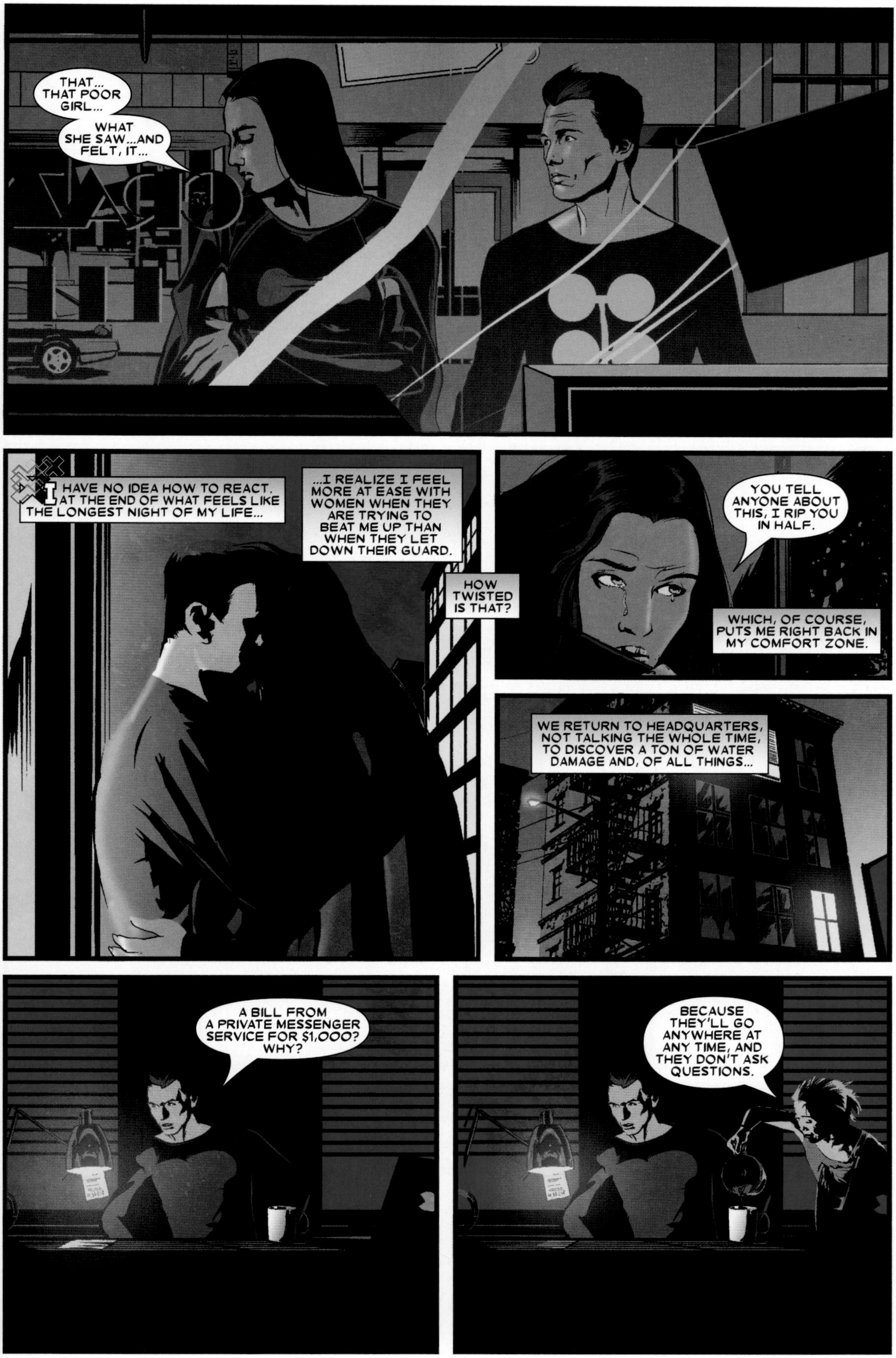
THAT... THAT POOR GIRL...
WHAT SHE SAW...AND FELT, IT...
I HAVE NO IDEA HOW TO REACT. AT THE END OF WHAT FEELS LIKE THE LONGEST NIGHT OF MY LIFE...
...I REALIZE I FEEL MORE AT EASE WITH WOMEN WHEN THEY ARE TRYING TO BEAT ME UP THAN WHEN THEY LET DOWN THEIR GUARD.
HOW TWISTED IS THAT?
YOU TELL ANYONE ABOUT THIS, I RIP YOU IN HALF.
WHICH, OF COURSE, PUTS ME RIGHT BACK IN MY COMFORT ZONE.
WE RETURN TO HEADQUARTERS, NOT TALKING THE WHOLE TIME, TO DISCOVER A TON OF WATER DAMAGE AND, OF ALL THINGS...
A BILL FROM A PRIVATE MESSENGER SERVICE FOR $1,000? WHY?
BECAUSE THEY'LL GO ANYWHERE AT ANY TIME, AND THEY DON'T ASK QUESTIONS.

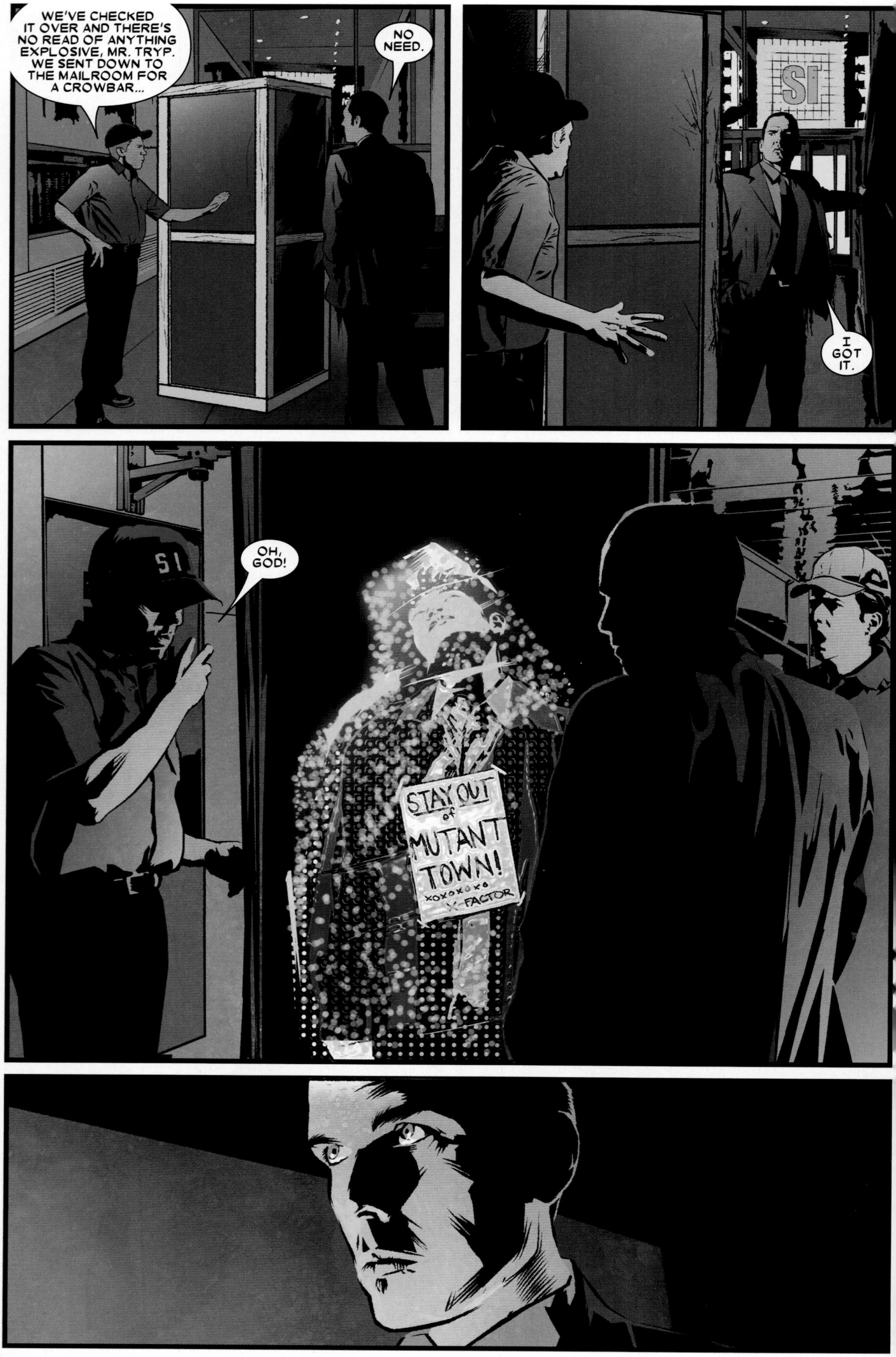
WE'VE CHECKED IT OVER AND THERE'S NO READ OF ANYTHING EXPLOSIVE, MR. TRYP. WE SENT DOWN TO THE MAILROOM FOR A CROWBAR...
NO NEED.
SI
I GOT IT.
SI
OH, GOD!
STAY OUT of MUTANT TOWN!
xoxoxoxo
X-FACTOR

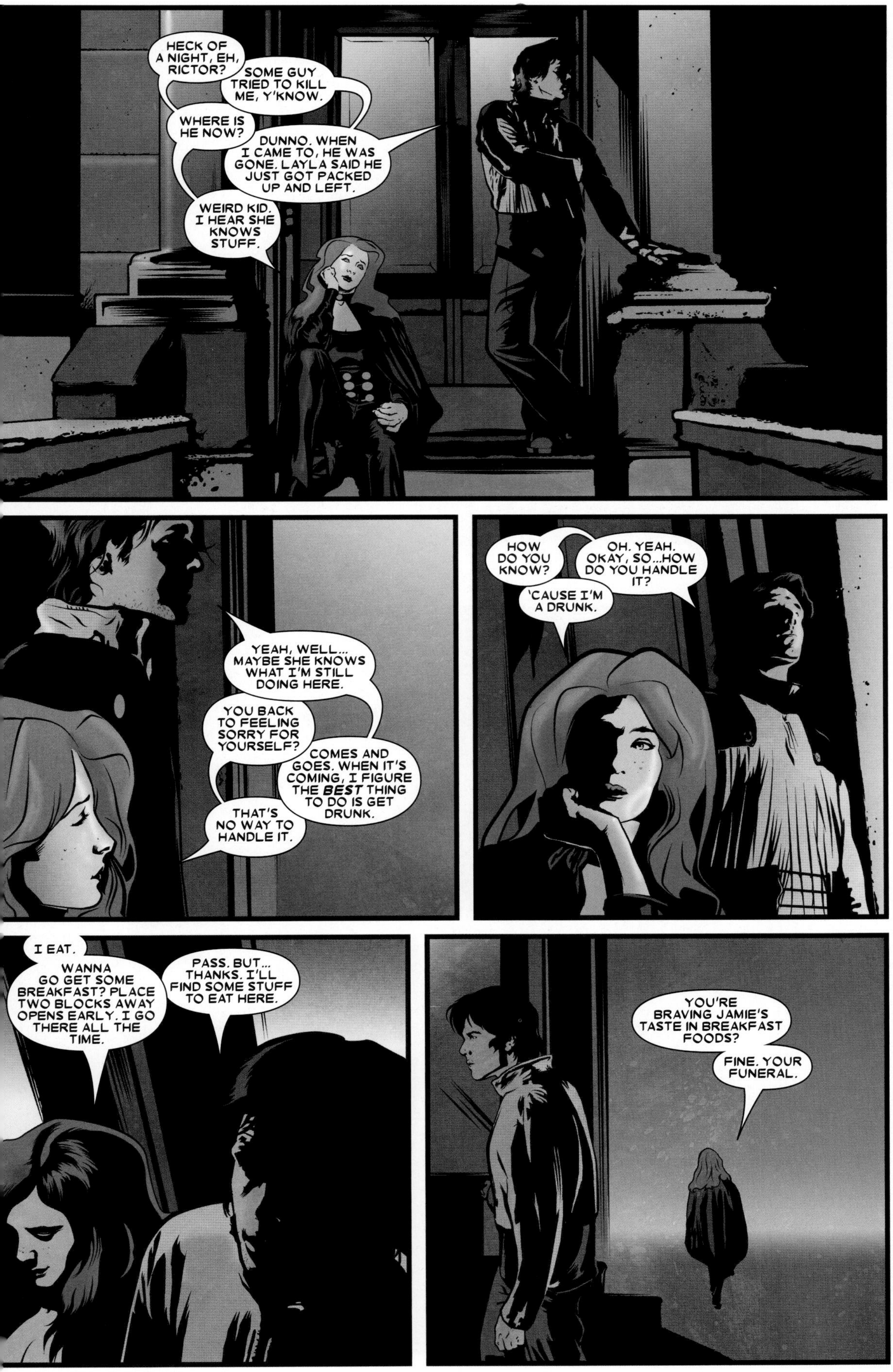
HECK OF A NIGHT, EH, RICTOR?
SOME GUY TRIED TO KILL ME, Y'KNOW.
WHERE IS HE NOW?
DUNNO. WHEN I CAME TO, HE WAS GONE. LAYLA SAID HE JUST GOT PACKED UP AND LEFT.
WEIRD KID. I HEAR SHE KNOWS STUFF.
YEAH, WELL... MAYBE SHE KNOWS WHAT I'M STILL DOING HERE.
YOU BACK TO FEELING SORRY FOR YOURSELF?
COMES AND GOES. WHEN IT'S COMING, I FIGURE THE *BEST* THING TO DO IS GET DRUNK.
THAT'S NO WAY TO HANDLE IT.
HOW DO YOU KNOW?
'CAUSE I'M A DRUNK.
OH. YEAH. OKAY, SO...HOW DO YOU HANDLE IT?
I EAT.
WANNA GO GET SOME BREAKFAST? PLACE TWO BLOCKS AWAY OPENS EARLY. I GO THERE ALL THE TIME.
PASS. BUT... THANKS. I'LL FIND SOME STUFF TO EAT HERE.
YOU'RE BRAVING JAMIE'S TASTE IN BREAKFAST FOODS?
FINE. YOUR FUNERAL.

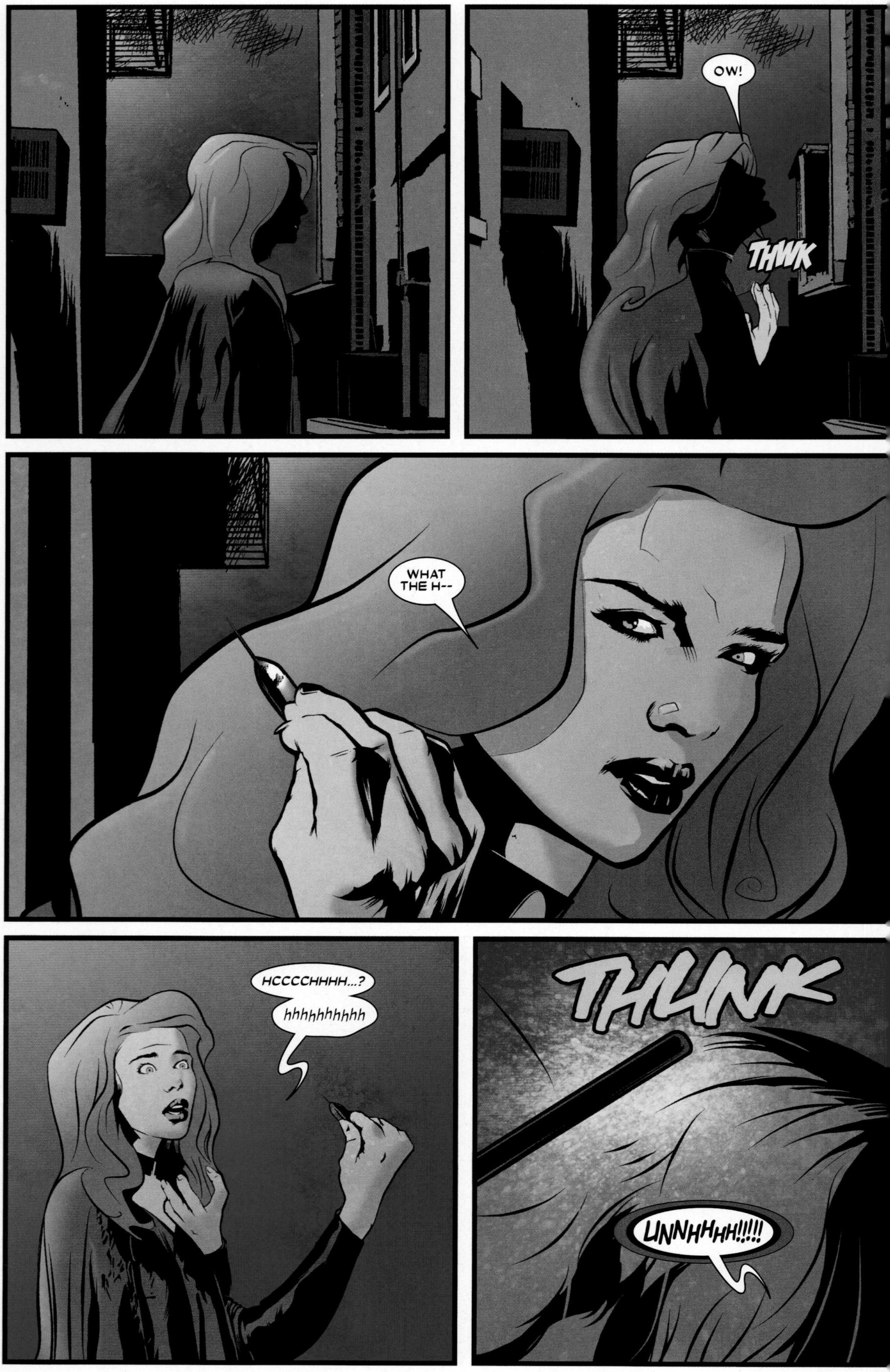

OW!
THWK
WHAT THE H--
HCCCCHHHH...?
hhhhhhhhhh
THUNK
UNNHHHH!!!!!

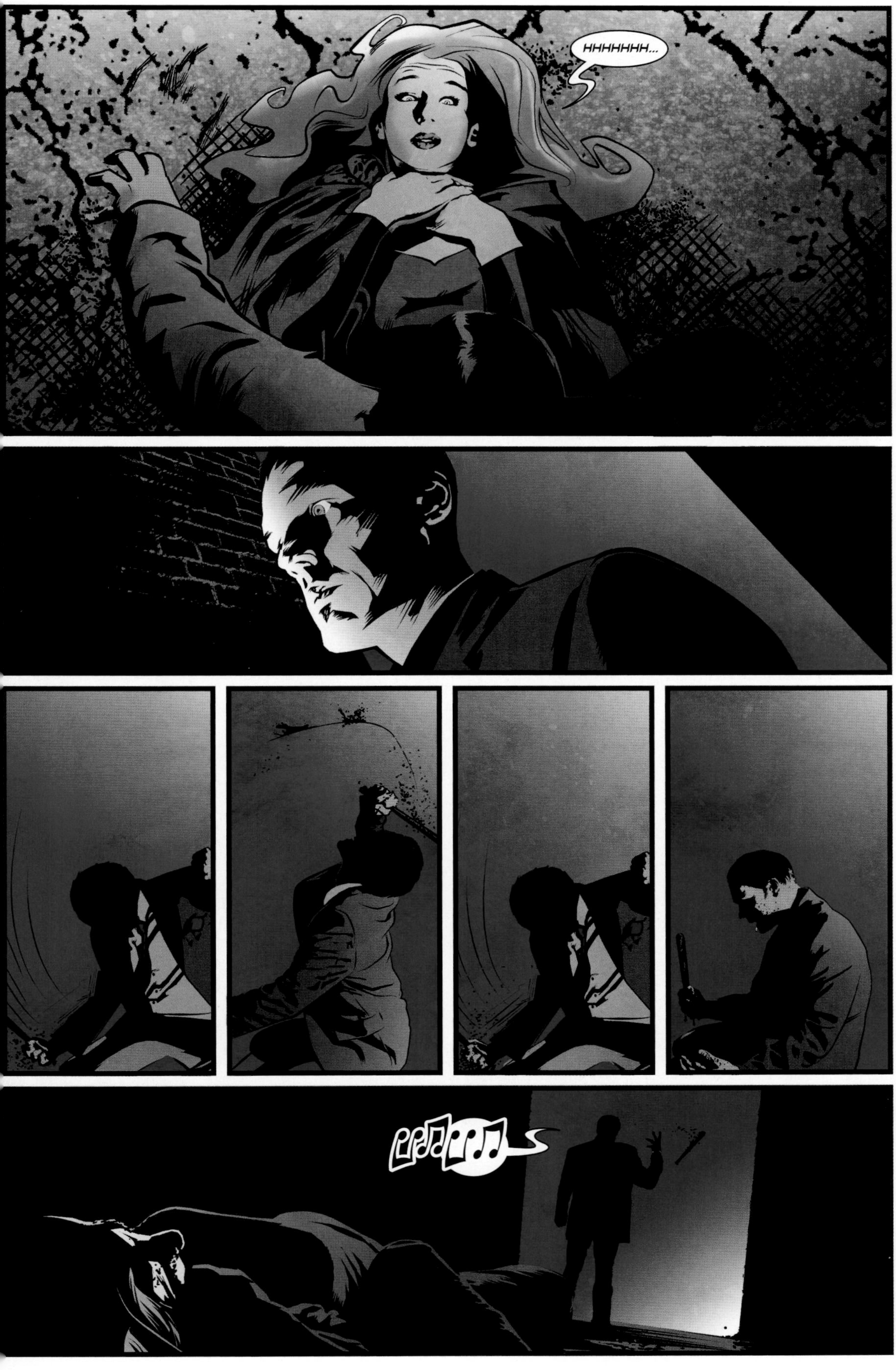
HHHHHHH...

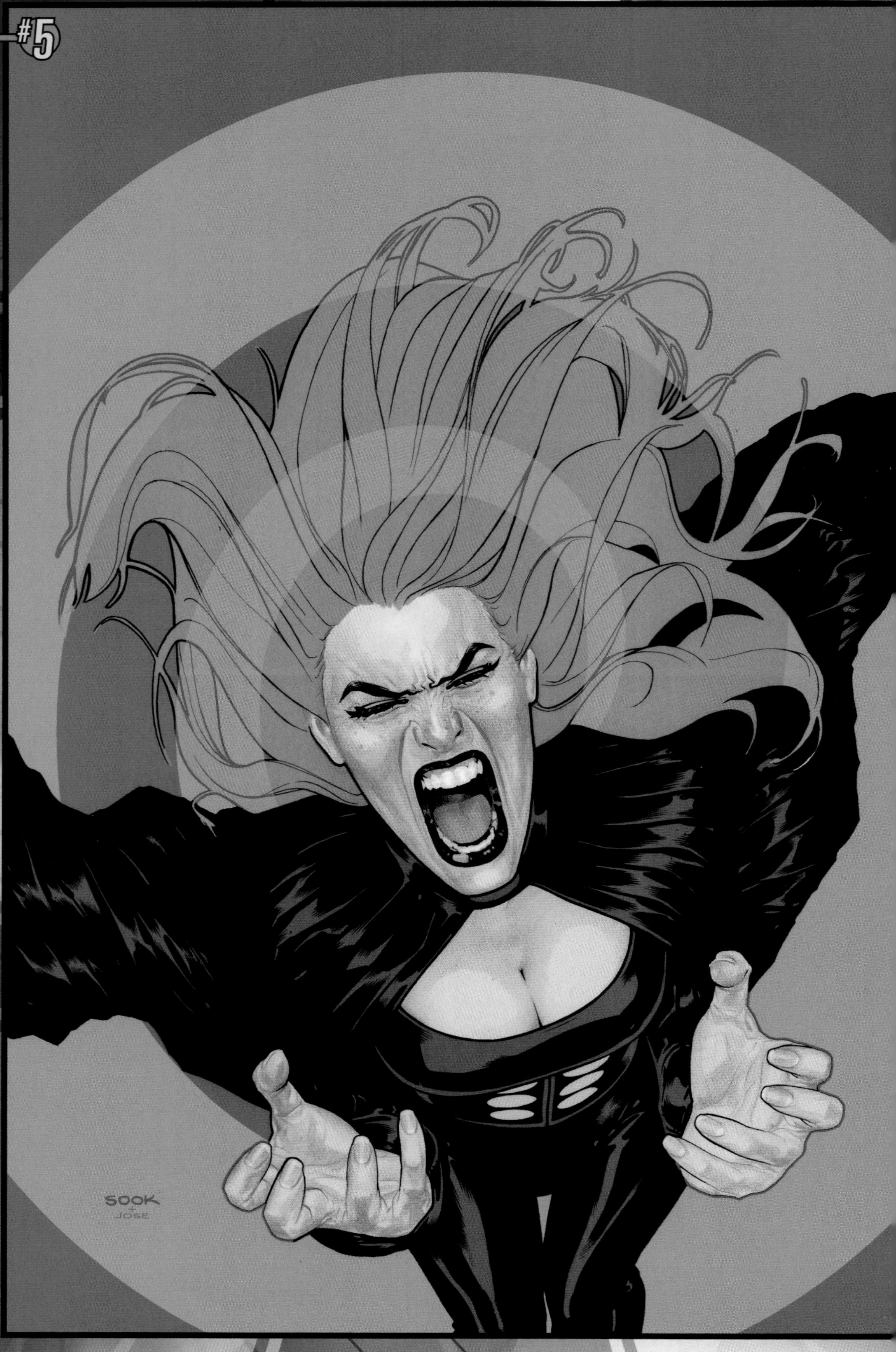
#5
SOOK + JOSE

EXCUSE ME.

NO, UH...

JUST SIT ANYWHERE, HONEY.

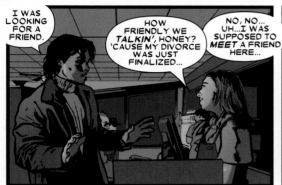

I WAS LOOKING FOR A FRIEND.

HOW FRIENDLY WE *TALKIN'*, HONEY? 'CAUSE MY DIVORCE WAS JUST FINALIZED...

NO, NO... UH...I WAS SUPPOSED TO *MEET* A FRIEND HERE...

WELL...NOT MEET HER, EXACTLY. SHE SAID SHE COMES HERE ALL THE TIME FOR BREAKFAST, AND INVITED ME, BUT I PASSED...

...AND THEN I CHANGED MY MIND AND CAME HERE, BUT I DON'T SEE HER.

HER NAME'S THERESA CASSIDY...

OH, SY-*REEN*. LOVELY GIRL. COMES HERE ALL A TIME.

COCKROACH JUMPED OUT OF HER OMELET ONCE. HER SCREAM BROKE EVERY GLASS IN THE JOINT.

COMPED THE OMELET, OF COURSE.

DIDN'T SEE HER *TODAY*, THOUGH.

HAVE YOU BEEN HERE THE WHOLE MORNING?

SURE HAVE, HONEY.

YOU DON'T THINK SOMETHING *BAD* HAPPENED TO--?

OH, *NO*, NO, I'M SURE IT'S FINE.

WELL, TELL HER CANDY SAYS "HI."

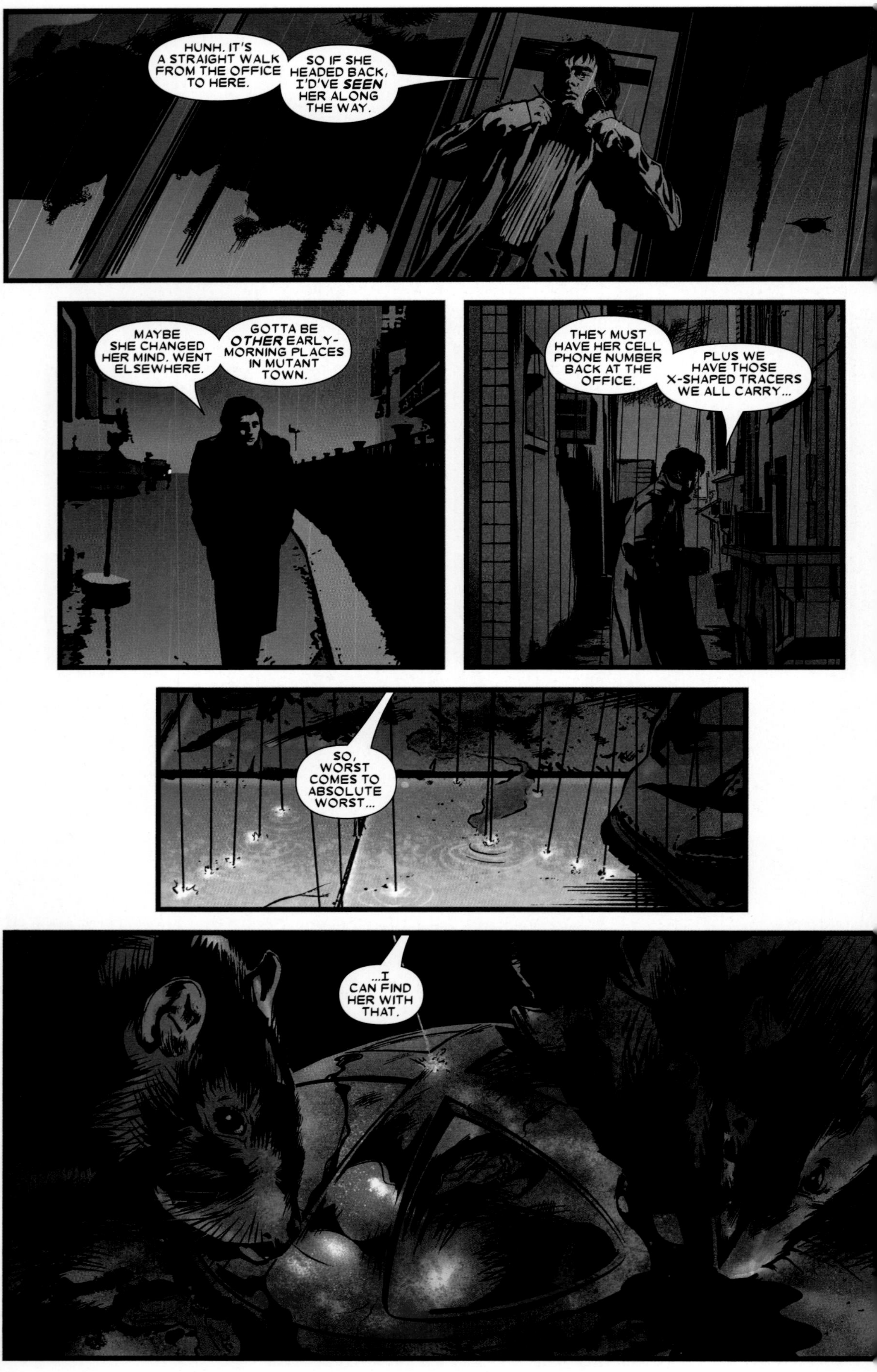
HUNH. IT'S A STRAIGHT WALK FROM THE OFFICE TO HERE.
SO IF SHE HEADED BACK, I'D'VE SEEN HER ALONG THE WAY.
MAYBE SHE CHANGED HER MIND. WENT ELSEWHERE.
GOTTA BE OTHER EARLY-MORNING PLACES IN MUTANT TOWN.
THEY MUST HAVE HER CELL PHONE NUMBER BACK AT THE OFFICE.
PLUS WE HAVE THOSE X-SHAPED TRACERS WE ALL CARRY...
SO, WORST COMES TO ABSOLUTE WORST...
...I CAN FIND HER WITH THAT.

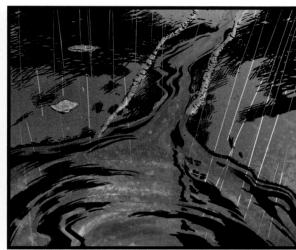

"YOU'RE LUCKY I HAPPENED BY.

"WITH YOU JUST LYIN' HELPLESS IN THE ALLEY...

"...ANYTHING COULDA HAPPENED TO YOU.

"GOOD THING I FOUND YOU.

"REAL GOOD THING.

STAGE DOOR
cast and crew
only

"ME BEING A DOCTOR AND ALL."

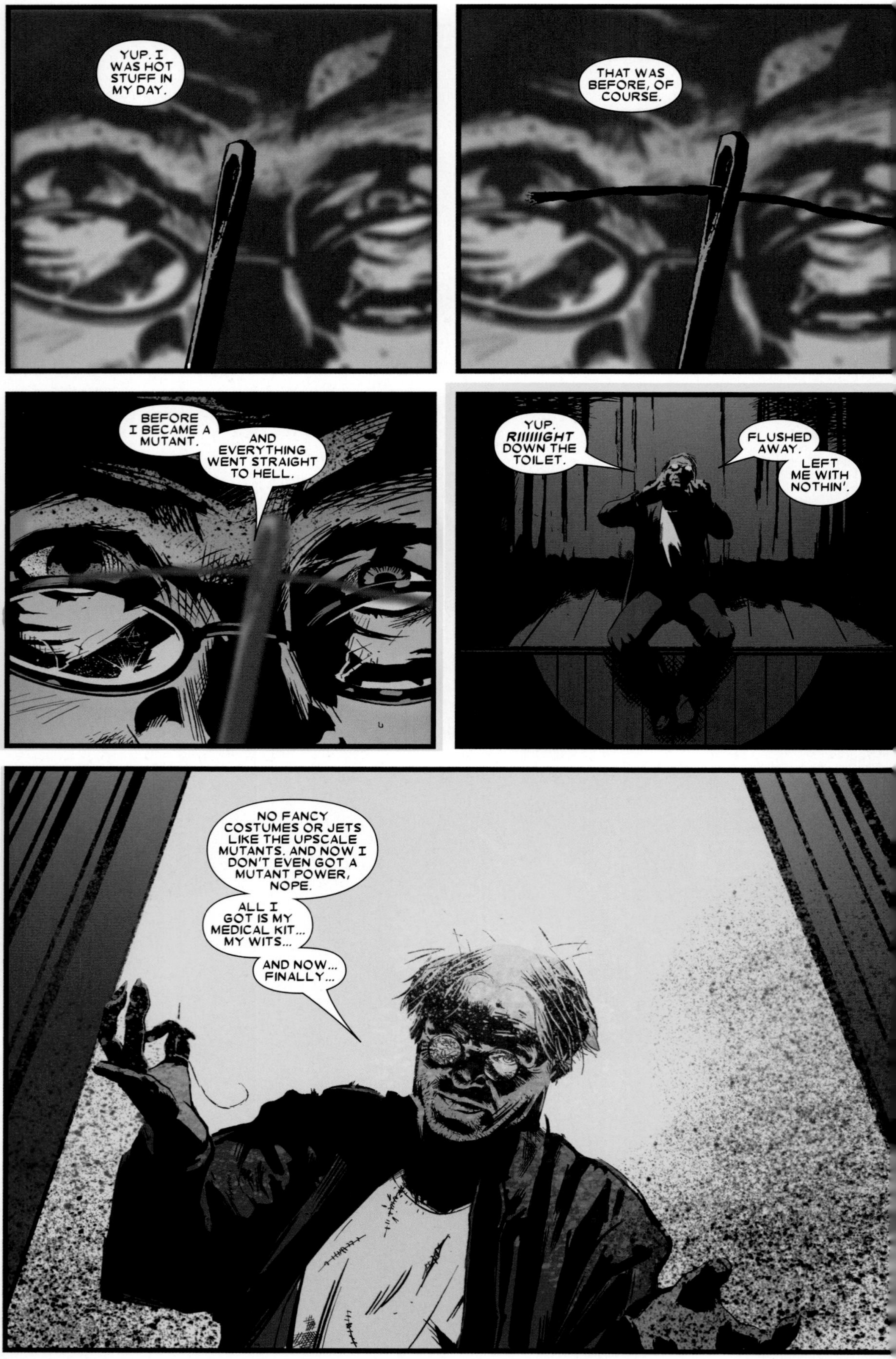

YUP. I WAS HOT STUFF IN MY DAY.
THAT WAS BEFORE, OF COURSE.
BEFORE I BECAME A MUTANT.
AND EVERYTHING WENT STRAIGHT TO HELL.
YUP. RIIIIIIGHT DOWN THE TOILET.
FLUSHED AWAY.
LEFT ME WITH NOTHIN'.
NO FANCY COSTUMES OR JETS LIKE THE UPSCALE MUTANTS. AND NOW I DON'T EVEN GOT A MUTANT POWER, NOPE.
ALL I GOT IS MY MEDICAL KIT... MY WITS...
AND NOW... FINALLY...

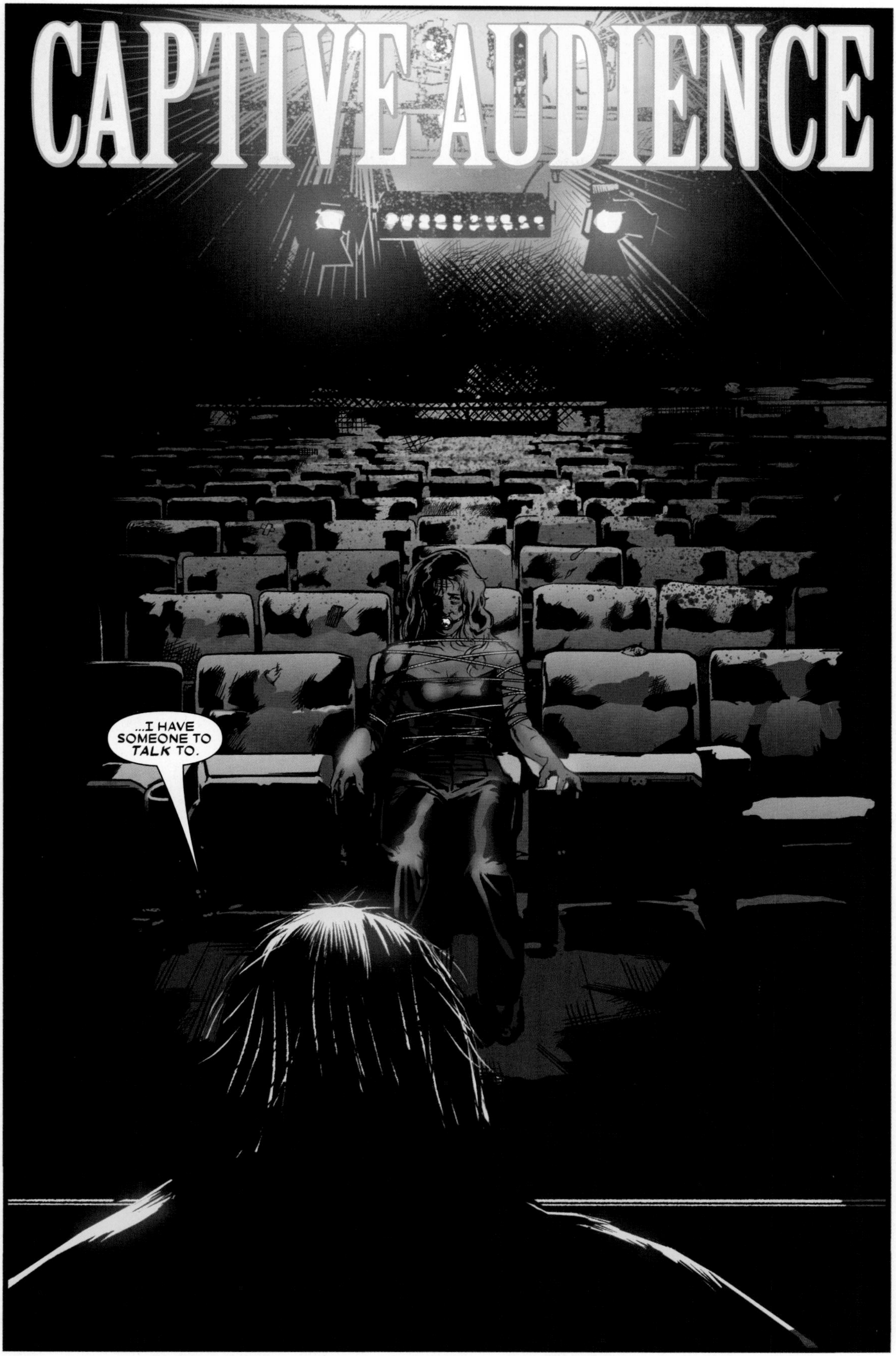
CAPTIVE AUDIENCE
...I HAVE SOMEONE TO *TALK* TO.

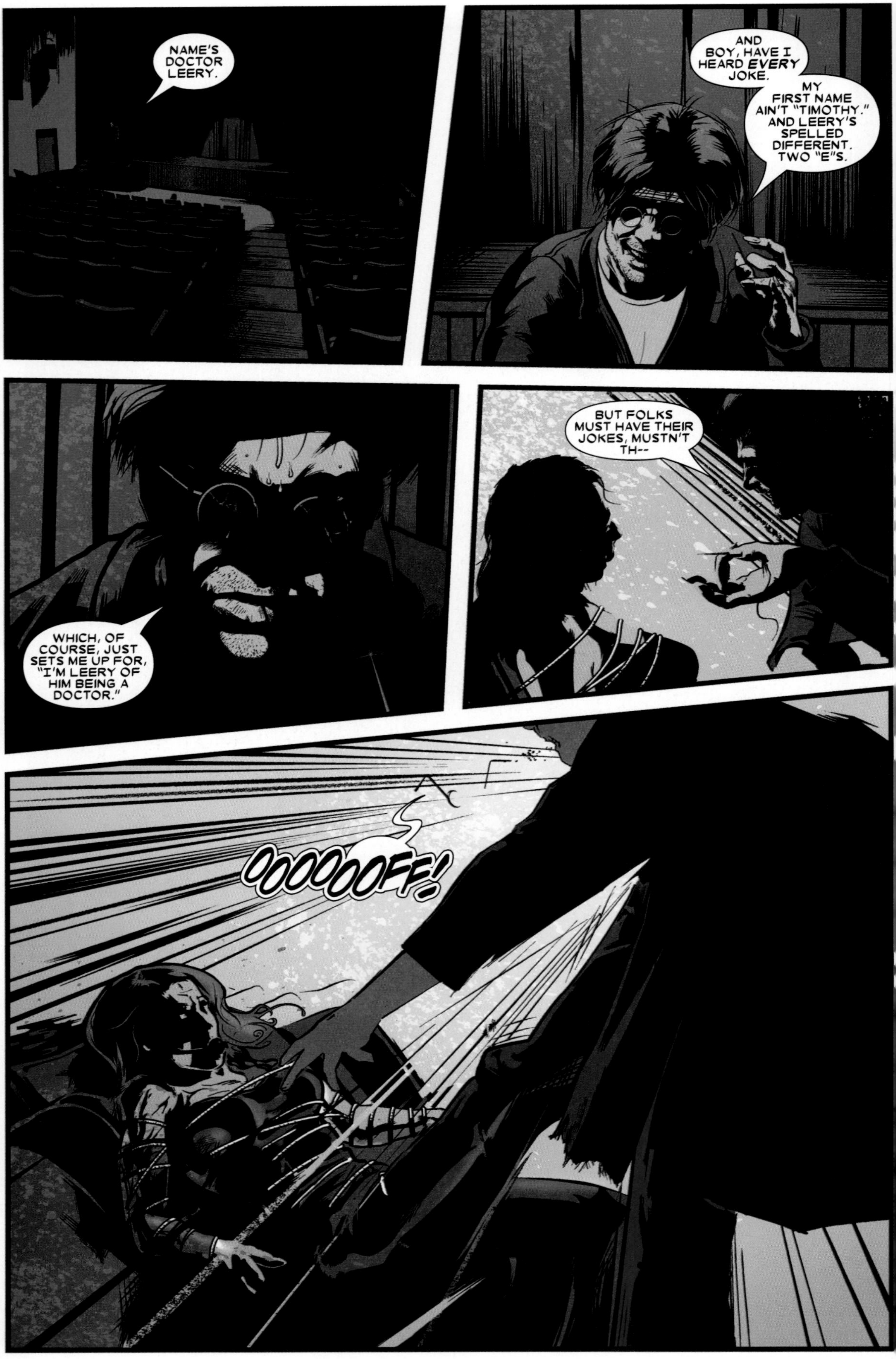
NAME'S DOCTOR LEERY.
AND BOY, HAVE I HEARD EVERY JOKE.
MY FIRST NAME AIN'T "TIMOTHY." AND LEERY'S SPELLED DIFFERENT. TWO "E"S.
WHICH, OF COURSE, JUST SETS ME UP FOR, "I'M LEERY OF HIM BEING A DOCTOR."
BUT FOLKS MUST HAVE THEIR JOKES, MUSTN'T TH--
OOOOOOFF!

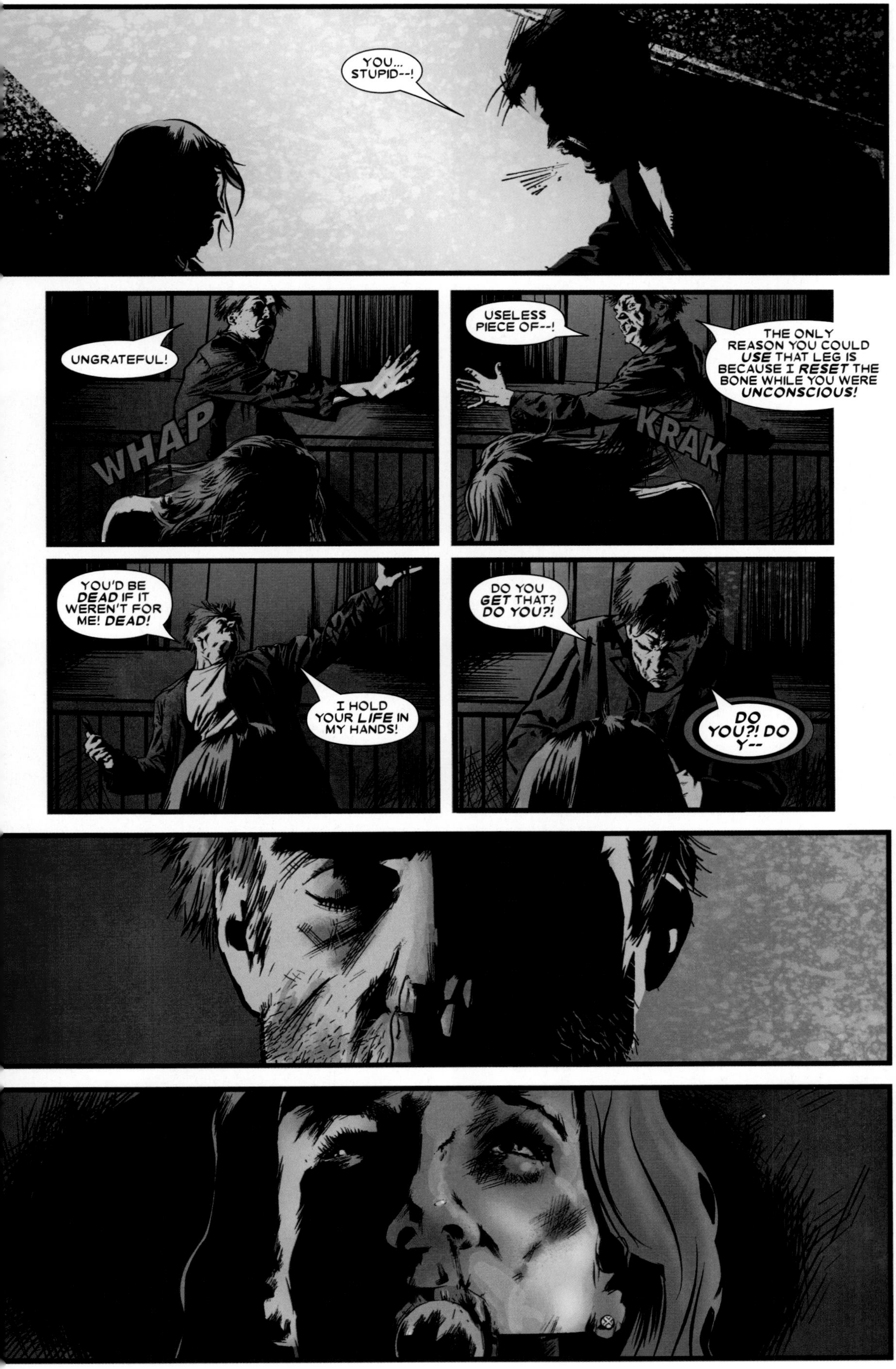
YOU... STUPID--!
UNGRATEFUL!
WHAP
USELESS PIECE OF--!
THE ONLY REASON YOU COULD USE THAT LEG IS BECAUSE I RESET THE BONE WHILE YOU WERE UNCONSCIOUS!
KRAK
YOU'D BE DEAD IF IT WEREN'T FOR ME! DEAD!
I HOLD YOUR LIFE IN MY HANDS!
DO YOU GET THAT? DO YOU?!
DO YOU?! DO Y--

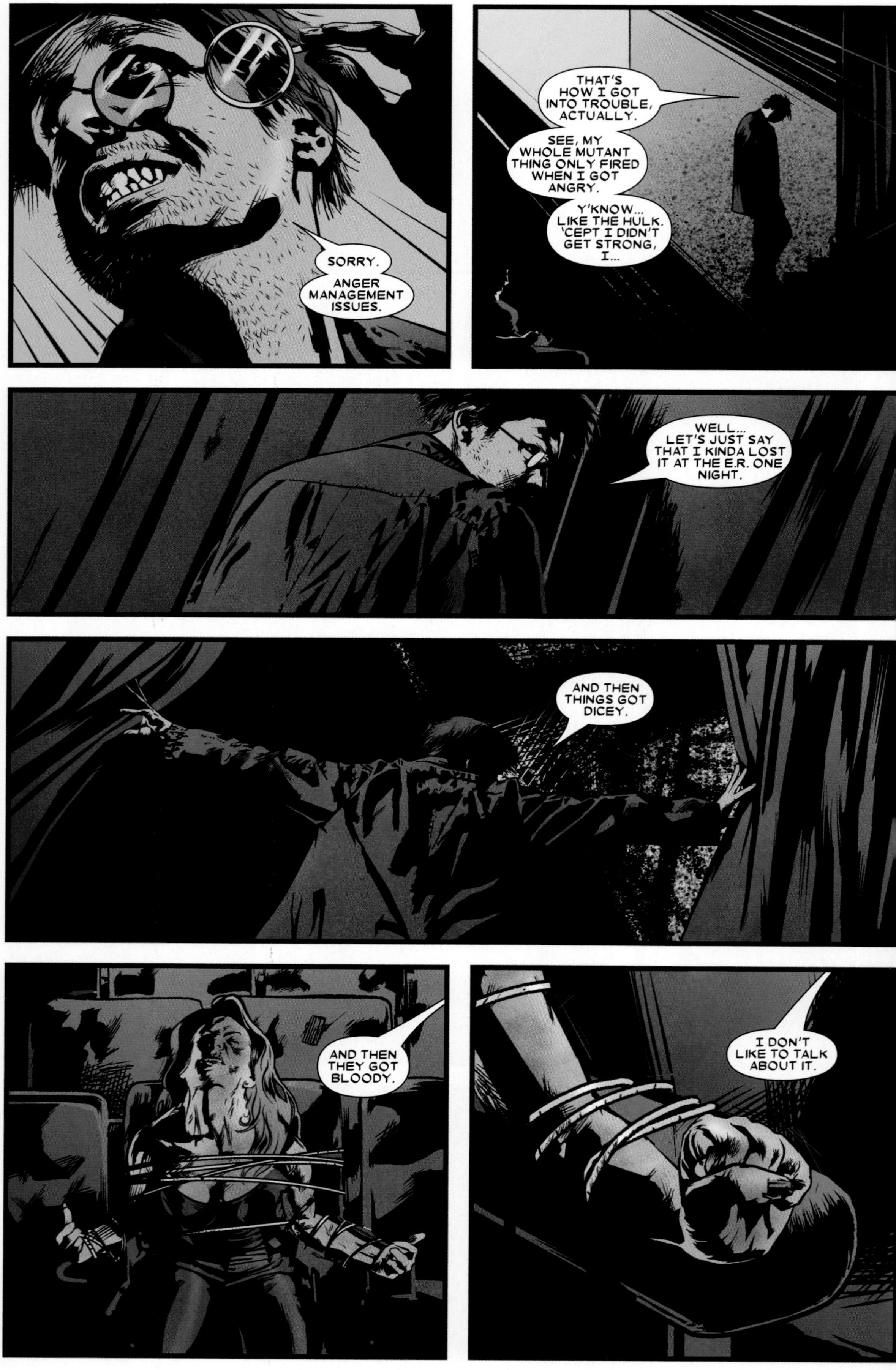
SORRY.
ANGER MANAGEMENT ISSUES.
THAT'S HOW I GOT INTO TROUBLE, ACTUALLY.
SEE, MY WHOLE MUTANT THING ONLY FIRED WHEN I GOT ANGRY.
Y'KNOW... LIKE THE HULK. 'CEPT I DIDN'T GET STRONG, I...
WELL... LET'S JUST SAY THAT I KINDA LOST IT AT THE E.R. ONE NIGHT.
AND THEN THINGS GOT DICEY.
AND THEN THEY GOT BLOODY.
I DON'T LIKE TO TALK ABOUT IT.

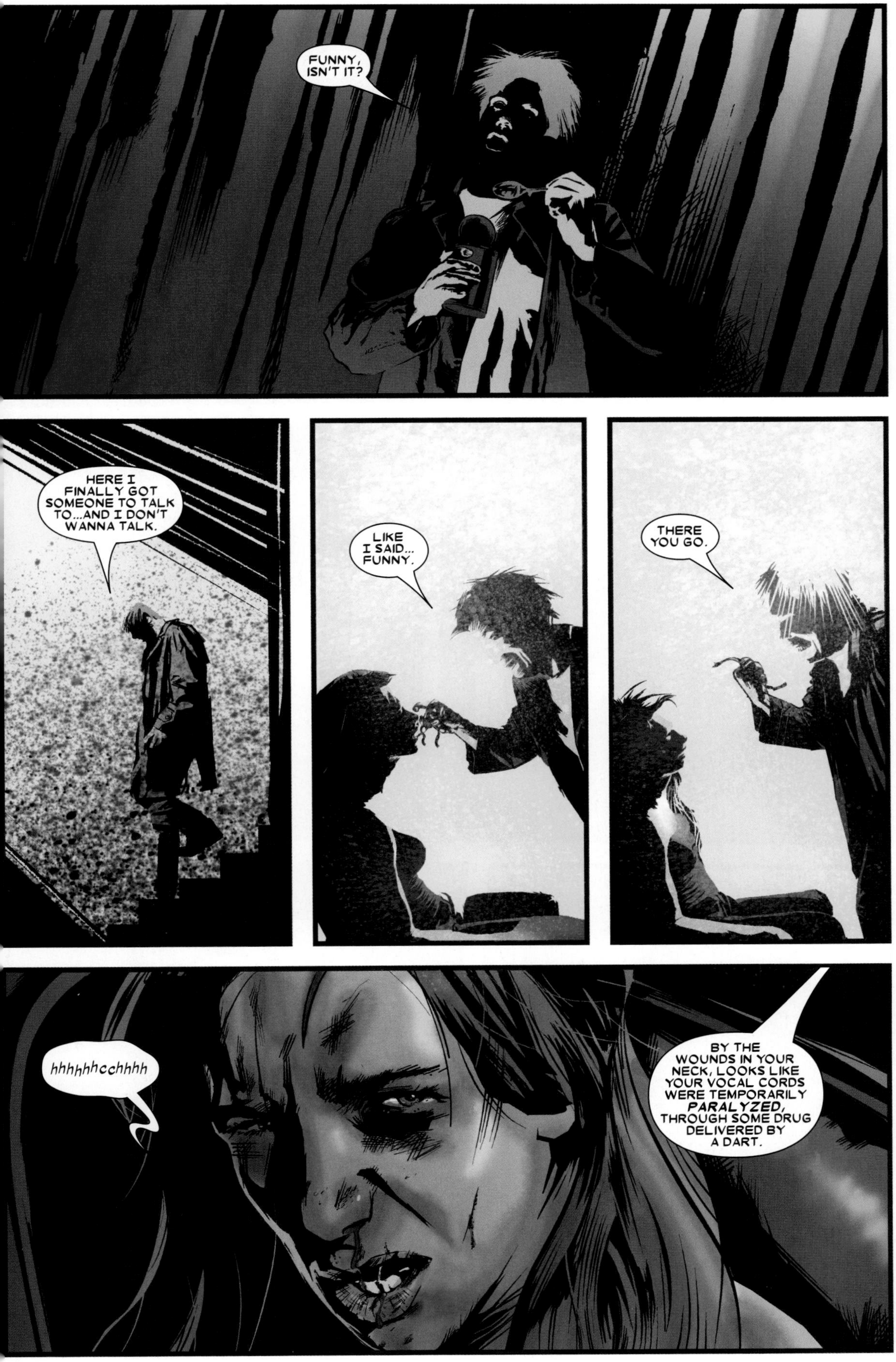
FUNNY, ISN'T IT?
HERE I FINALLY GOT SOMEONE TO TALK TO...AND I DON'T WANNA TALK.
LIKE I SAID... FUNNY.
THERE YOU GO.
hhhhhhcchhhh
BY THE WOUNDS IN YOUR NECK, LOOKS LIKE YOUR VOCAL CORDS WERE TEMPORARILY PARALYZED, THROUGH SOME DRUG DELIVERED BY A DART.

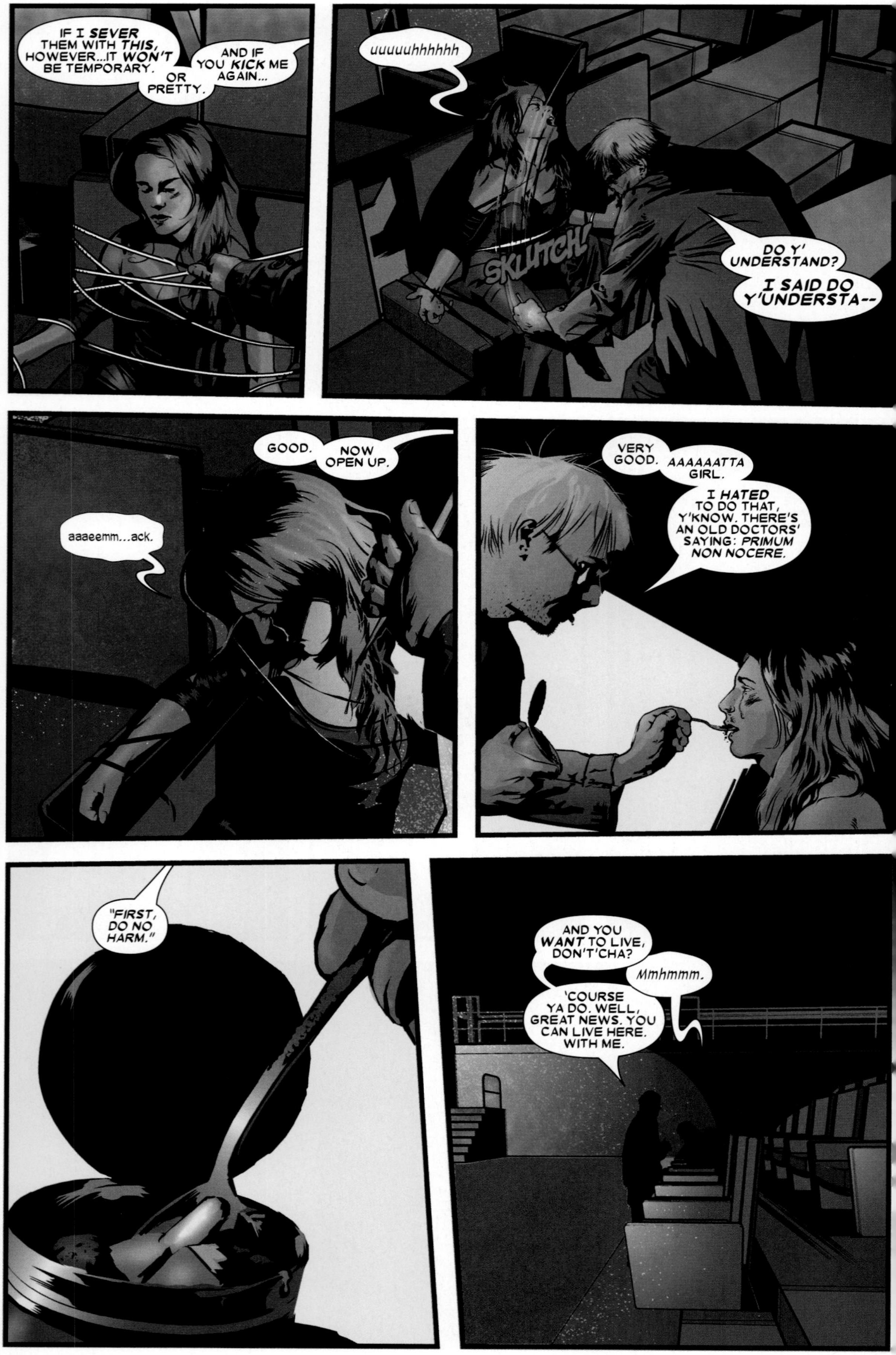
IF I SEVER THEM WITH THIS, HOWEVER...IT WON'T BE TEMPORARY.
OR PRETTY.
AND IF YOU KICK ME AGAIN...
uuuuuhhhhhh
SKLUTCH!
DO Y' UNDERSTAND?
I SAID DO Y'UNDERSTA--
GOOD.
NOW OPEN UP.
aaaeemm...ack.
VERY GOOD.
AAAAAATTA GIRL.
I HATED TO DO THAT, Y'KNOW. THERE'S AN OLD DOCTORS' SAYING: PRIMUM NON NOCERE.
"FIRST, DO NO HARM."
AND YOU WANT TO LIVE, DON'T'CHA?
Mmhmmm.
'COURSE YA DO. WELL, GREAT NEWS. YOU CAN LIVE HERE. WITH ME.

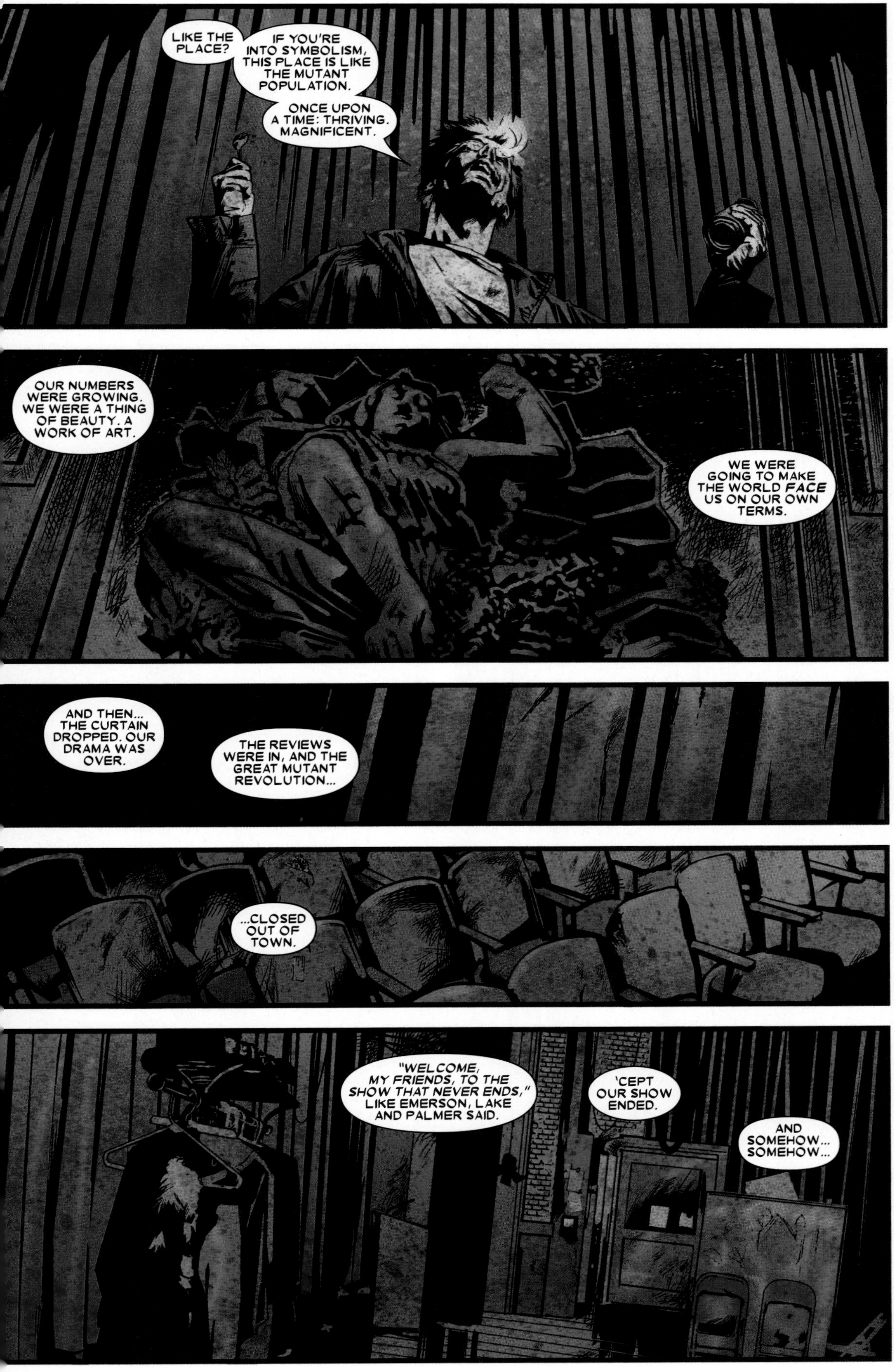
LIKE THE PLACE?
IF YOU'RE INTO SYMBOLISM, THIS PLACE IS LIKE THE MUTANT POPULATION.
ONCE UPON A TIME: THRIVING. MAGNIFICENT.
OUR NUMBERS WERE GROWING. WE WERE A THING OF BEAUTY. A WORK OF ART.
WE WERE GOING TO MAKE THE WORLD *FACE* US ON OUR OWN TERMS.
AND THEN... THE CURTAIN DROPPED. OUR DRAMA WAS OVER.
THE REVIEWS WERE IN, AND THE GREAT MUTANT REVOLUTION...
...CLOSED OUT OF TOWN.
"WELCOME, MY FRIENDS, TO THE SHOW THAT NEVER ENDS," LIKE EMERSON, LAKE AND PALMER SAID.
'CEPT OUR SHOW ENDED.
AND SOMEHOW... SOMEHOW...

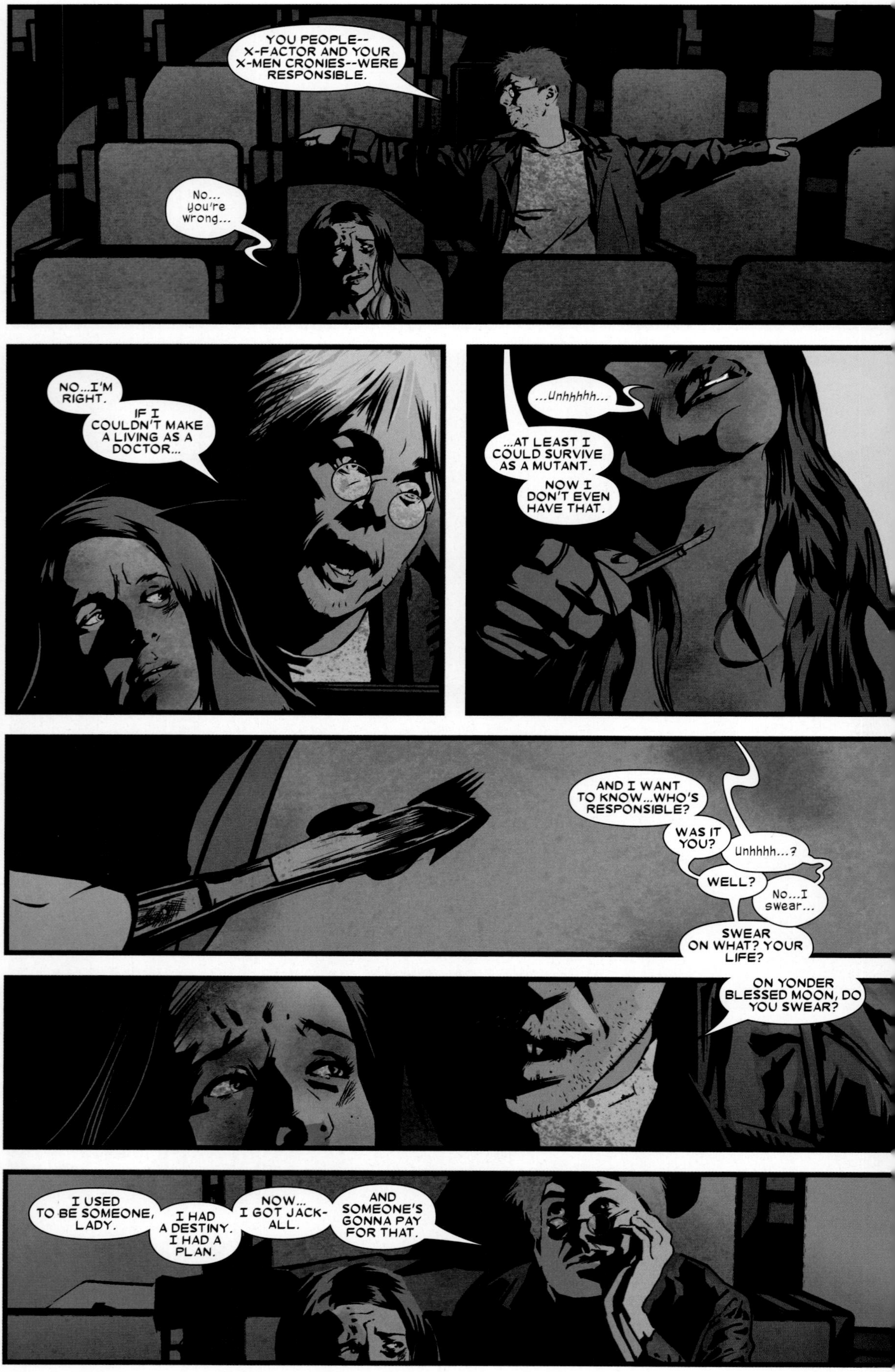
YOU PEOPLE-- X-FACTOR AND YOUR X-MEN CRONIES--WERE RESPONSIBLE.
No... you're wrong...
NO...I'M RIGHT.
IF I COULDN'T MAKE A LIVING AS A DOCTOR...
...Unhhhhh...
...AT LEAST I COULD SURVIVE AS A MUTANT.
NOW I DON'T EVEN HAVE THAT.
AND I WANT TO KNOW...WHO'S RESPONSIBLE?
WAS IT YOU?
Unhhhh...?
WELL?
No...I swear...
SWEAR ON WHAT? YOUR LIFE?
ON YONDER BLESSED MOON, DO YOU SWEAR?
I USED TO BE SOMEONE, LADY.
I HAD A DESTINY. I HAD A PLAN.
NOW... I GOT JACK-ALL.
AND SOMEONE'S GONNA PAY FOR THAT.

"I BET YOU THINK I'M VERMIN. THAT I'M LOWER THAN ANY FORM OF LIFE. BUT YOU'RE WRONG.

"I'M A PERSON. A PERSON WITH DREAMS AND HOPES THAT KEEP GETTING SMACKED AROUND BY THE HAND OF FATE. I NEED SOMETHING TO GRAB ONTO.

"AND YOU'RE IT.

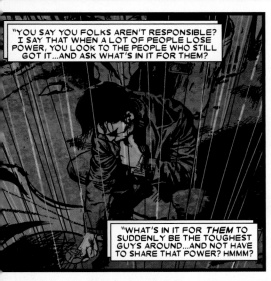

"YOU SAY YOU FOLKS AREN'T RESPONSIBLE? I SAY THAT WHEN A LOT OF PEOPLE LOSE POWER, YOU LOOK TO THE PEOPLE WHO STILL GOT IT...AND ASK WHAT'S IN IT FOR THEM?

"WHAT'S IN IT FOR *THEM* TO SUDDENLY BE THE TOUGHEST GUYS AROUND...AND NOT HAVE TO SHARE THAT POWER? HMMM?

"WHICH IS WHY I KINDA DOUBT YOU'LL BE GIVING THE INVESTIGATION YOUR BEST EFFORTS.

"SO I'M FIGURING...

"...YOUR GUYS MIGHT NEED SOME, Y'KNOW... *INCENTIVE.*

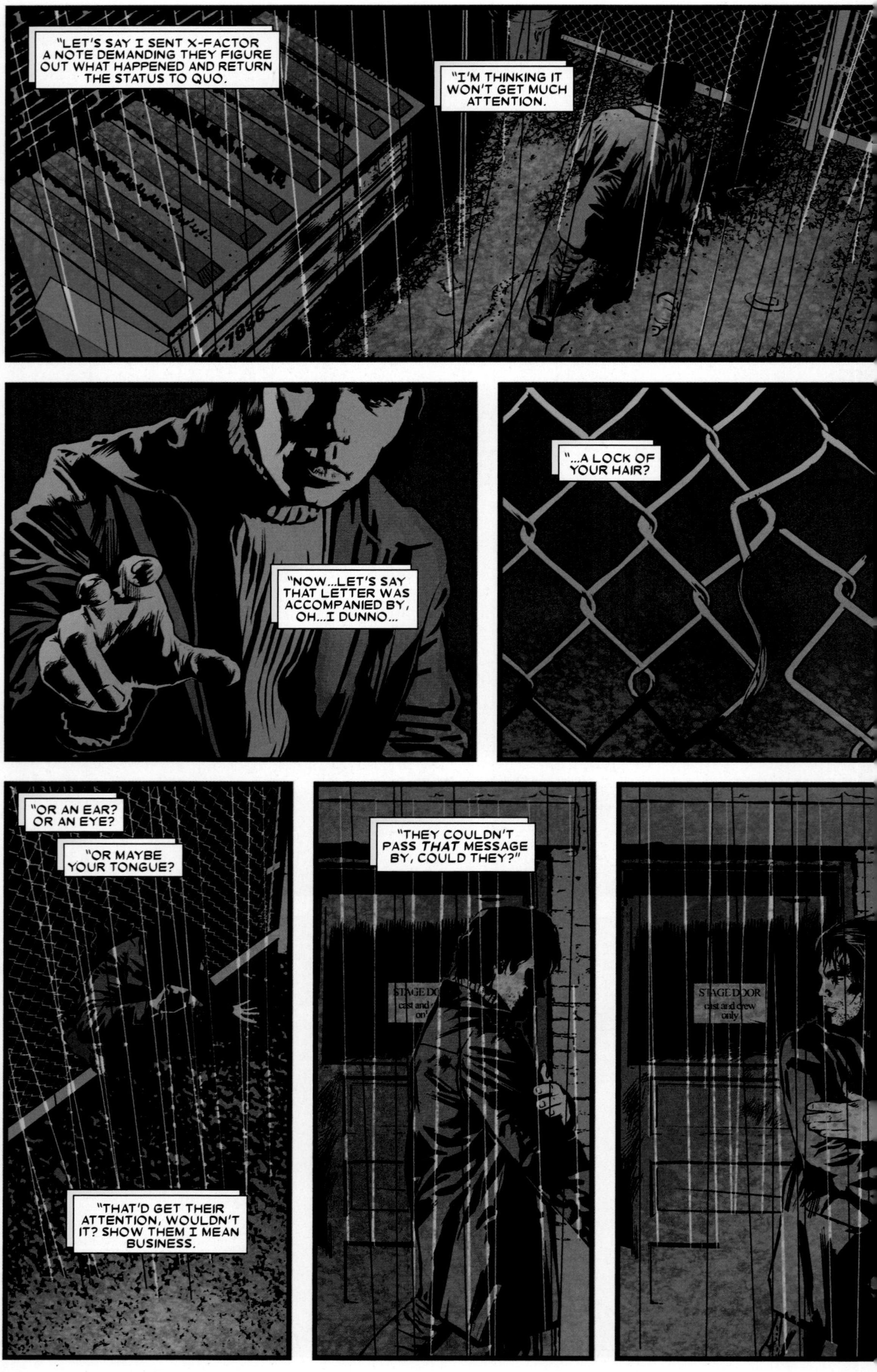
"LET'S SAY I SENT X-FACTOR A NOTE DEMANDING THEY FIGURE OUT WHAT HAPPENED AND RETURN THE STATUS TO QUO.
"I'M THINKING IT WON'T GET MUCH ATTENTION.
"NOW...LET'S SAY THAT LETTER WAS ACCOMPANIED BY, OH...I DUNNO...
"...A LOCK OF YOUR HAIR?
"OR AN EAR? OR AN EYE?
"OR MAYBE YOUR TONGUE?
"THAT'D GET THEIR ATTENTION, WOULDN'T IT? SHOW THEM I MEAN BUSINESS.
"THEY COULDN'T PASS THAT MESSAGE BY, COULD THEY?"
STAGE DOOR
cast and crew only

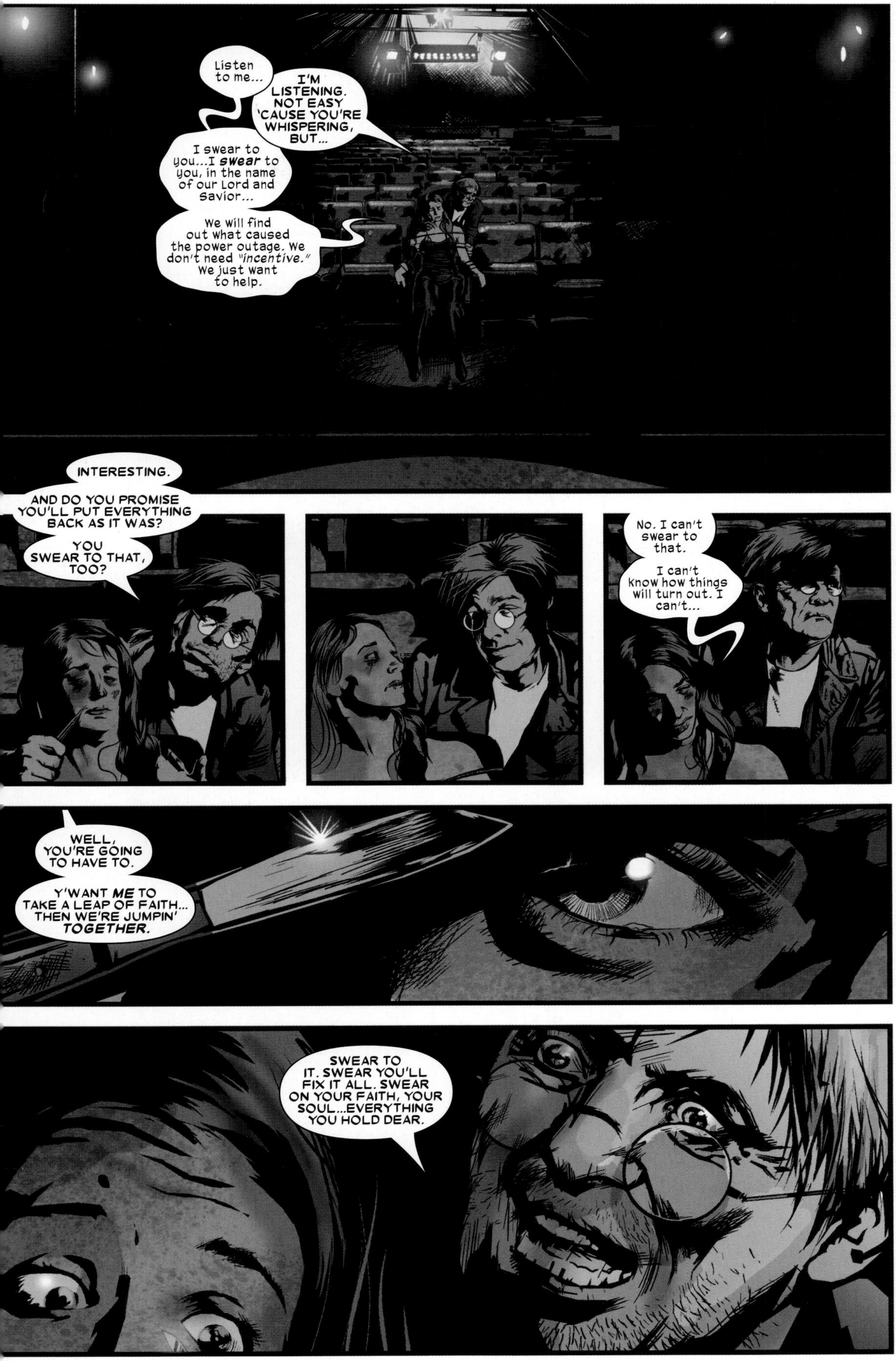
Listen to me...
I'M LISTENING. NOT EASY 'CAUSE YOU'RE WHISPERING, BUT...
I swear to you...I *swear* to you, in the name of our Lord and Savior...
We will find out what caused the power outage. We don't need *"incentive."* We just want to help.
INTERESTING.
AND DO YOU PROMISE YOU'LL PUT EVERYTHING BACK AS IT WAS?
YOU SWEAR TO THAT, TOO?
No. I can't swear to that.
I can't know how things will turn out. I can't...
WELL, YOU'RE GOING TO HAVE TO.
Y'WANT **ME** TO TAKE A LEAP OF FAITH... THEN WE'RE JUMPIN' ***TOGETHER.***
SWEAR TO IT. SWEAR YOU'LL FIX IT ALL. SWEAR ON YOUR FAITH, YOUR SOUL...EVERYTHING YOU HOLD DEAR.

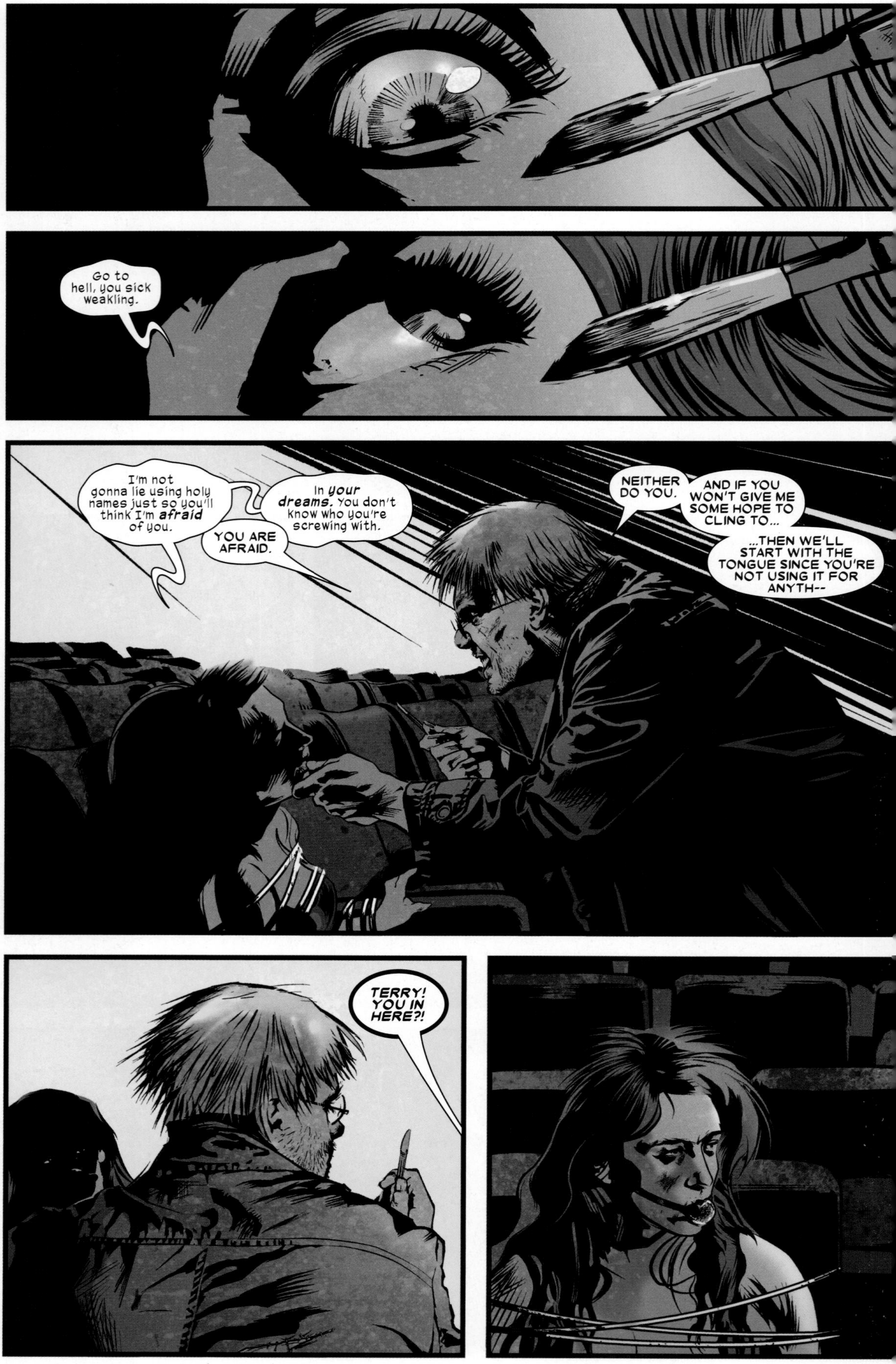
Go to hell, you sick weakling.
I'm not gonna lie using holy names just so you'll think I'm *afraid* of you.
YOU ARE AFRAID.
In *your dreams.* You don't know who you're screwing with.
NEITHER DO YOU.
AND IF YOU WON'T GIVE ME SOME HOPE TO CLING TO...
...THEN WE'LL START WITH THE TONGUE SINCE YOU'RE NOT USING IT FOR ANYTH--
TERRY! YOU IN HERE?!

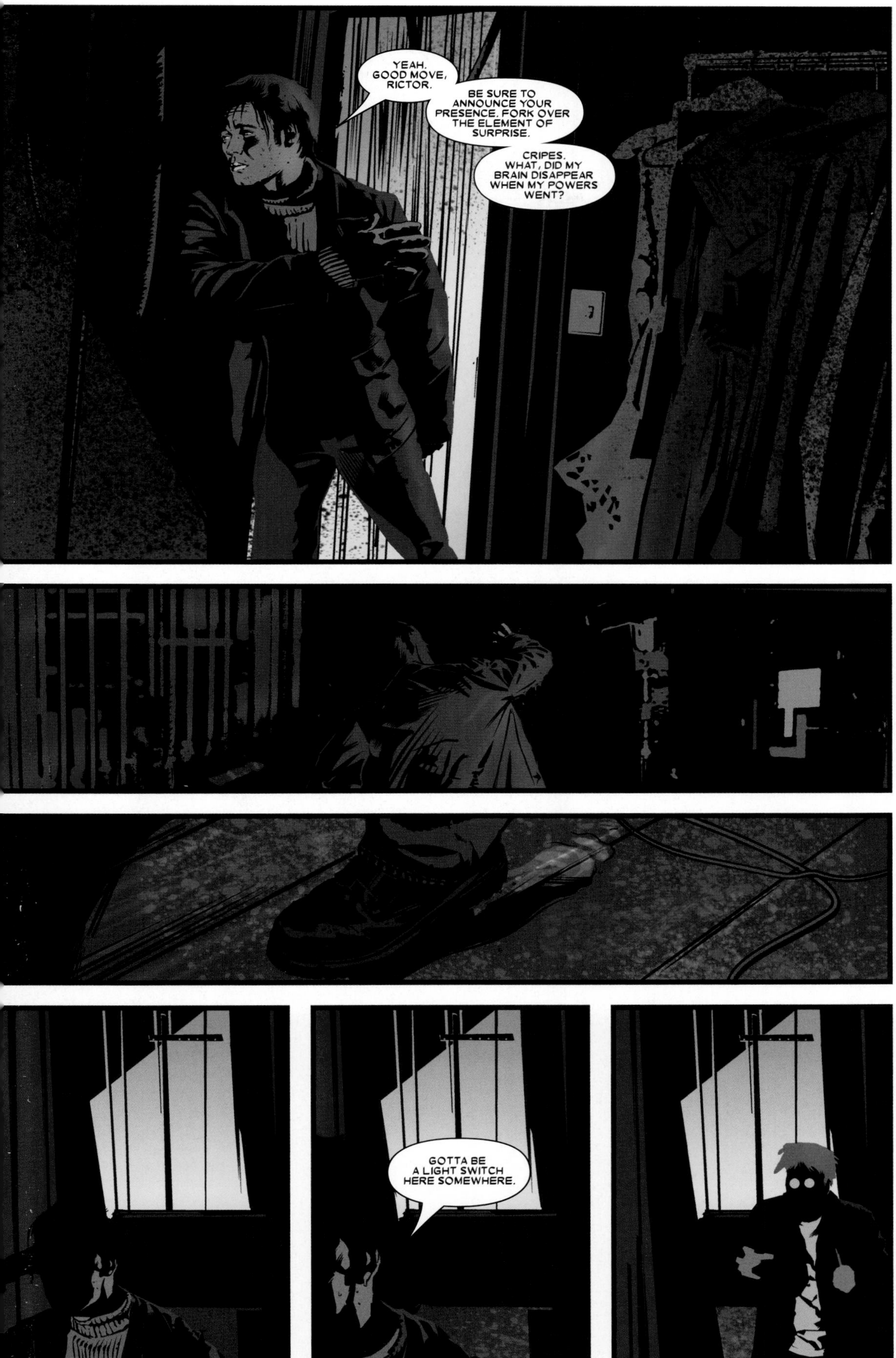
YEAH. GOOD MOVE, RICTOR.
BE SURE TO ANNOUNCE YOUR PRESENCE. FORK OVER THE ELEMENT OF SURPRISE.
CRIPES. WHAT, DID MY BRAIN DISAPPEAR WHEN MY POWERS WENT?
GOTTA BE A LIGHT SWITCH HERE SOMEWHERE.

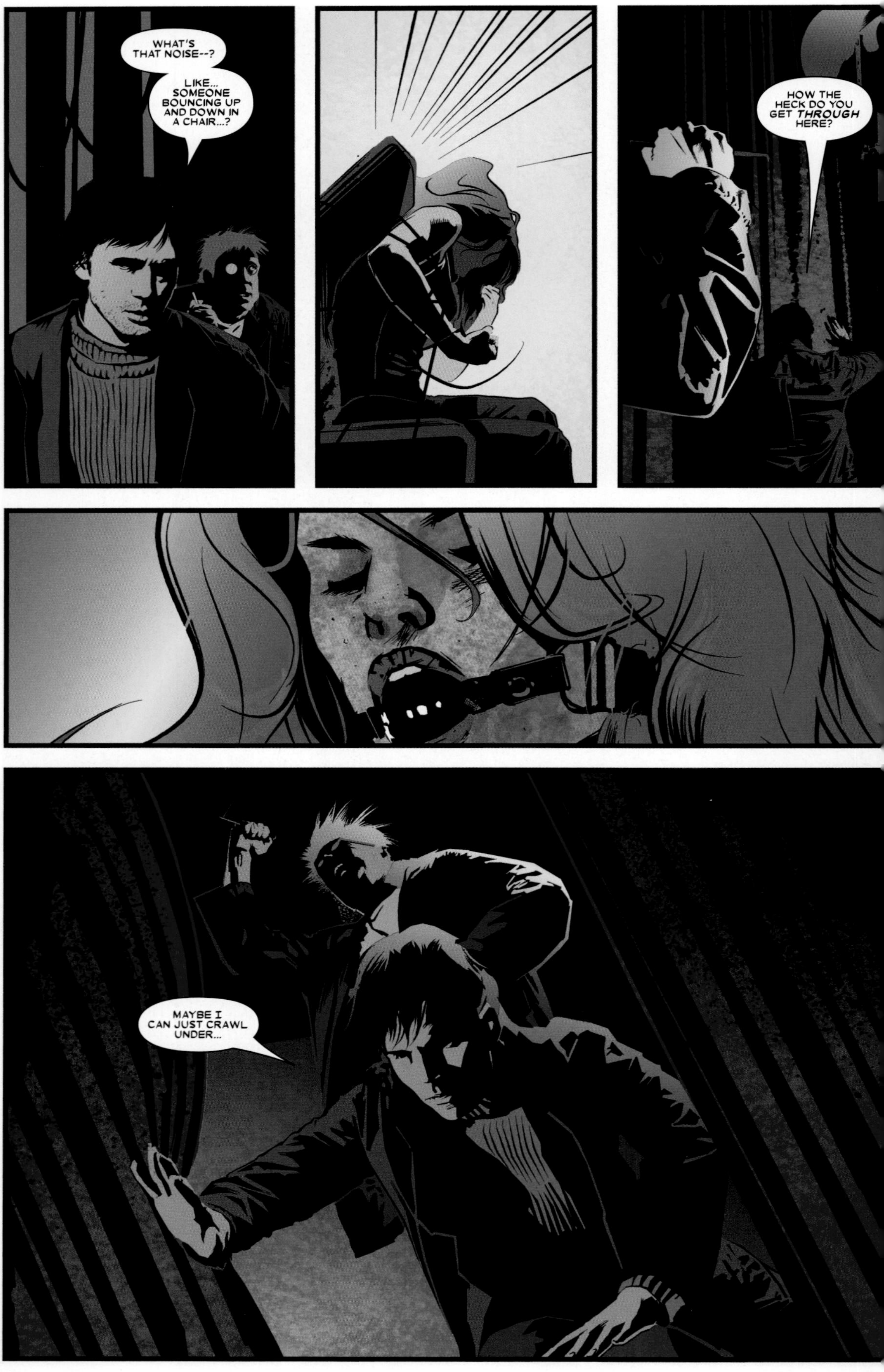
WHAT'S THAT NOISE--?
LIKE... SOMEONE BOUNCING UP AND DOWN IN A CHAIR...?
HOW THE HECK DO YOU GET *THROUGH* HERE?
MAYBE I CAN JUST CRAWL UNDER...

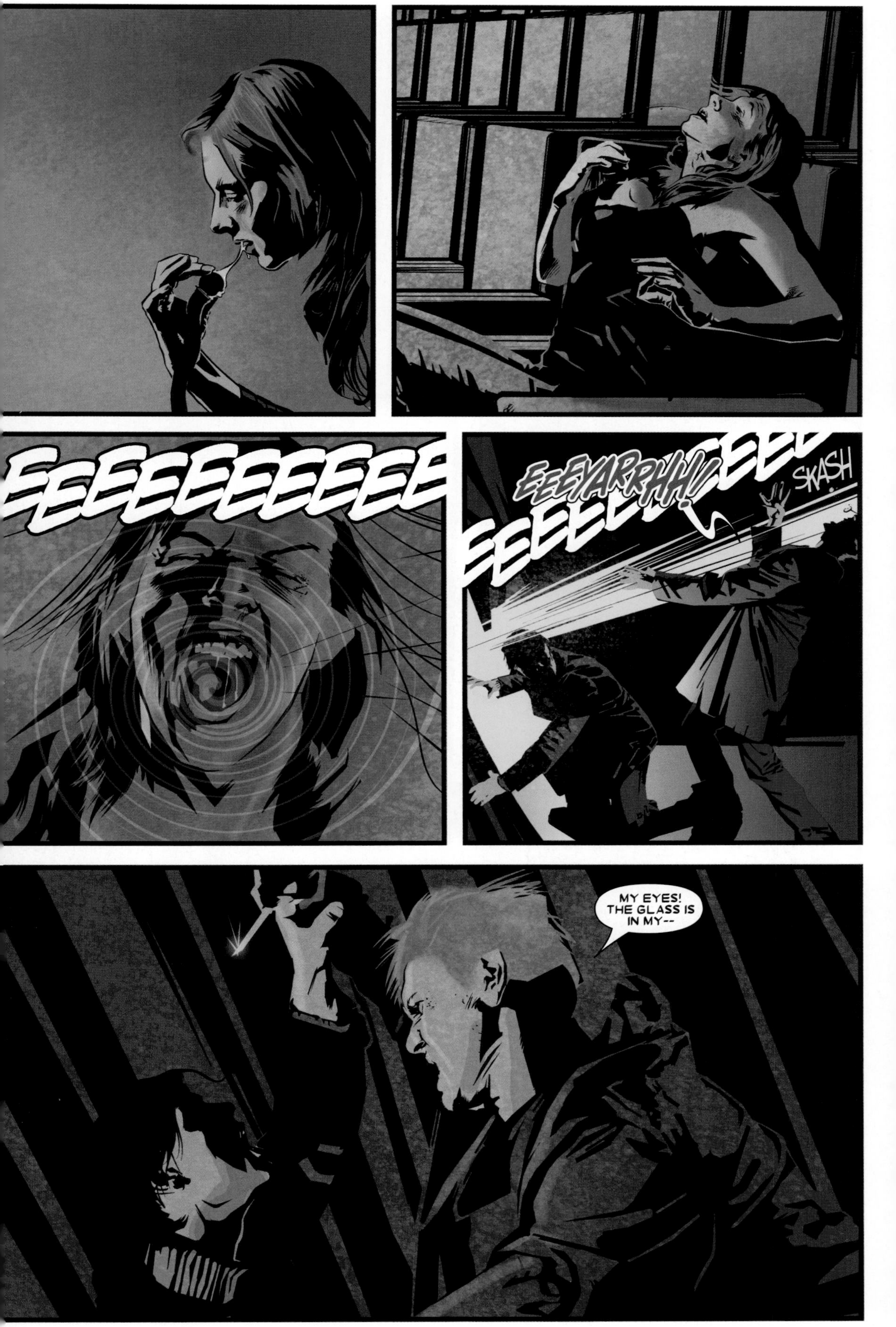
EEEEEEEEEEE
EEEYARRHH!
EEEEEEEEEEE
SKASH
MY EYES! THE GLASS IS IN MY--

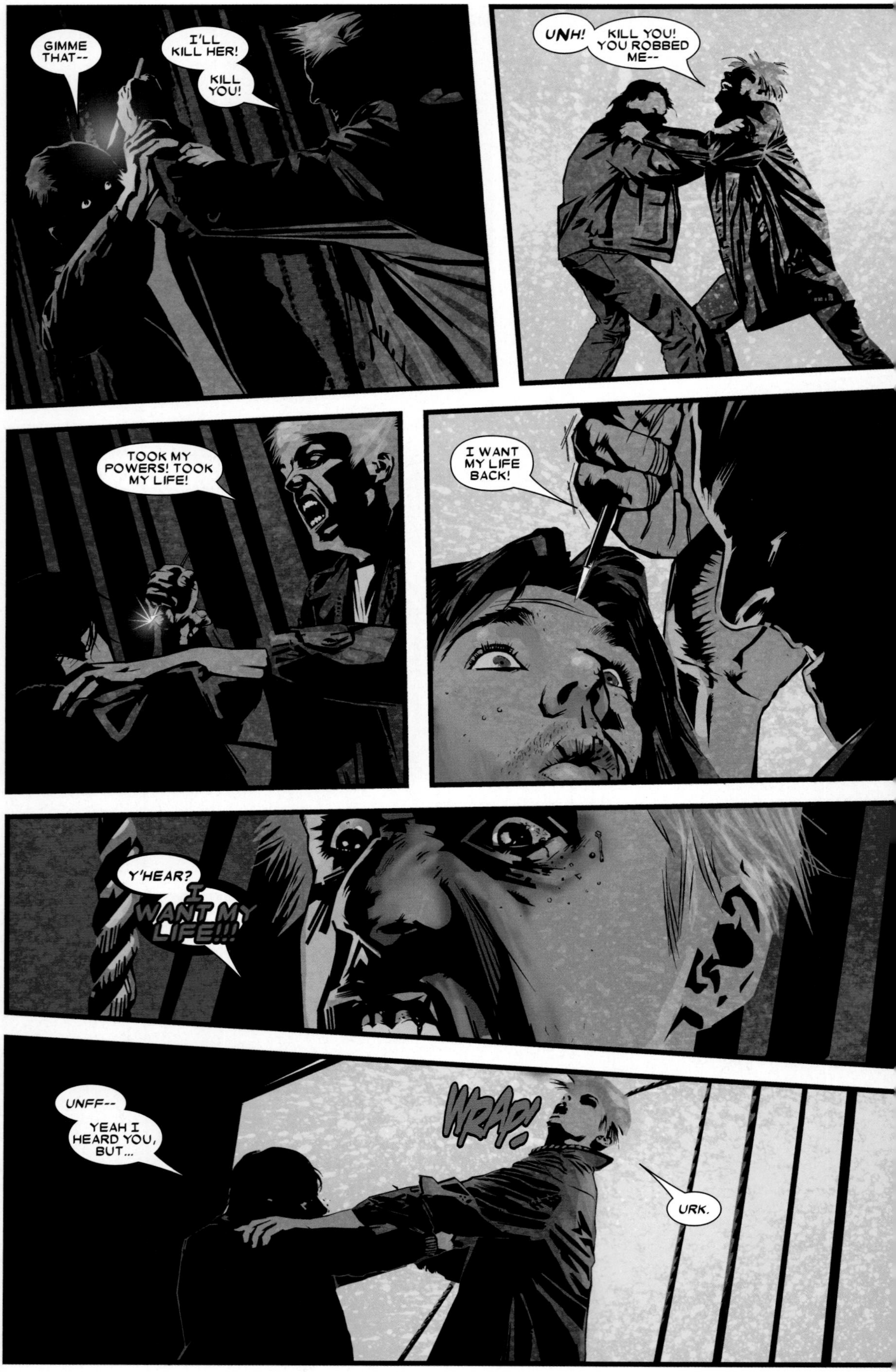
GIMME THAT--
I'LL KILL HER!
KILL YOU!
UNH!
KILL YOU! YOU ROBBED ME--
TOOK MY POWERS! TOOK MY LIFE!
I WANT MY LIFE BACK!
Y'HEAR? I WANT MY LIFE!!!
UNFF--
YEAH I HEARD YOU, BUT...
WRAP!
URK.

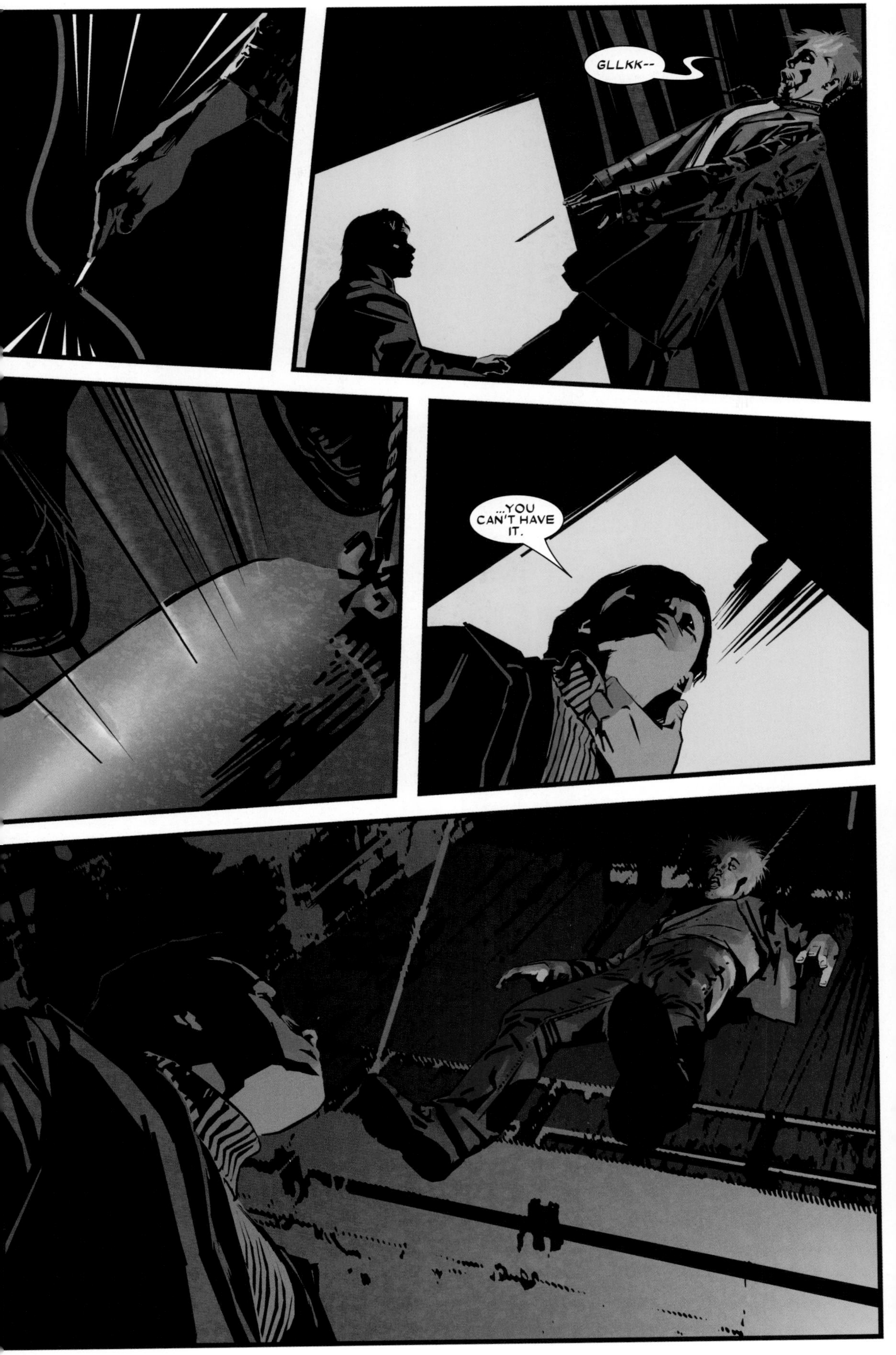
GLLKK--
...YOU CAN'T HAVE IT.

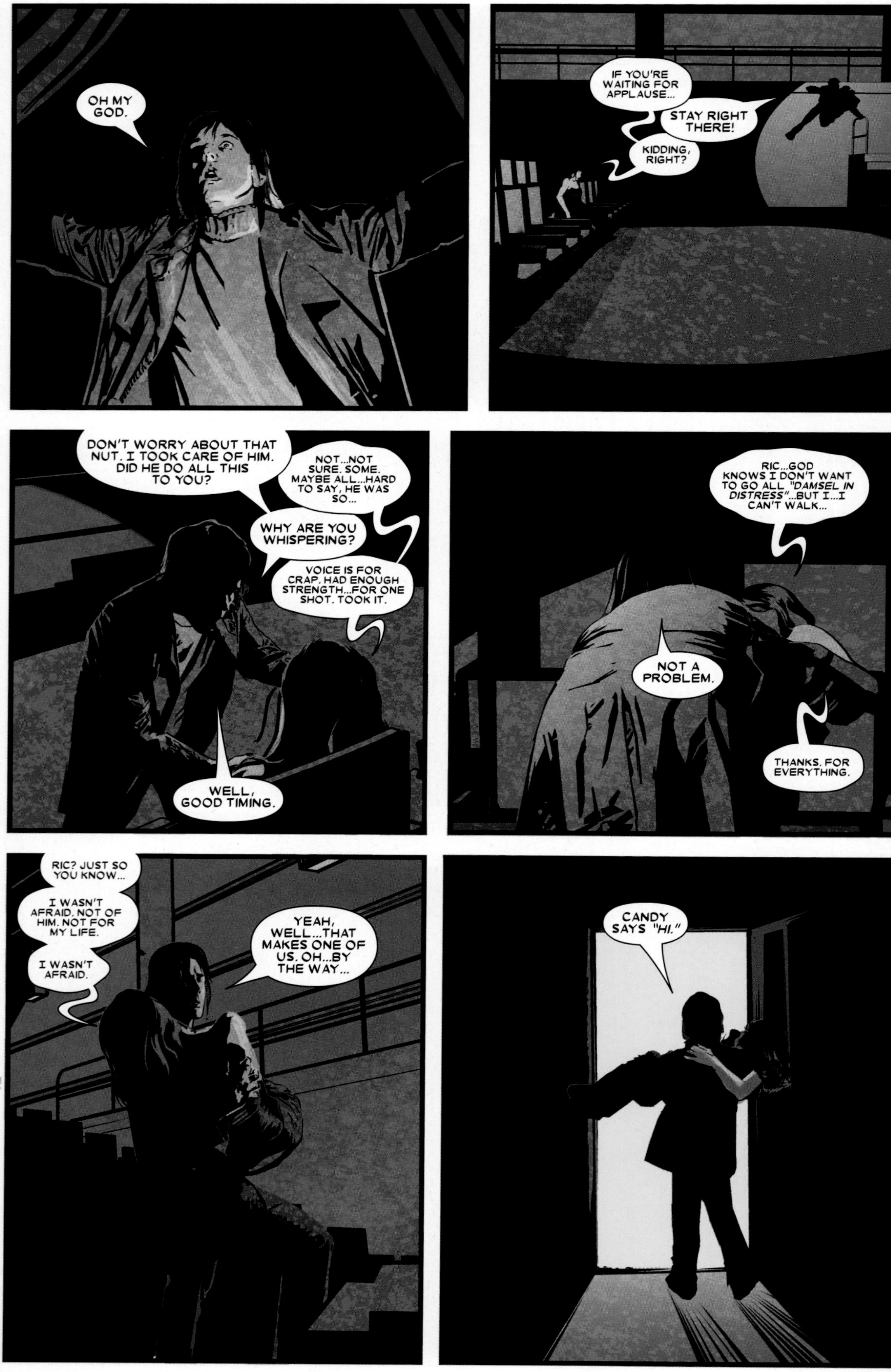
OH MY GOD.
IF YOU'RE WAITING FOR APPLAUSE...
STAY RIGHT THERE!
KIDDING, RIGHT?
DON'T WORRY ABOUT THAT NUT. I TOOK CARE OF HIM. DID HE DO ALL THIS TO YOU?
NOT...NOT SURE. SOME. MAYBE ALL...HARD TO SAY, HE WAS SO...
WHY ARE YOU WHISPERING?
VOICE IS FOR CRAP. HAD ENOUGH STRENGTH...FOR ONE SHOT. TOOK IT.
WELL, GOOD TIMING.
RIC...GOD KNOWS I DON'T WANT TO GO ALL "DAMSEL IN DISTRESS"...BUT I...I CAN'T WALK...
NOT A PROBLEM.
THANKS. FOR EVERYTHING.
RIC? JUST SO YOU KNOW...
I WASN'T AFRAID. NOT OF HIM. NOT FOR MY LIFE.
I WASN'T AFRAID.
YEAH, WELL...THAT MAKES ONE OF US. OH...BY THE WAY...
CANDY SAYS "HI."

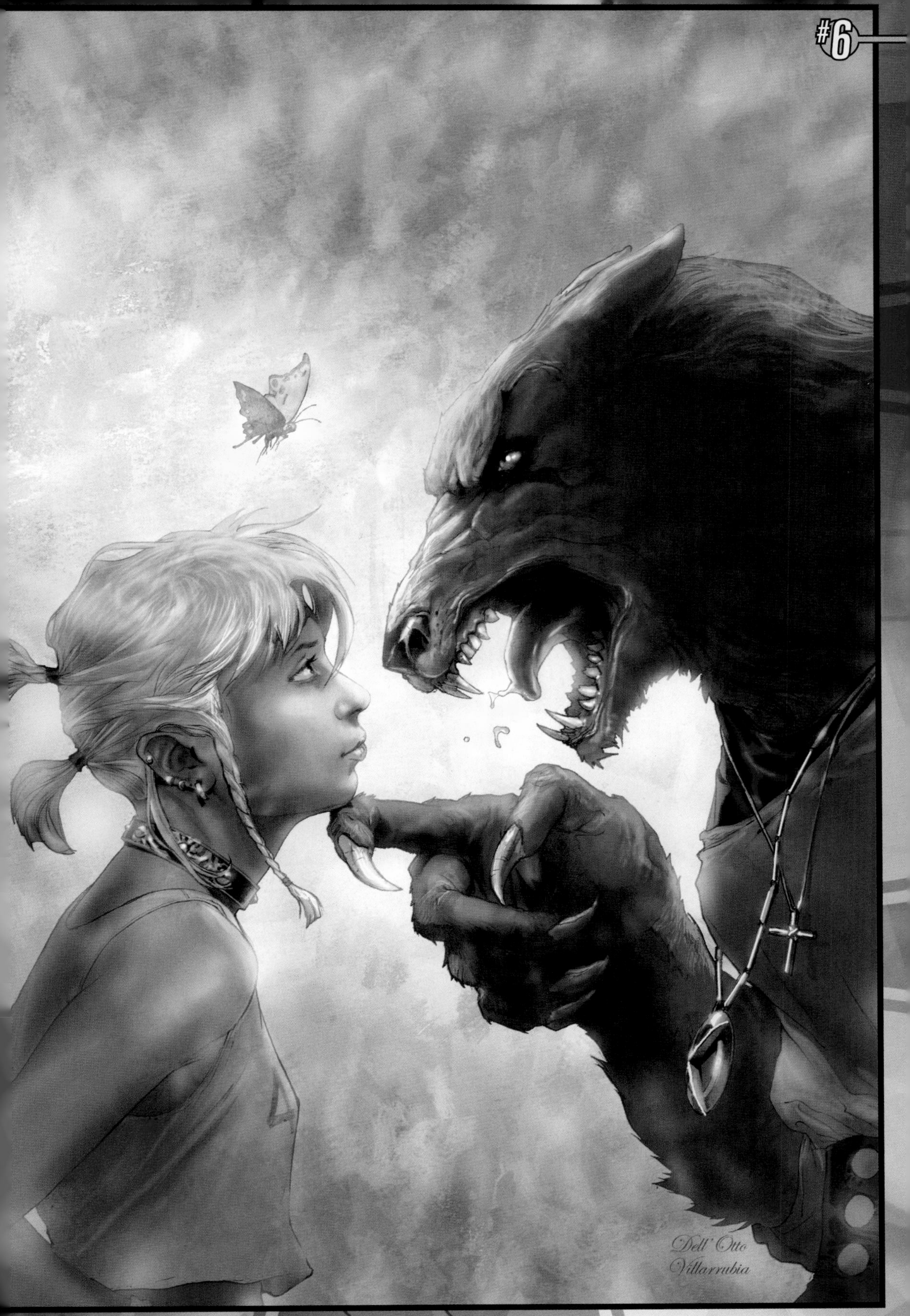
#6
Dell' Otto
Villarrubia

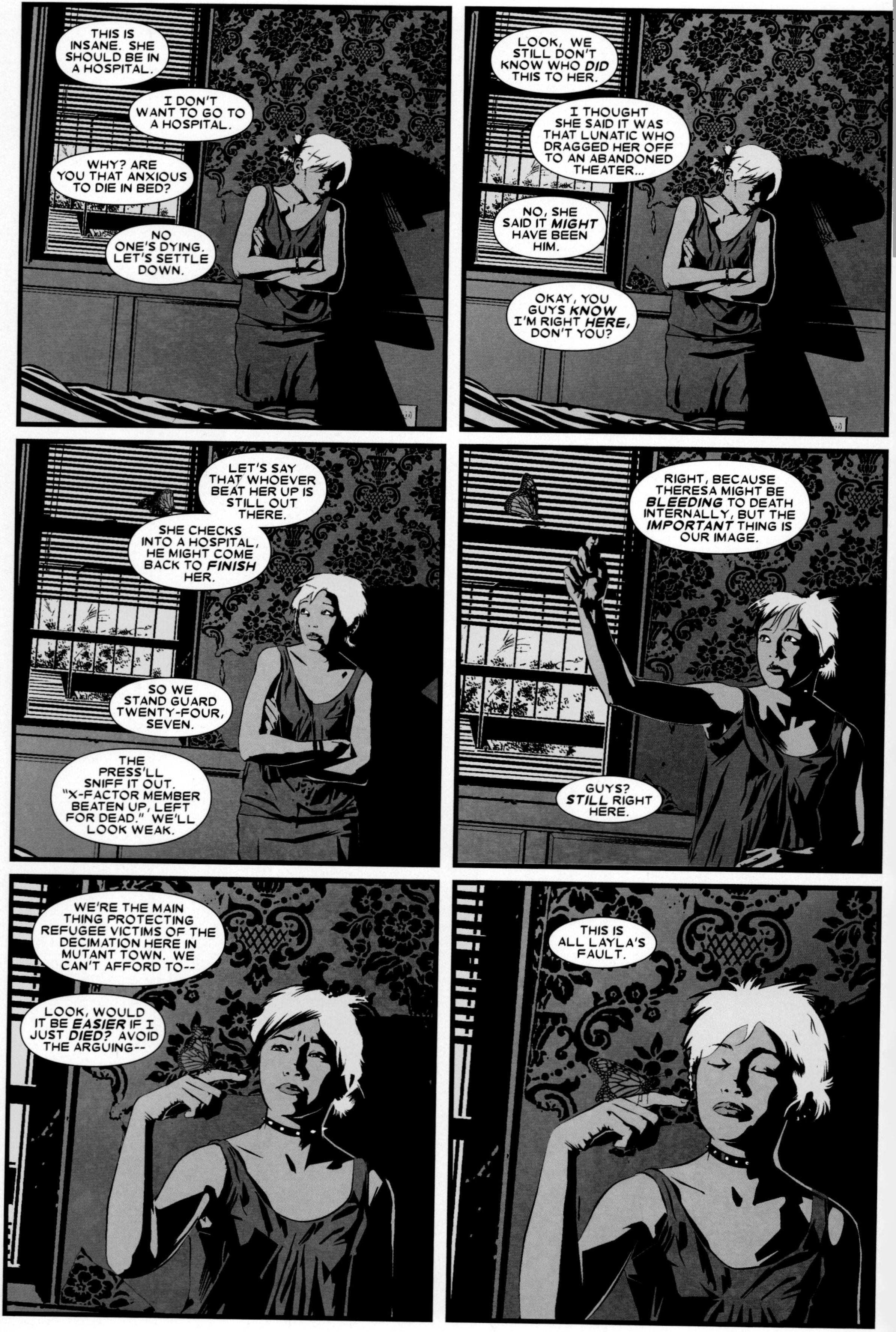
THIS IS INSANE. SHE SHOULD BE IN A HOSPITAL.
I DON'T WANT TO GO TO A HOSPITAL.
WHY? ARE YOU THAT ANXIOUS TO DIE IN BED?
NO ONE'S DYING. LET'S SETTLE DOWN.
LOOK, WE STILL DON'T KNOW WHO DID THIS TO HER.
I THOUGHT SHE SAID IT WAS THAT LUNATIC WHO DRAGGED HER OFF TO AN ABANDONED THEATER...
NO, SHE SAID IT MIGHT HAVE BEEN HIM.
OKAY, YOU GUYS KNOW I'M RIGHT HERE, DON'T YOU?
LET'S SAY THAT WHOEVER BEAT HER UP IS STILL OUT THERE.
SHE CHECKS INTO A HOSPITAL, HE MIGHT COME BACK TO FINISH HER.
SO WE STAND GUARD TWENTY-FOUR, SEVEN.
THE PRESS'LL SNIFF IT OUT. "X-FACTOR MEMBER BEATEN UP, LEFT FOR DEAD." WE'LL LOOK WEAK.
RIGHT, BECAUSE THERESA MIGHT BE BLEEDING TO DEATH INTERNALLY, BUT THE IMPORTANT THING IS OUR IMAGE.
GUYS? STILL RIGHT HERE.
WE'RE THE MAIN THING PROTECTING REFUGEE VICTIMS OF THE DECIMATION HERE IN MUTANT TOWN. WE CAN'T AFFORD TO--
LOOK, WOULD IT BE EASIER IF I JUST DIED? AVOID THE ARGUING--
THIS IS ALL LAYLA'S FAULT.

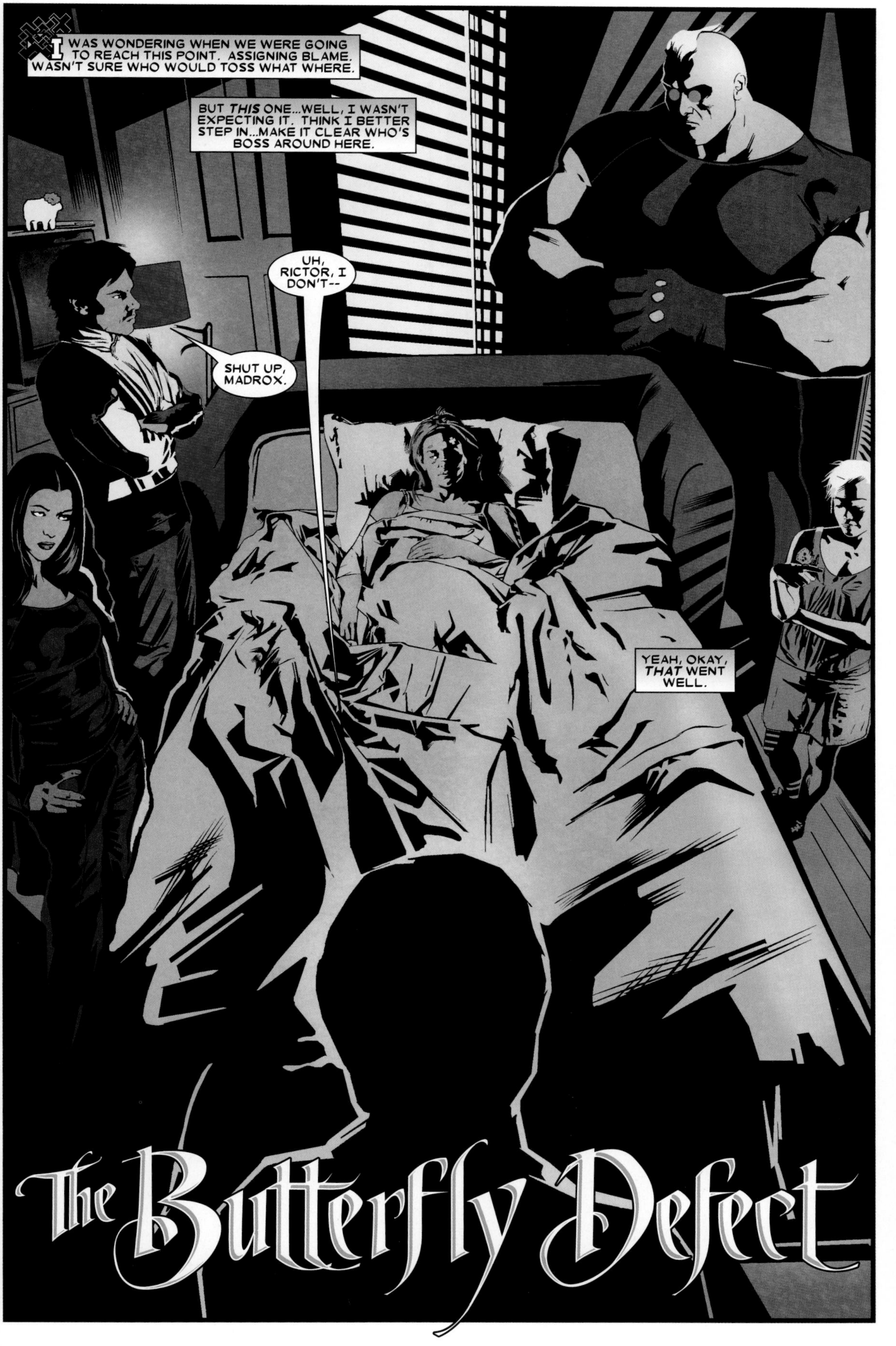
I WAS WONDERING WHEN WE WERE GOING TO REACH THIS POINT. ASSIGNING BLAME. WASN'T SURE WHO WOULD TOSS WHAT WHERE.
BUT THIS ONE...WELL, I WASN'T EXPECTING IT. THINK I BETTER STEP IN...MAKE IT CLEAR WHO'S BOSS AROUND HERE.
UH, RICTOR, I DON'T--
SHUT UP, MADROX.
YEAH, OKAY, THAT WENT WELL.
The Butterfly Defect

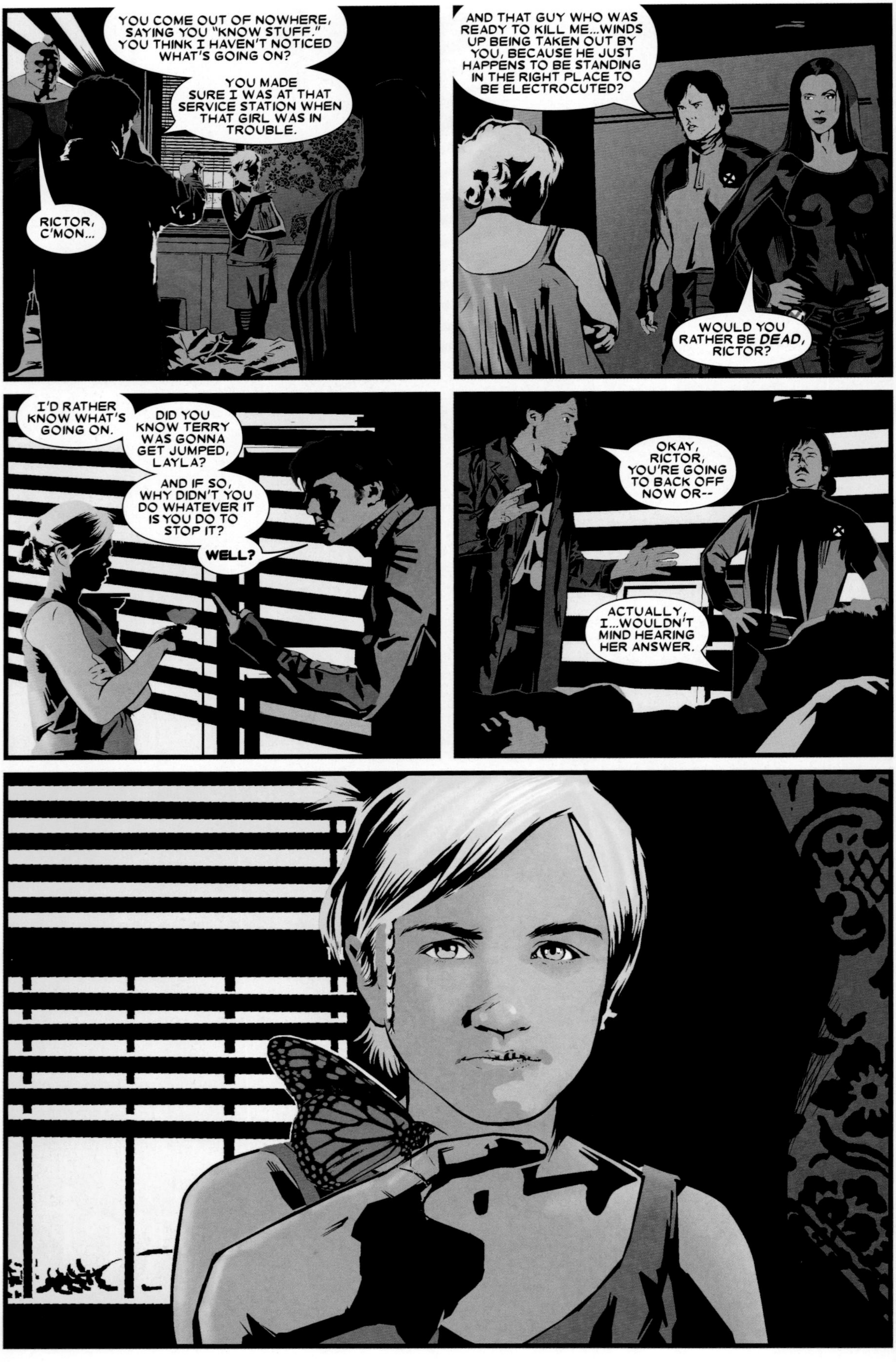

YOU COME OUT OF NOWHERE, SAYING YOU "KNOW STUFF." YOU THINK I HAVEN'T NOTICED WHAT'S GOING ON?
YOU MADE SURE I WAS AT THAT SERVICE STATION WHEN THAT GIRL WAS IN TROUBLE.
RICTOR, C'MON...
AND THAT GUY WHO WAS READY TO KILL ME...WINDS UP BEING TAKEN OUT BY YOU, BECAUSE HE JUST HAPPENS TO BE STANDING IN THE RIGHT PLACE TO BE ELECTROCUTED?
WOULD YOU RATHER BE *DEAD*, RICTOR?
I'D RATHER KNOW WHAT'S GOING ON.
DID YOU KNOW TERRY WAS GONNA GET JUMPED, LAYLA?
AND IF SO, WHY DIDN'T YOU DO WHATEVER IT IS YOU DO TO STOP IT?
WELL?
OKAY, RICTOR, YOU'RE GOING TO BACK OFF NOW OR--
ACTUALLY, I...WOULDN'T MIND HEARING HER ANSWER.

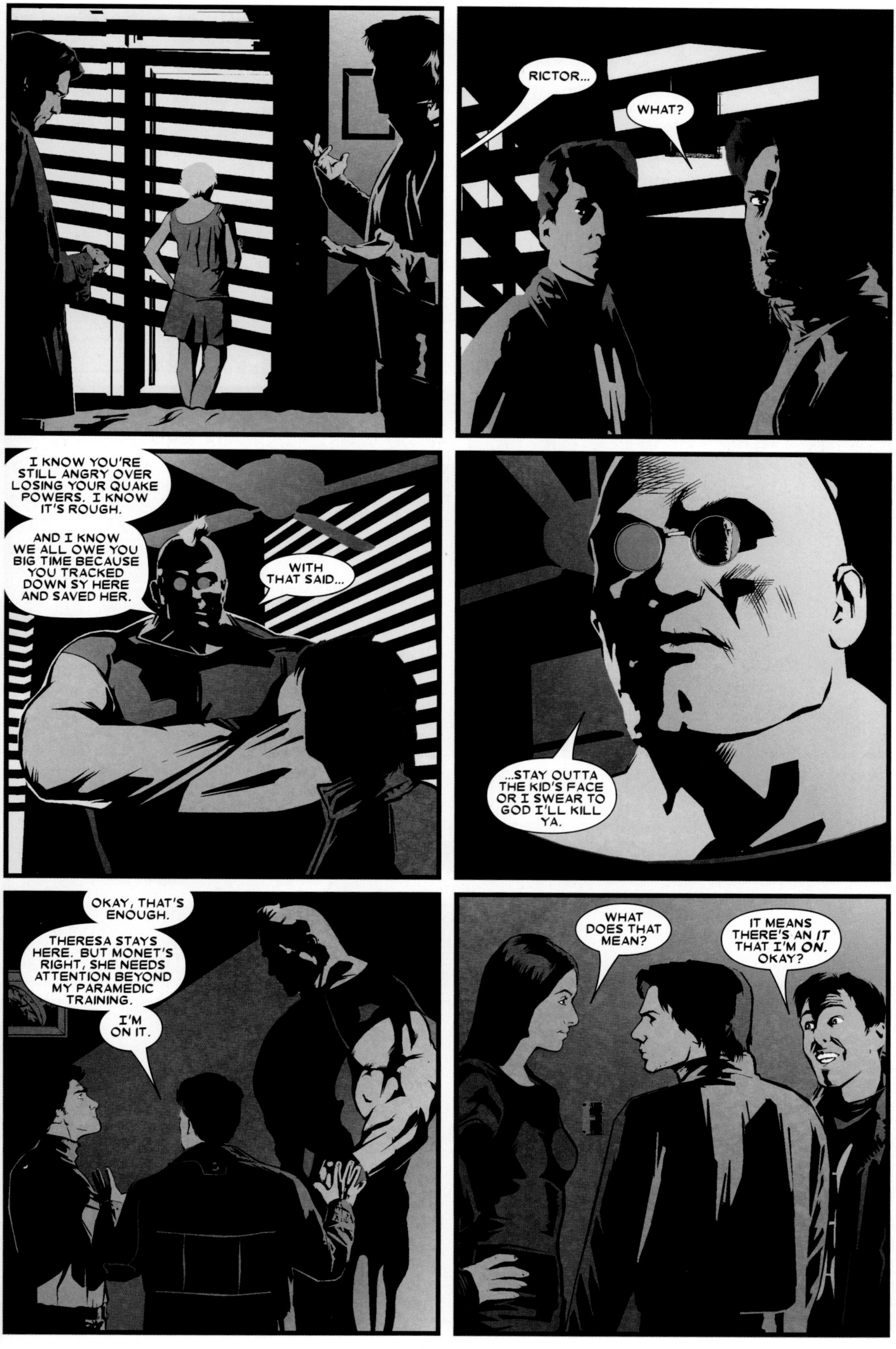
RICTOR...
WHAT?
I KNOW YOU'RE STILL ANGRY OVER LOSING YOUR QUAKE POWERS. I KNOW IT'S ROUGH.
AND I KNOW WE ALL OWE YOU BIG TIME BECAUSE YOU TRACKED DOWN SY HERE AND SAVED HER.
WITH THAT SAID...
...STAY OUTTA THE KID'S FACE OR I SWEAR TO GOD I'LL KILL YA.
OKAY, THAT'S ENOUGH.
THERESA STAYS HERE. BUT MONET'S RIGHT, SHE NEEDS ATTENTION BEYOND MY PARAMEDIC TRAINING.
I'M ON IT.
WHAT DOES THAT MEAN?
IT MEANS THERE'S AN *IT* THAT I'M *ON*. OKAY?

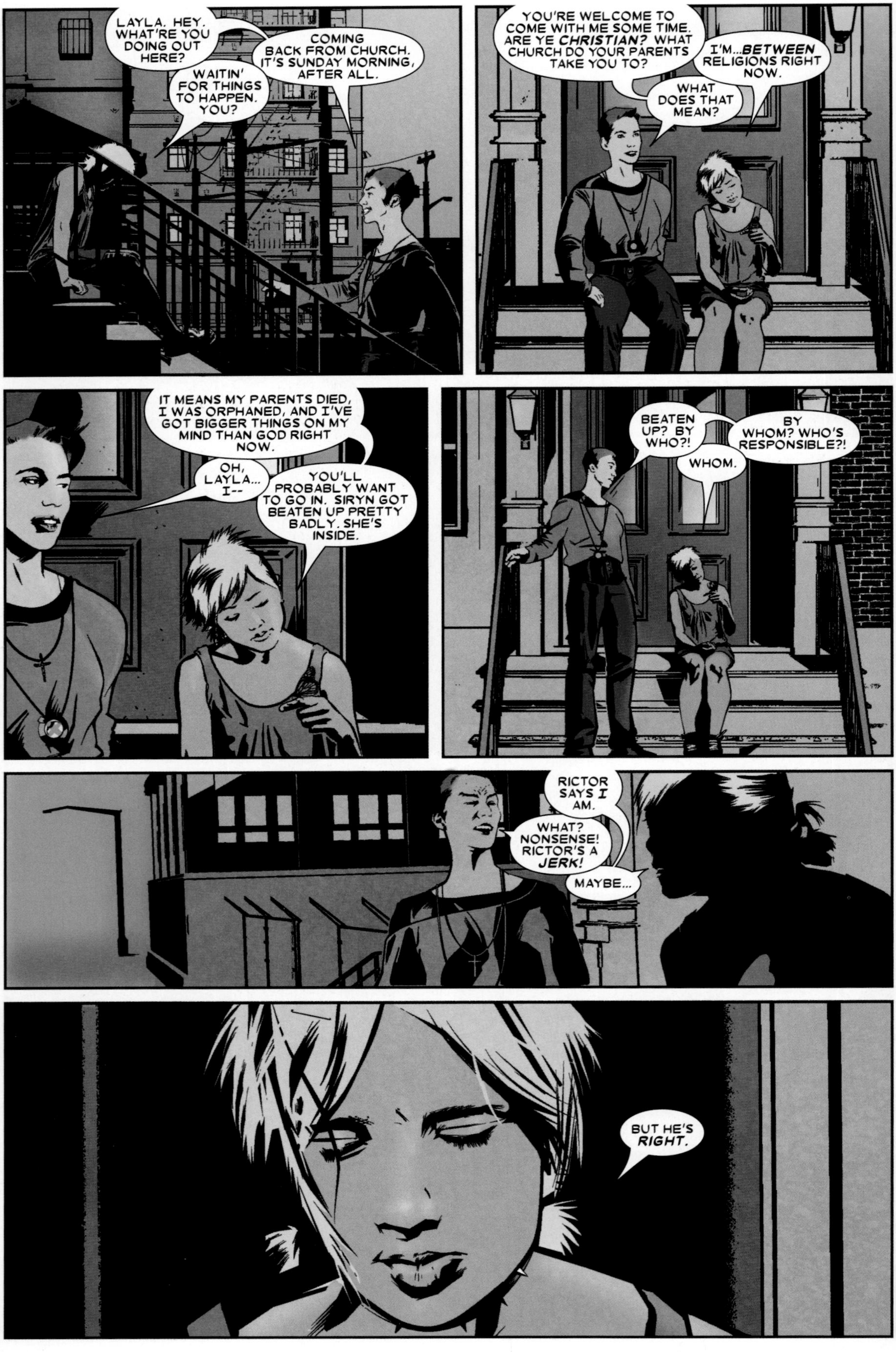
LAYLA. HEY. WHAT'RE YOU DOING OUT HERE?
WAITIN' FOR THINGS TO HAPPEN. YOU?
COMING BACK FROM CHURCH. IT'S SUNDAY MORNING, AFTER ALL.
YOU'RE WELCOME TO COME WITH ME SOME TIME. ARE YE CHRISTIAN? WHAT CHURCH DO YOUR PARENTS TAKE YOU TO?
I'M...BETWEEN RELIGIONS RIGHT NOW.
WHAT DOES THAT MEAN?
IT MEANS MY PARENTS DIED, I WAS ORPHANED, AND I'VE GOT BIGGER THINGS ON MY MIND THAN GOD RIGHT NOW.
OH, LAYLA... I--
YOU'LL PROBABLY WANT TO GO IN. SIRYN GOT BEATEN UP PRETTY BADLY. SHE'S INSIDE.
BEATEN UP? BY WHO?!
WHOM.
BY WHOM? WHO'S RESPONSIBLE?!
RICTOR SAYS I AM.
WHAT? NONSENSE! RICTOR'S A JERK!
MAYBE...
BUT HE'S RIGHT.

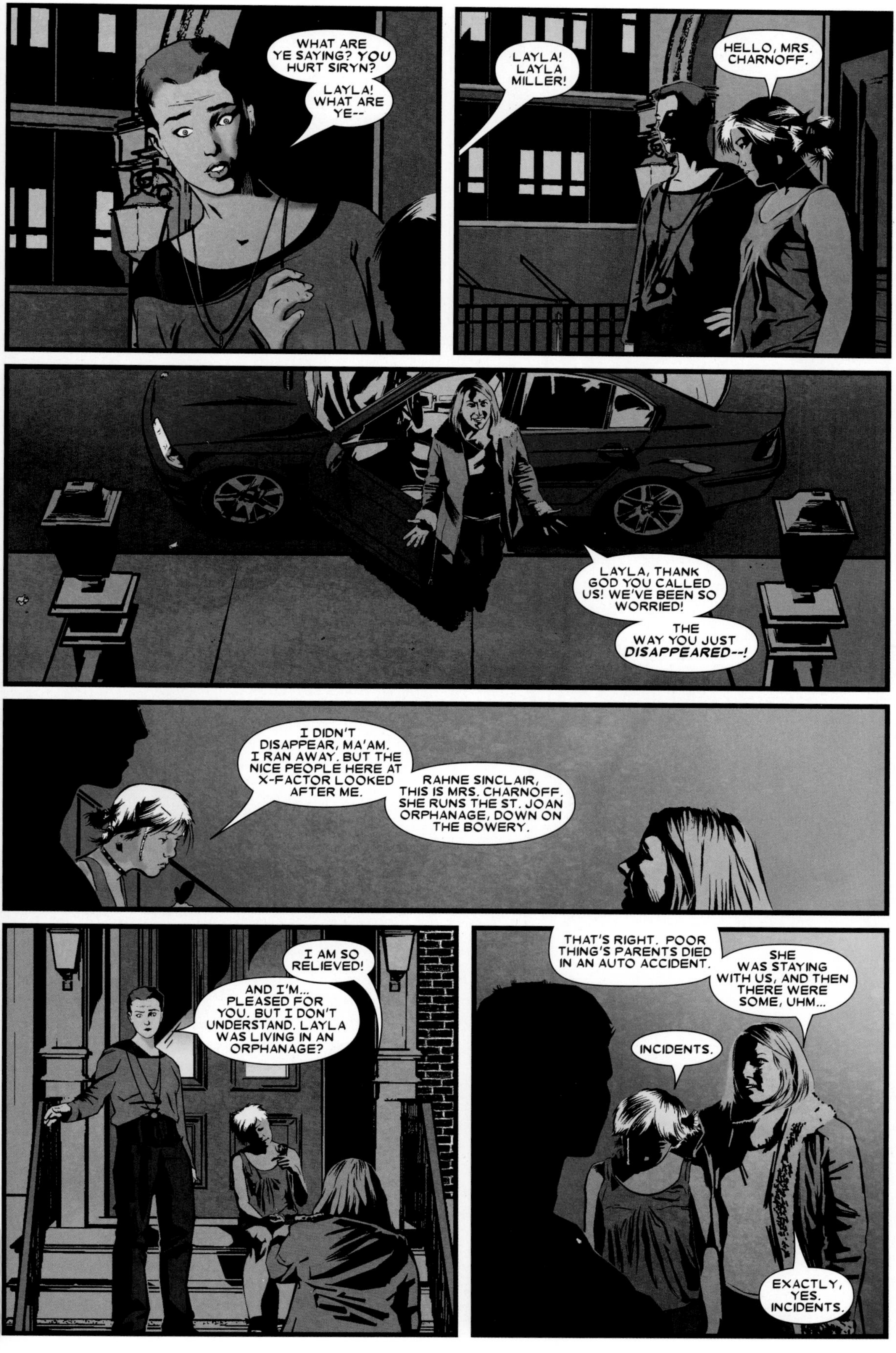
WHAT ARE YE SAYING? YOU HURT SIRYN?
LAYLA! WHAT ARE YE--
LAYLA! LAYLA MILLER!
HELLO, MRS. CHARNOFF.
LAYLA, THANK GOD YOU CALLED US! WE'VE BEEN SO WORRIED!
THE WAY YOU JUST DISAPPEARED--!
I DIDN'T DISAPPEAR, MA'AM. I RAN AWAY. BUT THE NICE PEOPLE HERE AT X-FACTOR LOOKED AFTER ME.
RAHNE SINCLAIR, THIS IS MRS. CHARNOFF. SHE RUNS THE ST. JOAN ORPHANAGE, DOWN ON THE BOWERY.
I AM SO RELIEVED!
AND I'M... PLEASED FOR YOU. BUT I DON'T UNDERSTAND. LAYLA WAS LIVING IN AN ORPHANAGE?
THAT'S RIGHT. POOR THING'S PARENTS DIED IN AN AUTO ACCIDENT.
SHE WAS STAYING WITH US, AND THEN THERE WERE SOME, UHM...
INCIDENTS.
EXACTLY, YES. INCIDENTS.

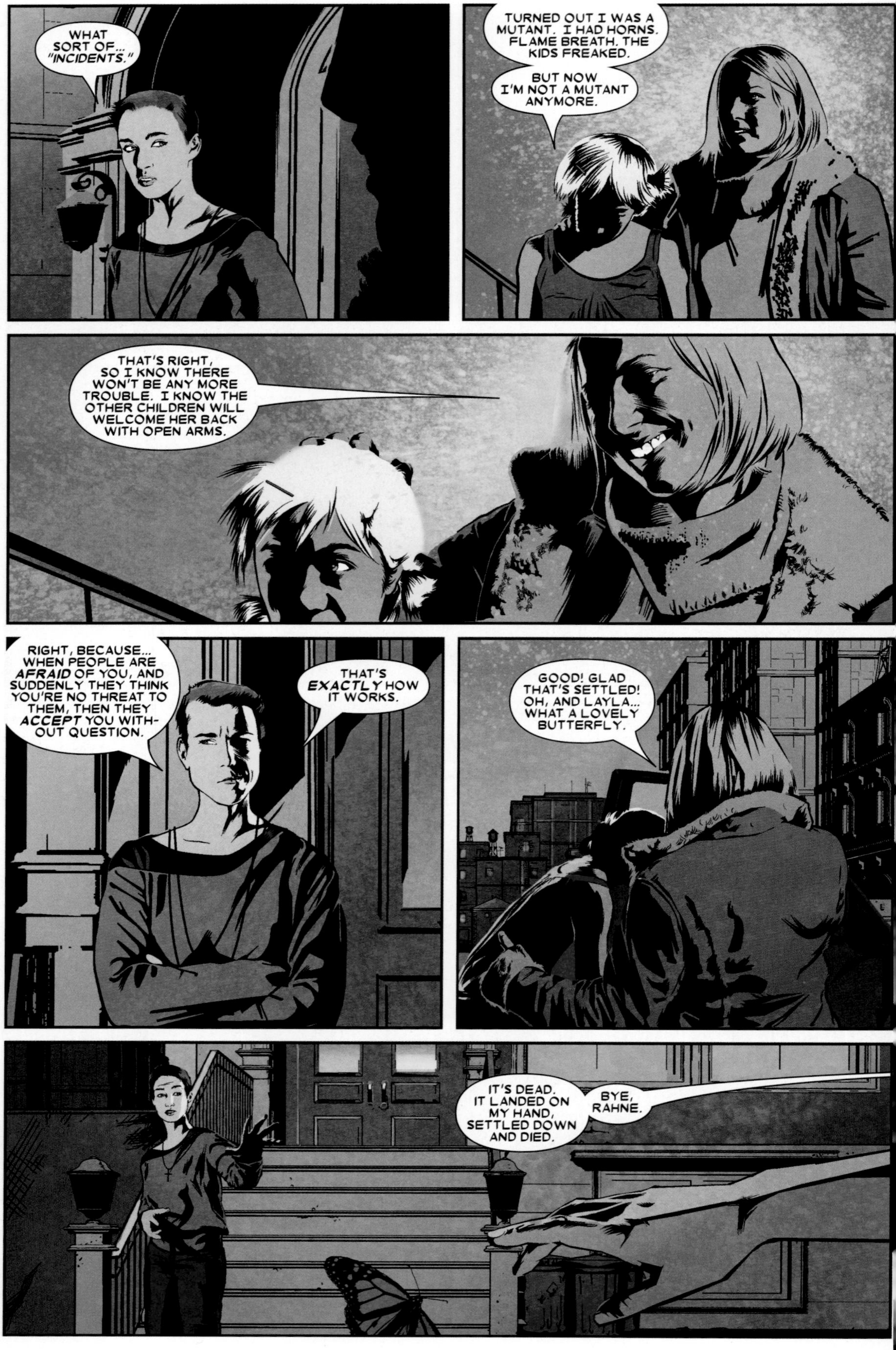
WHAT SORT OF... "INCIDENTS."
TURNED OUT I WAS A MUTANT. I HAD HORNS. FLAME BREATH. THE KIDS FREAKED.
BUT NOW I'M NOT A MUTANT ANYMORE.
THAT'S RIGHT, SO I KNOW THERE WON'T BE ANY MORE TROUBLE. I KNOW THE OTHER CHILDREN WILL WELCOME HER BACK WITH OPEN ARMS.
RIGHT, BECAUSE... WHEN PEOPLE ARE AFRAID OF YOU, AND SUDDENLY THEY THINK YOU'RE NO THREAT TO THEM, THEN THEY ACCEPT YOU WITHOUT QUESTION.
THAT'S EXACTLY HOW IT WORKS.
GOOD! GLAD THAT'S SETTLED! OH, AND LAYLA... WHAT A LOVELY BUTTERFLY.
IT'S DEAD. IT LANDED ON MY HAND, SETTLED DOWN AND DIED.
BYE, RAHNE.

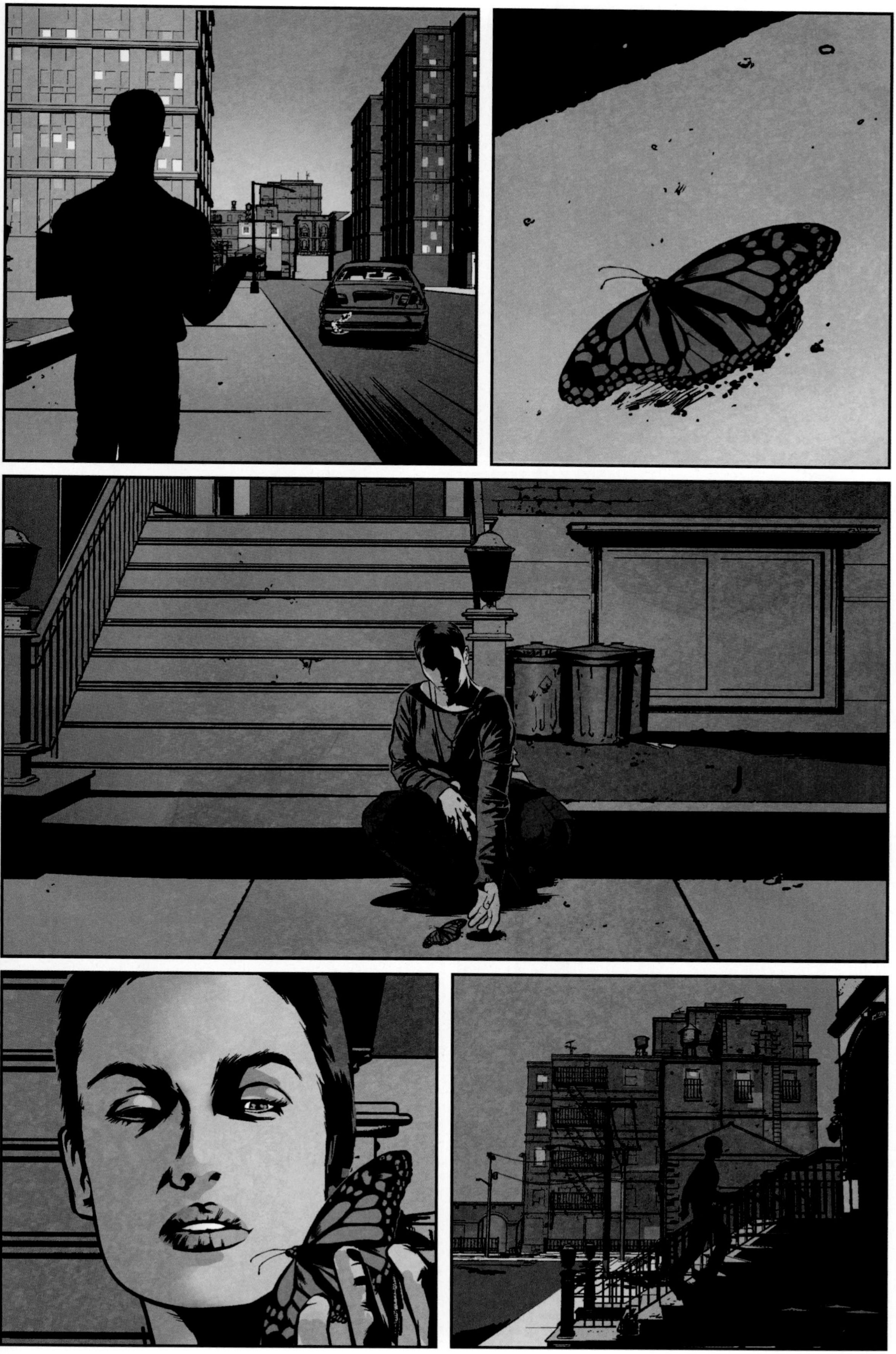

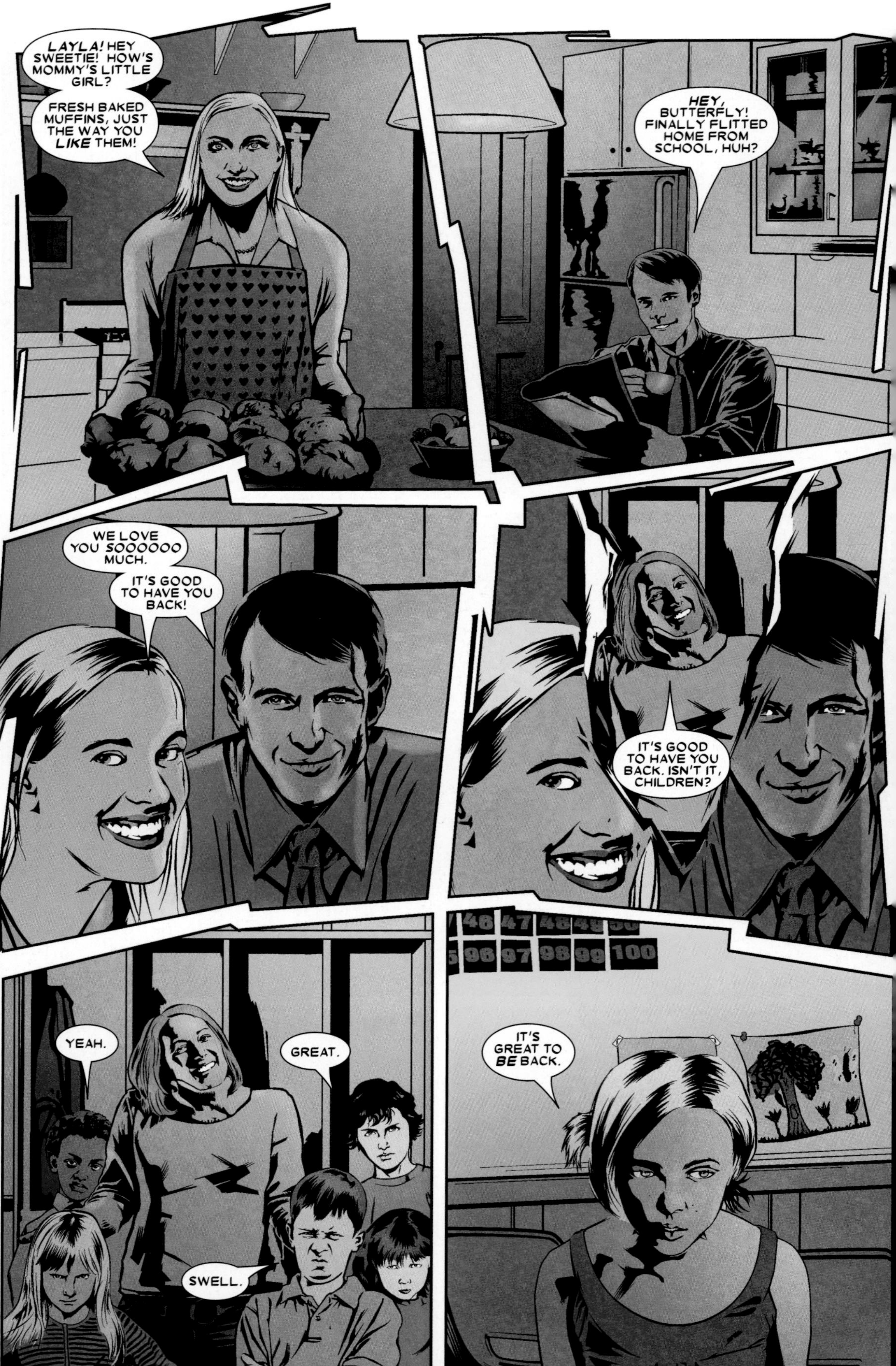
LAYLA! HEY SWEETIE! HOW'S MOMMY'S LITTLE GIRL?
FRESH BAKED MUFFINS, JUST THE WAY YOU LIKE THEM!
HEY, BUTTERFLY! FINALLY FLITTED HOME FROM SCHOOL, HUH?
WE LOVE YOU SOOOOOO MUCH.
IT'S GOOD TO HAVE YOU BACK!
IT'S GOOD TO HAVE YOU BACK. ISN'T IT, CHILDREN?
YEAH.
GREAT.
SWELL.
IT'S GREAT TO BE BACK.

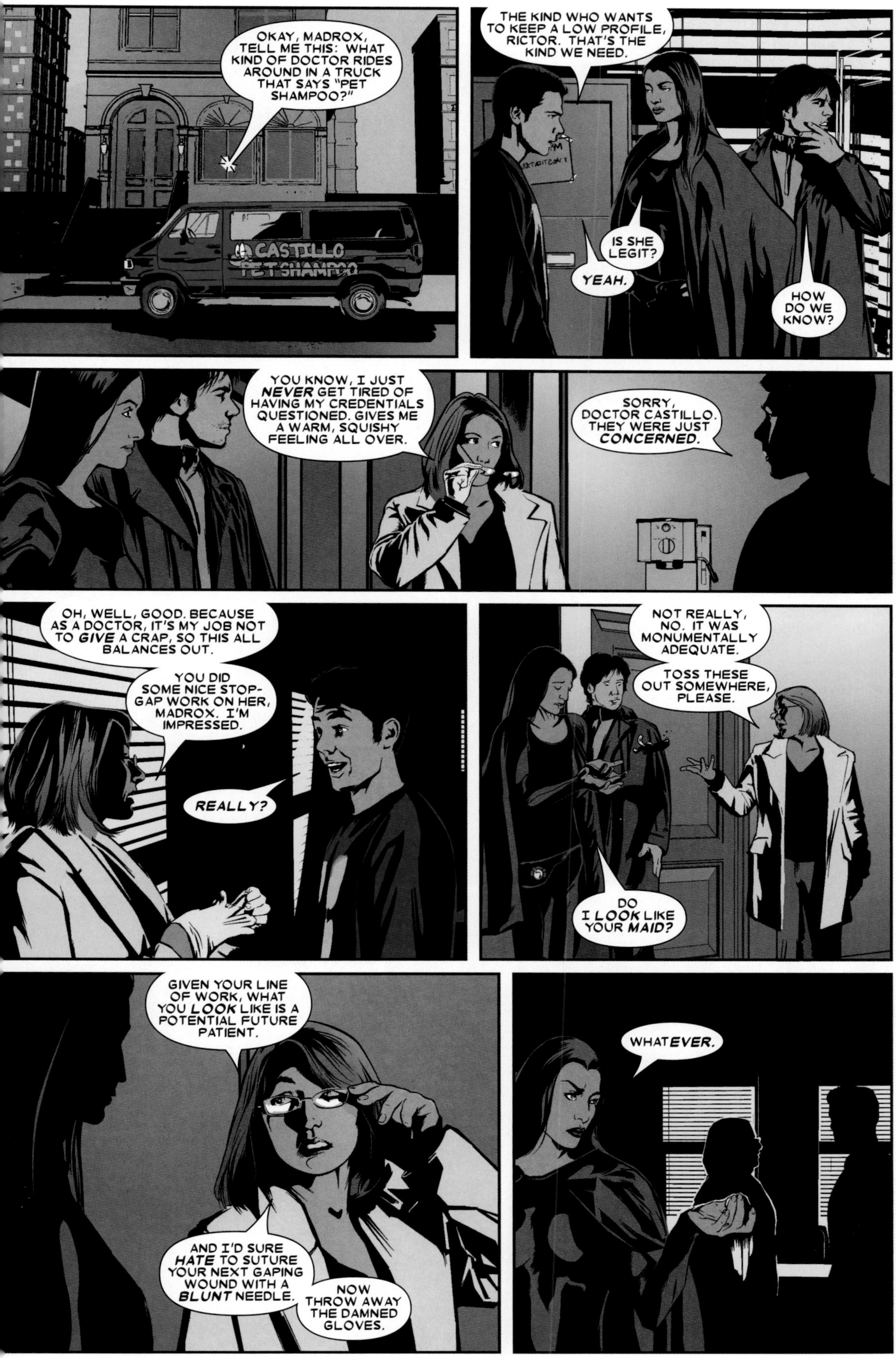
OKAY, MADROX, TELL ME THIS: WHAT KIND OF DOCTOR RIDES AROUND IN A TRUCK THAT SAYS "PET SHAMPOO?"
CASTILLO PET SHAMPOO
THE KIND WHO WANTS TO KEEP A LOW PROFILE, RICTOR. THAT'S THE KIND WE NEED.
IS SHE LEGIT?
YEAH.
HOW DO WE KNOW?
YOU KNOW, I JUST NEVER GET TIRED OF HAVING MY CREDENTIALS QUESTIONED. GIVES ME A WARM, SQUISHY FEELING ALL OVER.
SORRY, DOCTOR CASTILLO. THEY WERE JUST CONCERNED.
OH, WELL, GOOD. BECAUSE AS A DOCTOR, IT'S MY JOB NOT TO GIVE A CRAP, SO THIS ALL BALANCES OUT.
YOU DID SOME NICE STOP-GAP WORK ON HER, MADROX. I'M IMPRESSED.
REALLY?
NOT REALLY, NO. IT WAS MONUMENTALLY ADEQUATE.
TOSS THESE OUT SOMEWHERE, PLEASE.
DO I LOOK LIKE YOUR MAID?
GIVEN YOUR LINE OF WORK, WHAT YOU LOOK LIKE IS A POTENTIAL FUTURE PATIENT.
AND I'D SURE HATE TO SUTURE YOUR NEXT GAPING WOUND WITH A BLUNT NEEDLE.
NOW THROW AWAY THE DAMNED GLOVES.
WHATEVER.

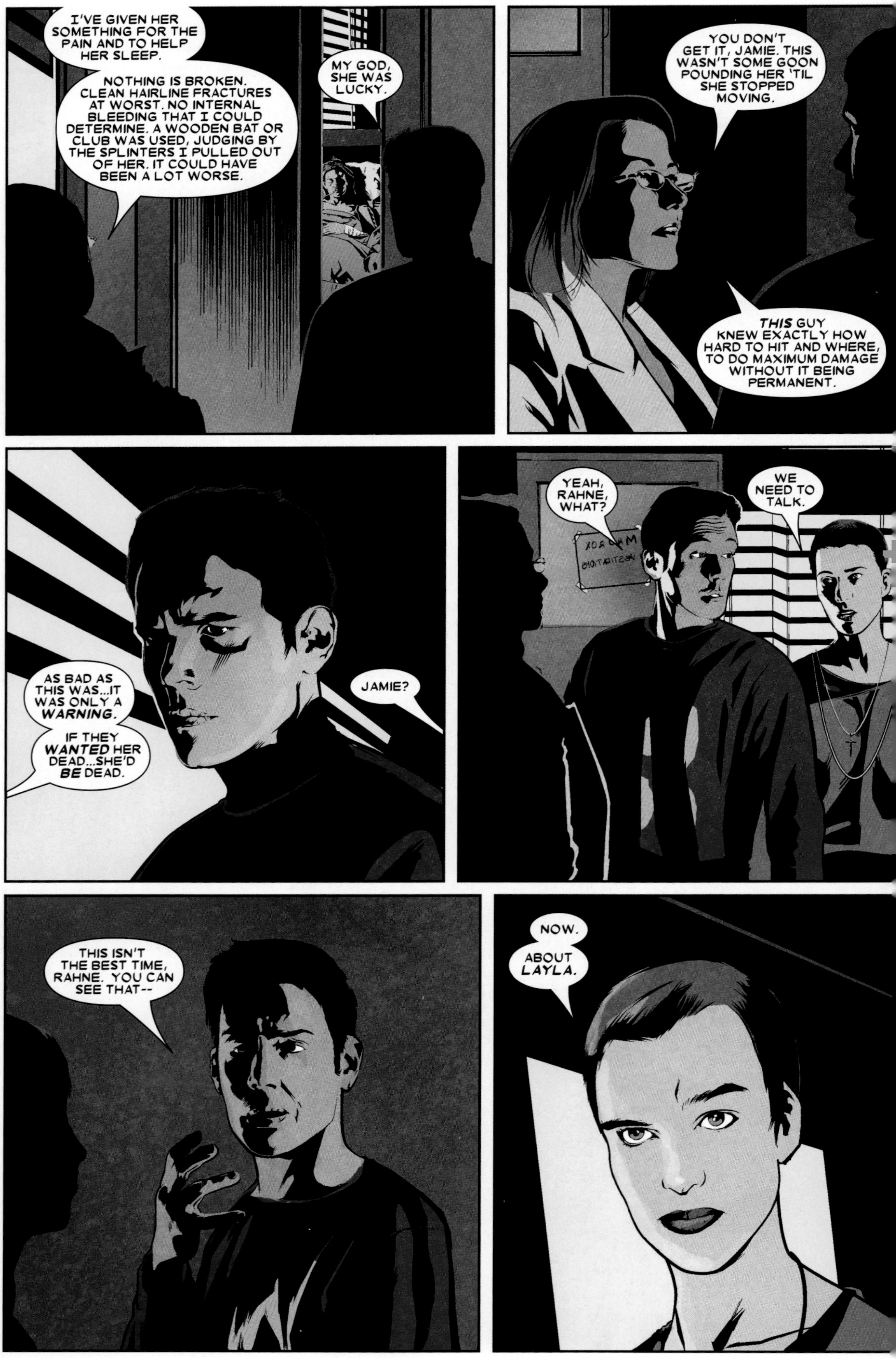
I'VE GIVEN HER SOMETHING FOR THE PAIN AND TO HELP HER SLEEP.
NOTHING IS BROKEN. CLEAN HAIRLINE FRACTURES AT WORST. NO INTERNAL BLEEDING THAT I COULD DETERMINE. A WOODEN BAT OR CLUB WAS USED, JUDGING BY THE SPLINTERS I PULLED OUT OF HER. IT COULD HAVE BEEN A LOT WORSE.
MY GOD, SHE WAS LUCKY.
YOU DON'T GET IT, JAMIE. THIS WASN'T SOME GOON POUNDING HER 'TIL SHE STOPPED MOVING.
THIS GUY KNEW EXACTLY HOW HARD TO HIT AND WHERE, TO DO MAXIMUM DAMAGE WITHOUT IT BEING PERMANENT.
AS BAD AS THIS WAS...IT WAS ONLY A WARNING.
IF THEY WANTED HER DEAD...SHE'D BE DEAD.
JAMIE?
YEAH, RAHNE, WHAT?
WE NEED TO TALK.
THIS ISN'T THE BEST TIME, RAHNE. YOU CAN SEE THAT--
NOW.
ABOUT LAYLA.

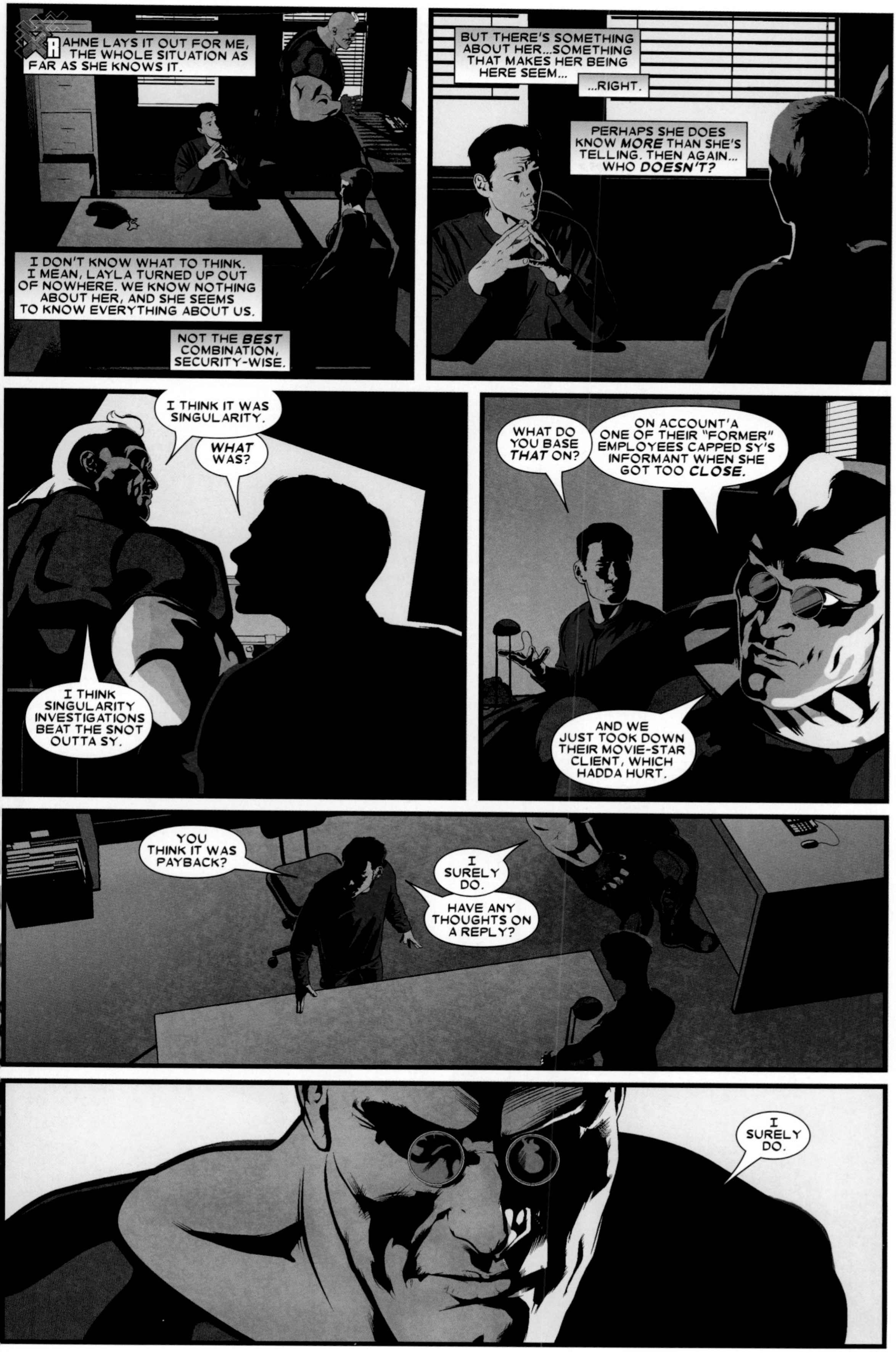
RAHNE LAYS IT OUT FOR ME, THE WHOLE SITUATION AS FAR AS SHE KNOWS IT.
I DON'T KNOW WHAT TO THINK. I MEAN, LAYLA TURNED UP OUT OF NOWHERE. WE KNOW NOTHING ABOUT HER, AND SHE SEEMS TO KNOW EVERYTHING ABOUT US.
NOT THE BEST COMBINATION, SECURITY-WISE.
BUT THERE'S SOMETHING ABOUT HER...SOMETHING THAT MAKES HER BEING HERE SEEM...
...RIGHT.
PERHAPS SHE DOES KNOW MORE THAN SHE'S TELLING. THEN AGAIN... WHO DOESN'T?
I THINK IT WAS SINGULARITY.
WHAT WAS?
I THINK SINGULARITY INVESTIGATIONS BEAT THE SNOT OUTTA SY.
WHAT DO YOU BASE THAT ON?
ON ACCOUNT'A ONE OF THEIR "FORMER" EMPLOYEES CAPPED SY'S INFORMANT WHEN SHE GOT TOO CLOSE.
AND WE JUST TOOK DOWN THEIR MOVIE-STAR CLIENT, WHICH HADDA HURT.
YOU THINK IT WAS PAYBACK?
I SURELY DO.
HAVE ANY THOUGHTS ON A REPLY?
I SURELY DO.

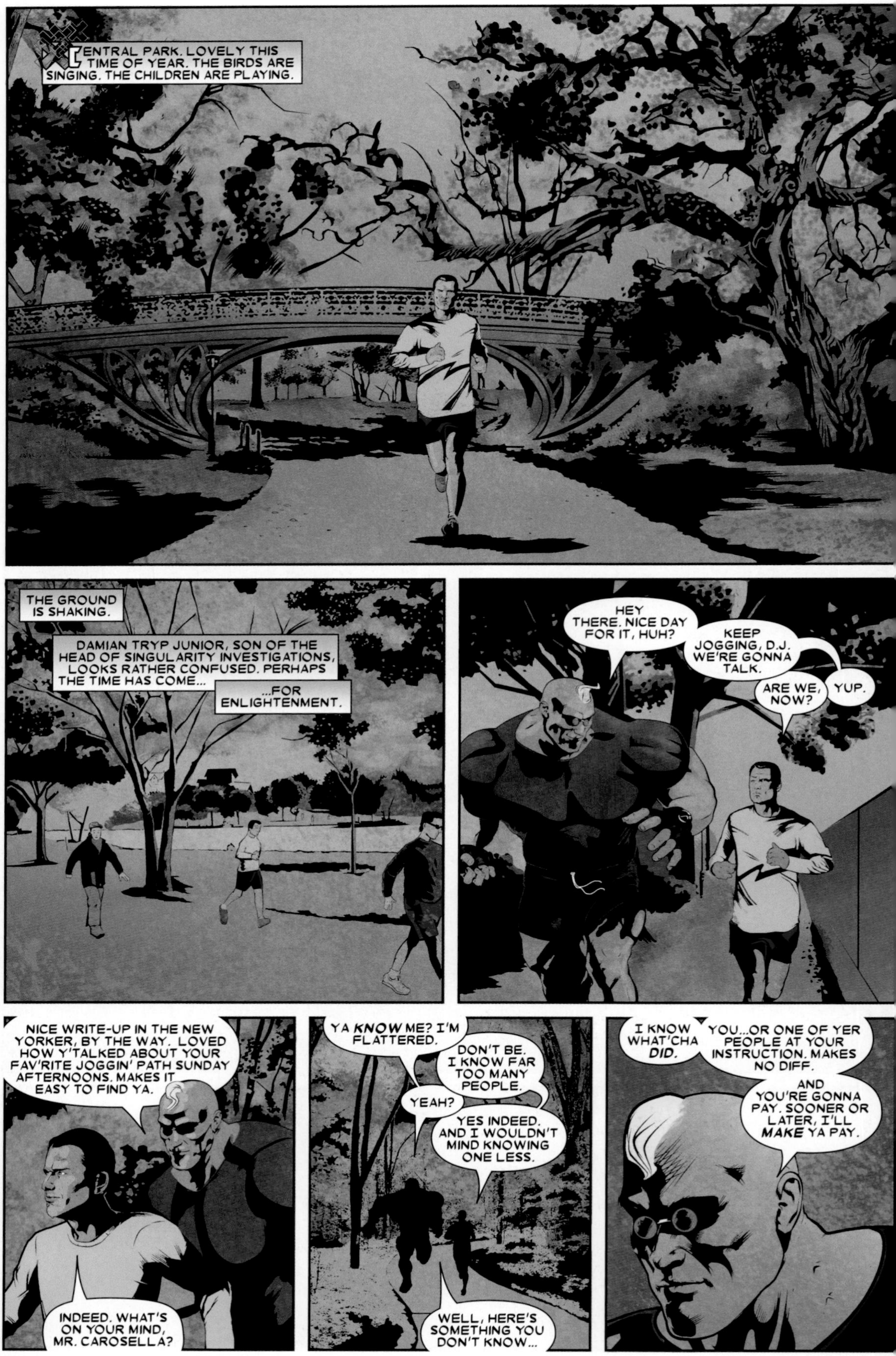
CENTRAL PARK. LOVELY THIS TIME OF YEAR. THE BIRDS ARE SINGING. THE CHILDREN ARE PLAYING.
THE GROUND IS SHAKING.
DAMIAN TRYP JUNIOR, SON OF THE HEAD OF SINGULARITY INVESTIGATIONS, LOOKS RATHER CONFUSED. PERHAPS THE TIME HAS COME...
...FOR ENLIGHTENMENT.
HEY THERE. NICE DAY FOR IT, HUH?
KEEP JOGGING, D.J. WE'RE GONNA TALK.
ARE WE, NOW?
YUP.
NICE WRITE-UP IN THE NEW YORKER, BY THE WAY. LOVED HOW Y'TALKED ABOUT YOUR FAV'RITE JOGGIN' PATH SUNDAY AFTERNOONS. MAKES IT EASY TO FIND YA.
INDEED. WHAT'S ON YOUR MIND, MR. CAROSELLA?
YA KNOW ME? I'M FLATTERED.
DON'T BE. I KNOW FAR TOO MANY PEOPLE.
YEAH?
YES INDEED. AND I WOULDN'T MIND KNOWING ONE LESS.
WELL, HERE'S SOMETHING YOU DON'T KNOW...
I KNOW WHAT'CHA DID.
YOU...OR ONE OF YER PEOPLE AT YOUR INSTRUCTION. MAKES NO DIFF.
AND YOU'RE GONNA PAY. SOONER OR LATER, I'LL MAKE YA PAY.

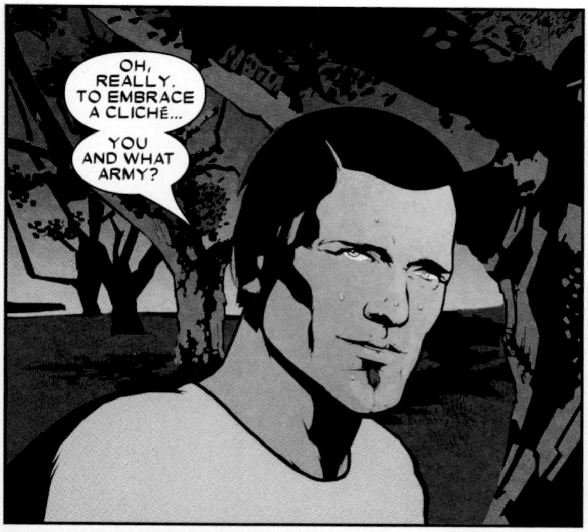
OH, REALLY. TO EMBRACE A CLICHÉ...
YOU AND WHAT ARMY?

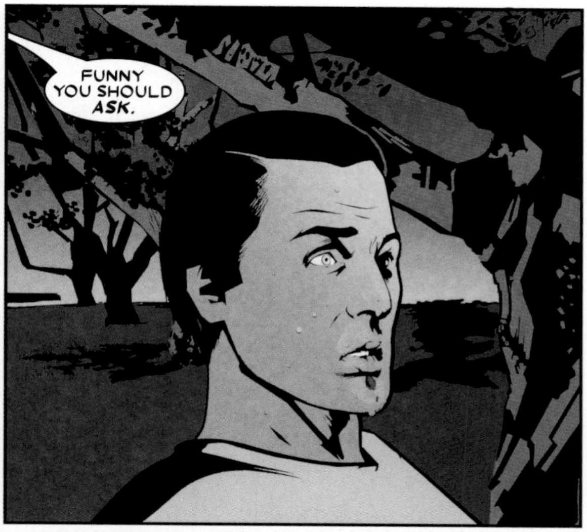
FUNNY YOU SHOULD ASK.

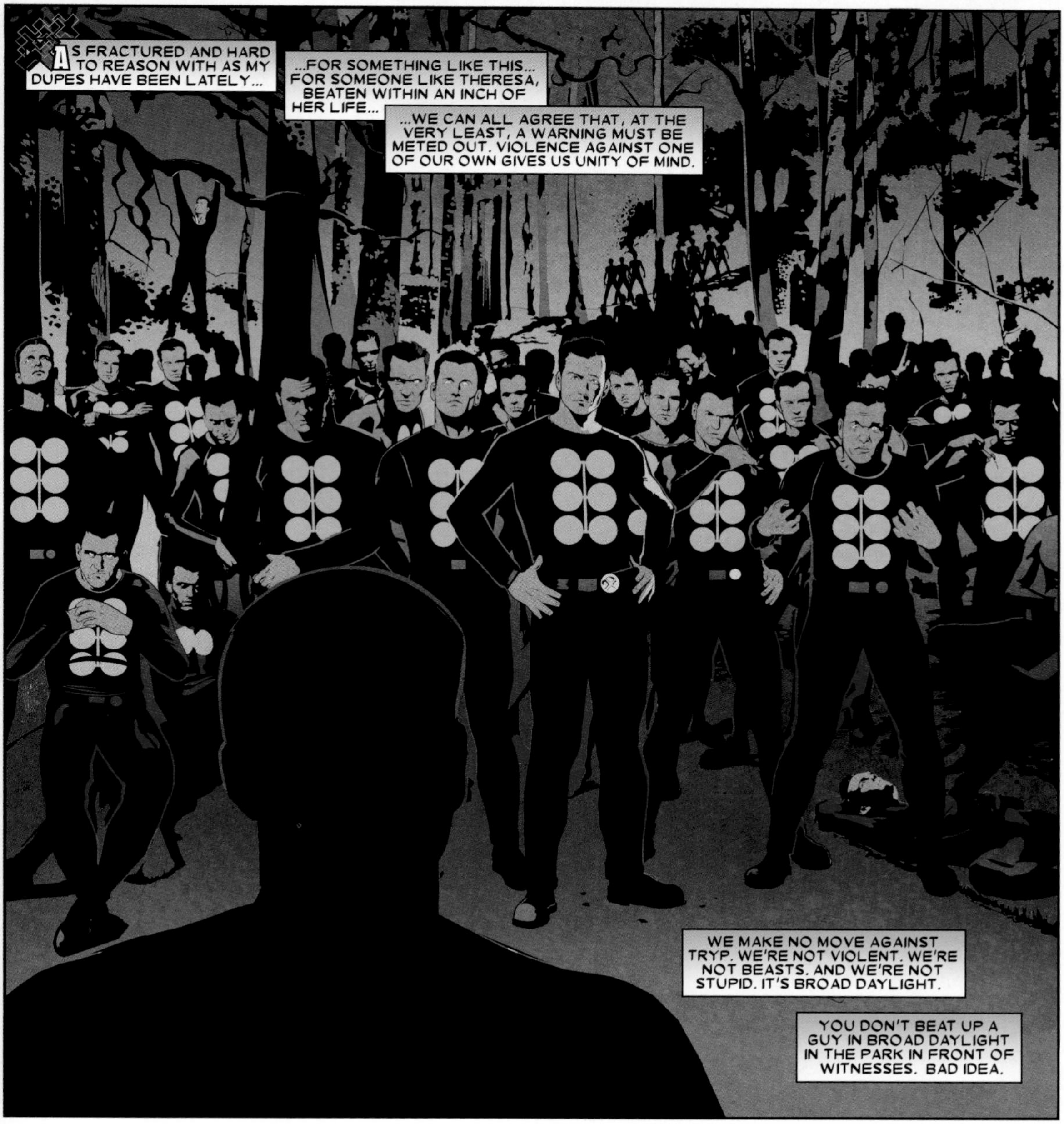
AS FRACTURED AND HARD TO REASON WITH AS MY DUPES HAVE BEEN LATELY...
...FOR SOMETHING LIKE THIS... FOR SOMEONE LIKE THERESA, BEATEN WITHIN AN INCH OF HER LIFE...
...WE CAN ALL AGREE THAT, AT THE VERY LEAST, A WARNING MUST BE METED OUT. VIOLENCE AGAINST ONE OF OUR OWN GIVES US UNITY OF MIND.
WE MAKE NO MOVE AGAINST TRYP. WE'RE NOT VIOLENT. WE'RE NOT BEASTS. AND WE'RE NOT STUPID. IT'S BROAD DAYLIGHT.
YOU DON'T BEAT UP A GUY IN BROAD DAYLIGHT IN THE PARK IN FRONT OF WITNESSES. BAD IDEA.

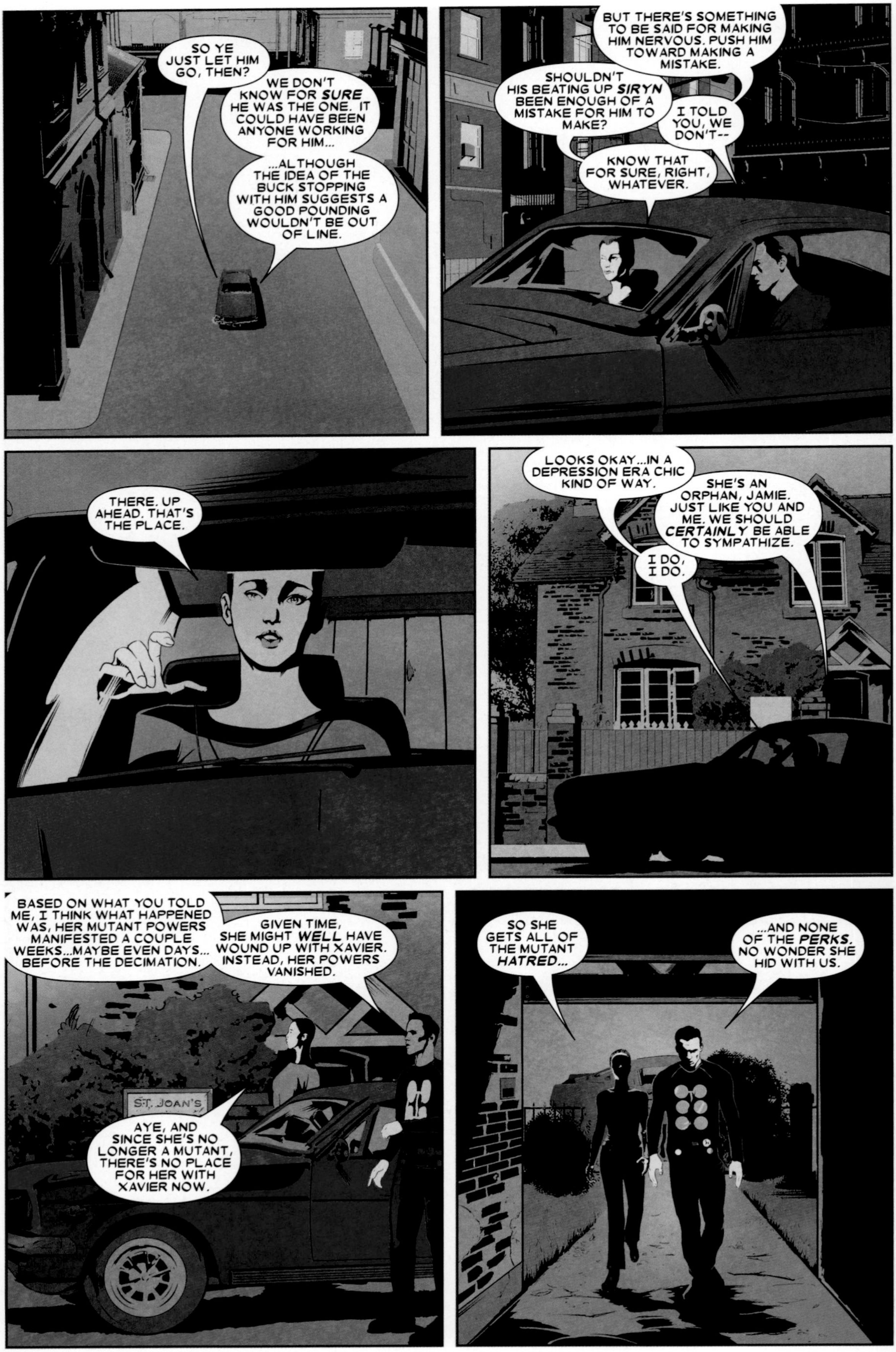
SO YE JUST LET HIM GO, THEN?
WE DON'T KNOW FOR SURE HE WAS THE ONE. IT COULD HAVE BEEN ANYONE WORKING FOR HIM...
...ALTHOUGH THE IDEA OF THE BUCK STOPPING WITH HIM SUGGESTS A GOOD POUNDING WOULDN'T BE OUT OF LINE.
BUT THERE'S SOMETHING TO BE SAID FOR MAKING HIM NERVOUS. PUSH HIM TOWARD MAKING A MISTAKE.
SHOULDN'T HIS BEATING UP SIRYN BEEN ENOUGH OF A MISTAKE FOR HIM TO MAKE?
I TOLD YOU, WE DON'T--
KNOW THAT FOR SURE, RIGHT, WHATEVER.
THERE. UP AHEAD. THAT'S THE PLACE.
LOOKS OKAY...IN A DEPRESSION ERA CHIC KIND OF WAY.
SHE'S AN ORPHAN, JAMIE. JUST LIKE YOU AND ME. WE SHOULD CERTAINLY BE ABLE TO SYMPATHIZE.
I DO, I DO.
BASED ON WHAT YOU TOLD ME, I THINK WHAT HAPPENED WAS, HER MUTANT POWERS MANIFESTED A COUPLE WEEKS...MAYBE EVEN DAYS... BEFORE THE DECIMATION.
GIVEN TIME, SHE MIGHT WELL HAVE WOUND UP WITH XAVIER. INSTEAD, HER POWERS VANISHED.
ST. JOAN'S
AYE, AND SINCE SHE'S NO LONGER A MUTANT, THERE'S NO PLACE FOR HER WITH XAVIER NOW.
SO SHE GETS ALL OF THE MUTANT HATRED...
...AND NONE OF THE PERKS. NO WONDER SHE HID WITH US.

I'M AFRAID THIS ISN'T A GOOD TIME FOR YOU TO SEE LAYLA.

IT'S WITHIN *VISITING* HOURS, ISN'T IT?

THIS ISN'T A HOSPITAL OR A PETTING ZOO, MR. MADROX. IT'S AN ORPHANAGE. LEGALLY SPEAKING, YOU'VE NO *STANDING* TO SEE HER.

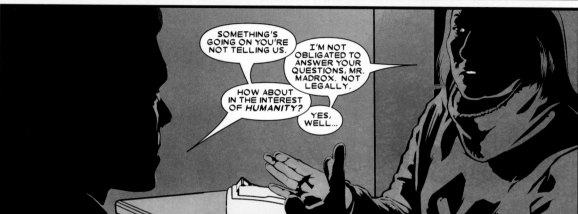

SOMETHING'S GOING ON YOU'RE NOT TELLING US.

I'M NOT OBLIGATED TO ANSWER YOUR QUESTIONS, MR. MADROX. NOT LEGALLY.

HOW ABOUT IN THE INTEREST OF *HUMANITY?*

YES, WELL...

FROM WHAT I HEAR, YOU'RE NOT QUITE... *HUMAN,* ARE YOU.

YE HEARD RIGHT.

C'MON, JAMIE. WE DON'T *NEED* HER. AH KNOW LAYLA'S SCENT. I'LL BRING YE RIGHT TO HER.

SORRY. SHE GETS A LITTLE... TESTY.

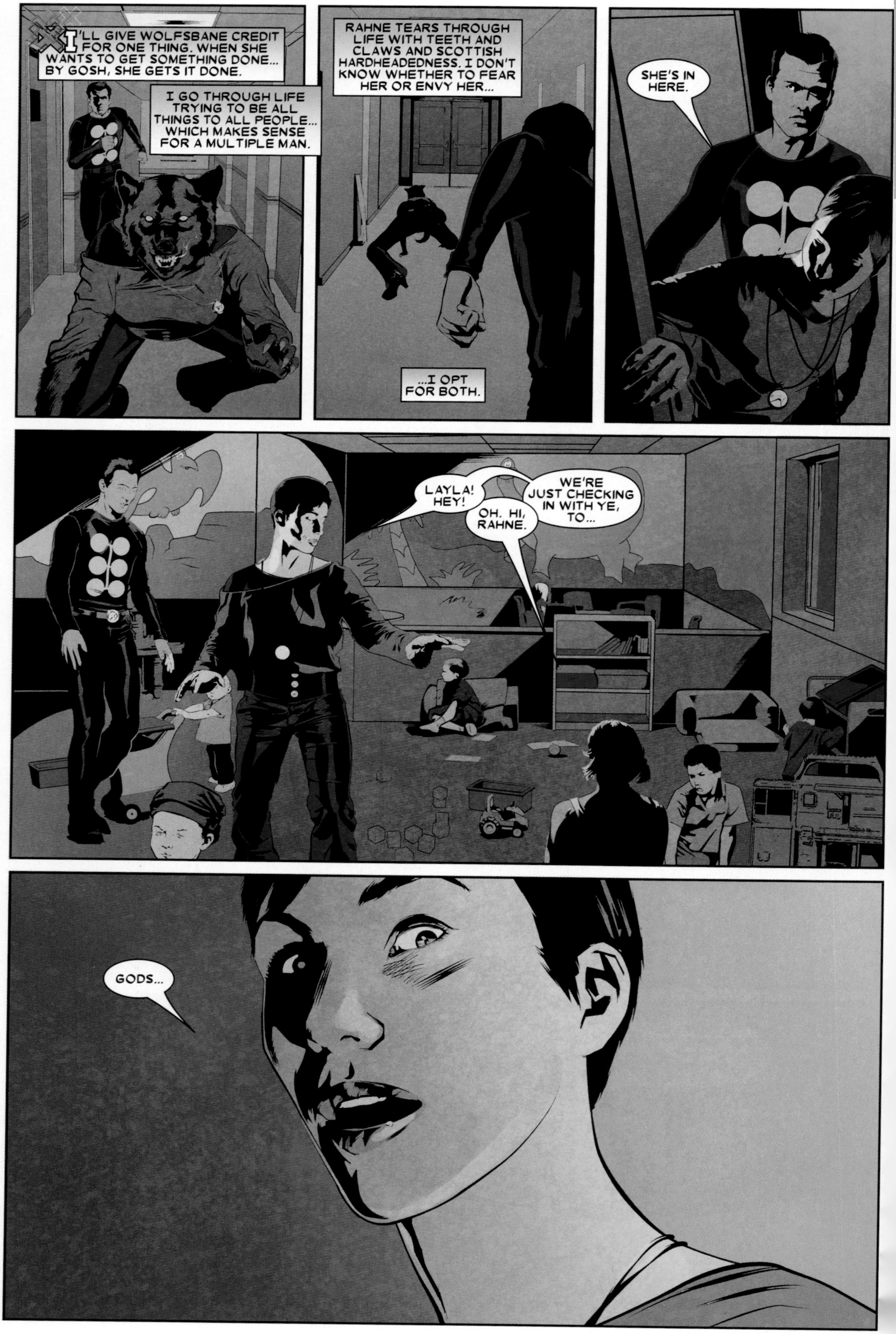
I'LL GIVE WOLFSBANE CREDIT FOR ONE THING. WHEN SHE WANTS TO GET SOMETHING DONE... BY GOSH, SHE GETS IT DONE.
I GO THROUGH LIFE TRYING TO BE ALL THINGS TO ALL PEOPLE... WHICH MAKES SENSE FOR A MULTIPLE MAN.
RAHNE TEARS THROUGH LIFE WITH TEETH AND CLAWS AND SCOTTISH HARDHEADEDNESS. I DON'T KNOW WHETHER TO FEAR HER OR ENVY HER...
...I OPT FOR BOTH.
SHE'S IN HERE.
LAYLA! HEY!
WE'RE JUST CHECKING IN WITH YE, TO...
OH. HI, RAHNE.
GODS...

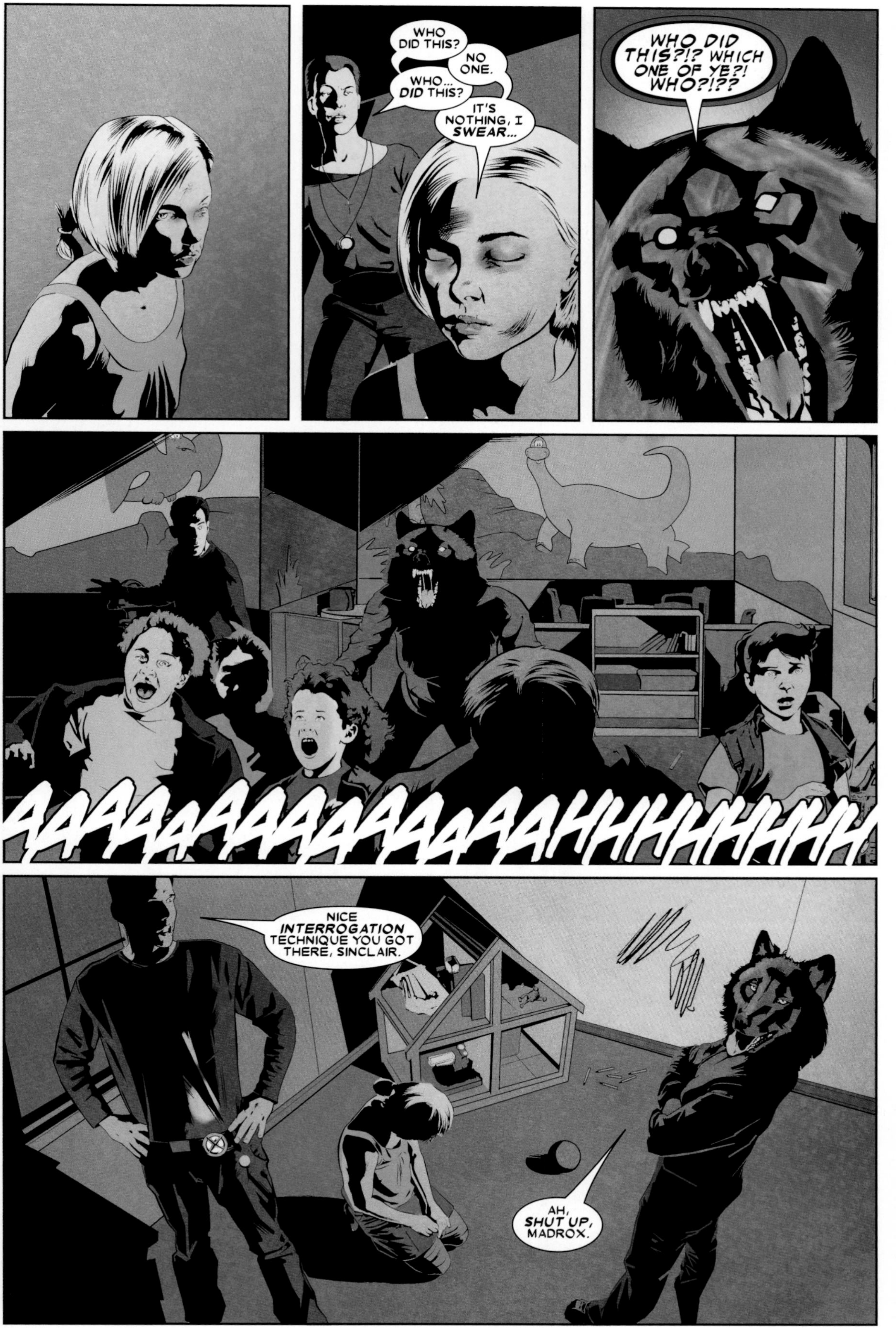
WHO DID THIS?
NO ONE.
WHO... DID THIS?
IT'S NOTHING, I SWEAR...
WHO DID THIS?!? WHICH ONE OF YE?! WHO?!??
AAAAAAAAAAAAAAAAHHHHHHHHH
NICE INTERROGATION TECHNIQUE YOU GOT THERE, SINCLAIR.
AH, SHUT UP, MADROX.

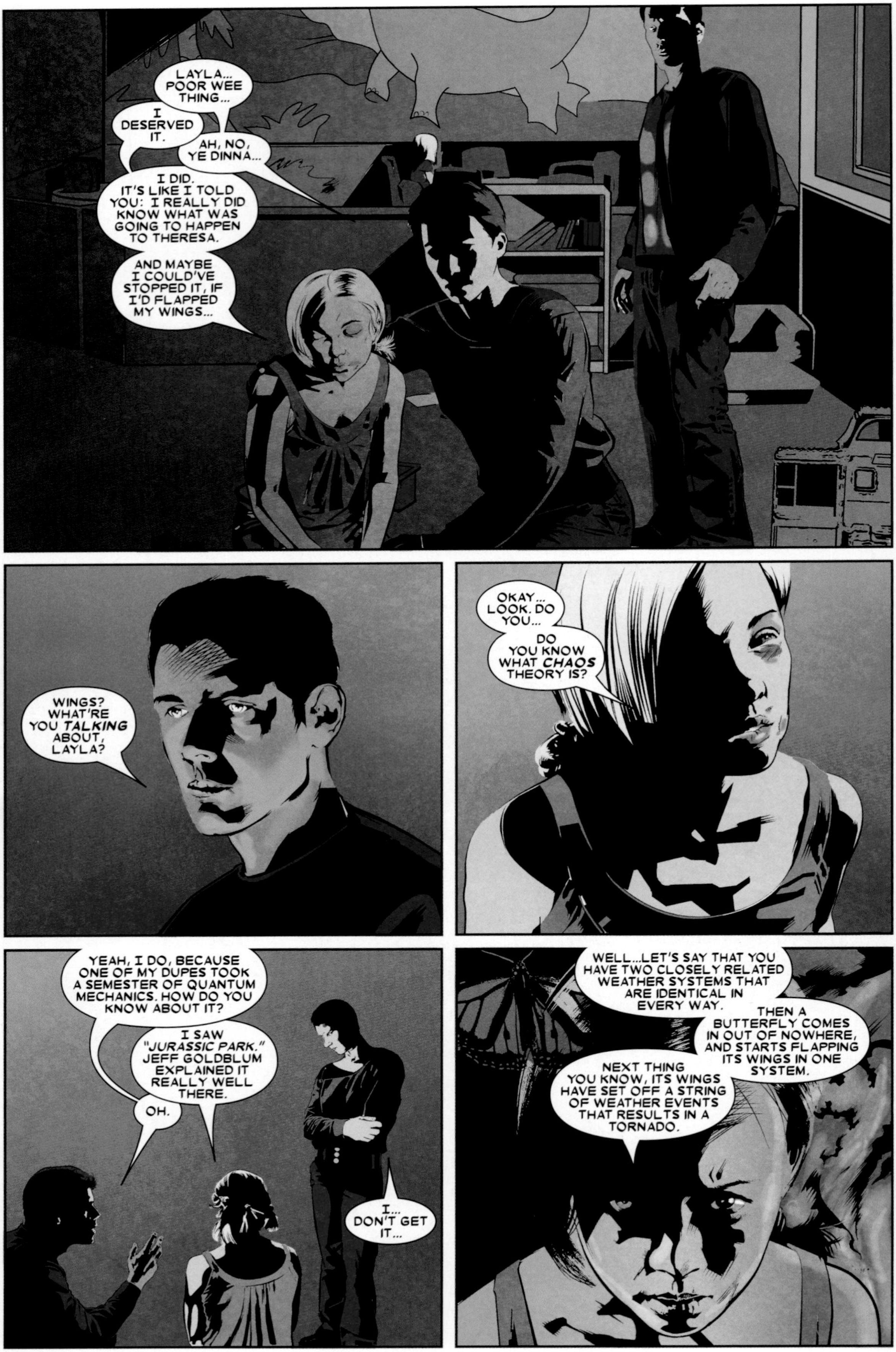

LAYLA... POOR WEE THING...
I DESERVED IT.
AH, NO, YE DINNA...
I DID. IT'S LIKE I TOLD YOU: I REALLY DID KNOW WHAT WAS GOING TO HAPPEN TO THERESA.
AND MAYBE I COULD'VE STOPPED IT, IF I'D FLAPPED MY WINGS...
WINGS? WHAT'RE YOU *TALKING* ABOUT, LAYLA?
OKAY... LOOK. DO YOU...
DO YOU KNOW WHAT *CHAOS* THEORY IS?
YEAH, I DO, BECAUSE ONE OF MY DUPES TOOK A SEMESTER OF QUANTUM MECHANICS. HOW DO YOU KNOW ABOUT IT?
I SAW "*JURASSIC PARK.*" JEFF GOLDBLUM EXPLAINED IT REALLY WELL THERE.
OH.
I... DON'T GET IT...
WELL...LET'S SAY THAT YOU HAVE TWO CLOSELY RELATED WEATHER SYSTEMS THAT ARE IDENTICAL IN EVERY WAY.
THEN A BUTTERFLY COMES IN OUT OF NOWHERE, AND STARTS FLAPPING ITS WINGS IN ONE SYSTEM.
NEXT THING YOU KNOW, ITS WINGS HAVE SET OFF A STRING OF WEATHER EVENTS THAT RESULTS IN A TORNADO.

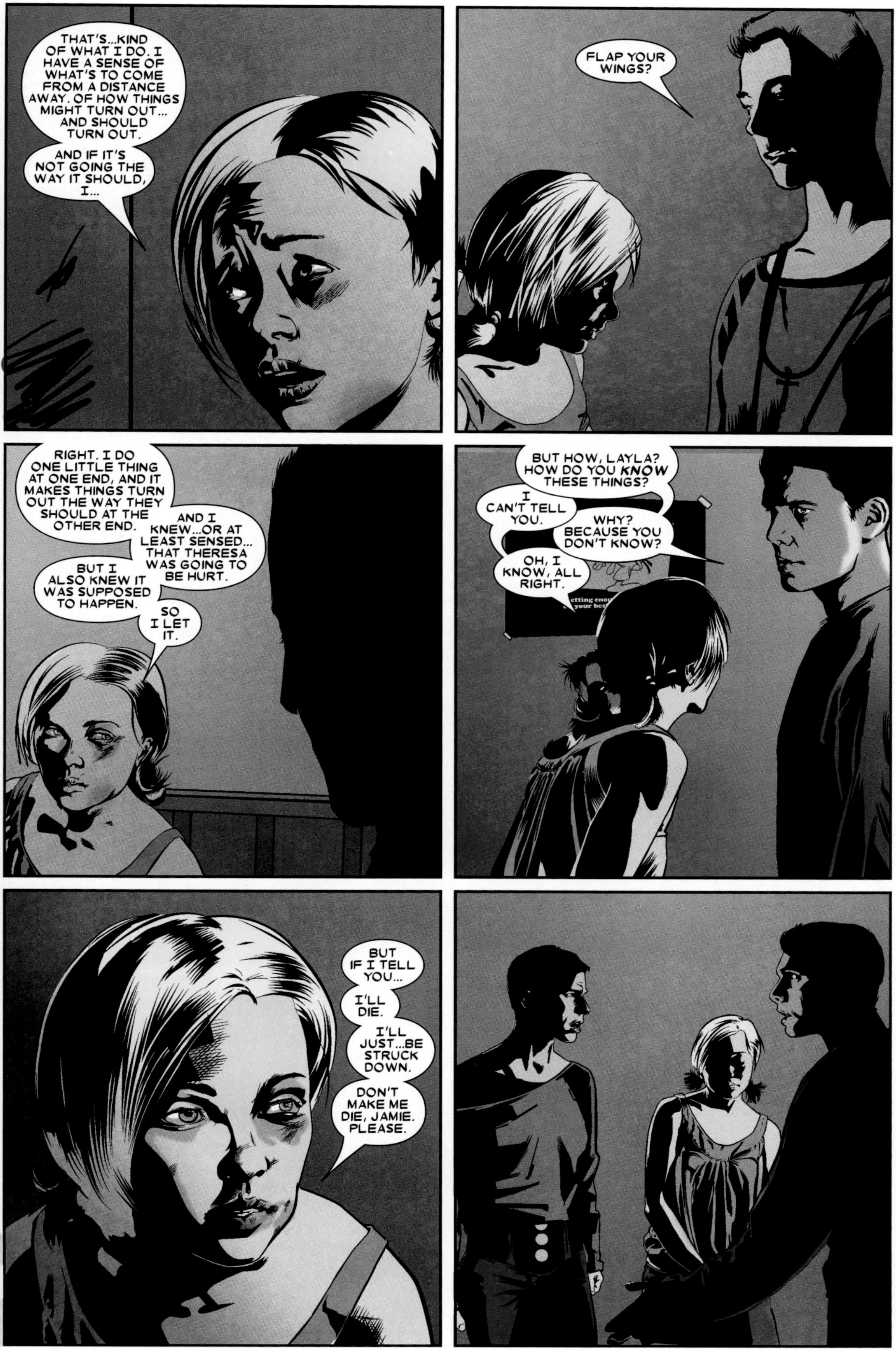
THAT'S...KIND OF WHAT I DO. I HAVE A SENSE OF WHAT'S TO COME FROM A DISTANCE AWAY. OF HOW THINGS MIGHT TURN OUT... AND SHOULD TURN OUT.
AND IF IT'S NOT GOING THE WAY IT SHOULD, I...
FLAP YOUR WINGS?
RIGHT. I DO ONE LITTLE THING AT ONE END, AND IT MAKES THINGS TURN OUT THE WAY THEY SHOULD AT THE OTHER END.
AND I KNEW...OR AT LEAST SENSED... THAT THERESA WAS GOING TO BE HURT.
BUT I ALSO KNEW IT WAS SUPPOSED TO HAPPEN.
SO I LET IT.
BUT HOW, LAYLA? HOW DO YOU *KNOW* THESE THINGS?
I CAN'T TELL YOU.
WHY? BECAUSE YOU DON'T KNOW?
OH, I KNOW, ALL RIGHT.
BUT IF I TELL YOU...
I'LL DIE.
I'LL JUST...BE STRUCK DOWN.
DON'T MAKE ME DIE, JAMIE. PLEASE.

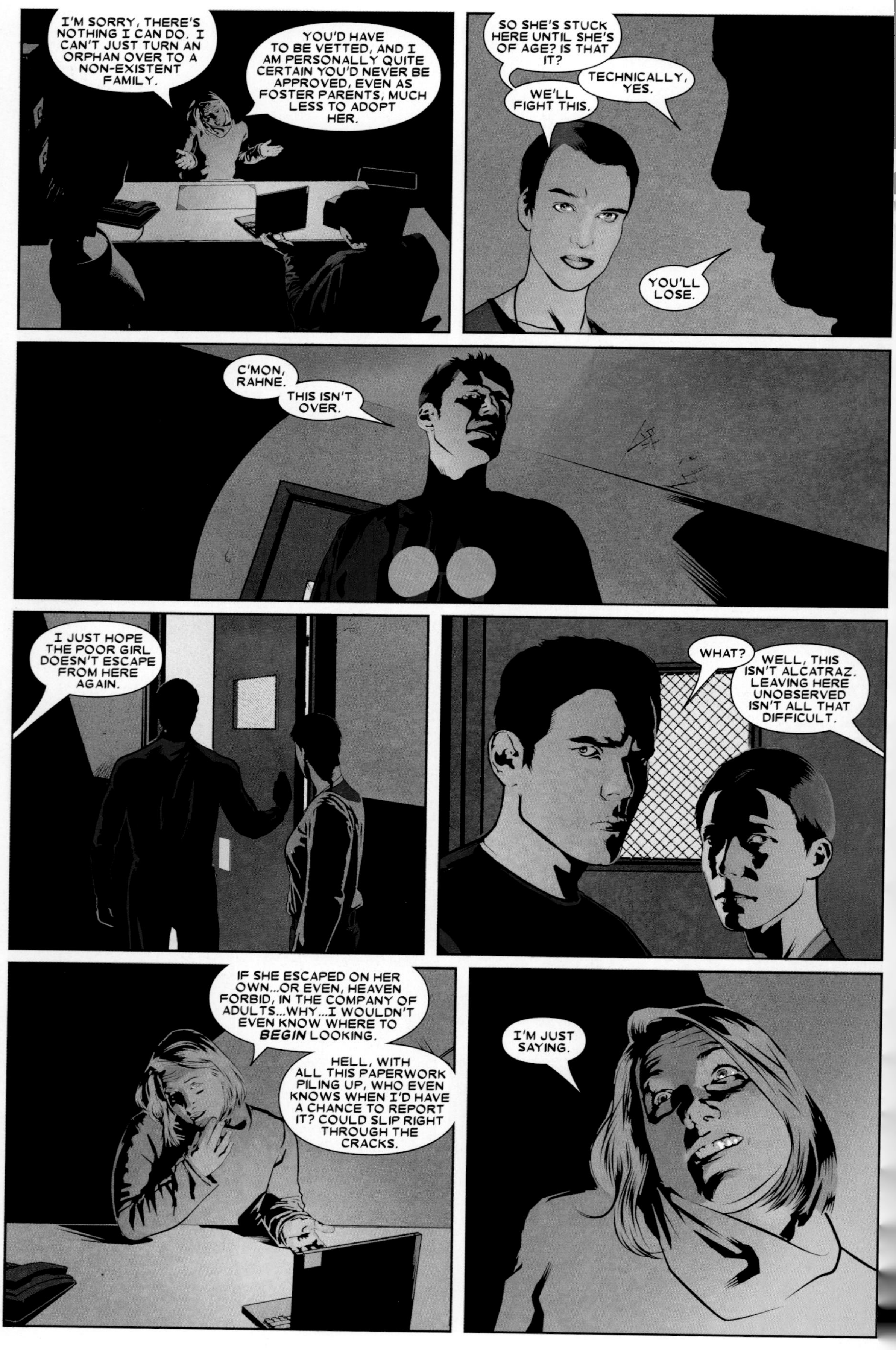
I'M SORRY, THERE'S NOTHING I CAN DO. I CAN'T JUST TURN AN ORPHAN OVER TO A NON-EXISTENT FAMILY.
YOU'D HAVE TO BE VETTED, AND I AM PERSONALLY QUITE CERTAIN YOU'D NEVER BE APPROVED, EVEN AS FOSTER PARENTS, MUCH LESS TO ADOPT HER.
SO SHE'S STUCK HERE UNTIL SHE'S OF AGE? IS THAT IT?
TECHNICALLY, YES.
WE'LL FIGHT THIS.
YOU'LL LOSE.
C'MON, RAHNE.
THIS ISN'T OVER.
I JUST HOPE THE POOR GIRL DOESN'T ESCAPE FROM HERE AGAIN.
WHAT?
WELL, THIS ISN'T ALCATRAZ. LEAVING HERE UNOBSERVED ISN'T ALL THAT DIFFICULT.
IF SHE ESCAPED ON HER OWN...OR EVEN, HEAVEN FORBID, IN THE COMPANY OF ADULTS...WHY...I WOULDN'T EVEN KNOW WHERE TO *BEGIN* LOOKING.
HELL, WITH ALL THIS PAPERWORK PILING UP, WHO EVEN KNOWS WHEN I'D HAVE A CHANCE TO REPORT IT? COULD SLIP RIGHT THROUGH THE CRACKS.
I'M JUST SAYING.

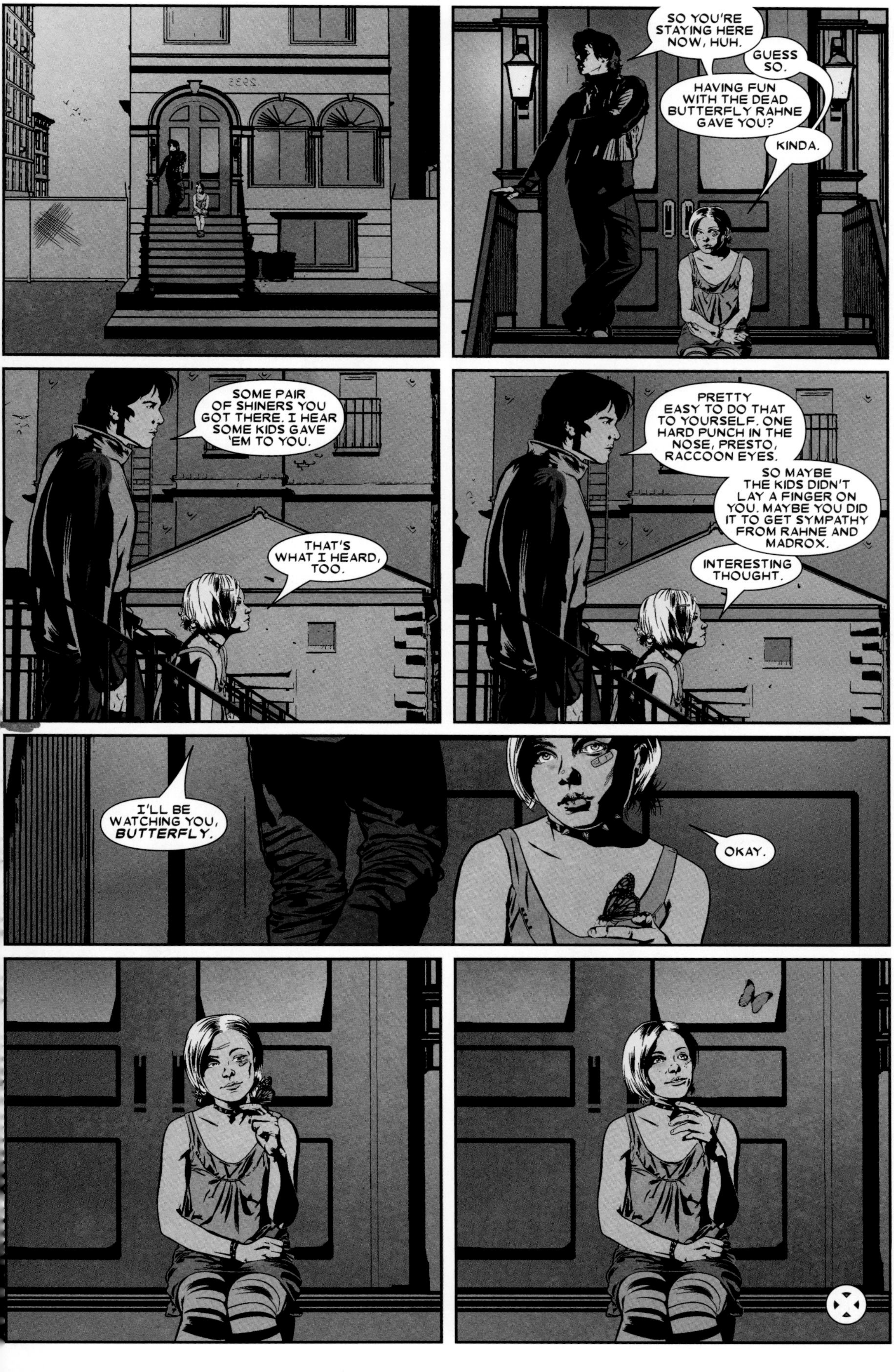

SO YOU'RE STAYING HERE NOW, HUH.
GUESS SO.
HAVING FUN WITH THE DEAD BUTTERFLY RAHNE GAVE YOU?
KINDA.
SOME PAIR OF SHINERS YOU GOT THERE. I HEAR SOME KIDS GAVE 'EM TO YOU.
THAT'S WHAT I HEARD, TOO.
PRETTY EASY TO DO THAT TO YOURSELF. ONE HARD PUNCH IN THE NOSE, PRESTO, RACCOON EYES.
SO MAYBE THE KIDS DIDN'T LAY A FINGER ON YOU. MAYBE YOU DID IT TO GET SYMPATHY FROM RAHNE AND MADROX.
INTERESTING THOUGHT.
I'LL BE WATCHING YOU, BUTTERFLY.
OKAY.

Character Designs by Ryan Sook

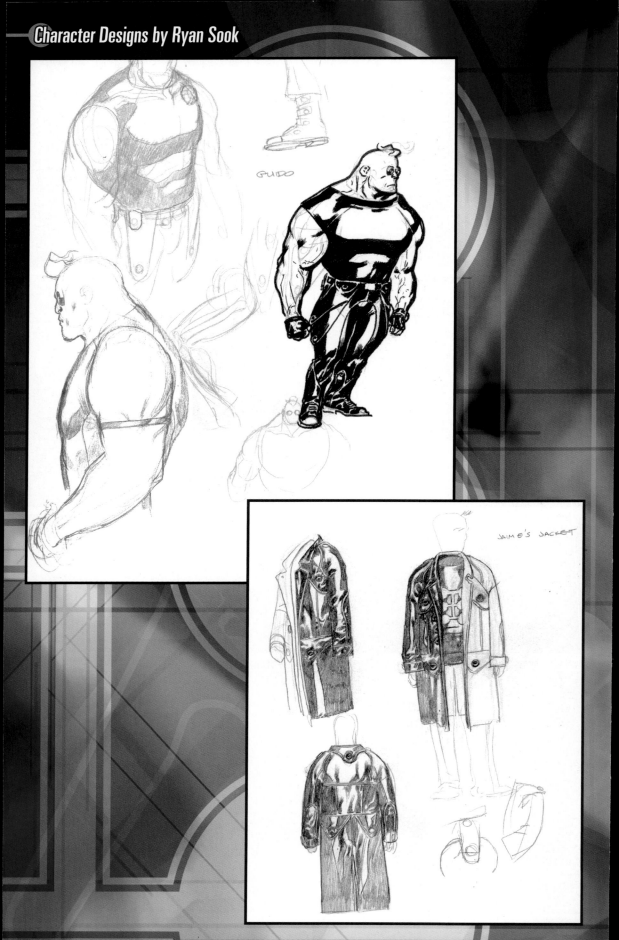

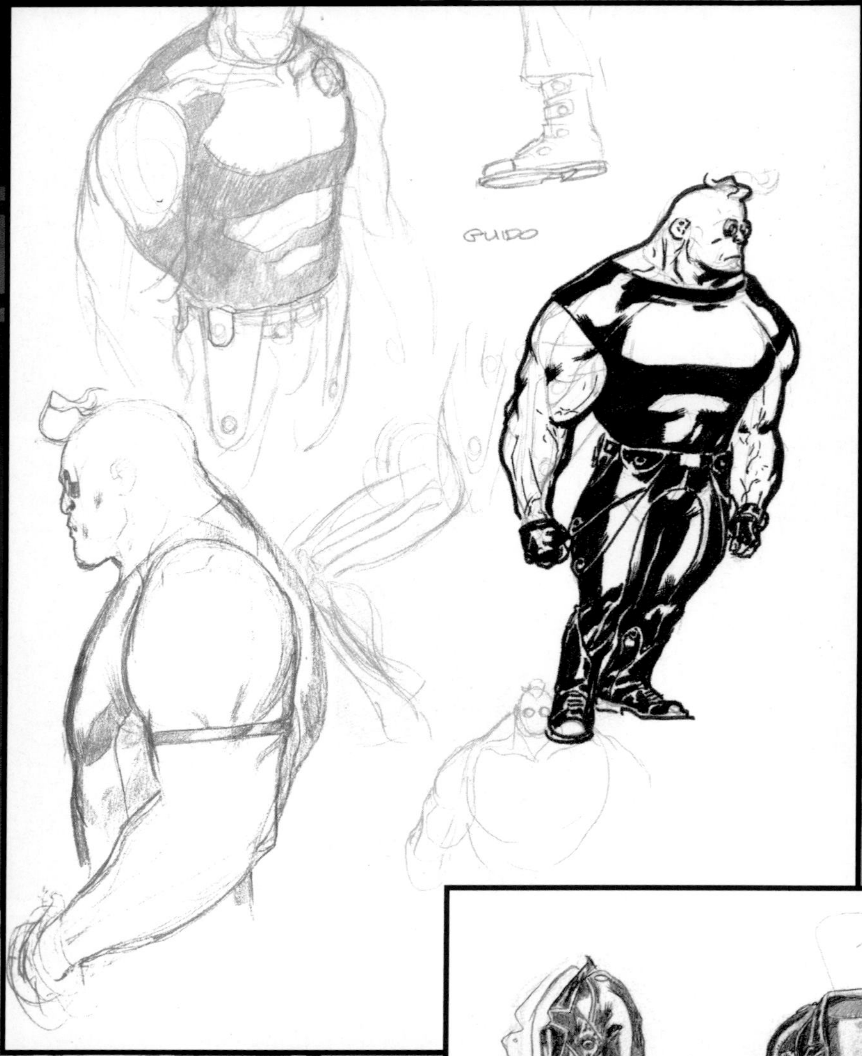
GUIDO

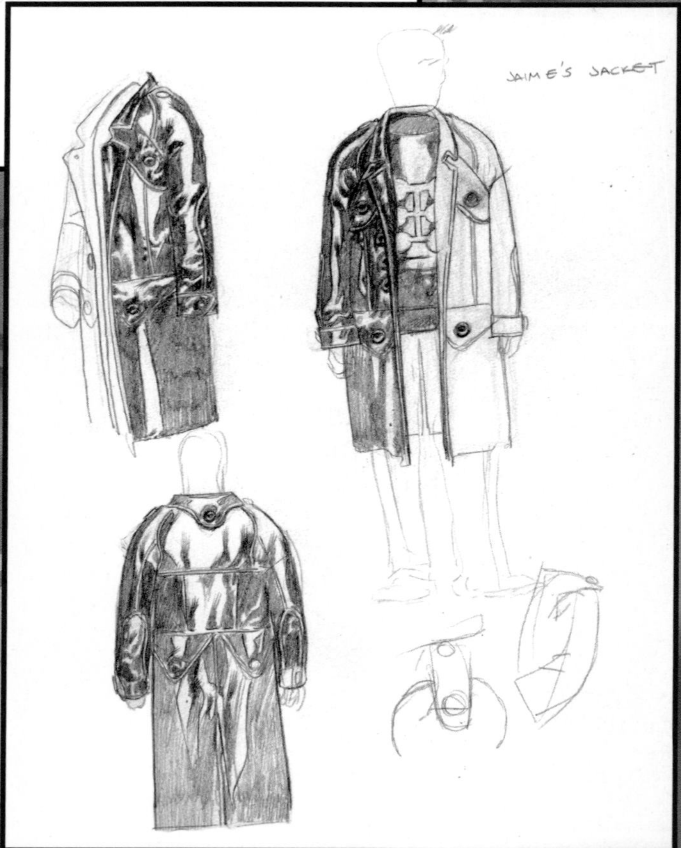
JAIME'S JACKET

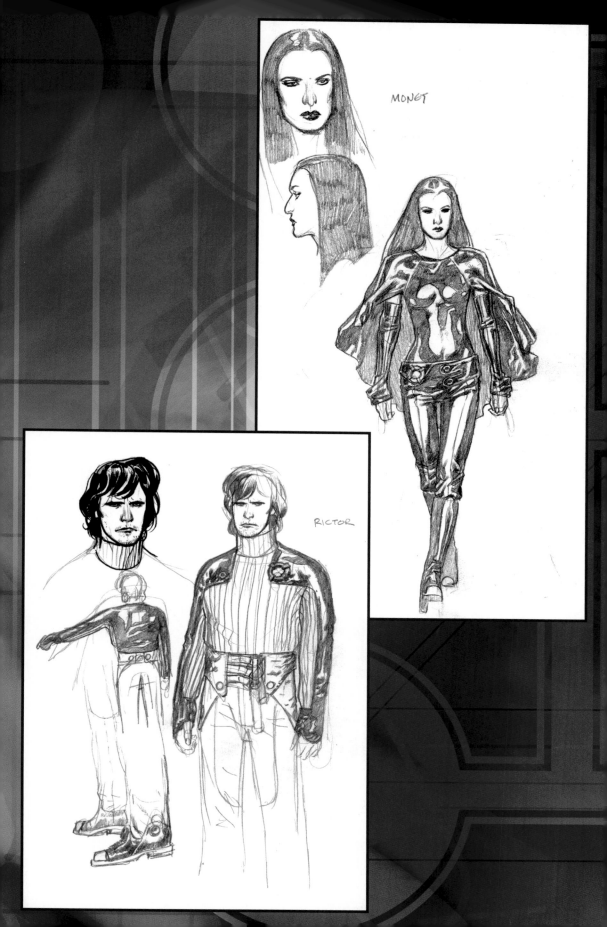

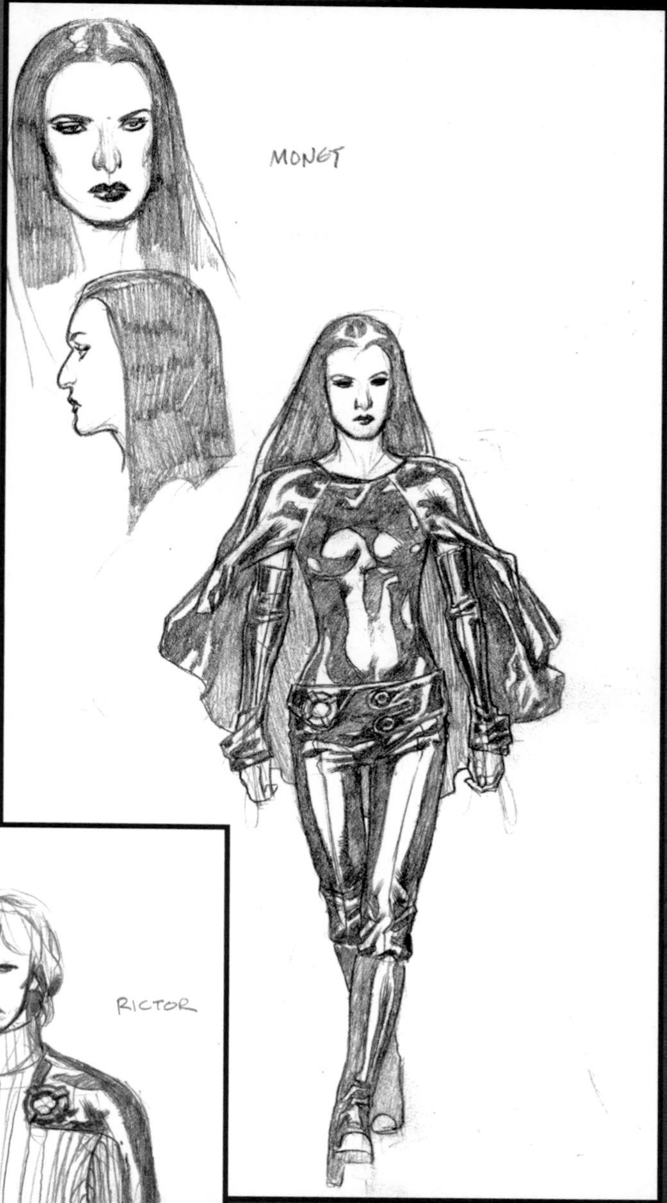
MONET

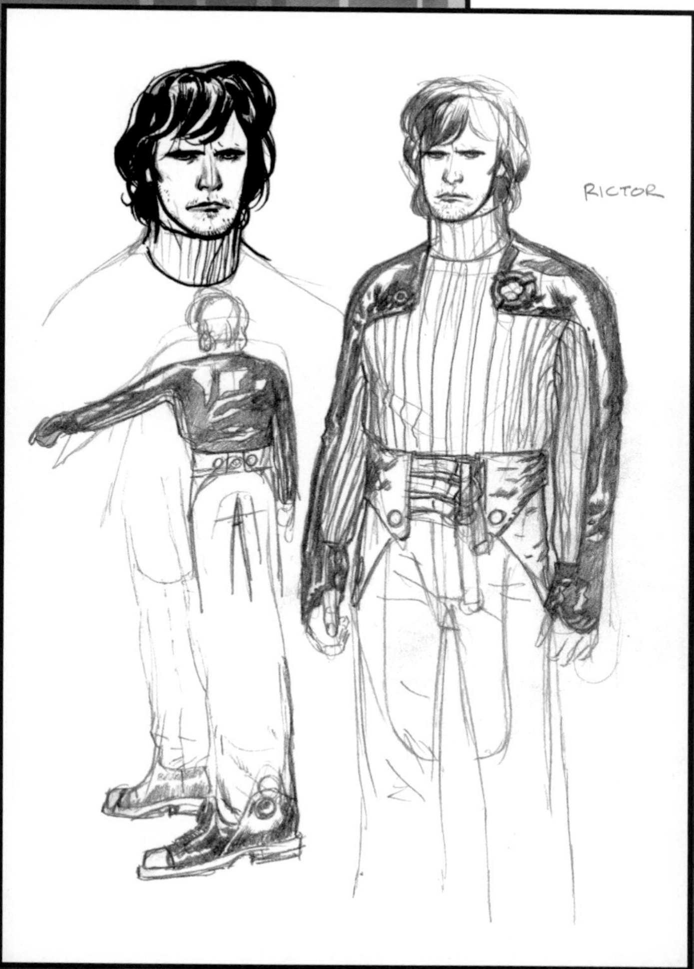
RICTOR

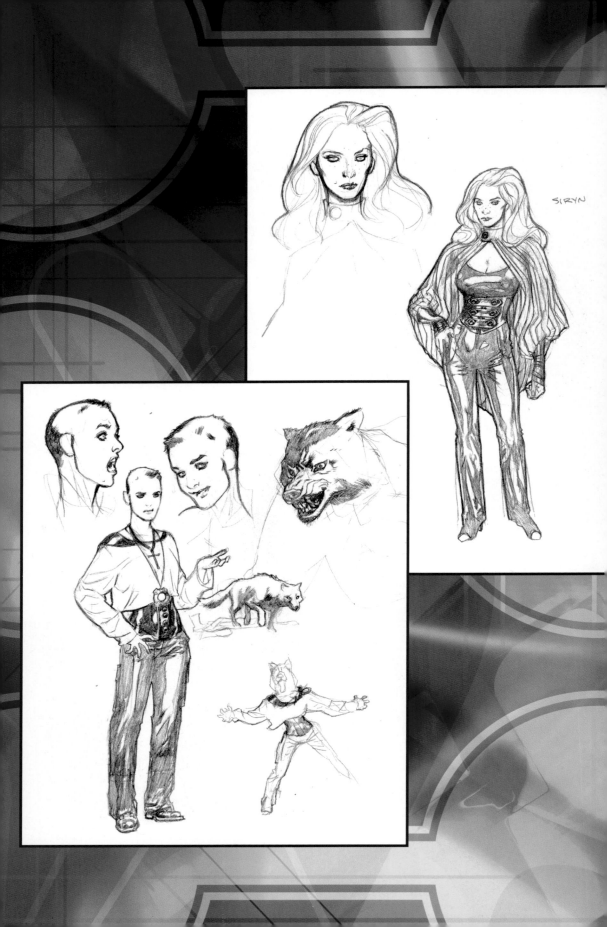

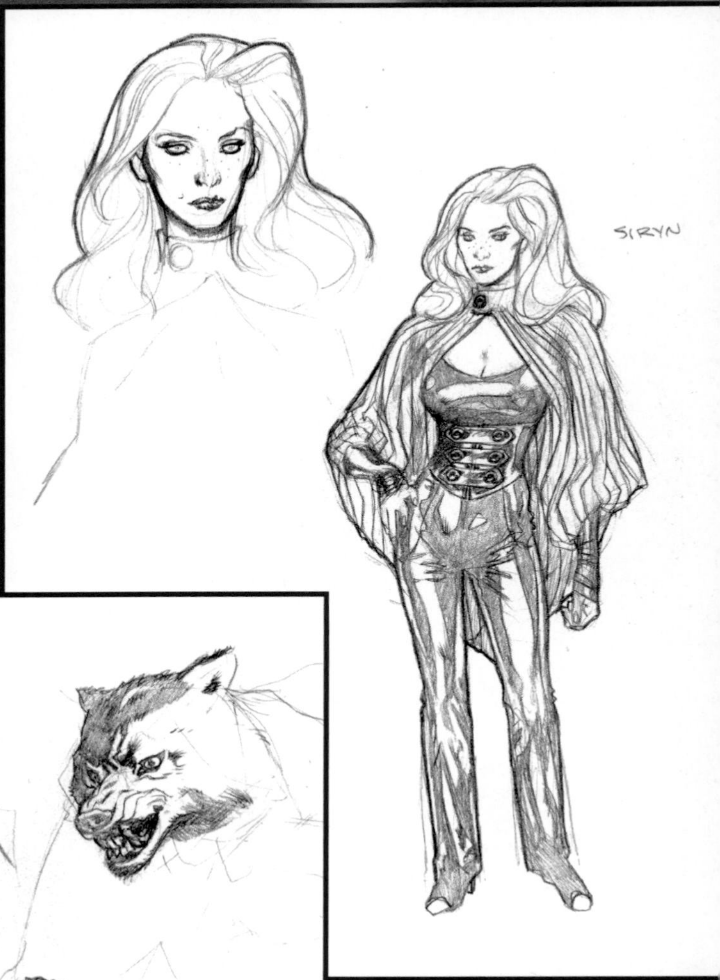
SIRYN

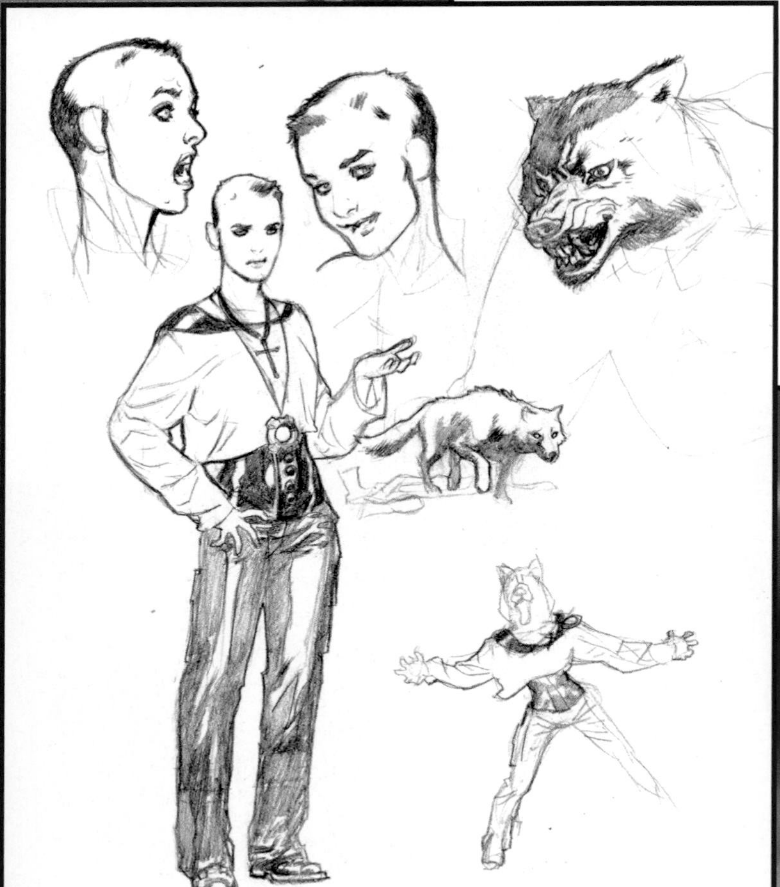